Teilhard de Chardin and Eastern Religions

Spirituality and Mysticism in an Evolutionary World

Ursula King

Foreword by Joseph Needham

Paulist Press
New York / Mahwah, NJ

To Tony,
with deepest thanks for your love, companionship,
and always-welcome advice

Excerpts from *Letters from a Traveler* by Pierre Teilhard de Chardin, English translation © Collins, 1962. Originally published in France as *Lettres de voyage* by Pierre Teilhard de Chardin. © Éditions Grasset & Fasquelle, 1956.

Cover design by Cynthia Dunne, www.bluefarmdesign.com
Book design by Lynn Else

Library of Congress Cataloging-in-Publication Data

King, Ursula.
    Teilhard de Chardin and Eastern religions / Ursula King ; foreword by Joseph Needham.
        p. cm.
    Includes bibliographical references (p.   ) and index.
    ISBN 978-0-8091-4704-5 (alk. paper)
    1. Religions—History. 2. Mysticism—History. 3. Teilhard de Chardin, Pierre. I. Title.
    BL98.K56 2011
    261.2′995—dc22

                                                                            2010044154

Published by Paulist Press
997 Macarthur Boulevard
Mahwah, New Jersey 07430

www.paulistpress.com

Printed and bound in the
United States of America

CONTENTS

PREFACE AND
ACKNOWLEDGMENTS

This is a revised edition of my earlier book *Toward a New Mysticism: Teilhard de Chardin and Eastern Religions*, originally published in 1980 but out of print for more than twenty years. Although widely reviewed and cited in studies on mysticism, interfaith dialogue, and the theology of religions, it was in some ways a book ahead of its time. When it originally appeared, there existed far less interest in mysticism and spirituality than is the case today. Moreover, the global awareness and context of the twenty-first century, with its myriad challenges and problems, has opened up new opportunities for intercultural dialogue and encounter, and for closer collaboration in all fields of endeavor to ensure the future of humanity and the Earth. It is here that Teilhard de Chardin's work makes a major contribution by supplying seminal ideas for personal, social, and planetary transformation. I am therefore delighted that the Paulist Press has agreed to publish this revised edition of my earlier book.

Many themes that Teilhard wrestled with during the first half of the twentieth century—how to understand eastern religions and cultures, the modernization of China, the future of humanity, the reinterpretation of Christianity, spirituality, and mysticism in an evolutionary world, the urgency of ecological and environmental concerns—are debated far more widely now than they ever were during his own life or even thirty years ago. My own ideas have also greatly expanded since this book was first published. I have therefore incorporated some new perspectives without writing an altogether new book. On rereading Teilhard I have been surprised to discover how many of his religious and philosophical questions, his cross-cultural experiences, and his profound reflections on science and religion relate even more strikingly to contemporary cultural concerns than they did to those of earlier years. This is especially true in relation to questions of religion and evolution, ecology, spirituality, and the significance of China in a globalized world.

In updating this book, I have cut some parts and enlarged others. I have also made some linguistic changes to express inclusive rather than exclusive ways of thinking. However, most of the material that follows retains the original structure of the first edition.

Dr. Joseph Needham's foreword, with which the book opens, has been retained in its original form with the permission of the Needham Research Institute, Cambridge. The introduction and epilogue contain some new material, as do several chapters of the book. An entirely new addition is the separate annotated study guide at the end, designed to help students and other readers new to Teilhard's thought to gain an overview and deepen their understanding of his ideas. Those already acquainted with his work can take up the more specialized references in order to carry out research of their own.

Writing this book was made possible through the serendipitous coming together of several experiences. I was first introduced to Teilhard's thought during my theological studies in France in the early 1960s. The first essay I ever read was one that Teilhard wrote during the last years of his life, his spiritual autobiography, "The Heart of Matter" (1950). This essay was only available in cyclostyled form during the 1960s and was one of the last of his essays to be published in France (1976), soon followed by an English translation (1978). Reading this vivid account aroused both my curiosity and enthusiasm, though without leading immediately to any detailed study. This happened later, during the five years I lived in India (1965–70), where I read many of Teilhard's essays and discussed his thought on religion, evolution, spirituality, mysticism, and the future of humanity with many Indian friends and colleagues. My study of Indian religions, and the subsequent teaching of this subject within university courses on religious studies, together with the comparative study of mysticism, led to the initial formulation and further development of the ideas contained in this book.

Over several years, I analyzed Teilhard's published and

unpublished writings in their original French versions. Correspondence and personal interviews with Teilhard's former friends and family members helped to elucidate this material. It would have been impossible to write this book without the collaboration of many people who willingly replied to my questions and letters. While it is impossible to list them all, I record here my gratitude to several individuals, all sadly deceased by now. In particular, I want to thank my former professor at the Institut Catholique, Professor Paul Henry, SJ, whose stimulating lectures first inspired me to read Teilhard's work. Later, help was given by Father Pierre Leroy, SJ, Teilhard's close collaborator and friend, and also by Father Henri de Lubac, SJ, who has written extensively on Teilhard's thought.

Dr. Claude Cuénot, Teilhard's first biographer, and Mademoiselle Jeanne Mortier, the literary executrix of his papers, answered many of my queries and drew attention to additional material. Madame Béatrice d'Hauteville kindly put at my disposal papers relating to Teilhard's work for the French branch of the World Congress of Faiths and also his unpublished correspondence with Madame Solange Lemaître. Special thanks go to Teilhard's youngest brother, Monsieur Joseph Teilhard de Chardin, and his wife, who so hospitably received me in the family's ancestral houses at Les Moulins and Sarcenat in the Auvergne in France, and in their Paris home, thereby enabling me to gain a better understanding of Teilhard's background and family milieu.

I will always gratefully remember the encouragement given by the late Professor E. G. Parrinder in London; the comments provided by the late Professor R. C. Zaehner in Oxford; and the inspiration, generosity, and kindness of the late Dr. Joseph Needham in Cambridge in sharing many discussions with me during my year's fellowship at Gonville and Caius College, Cambridge, and especially in agreeing to write the foreword for this book. I am most grateful to both the director and librarian of the Needham Research Institute, Cambridge, for permission to reprint this foreword in its original form.

More recently, the help of Professor Francois Euvé, SJ, from the Centre Sèvres, Facultés Jésuites de Paris, has been greatly appreciated. I have also much valued the friendship and advice of

Father Richard Brüchsel, SJ, in Basel, Switzerland, with whom I have shared many stimulating discussions on Teilhard de Chardin. In addition I express my deep thanks to Arthur Fabel, the editor of the *Teilhard Perspective* newsletter of the American Teilhard Association, and to Dr. Kathleen Duffy, SSJ, from Chestnut Hill College, Philadelphia, editor of the Teilhard Studies series, for their generous, helpful advice given at the final editing stage of this work.

This book is dedicated to my family and the numerous participants in dialogue who in England, France, India, Germany, Switzerland, the United States, and China inspired me to develop the ideas presented here. Also included are all those who through their writing and work in many fields help to advance the emergence of a more spiritually aware and awakened humanity. This includes the fostering of a better understanding between East and West, of greater peace and justice, and countless efforts around the world to establish a more united humanity and a more ecologically balanced community on our planet.

Ursula King
Bristol, England
December 2010

FOREWORD

Dr. Joseph Needham

Author's note: The Foreword has been reproduced as written for the first edition of this book in 1980.

It is a great privilege for me to be invited to write a foreword for the book of my friend Ursula King on Teilhard de Chardin in relation to the religions of Asia, that part of the world in which he himself lived so long. I should say without any hesitation that Father Teilhard was called to be the greatest prophet of this age. That will become more and more clear, I believe, as time goes on. How then did such a man, arising from the relatively narrow environment of provincial Latin Catholic France and yet generating a view which surveyed the infinities of time and space with undimmed theistic conviction, react to the philosophies and religions of the eastern world far beyond the confines of Christendom? Such a book as Ursula King's has become an urgent necessity, and I think she has made a great success of it. Although many of Teilhard's notes and travel diaries are unfortunately lost, a large amount of material remains, and the author has laid it fully under contribution. She produces a flood of facts hitherto not known—such as Teilhard's meeting with Edgar Snow and his wife, or talking with Living Buddhas, or admiring the numinous quality of Mahayana Buddhist liturgies. Most of us had no idea how much reading he did in comparative religion, especially as regards Asia, nor did we know how active he was in the World Congress of Faiths.

From my student days onwards, I gradually developed a view of the world which had two principal aspects. On the one hand, following Rudolf Otto and R. G. Collingwood, I became profoundly convinced that man gains true apprehension of the universe only through the exercise of several different forms of experience, science, religion, art, history, philosophy and so on. Even though these forms of experience are liable to contradict each other, no one will do alone, certainly not science which tends to be supreme today. As C. G. Jung said, "science should always be man's servant; when it usurps the throne it leads to tyranny." On the other hand, I was convinced that Christianity must take evolution seriously. Modern knowledge about cosmic, biological and social evolution made it absolutely impossible to maintain any longer the medieval Christian worldviews. In other words, in a way I had become a "process theologian" without knowing it.

Consequently I ought to have been well prepared to understand Teilhard de Chardin when I met him personally in Paris in 1947 at a time when I was working to establish the Natural Sciences Division of UNESCO. He and I used to dine together from time to time, and I found him a charismatic as well as a lovable person, but I didn't quite understand what exactly he was driving at; and it was only after the appearance of his many books, and after he himself was dead, that I realized we had been travelling on very similar main lines. Actually I have never been able to reread some of his books, because they move me too much, and I prefer to remain calm and clear-headed though quite conscious of Pascal's frightening infinite empty spaces.

I also had much in common of course with another great friend, Julian Huxley, at that time Director-General of UNESCO, but where I differed from his evolutionary humanism was that I thought the numinous was very important, and I could find it best in my own traditional religion. I had begun as an Anglo-Catholic and an Anglo-Catholic I remained, though deeply attached to Orthodoxy and at the same time by my own confession, an "honorary Taoist."

Now I always supposed that Teilhard de Chardin had been very little influenced by the Asian religions. It is admitted that although he lived in China a long time he knew very little Chinese, and in fact inhabited a kind of expatriate colonial milieu, both in Egypt and in China. The impression people got that he was rather hostile to Asian religions probably originated from a distinction which he drew (and which Ursula King discusses in chapter 6) between "the eastern" and "the western" modes of spirituality and mysticism. He was against the former because it was too much given to renunciation, the negation of the world of matter, and the belief that the material world was nothing but an illusion of Mara the Tempter. The "eastern" way, he felt, was anti-time and anti-evolution; he repudiated the attraction of pure nature-mysticism, and did not like the idea of return or fusion with the One, identification with the universe without the presence of any love. Similarly the "western" way for him was a way of convergence including love, of progress, synthesis, taking time as real and evolution as real, and recognizing the world as an organic whole. He sought for a spirituality which feeds social action rather than eschewing it. This was, he felt, a new road which religious men could follow, leading to an ultra-personal or supra-personal God to be loved in and through all things rather than *above* all things.

It seems to have been unfortunate that Teilhard chose "eastern" and "western" as names for these different ways. A good deal of what he disliked belonged to Hinduism and Buddhism, not at all to Taoism and Confucianism. Both the great Chinese religions were strongly world-affirming. The Tao or "Order of Nature" could be understood as immanent deity. If Teilhard had been able to get so far as an analysis of Chinese conceptions of time, he would have found that they were not at all cyclical, but much more similar to the one-way time of Hebrew monotheism, a time in which real permanent change can happen and where there can be, for instance, a "plan of salvation." But of course he could not expect to have found the evolutionary view of the world in its fullness, because that was a product of modern science, and modern science originated only in the western world. Still, Teilhard would have been very encouraged if he had been able to get to the foundations of Taoism and Confucianism, because the principle of ethics and ethical love was tremendously there, quite different from any loveless "fusion with the One" such as might be found in pure nature mysticism, or in some of the Indian, Platonic or Neo-Platonic forms of mystical experience. A valuable short book by Marie-Ina Bergeron, *La Chine et Teilhard*, complementary to Ursula King's, has explored some of the basic Taoist-Confucian ideas which Teilhard would have appreciated greatly if he could have got access to them.

What was misleading was that by "eastern" Teilhard really meant all "other-worldly spirituality." The fact is that as a Christian he was bound to the traditions of the "Peoples of the Book." As the Great Church says every day, *pistevō eis ena theou patera pantokratora; credo in unum deum patrem omnipotentem....*Therefore no nontheistic universe, however immense or glorious, would suffice for such a soul to be one-ed with. At the same time, the knowledge of evolution was a product of modern science and only Europe gave rise to that, so that Teilhard was really a fundamentally post-Newtonian and post-Darwinian theologian. Taoism and Confucianism, however, are only ambiguously nontheistic, in so far as the Tao is the deity immanent in the universe, and remembering that for the Sage, "Heaven" (nonpersonal, but not nontheistic) blessed and authorized the ethics which he taught. Moreover, one could go further and say that many currents in Indian religious thought and practice don't agree with the impression one might get from Teilhard that the "eastern" road was wrong or imperfect. To mention only one aspect, Tantrism, whether in its Hindu or Buddhist forms, was also world-affirming.

The fact seems to be that Teilhard de Chardin never acquired a detailed knowledge of Asian religious beliefs and practices, although his general acquaintance with the peoples and cultures of Asia was much greater than is usually supposed. It is truly important that his ideas on the religions of Asia should be expounded as thoroughly as Ursula King has succeeded in doing in this present book, for I end as I began with the conviction that Teilhard de Chardin is the prophet of this age, a prophet not for the western world alone but for all men everywhere, so that his insights will need translation into the idioms of the eastern nations. I suspect that in the last resort no insights fundamentally true will be irremediably untranslatable. All success to Ursula King's book.

Joseph Needham, FRS, FBA
Director of the East Asian History of Science Library, Cambridge
President, Teilhard Centre for the Future of Man, London

Author's note: The East Asian History of Science Library is now known as the Needham Research Institute after its founder, Dr. Joseph Needham (1900–95). For further information on the Institute and its founder, see www. nri.org.uk. The "Teilhard Centre for the Future of Man" no longer exists, but there is still a British Teilhard Association. For details see www.teilhard.org.uk.

INTRODUCTION

Eastern religions are of increasing interest to people in the West,[1] where many religious traditions from the East have now found a permanent home through the global migration of people and the transplantation of religious beliefs and practices all over the world. Yet many western people remain uncertain how to relate eastern religious teachings to their own western backgrounds. How do we respond to cultural and religious pluralism in a globalized world? And what do we make of the growing interest in spirituality, meditation, and mysticism at a time when so many vigorous debates about agnosticism, atheism, and the irrelevance of faith of any kind catch the headlines?

Watching the growth of eastern-inspired cults, some anxiously ask whether eastern religions will eventually supersede western religious traditions. Do the religions of the East really possess a richer spirituality, a deeper mysticism? Or will all religions ultimately disappear from the modern world, with its marked secularity and militant irreligiosity, at least in large parts of the West? Other people perceive new, exciting possibilities through the closer coming together of the great world faiths, the growth of interreligious dialogue, and of a truly worldwide ecumenism.

The French Jesuit Pierre Teilhard de Chardin (1881–1955) first traveled eastward almost a hundred years ago. Like many people today, he felt a strong attraction to the East. Although he sharply criticized some aspects of eastern religions, it is perhaps less well known that from the moment of his first encounter with the East—first through living in the Middle East, in Egypt from 1905 to 1908, and then from 1923 onward in the Far East, in China—he looked for seeds of religious renewal for the West, especially for Christianity, and he also sensed the need for a higher unity of faiths beyond existing religious diversity. Yet he

1

lived at a time when interreligious dialogue was in its infancy. The willingness to listen to adherents of religious traditions other than one's own at that time existed only among a few individuals, but it was not the predominant spirit in the West generally or in the Christian churches. In his thinking and writing, Teilhard ventured considerably beyond the official boundaries of his own Roman Catholic Church. Consequently, he suffered much for being a pioneer, since almost none of his essays on religion and philosophy were allowed to be published while he was alive.

Throughout his extensive travels in the East, Teilhard encountered members of different faiths, especially adherents of Buddhism, Hinduism, and Islam. At first, his writings seem to make little reference to these encounters. Yet as a religious thinker he was deeply interested in what he called the "active currents of faith," now more often referred to as "living religions." What is their role and relevance in the contemporary world? How can the religions of the past help us to solve the problems of the present? What contribution can the world faiths make to the development of the Earth and to the future of humanity? What kind of spirituality do we need today, and what is the place of mysticism in religion? Are we approaching a critical threshold toward a new consciousness and a new humanity that requires the emergence of a new spirit, a new ethic, and a new world order? It is largely with these questions that the present book is concerned.

During the years since his death in 1955, many important works on Teilhard de Chardin have appeared in different languages, including Russian and Chinese. None of them, however, has included a close examination of his contacts with the East and its religions, at least not before the first edition of this book was published.[2] Most writers have interpreted Teilhard's thought from the perspective of either traditional or contemporary Christian theology, but few have related his reflections on religion and mysticism to the wider study of religions[3] or to the ongoing processes of global cultural and social evolution.

Teilhard de Chardin expressed his fascination with eastern thought more than once. In 1934 he wrote, "My own individual faith was inevitably peculiarly sensitive to eastern influences; and I am perfectly conscious of having felt their attraction...." It

2

appears even more surprising, therefore, that in spite of many years in the East, his writings seem to value eastern religions so little and judge them to be in opposition to his own worldview. The passage just quoted continues:

> The East fascinates me by its faith in the ultimate unity of the universe; but the fact remains that the two of us, the East and I, have two diametrically opposed conceptions....For the East, the One is seen as a suppression of the multiple; for me, the One is born from the concentration of the multiple. Thus, under the same monist appearances, there are two moral systems, two metaphysics and two mysticisms.[4]

Why did he perceive such an opposition, and what did he mean by it? This important question relates to many others. What historical, philosophical, or theological knowledge of eastern religions did he possess when comparing them with his own faith? Can the initial impression of his complete ignorance of these religions, assumed by many critics, be shown to be correct? Or will a closer examination of his works require us to modify such an assumption?

To assess Teilhard's statements in their proper context, his knowledge of eastern religions needs to be more carefully examined. This is less a question of describing some formally pursued course of study than of tracing his experience of the East and its religions. If the rich texture of lived experience is accepted as knowledge in a wider sense, then his extensive acquaintance with several Asian countries and their populations may have provided more influences on his thought than is generally recognized.

Teilhard de Chardin was not just an ordinary traveler journeying eastward, but someone particularly receptive to religious insights. He was therefore likely to reflect more than most on the religious beliefs and practices of the people he met. We must also remember that, in the presentation of his thought, he assigns a central place to "seeing." This applies to both the visual perception of the many phenomena that constitute the outer world as well as to the development of an inner vision. One might therefore expect that, although he never systematically pursued a historical or textual study of eastern religions, he nonetheless acquired a certain amount of knowledge about them, according to what time and circumstances permitted.

The examination of Teilhard's knowledge and experience of eastern religions has to be undertaken in a broad context. The expression "eastern religions" refers here to some of the major religions outside Judaism and Christianity whose beliefs and practices Teilhard encountered in Egypt, China, India, and elsewhere in Asia.

It is not enough, however, to consider only the years Teilhard spent in the Middle and Far East. Certain formative influences occurred earlier in his life. These permanently shaped his approach to religion and mysticism. Indeed, it is only through these experiences that he became interested in eastern mysticism at all. To elucidate the web of experiences and influences that affected Teilhard's ideas on eastern religions, I have gathered much relevant information about his early background, travels, and fieldtrips in the Middle and Far East, as well as his acquaintances, encounters, and readings about eastern religions.

His contacts and impressions of the East, especially of China, are described to give something of the flavor of his experiences and relate his thought on eastern religions and mysticism to the context of his life; in other words, to find the *Sitz im Leben* of his ideas. Here, as elsewhere, it is true to say that no study of Teilhard de Chardin's works makes sense "if one does not attempt to retrace the historical conditions of the milieu wherein his personality became conscious of itself."[5]

It must be stressed at the start that Teilhard's approach to eastern religions is directly dependent on his understanding of mysticism. This was not primarily theoretical but proceeded from a personal vision that was grounded in mystical experience. The patterns of this inner realization appear clearly when his writings are studied in chronological order. He first expressed his basic understanding of mysticism in his early essays, written before he went to the Far East. They introduce an important distinction between different forms of mysticism that, in essence, he maintained throughout his life. It is significant, however, that with his stay in the Far East, further references to this distinction usually include comparisons with eastern forms of mysticism. I discuss his comparative evaluation of eastern and western mysticism; in particular, I ask what he meant by his distinction between the "road of the East," and the "road of the West." What is the difference between these two "roads," and can there be a convergence between them that may eventually overcome their former separation?

Seen from a contemporary perspective, Teilhard's approach to eastern religions remains limited and undeveloped since he frequently expresses himself in rather oppositional terms that can be easily misunderstood. Yet a sympathetic as well as critical study of his thought reveals several convergent perspectives that transcend existing differences by pointing to the possibility of a greater unity between East and West. It is certainly worth investigating how a leading western religious thinker who spent nearly twenty years of his life and work in the East reacted to and reflected on eastern religions and, even more, why he assigned such a central place to what he called a "new mysticism" or a "mysticism of evolution."

Few contemporary writers have seen the importance of spirituality and mysticism for today with such great clarity. Teilhard was a man who felt passionately about the contemporary world and the radical transformation of human consciousness through the modern discovery of the immense process of evolution. His sensibility was searching for a spirituality commensurate with the dynamic of the world we live in. A prophet of hope, his mystical spirituality was firmly rooted in the Christian tradition, but it is without doubt that the experience of the East and its religions both influenced and enriched his fundamental vision of unity and convergence.

He experienced the world with a great sense of wonder, as a gracious gift, beckoning him to discover, praise, and adore something, or rather Someone, greater than himself. This numinous experience has been the primary matrix of all poetic vision and philosophic insight, and of humanity's ongoing religious and scientific quest, which has always meant far more than just a search for knowledge. For Teilhard, the whole of the natural world and the cosmos, but also the human world, was a "divine milieu," suffused with divine presence and power. As a highly trained scientist, he did not simply *look* at the world from the outside to understand its laws and facts of existence, but he traced the stirrings and struggles of life from within, from its very beginnings to its most complex developments. The integration of his scientific work with his deeply mystical faith made him *see* something great and wonderful, revealing all life as being held within the life of God.

Better known and rightly understood, Teilhard's mystical experience and vision may prove a stimulus and challenge to others who also want to know and to see, longing for oneness and connections deep within and without. Teilhard wrestled with science and religion but always experienced them as profoundly interconnected. He understood the tremendous challenge of evolution and felt that religion must take this very seriously and become transformed by engaging with it. It is right to call Teilhard a "post-Darwinian theologian," even though he never worked with theology as a specialized discipline or field of knowledge. Even more than this, he is a true "prophet" for our age, as Joseph Needham has so appropriately called him. A prophet not only for the western world, but for all people on our planet.

There exists a certain tension, even contradiction, between the open universalism and inclusiveness of Teilhard's world vision and the narrow constraints of his western-derived perspectives and exclusiveness as reflected in his interpretations of eastern religions and cultures. But this tension can be made to work as a fruitful and constructive combination of possibilities rather than be negative and destructive. His attitudes were rooted in, and limited by, many of the understandings prevalent during the late nineteenth and early twentieth centuries. Moreover, like other westerners of his time, he spent part of his life in the East in an expatriate, still largely colonial, milieu, although his numerous scientific expeditions in China and elsewhere enabled him to break the shackles and narrow limitations of this environment. His continual travels between West and East, and the rich textures of his many relationships with scientific colleagues and personal friends from different professional, religious, and ethnic backgrounds and cultures, opened up to him the diversity and complexities of contemporary life. He realized early on the profound

6

changes taking place in modern living and communications. He was acutely aware of the great need for closer collaboration between the different human groups in order to "build the earth" and share its resources equitably between its peoples. There is, in the words of Thomas Berry, a "great work" to be done,[6] an idea spelled out in even greater detail in Berry's own writings than in Teilhard's.

While retracing Teilhard's experience of the East and his knowledge of eastern religions, I hope to convey to readers something of the grandeur, strength, and beauty of his holistic vision, his firm faith in the future, and his zest and love of life. I hope readers will understand how his spirituality and mysticism are not only fed by the living sources of traditional religion, but also by the tremendous dynamic of an evolutionary worldview so radically new that its profoundly transformative impact is not always fully recognized by Teilhard's commentators.

William James once said that a man's vision is the great fact about him. It is the ultimate key for understanding someone's life and work. I hope to convey something of this in the present book while speaking at the same time to those engaged in the comparative study of religions, or actively involved in the meeting of world faiths in East and West, or searching for new directions in contemporary spirituality.

The book is in two parts. The first deals with the unity of life and thought in Teilhard's work. Its four chapters pursue a more or less chronological path by first tracing the emergence of Teilhard's great vision of faith, followed by his early contacts with the East, then his scientific work and travels between East and West, accompanied by his reflections on unity and oneness.

The second part is concerned with a discussion of the relationship between eastern and western religions in a converging world. It consists of five chapters, three of which examine Teilhard's understanding of monism, pantheism, and mysticism. They also analyze the meaning of his expressions "road of the East" and "road of the West," understood as two different roads to ultimate unity, and discuss how the contemporary global situation requires a convergence of these two roads. Chapter 8 deals with religion and evolution, a pivotal theme that shapes Teilhard's approach to all other issues and culminates in the evolution of mysticism. Chapter 9 is devoted to Teilhard's understanding of a new evolutionary "mysticism of action" and its implications for the contemporary world. The concluding epilogue raises several issues concerning spirituality in the twenty-first century, emphasizing the need to go beyond Teilhard by a critical engagement with his ideas and their further development.

Additional material is in the appendices, which list some of the important findings and ideas of this study in tabular form. It also includes an extended commentary on Teilhard's reading notes of some books on eastern religions. Following the notes, bibliography, and index, a separate annotated study guide has been included. This provides guidance for further reading and reflection, in order that additional study of key themes raised in this book can be pursued if so desired.

Wherever possible, I have used gender-inclusive language. This means that some quotations from Teilhard's writings, which, in common with the style of the previous century, usually are expressed in gender-exclusive terms, have been paraphrased or replaced by an inclusive word. It is only in this way that Teilhard can speak to contemporary sensibilities and his words be reinscribed with the inherent power of their original meaning.

I
UNITY OF LIFE AND THOUGHT

The greatest success I can hope for in my life—to have published a new vision of the world.

Pierre Teilhard de Chardin

A GREAT VISION OF FAITH

Pierre Teilhard de Chardin's deep Christian faith shaped his approach to all aspects of life, whether inner or outer, past, present, or future. He was a strong believer, one of the great modern mystics, whose inspiring spiritual vision remains unfortunately far too little known. But he was also an eminent scientist, a specialist in biology, geology, and paleontology, who devoted his life to research in geology and human origins. His vision is a synthesis of personal faith and evolutionary science, as understood in his day. Short passages from Teilhard's collected works are often quoted in isolation without revealing this overall dynamic and evolutionary perspective. Yet what matters most is his all-embracing mystical vision of the world, humanity, and God. He described this as a new way of seeing, acquired through formative personal experiences, great intellectual attainments, and a depth of new understanding grounded in the combined insights of both religion and science, and expressed through deep wisdom and love.

Seeing the World Anew

The unfolding of this vision can be traced, stage by stage, in the development of Teilhard's life and in the lifelong expression of his thought in scientific publications, letters, diaries, and in philosophical and religious essays collected and published after his death. There are few whose life and work are so closely intertwined into a coherent unity that radiates a breathtaking vision spanning an entire life. When he wrote the essay "My Fundamental Vision" (1948), he presented his worldview in a fairly schematic manner, but elsewhere the elements of this vision are expressed in a more personal and autobiographical form, especially in the beautiful late essays "The Heart of Matter" (1950) and "The Christic" (1955).[1]

"My Fundamental Vision" is the translation of the French essay "*Comment Je Vois*," which literally means "How I See." It is indeed the importance of "seeing" that here, as elsewhere in his works, is often emphasized in Teilhard's approach. The essay is prefaced by the sentence: "It seems to me that a whole life-time of continued hard work would be as nothing to me, if only I could, just for one moment, give a true picture of what I see."[2]

The foreword to Teilhard's major work, which first became widely known as *The Phenomenon of Man* but has now been more accurately retranslated as *The Human Phenomenon*, is also devoted to "Seeing." In fact, the entire book is an attempt to let people see more, for "to see is really to become more," a deeper vision "is really fuller being."[3] To learn to see in this sense means "to develop a *homogeneous* and *coherent* perspective of our general extended experience of man."[4] Many passages in his work emphasize that "it is essential to see—to see things as they are and to see them really and intensely."[5] *Seeing* is used in an extended sense here; to see means to discern, apprehend, and understand, to develop an overall perspective of looking at life and constructing an all-encompassing worldview. However, Teilhard does not merely mean natural seeing, but a seeing of an altogether different order:

> The perception of the divine omnipresence is essentially a seeing, a taste, that is to say a sort of intuition bearing upon certain superior qualities in things. It cannot, therefore, be attained directly by any process of reasoning, nor by any human artifice. It is a gift like life itself, of which it is undoubtedly the supreme experiential perfection.[6]

In other words, seeing is not simply a human activity but something we are endowed with, something given to us like an innate treasure from which we can draw immeasurable benefits.

Teilhard's understanding of what he called "the human phenomenon," that is to say all aspects of what it means to be fully human—including all the processes by which human beings emerged during the long drawn-out history of evolutionary becoming—refers at its deepest level also to the phenomena of religion, spirituality, and mysticism. The nature of human beings cannot be fully understood without recognizing the central significance of these developments. When Teilhard first went to China in 1923, he wrote in a letter from the Ordos Desert that "mysticism remains the great science and the great art, the only power capable of synthesizing the riches accumulated by other forms of human activity."[7]

What did Teilhard see in retracing human origins and the evolution of the human species within the great story of life? The physical evidence of stones, fossil plants, and bones that spoke to him so palpably can be traced in his meticulously assembled fossil collections, scientific lectures, and memoirs. The deeply spiritual interpretation given to this painstaking scientific work is revealed in his numerous philosophical and religious writings. These disclose a deeply poetic and mystical soul for whom the living universe was ablaze with the fire of divine love, suffused with the elements of a presence that beckons, summons, and embraces us; a world intimately united with God in all its fibers and phases of development, but a world that had emerged through an immense process of evolution during eons of time.

This "world" meant for him the natural and cosmic world as well as the personal and social world, the large sphere of human action, where the smallest effort contributes something to a higher reality being born and emerging. Teilhard refers already in his earliest writings to the experience of the mystic seer, the *voyant*, whose vision constructs the world anew. In the very last of his essays, "The Christic," after describing the coherence and beauty of his vision of faith, a deeply spiritual and mystical vision arising out of the intimate conjunction of material and spiritual aspects of life, he movingly asks whether he is the only person to have seen such a vision or whether other people share it and may be similarly transformed by such seeing anew. To understand the depth and power of Teilhard's amazing spiritual and mystical vision, to be

13

grasped by the great synthesis of so many diverse and dynamic elements, it is essential to trace step by step the unfolding of a lifelong process of outer and inner experiences and reflection.

Major Elements of Teilhard's Vision

Let me try to recapture some elements of this vision. Since Teilhard's life and thought are so closely interwoven, both illuminate each other and have to be examined together. This is difficult, since almost none of his works were published during his lifetime. Although his ideas and essays circulated among friends, students, and colleagues, their publication occurred only after his death and was arranged by others. Moreover, his many essays were not published in chronological order but were arranged thematically and grouped into a collection of thirteen books whose titles were also chosen by others, not by Teilhard. The complex process of publication over more than twenty years can appear to be quite arbitrary and makes it difficult to trace the historical development of Teilhard's ideas. Apart from the two books, *The Human Phenomenon* and *The Divine Milieu*, the other eleven volumes of the French edition, on which the English translations are based, each contain collection of essays selected from his entire life. Unfortunately, no critical edition of Teilhard's works has been published so far, although his writings have been digitalized by the French Fondation Teilhard de Chardin and are accessible by subscription via an Internet site.[8]

Numerous letters written each year are also scattered over many volumes of a large correspondence or remain unpublished. To arrive at a detailed analysis of the development of Teilhard's thought, one therefore has to piece together many fragments from different sources, and this requires careful detective work. Only in this way can we reconstruct a chronological sequence that reveals the fundamental vision of a modern man of faith who attempted to chart a new road for contemporary Christian spirituality. It is a vision nourished by the deepest sources of the Christian tradition while enlivened and strengthened by the discoveries of modern science, especially the new understanding of evolution that appeals so much to many people outside the Christian faith.

The development of Teilhard's inner vision is linked to certain formative experiences of his life, mystical experiences that can be inferred from allusions in his letters, diaries, and essays, particularly when they are read in conjunction with his essay "The Heart of Matter" (1950), written late in his life. This spiritual autobiography is of immense significance, for it is here that Teilhard, in his old age, describes the early emergence and subsequent growth of a powerful mystical vision that sustained him throughout his life. For those who can decipher them, there are many clues to this vision in his earlier writings. Teilhard's earliest attempt to outline some kind of spiritual autobiography goes back as far as 1918, to the first version of his essay "My Universe,"[9] which already sets out the elements of his mystical experience and vision.

The experience came first; it provided the nucleus from which he developed a philosophy, a theology, and an integral worldview rooted in both science and religion, and that included a partly new understanding of spirituality and mysticism. He emphasizes this primacy of experience in an early diary entry that reads, "The true interest of life does not lie in discovery and knowledge,—but in *realization*...."[10]

In the essay "The Heart of Matter," Teilhard relates how from his earliest childhood onward, he had decisive inner experiences that made him seek some Absolute, some universal unity and coherence that was both tangible and concrete at the same time. At first, this search expressed itself in a passion for collecting rocks and stones; later, it was the wider contact with many different aspects of nature that developed in him the ardent desire for communion with an All. His father nurtured in him an early interest in science, whereas his mother transmitted to him the ardor of a religious faith that was deeply nourished by the Christian mystics.

As a child and young adult, Teilhard had several mystic experiences that may be described as a realization of cosmic consciousness, an experience where the oneness, the beauty, and the divine vibrations running through all of nature were felt with great intensity. Years later, when he was able to describe these experiences in words and reflect upon their significance, he noted, "All I shall ever write will only be a feeble part of what I feel."[11]

This nature mysticism, which had its roots in his childhood, first found its full flowering in Jersey, an island in the English Channel where the French Jesuits had moved their study house after being driven out of France by an anticlerical government. Teilhard spent the years 1901–5 there as a philosophy student and fell in love with the coast and the sea. His strong attraction to the beauty of nature revealed a pantheistic inclination that was to remain with him all his life, although it later underwent several important modifications.

While the wide open sea and lonely rock-strewn shores of Jersey impressed upon Teilhard the beauty and grandeur of nature, it was the strange, exotic features of an eastern landscape on a vaster scale that led to the full awakening of his mystic search. The first contact with the East was experienced through a stay in Egypt, which left a lasting influence and mark on him. During 1905–8, Teilhard taught physics at a Jesuit school, the College of the Holy Family in Cairo. When he had time, he undertook expeditions into the Egyptian desert in order to pursue geological and archaeological field research. This gave him the opportunity to discover new fossils, and he was thrilled when the French Geological Society named one specimen after him.

There is ample evidence in his later works that the experience of the desert, especially eight days spent with a Jesuit friend in an expedition to the West of the Nile in 1907, left an indelible impression on him. Numerous passages exist in his writings where the solitude, vastness, and entrancing beauty of the desert are alluded to as the place where the mystic seer is closest to a vision of unity and all-embracing oneness. It was in the desert of Egypt that he "experienced such sense of wonder."[12]

While forever indebted to the positive aspects of this experience, Teilhard nevertheless soon recognized its negative features, which he repudiated as a pantheistic temptation, luring him away from the world of human beings in order to become fused with an impersonal All. Teilhard's first biographer, the French scholar Claude Cuénot, has said that Teilhard underwent his biggest religious crisis in Egypt, meeting there a very subtle and heavy temptation to dissolve himself in nature. If one reflects for a moment on the role of the desert in the history of spirituality, not only as the place of temptation and encounter with God—as for example in the Christian desert fathers, or more recently in the life of Charles de Foucault—but also as a place of solitude, silence, and emptiness, a motif found in religions other than Christianity, one realizes the crucial importance that the desert experience had for Teilhard's inner development and understanding of mysticism. As a type, the desert experience was later repudiated; it led to a cul-de-sac and was subsequently described as an "eastern vision," understood as a negative road of fusion and escape. From early on, Teilhard also enquired into the mystical experiences of others, both in Christianity and outside it. He widened his vision by reading different mystics and studies about mysticism through which he discovered mystics of different faiths.

The Discovery of Evolution

After his stay in Egypt, Teilhard spent four years studying theology in a Jesuit house based in Hastings (1908–12), a seaside town on the English Channel in the south of England. The French Jesuits had sought refuge here, in addition to Jersey, when an anti-clerical government expelled them from France. Besides intensive theological studies, Teilhard found enough time to undertake geological field trips around the English coast. Again, he collected many fossils, now mainly housed in the Hastings Museum. The field trips also provided an opportunity to establish contact with the Kensington Science Museum in London. He was thrilled when a British scientist later published a description of the fossil plants collected by Teilhard in Hastings, naming among others a genus *Teilhardia* and a species *Teilhardi*.

During the time at Hastings, "the attraction of matter" still predominated, since he experienced a strong inclination toward nature and to what he later described as "cosmic life." Yet he could not go on studying fossil remains and contemporary understandings of nature without coming across theories of evolution. Combining these with the static views of theology and philosophy presented considerable problems that he discussed with Jesuit friends who were similarly interested in the physical and natural sciences. The transformation of Teilhard's thinking happened gradually, until his religious and scientific views suddenly all came together, fusing into a new vision when he read Henri Bergson's inspiring book, *Creative Evolution,* published in 1907. Even forty years later, Teilhard could clearly remember how avidly he had read that book. It made him discover the dynamic pattern and rhythm running through the whole universe. God's creation acquired a new meaning, and the attraction of nature grew stronger still. He rejected Bergson's idea of a vital impulse, of a cosmos originating from a central source developing in divergent directions. Instead, he understood the cosmos as coming into being through a process of evolutionary creation, a convergent cosmogenesis, unfolding in space–time.

In his spiritual autobiography "The Heart of Matter" (1950), Teilhard reflected on the influence of Bergson's book on him:

> I can now see quite clearly that the only effect that bril-liant book had upon me was to provide fuel just at the right moment, and very briefly, for a fire that was already consuming my heart and mind. And that fire had been kindled, I imagine, simply by the coincidence in me...of the three inflammable elements that had slowly piled up in the depths of my soul over a period of thirty years. These were the cult of Matter, the cult of Life, and the cult of Energy. All three found a poten-tial outlet and synthesis in a world which had suddenly acquired a new dimension and had thereby moved from the fragmented state of static Cosmos to the organic state and dignity of Cosmogenesis.
>
> At first, naturally enough, I was far from under-standing and clearly appreciating the importance of the change I was undergoing.[13]

Under Bergson's powerful influence the perception of the greatness and oneness of nature—the sea, the sky, the cliffs and their abundant fossils, the colorful countryside and its rich vegetation—grew so intense that it became almost overwhelming. As in Egypt before, the study of, and personal immersion in, nature became fused into an overriding experience of mystical attraction. He often expressed this exuberant nature mysticism in his early essays, and it is beautifully summed up in "The Heart of Matter," written so many years later:

> All that I can remember of those days (apart from that magic word "evolution", which haunted my thoughts like a tune: which was to me like an unsatisfied hunger, like a promise held out to me, like a summons to be answered)—all that I can remember is the extraordinary solidity and intensity I found then in the English countryside, particularly at sunset, when the Sussex woods were charged with all that "fossil" Life which I was then hunting for, from cliff to quarry, in the Wealden clay. There were moments, indeed, when it seemed to me that a sort of universal being was about to take shape suddenly in Nature before my very eyes.[14]

The period at Hastings marked for Teilhard a major turning point in his understanding of the world, of his faith, his method of working, and his interpretation of scientific data. The discovery of evolution meant that he had become conscious of a new dimension. It was no longer simply a hypothesis but was recognized as a condition of all life and experience, as he later often stated in his writings.

Evolution also assumed a central importance for the reinterpretation of his religious beliefs, particularly for his understanding of the figure of Christ. The "cosmic" and "christic sense" that he later described as the two sides of his being eventually converged into a powerful vision of the universal and cosmic "Christ," a symbol of great integrative force, which has its origin in this period.[15] It is a vision intrinsically related to the mystical quality of his nature experiences, but the initial experience of a monistic pantheism had gradually been prolonged and transcended into what Teilhard occasionally referred to as "pan-Christic monism," or what might be described as a person-centered theistic mysticism. Today this would be understood as a worldview of "panentheism," a term Teilhard himself did not use, although the word already existed at that time. But it was not in wide circulation.

Initially, the experience of nature seemed to be more important for Teilhard than the experience of an interpersonal world. The difficulty of interpersonal relationships was acutely felt by him when he described the "other" as an intruder into one's inner world, breaking the unity and self-contained coherence of the mystic's inner vision. The enriching experience of a personal *Thou* was probably first awakened in him through the love of his cousin Marguerite, well known to him since his childhood. He met up with her again during his years of scientific study in Paris (1912–14), where Marguerite, after completing an advanced university education in philosophy and literature, had become headmistress of a well-known Catholic girls' school. Initially drawn together by family ties, they discovered a close intellectual and spiritual affinity, deepened through their regular correspondence during the First World War (1914–18).

After having been ordained in Hastings in 1911, Teilhard performed many pastoral duties at the Front of what later came to be called the Great War. He chose to work as a simple stretcher-bearer, preferring to attend the many sick and wounded as an ordinary soldier rather than enjoy the relative privileges of an Army chaplain. No other period of his life is so closely documented as the war period. We possess the letters to his cousin, entitled *The Making of a Mind*, his war diaries, and the posthumously published essays *Writings in Time of War*, wherein he expresses his spiritual vision in a deeply moving, lyrical style.

His cousin Marguerite was a major friend and support during these difficult years. She shared and encouraged his literary interests in important ways and was, in fact, the only person who really understood his ideas at that time. One might even describe her as an attendant midwife to the birth of his literary work. Herself a writer, she was the first to receive his essays, and the two friends were mutual critics of each other's achievements.

The Great War: A Crucible of Fire

The war was a profoundly transforming experience for Teilhard. It brought home to him the complex realities of the social world, the impact of human masses in movement and action, and the great diversity of people, especially in terms of the recruits drawn from French imperial territories in North Africa and South East Asia.

Working as a stretcher-bearer in the First World War, Teilhard was always close to military action at the Front. Almost daily, he experienced the savage, fiery battles of the trenches. Repeatedly, he was immersed in experiences of battle between life and death. This drove him to leave a "testament," to find an intellectual expression of his inner vision, to articulate a philosophical elaboration of his pantheistic and mystic experiences. Whenever there was a respite from battle, a temporary withdrawal from fighting, surprisingly, he could find enough time to set pen to paper and write down his thoughts. Through reading, reflection, and the comparison of his experience with that of others, he was able to formulate what, on one hand, he called his "vision" and, on the other, he attempted to preach as his "gospel." These were his first essays, written from 1916 onward and published much later as *Writings in Time of War*.[16] Generally far too little known, they contain the seeds of most of his later works. Commentators familiar with Teilhard's texts are well aware that he felt all his life that he had seen something new.

The expression of this vision in literary form began in 1916 and continued until his death in 1955. Studying his works from beginning to end, one cannot but be overawed, and feel immensely enriched, by the fundamental beauty, strength, and coherence of this consuming vision, which he often compared to a blazing fire. Throughout all his writings, the image of fire recurs with such regularity that I chose to call my biography of Teilhard's life and vision *Spirit of Fire*.[17]

The immensity of the war, the daily life at the Front, and face-to-face encounters with death provided a catalyzing influence through which the mystical seer turned writer. One might rightly wonder how, under such adverse conditions, Teilhard was able to reflect and write at all. The extreme circumstances of the war must have given Teilhard a compelling sense of urgency without which he might not have launched himself into writing.

The battle of the trenches was experienced as "a baptism of the real"[18] that brought about the focusing of his vision. With heightened sensibility and extraordinary detachment, he was able, between the battles, to go for lonely walks, reflect in solitude, and formulate his ideas. He even collected fossils to use for his scientific doctorate after the war!

The war impressions were so overwhelming that Teilhard felt neither the attractions of Egypt nor the stimulating activity of Paris were worth as much as his experience of the dirt of war. It was here, amid blood, death, and terror, that his tremendous vision of humanity as one, sharing a common origin and destiny and moving forward together, first began to take shape. When Teilhard's war letters were published in 1965, the well-known French Catholic writer, François Mauriac, commented:

> The most optimistic view a Christian thinker has ever held of this criminal world was conceived at Verdun; this frantic cry of hope has been uttered from an abyss....The same sort of courage which was necessary to hold out in the trenches of Verdun, was also necessary for conceiving thoughts as joyful as these, so permeated by hope.[19]

Teilhard's first essay, "Cosmic Life" (1916), was to be his "intellectual testament" in the event of his death. It spells out the attraction and abiding influence of a pantheistic vision, of being immersed in nature, while at the same time repudiating "the temptation of matter." The magic appeal of nature echoes through all the war writings, but especially through the powerful essays "The Mystical Milieu" (1917), "The Soul of the World" (1918), "The Great Monad" (1918), "My Universe" (1918), "The Universal Element" (1919), and "The Spiritual Power of Matter" (1919).[20] In 1916 Teilhard was for the first time able to fully articulate his earlier mystic experiences. Yet while describing the awakening to the cosmos, and the temptation to surrender

himself to the appeal of matter, he personally had already overcome this initial attraction and was searching for something
greater, more transcendent. Through the experience of nature he
discovered "as though in an ecstasy, that *through all nature I was
immersed in God.*" He felt that a vigorous effort was required to

> reverse my course and ascend....The true summons of
> the cosmos is a call consciously to share in the great
> work that goes on within it; it is not by drifting down
> the current of things that we shall be united with their
> one, single, soul, but by fighting our way, with them,
> towards some term still to come.[21]

This polarization of two tendencies in the mystic seeker,
expressed in "Cosmic Life," was to be a lasting feature of Teilhard's
approach to the interpretation of mysticism—the choice of reach-
ing ultimate unity either through return and fusion or through
progress and synthesis. In the following years these two tendencies became explicitly associated with an oversimplified, and ultimately misleading, polarization between eastern and western
mysticism. This emphasis on two types of mysticism, together
with the search for a higher unity, and a new mysticism, are examined later.

"Cosmic Life" is prefaced by an epigraph that expresses a
recurrent leitmotif of Teilhard's entire work. It reads, "There is a
communion with God, and a communion with earth, and a communion with God through earth." Initially the "communion with
earth" refers to the experience of a deeply felt unity with nature,
whereas later it stands for any immanent or inner-worldly attitude, but also for every close social engagement with the world
that leaves no room for transcendence. "Communion with God,"
by contrast, stands for an excessively otherworldly attitude, an
understanding of God and religion as separate from the world. In
Teilhard's view, the exclusive or nearly exclusive concern for a
transcendent reality, often regarded as the main characteristic of
the religious quest, does not place enough importance on the
value of human effort, on human responsibility and agency in the
development of the world. The two attitudes—communion with

earth, and communion with God—are regarded as incomplete. What is sought is the synthesis of both, not as a simple combination, but as something of a new order altogether. "Communion with God through earth" symbolizes, so to speak, Teilhard's life-long attempt to relate the Divine and the world in the most intimate manner, expressed through his efforts in seeing science and religion as part of the same quest for ultimate unity, and in relating mystical spirituality to creative effort and action.

But the synthesis he attempted was little understood. Of the thirteen essays composed during the war, all except one were judged unsuitable for publication. Teilhard realized then how difficult it would be for his ideas to see the light of day "except in conversation or manuscript form, passed surreptitiously from hand to hand."[22] Written at the end of 1916, this comment was truly prophetic, for this is exactly what happened during the next forty years. I cannot follow the vicissitudes of Teilhard's literary career here,[23] but I continue to trace the major stages of his inner development.

The Maturing of Teilhard's Vision in Asia

After the end of the First World War, Teilhard returned to Paris to finish his scientific studies in geology, botany, and zoology, followed by a doctorate on the mammals of the Lower Eocene in France. In 1922, he gave such a brilliant defense of his doctoral research that he was given a scientific medal and a prize by the Académie des Sciences in Paris.[24] He was promoted to the chair in geology at the Catholic Institute in Paris, where he had been lecturing since 1920, and soon afterward he was elected president of the French Geological Society. He was invited to international conferences in Basle and Brussels, where he met the codirector of the Chinese Geological Service without knowing then that he himself would later be associated with the pioneering scientific work of this organization.

It was however a fellow Jesuit who first invited him to China, to join him on a scientific mission in 1923. Teilhard greatly welcomed the opportunity to visit the Far East. He longed to see this part of the world, since it possessed many family associations for him. His oldest brother had visited China, and one of his sisters had worked as a missionary in Shanghai and had died there. Little did he know during his first visit that China would eventually become for him a place of exile, where he would spend most of his time, working there until 1946. The arrival in China completed Teilhard's inner development and brought his mystical vision into full focus. He has unequivocally stated that his pan-Christic mysticism matured "in the two great atmospheres of Asia and the War."[25] It found its full expression in two of his most important spiritual writings, "The Mass on the World" (1923) and *The Divine Milieu* (1927), which, together with the much later essay "The Christic" (1955), form a kind of mystical triptych.

During the initial contact with China, the experience of the desert was again decisive, as it had been earlier in Egypt. This time, it was the Ordos Desert inside the Yellow River bend that Teilhard and his Jesuit confrère, Père Licent, explored during an expedition to Mongolia. On several occasions, Teilhard compared the Ordos Desert with Egypt, which he had experienced more than fifteen years earlier. The period in Mongolia was likened to a retreat that led him "to the heart of the unique greatness of God."[26] During this expedition, Teilhard and his companion lived much of the time in a tent, camping in the desert. Under these conditions, it was not always possible to say Mass, so Teilhard continued his habit, begun during the war, to offer the world to God in a prayer that he at first referred to as a "Mass upon all things." It is from this prayer that the well-known "Mass on the World" developed, written down in the Ordos Desert, possibly on the Feast of the Transfiguration, but finalized at Tientsin in December 1923.[27]

This fervent hymn of praise is autobiographical. It presents a fully formed mystical vision based on a deep personal experience of union and communion with God. It is the offering of the world in all its concreteness to God who is "the universal milieu in which and through which all things live and have their being."[28] Thus, the world in its fullest extension becomes God's body, "the glorious living crucible in which everything melts away in order to be born anew."[29] Although not a pantheistic vision, this is a perspective that assumes into itself monistic and pantheistic aspirations, yet transcends them. It provides a sublime example of what philosophers and theologians today call "panentheism." Addressing himself intimately to God, Teilhard recalls the stages of his inner journey:

> Little by little, through the irresistible development of those yearnings you implanted in me as a child...and through the awakening of terrible and gentle initiations by which you made me transcend successive circles, through all these I have been brought to the point where I can no longer see anything, nor any longer breathe, outside that milieu in which all is made one.

And he goes on to explain:

> I shall savour with heightened consciousness the intense yet tranquil rapture of a vision whose coherence and harmonies I can never exhaust.[30]

His innermost being vibrates in accord with a single note of incredible richness wherein the most opposite tendencies find themselves united:

> The excitement of action and the delight of passivity; the joy of possessing and the thrill of reaching out beyond what one possesses; the pride in growing and the happiness of being lost in what is greater than oneself.[31]

The concluding prayer states unequivocally that, for Teilhard, everything depended on this fundamental vision of the union of God and the universe. If others proclaim the splendors of God as pure Spirit, he felt it his particular vocation to praise the innumerable prolongations of God's "incarnate Being in the world of matter," to preach the mystery of God's flesh.

From now on he maintained that the only thing that interested him was "the universe of the future—the world of living ideas and the mystical life."[32] He saw mysticism as "the great science and the great art" that was for him above all "the science of

Christ running through all things."[33] "The Mass on the World" can be said to contain a vision of the world as a cosmic sacrament. In Teilhard's words,

> The true substance to be consecrated each day is the world's development during that day—the bread symbolising appropriately what creation succeeds in producing, the wine what creation causes to be lost in exhaustion and suffering in the course of its effort.[34]

Teilhard later developed this theme systematically in *The Divine Milieu* (1927) as "the divinization of our activities" and "the divinization of our passivities." Bearing the subtitle "An Essay on the Interior Life," this book is a spiritual classic. However, the poetic approach of "The Mass on the World" may have more immediate appeal to many people than the rather treatise-like structure of *The Divine Milieu*.

The "divine milieu" is another name for what Teilhard had earlier called the "mystical milieu."[35] The mystical vision of communion and union with God gives human beings access to a new "milieu," a new environment and center where everything may potentially become divinized. As is said in the introduction of *The Divine Milieu*, "God truly waits for us in things."[36]

The Key for Understanding Teilhard's Vision

Fragments of Teilhard's inner vision are dispersed throughout all his essays. Sometimes, especially in the more abstract and scientific writings, it may only be a brief sentence, an allusion, a short paragraph that refers to his mystical understanding of world, humanity, and cosmic evolution. His well-known masterpiece, *The Human Phenomenon*, is more concerned with scientific than religious matters, so that it is not the easiest book for nonscientists to understand Teilhard's overall perspective or to gain full insight into his illuminating mystical vision. This large work is a *summa* of his comprehensive anthropological perspective presented in an overall evolutionary framework. As it is addressed primarily to the contemporary scientific temper, questions of spirituality are less touched upon.

The tremendous spiritual vision that radiates through Teilhard's entire life and undergirds all his writing finds its greatest expression in "The Heart of Matter" (1950). This moving essay provides an indispensable key for interpreting Teilhard's entire work. It celebrates a christo-cosmic vision, a "diaphany" of the Divine at the heart of the universe. The intimate union of the material and spiritual is affirmed by the words preceding the main text:

> At the heart of Matter
> A World-heart,
> The Heart of a God.[37]

The love of God and the love of the world are inextricably combined; their central focus is the universal and cosmic Christ, so that the essay culminates in a "Prayer to the ever greater Christ," remarkable for its mystical depth and beauty. It is a continuation of all that is most central to Christianity, and it reminds one of the hymn of the fourth-century Christian writer Prudentius who describes Christ as

> Of the Father's heart begotten
> Ere the world from chaos rose,
> He is Alpha: from the fountain
> All that is and has been, flows;
> He is Omega, of all things
> Yet to come the mystic Close
> Evermore and evermore.

Yet even after writing "The Heart of Matter," Teilhard still felt the need to express his Christ-centered vision once more. He labored for nearly five years to find an even more vivid description of what he had seen. In the essay "The Christic" (1955), completed a few weeks before his death, he presented his fundamental vision for the last time. This essay is of a very personal, almost confidential nature, a kind of quintessence of the "Mass on the World," *The Divine Milieu,* and "The Heart of Matter."

The final testament of Teilhard's pan-Christic mysticism, it also bears witness to an extraordinary psychological integration achieved through the close interweaving of profound religious and scientific insights.

Teilhard died on April 10, 1955. "The Christic" is signed "New York, March 1955," without giving a precise date.[38] It represents a singular summary of his vision, and a final confession of faith. He affirms with strong conviction:

> Today, after forty years of continuous thought, it is still exactly the same fundamental vision that I feel I must present, and enable others to share in its matured form—for the last time.
>
> It may not be expressed with the same freshness and exuberance as resulted from my first meeting with it—but the wonder and the passion will still be there, undimmed.[39]

It would be presumptuous to summarize this essay in a few words. It is not an easy work, but it deserves most careful attention since it expresses important thoughts that occupied Teilhard at the end of his life, as can be seen from his diaries of 1944–55. One of his central questions during this period was, "Is Christianity enough for today's world?" In "The Christic," he ponders over this and wonders whether the rise of the comparative study of religions has not led to the realization of the relativity of Christianity, bringing about its decline. This is a question of even greater concern today.

In 1955, Teilhard answered his own concern by stressing that while one has to be open to forces of renewal and insight from other sources, Christianity's specific contribution lies in its belief in God's incarnation in the world. Through this belief, Christianity has the extraordinary ability to engender an all-transforming, dynamic love that embraces both God and the world. It can connect to a world in movement and provide the activating energies for its further evolution.

The interpenetration of the spiritual and material, given through the incarnation, endows Christianity with a singular force of attraction and adoration, of worship, of human access to God via the world. Here is a universal presence, a living God, whose energy animates all matter and levels of life, an ultimate center where everything finds its consummation. Mystic seers who can perceive such intimate union discover new paths opening up before them.

The last section of "The Christic" is entitled "The Religion of Tomorrow." It makes the important point that only a new religious synthesis can provide the required psychic energy for the further evolution of humankind, that is to say, a synthesis that embraces a much wider perspective than in the past and takes into account the complementary insights of different faiths. Teilhard speaks of a "reborn Christianity" here, a faith that can energize to the full "both the powers of growth and life and the powers of diminishment and death," and is able "to provide the driving force in Evolution."[40]

In his personal conclusion he expresses the joy of having experienced the wonderful "diaphany" of God in and through the world, a vision that transforms everything and makes all things shine anew. The same passage also hints at Teilhard's suffering, doubt, and inner isolation through not being able to share his deepest thoughts with others. Perhaps he was, after all, only the victim of an "inner mirage"? Why is it that he seems to be the only person to have seen the force of such a cosmic, christic vision?

Teilhard thus questioned his own position. Notes of doubt and self-questioning could be quoted from other essays too. But in "The Christic" he ultimately affirms the internal coherence of his vision, the power of an all-embracing love, and the superiority of his new insights over traditional formulas of faith. The essay finishes therefore on an emphatic note of joy and hope: One day there will be others, similarly "ablaze" with the vision he saw: truth has to appear only once to spread like fire.

The Teilhard biography by the American writers Mary and Ellen Lukas, published in 1977,[41] begins by relating some folktales of the Auvergne, the region in France where Teilhard was born. These tales speak of the innocent seeker who leaves the land of his birth to look for the ultimate secret at the heart of reality, the single truth behind the multiple veil of illusion. In all the tales, the seeker who finds what he is looking for is wounded in the conquest and ends his life alone, without being able to communicate his secret to another living soul.

Is this true of Teilhard too?, the authors ask. It remains for each of us to answer this question. The Lukas biography was written with the intention to have Teilhard reexamined, for he remains outside the mainstream of contemporary thought. This is still true today, more than thirty years after the Lukas biography was published and more than fifty years after Teilhard's death. In the current situation of growing secularism and atheism in the West, the great potential of his ideas to inspire and advance current debates regarding humanity's scientific endeavors, religious thought, and mystical empowerment for a global world on the move has not been fully recognized yet. Within the global and ecological context of today, it is even more important than in earlier years to reexamine his understanding of spirituality and mysticism in an evolutionary world and trace his search for a new mysticism of action, especially in relation to modern science.

More than forty years ago, the great French theologian Henri de Lubac examined Teilhard's vision of faith;[42] so too have many other theological and philosophical authors since then. But only rarely has Teilhard's thought been linked to his experience of the East,[43] and his interpretation of eastern religions and mysticism has not been studied in depth. Did Teilhard's ideas about religion and mysticism, after passing through successive formulations, eventually transcend his own tradition and propose something new? If so, what contribution did the experience of eastern religions make to such a synthesis?

It is with these questions in mind that the following chapters were written. Beginning with early influences, they present a factual account of Teilhard's knowledge of the East and its religions as it developed through contacts, reading, and travels. Some key texts are then analyzed to show how he related his own mystic experiences to a particular interpretation of mysticism and eastern religions. This is followed by a discussion of the relevance of these ideas for contemporary spirituality.

2

EARLY CONTACTS WITH THE EAST

When Pierre Teilhard de Chardin began to write essays on religion and mysticism in 1916, he was in his mid-thirties. His reflections were primarily rooted in his personal experience, yet his ideas underwent continuous development in relation to important events of his life. Friendships, encounters, travels, and studies all helped to expand his vision and express what he felt and thought. He did not go to China until he was over forty. By this time he had developed certain views and expectations about the East due to his contacts and readings, and his earlier stay in Egypt.

How did his attitudes to eastern religions first develop? Is there any indication that early influences, even in his family background, kindled a certain interest in different countries of the East, and especially the Far East?

Early Family Influences

As a child, Teilhard was particularly close to his eldest brother Albéric and his sister Françoise, two years senior to him. Both exercised a strong influence on his early life. During the late nineteenth century, Albéric had joined the French Navy, with which he traveled widely in the Middle and Far East. He spent some time in Shanghai, Peking, and Japan and returned to France with many Chinese souvenirs for his parents and relatives. In the late twentieth century, some of these, such as paintings on silk and rice paper, were still kept in the family of Teilhard's youngest brother, Joseph. He showed them to me during a visit to Paris in the early 1970s, assuring me that in his view Pierre's interest in the East was first awakened through the travels of his brother Albéric (1876–1902).

There is plenty of evidence that these travels also influenced Pierre's sister Françoise (1879–1911). Like him, she had a religious vocation and joined a Catholic religious order, the Little Sisters of the Poor. She expressed a great desire to go to China, and she was eventually, in 1909, sent to a mission house in Shanghai where she worked among the urban poor. Sadly, she died from smallpox after just two years there. Her letters sent home between 1909 and 1911[1] provided another indirect source of information on China for Teilhard, as did some of the reports of Jesuits working in China and Japan.

Following his stay in the Far East at the end of the nineteenth century, Teilhard's brother Albéric was posted to Constantinople. There he developed a strong interest in the history of Byzantium, a subject about which he lectured extensively on his return to France in 1901–2. It seems that his younger brother Pierre became familiar with this material too. Teilhard's earliest impressions of both the Middle and the Far East were therefore mediated through his family. It is impossible to know whether these impressions created more than an initial curiosity or whether they influenced him in any way to seek further eastern contacts. There is no doubt, however, that the really formative experience of the East occurred initially when, as a young Jesuit, Teilhard had the opportunity to spend three years in the Middle East, in Egypt.

The Formative Experience of Egypt

The French Jesuit province of Lyons, to which Teilhard belonged, was particularly concerned with missions in the Middle East. A number of schools and educational institutions were in its charge, and it was to such a school in Cairo, the Jesuit Collège de la Sainte Famille, founded in 1888 and still in existence today, that Teilhard was sent in 1905. For three years, he taught physics and chemistry to Egyptian boys, many of them Muslims. Occasionally he accompanied his students home to their families in different parts of Egypt. He thus had an opportunity to get acquainted with the country and become familiar with both urban and rural parts, particularly with the striking landscape of the North African desert experienced on visits to classical sites and during several expeditions.

The discovery of the East was for Teilhard always connected with "the lonesome waste of the desert whose purple plains rose and fell one after another to a vanishing point on the wildly exotic horizon."[2] The unforgettable experience of magnificent sunsets, the vast spatial expanses of the desert whose calm and tranquility he later so much missed in Paris, echoed in him for the rest of his life. More than forty years later, he described this experience:

> The East flowed over me in a first wave of exoticism. I gazed at it and drank it in eagerly—the country itself, not its peoples or its history (which as yet held no interest for me), but its light, its vegetation, its fauna, its deserts....[3]

This passage suggests that Teilhard's primary interest at this time was in observing nature rather than society. We know few concrete details about this time in his life, which has been little researched. Besides allusions in later works, there exist only the rather formal letters sent home to his parents from Egypt. Although they have been described as being primarily a collection of natural history, they contain some information about Teilhard's contacts with both contemporary Islamic and ancient Egyptian culture. Excursions to the classical sites of Egypt were supplemented by attendance at monthly meetings of the Institute of Egyptology and repeated visits to the Museum of Egyptian Antiquities. Teilhard expressed his enthusiasm for the beauty of Egyptian art, which he preferred to the more abstract Islamic art, where he missed the portrayal of human life.

Contact with the Arab world was largely mediated through the Muslim pupils at the school. Some of the Jesuits in Cairo—particularly the later well-known Islamicist, Henri Lammens (1862–1937)—specialized in the study of Islam.[4] Teilhard saw him regularly during his stay in Egypt, although Lammens was almost twenty years his senior. Occasionally, Teilhard accompanied his friends in their explorations of the old Arab quarters of

Cairo. In his letters, he describes visits to mosques in Cairo and elsewhere, the experience of Ramadan, of meeting Muslim pilgrims returning from Mecca, and reading a thirteenth-century Arab poet. At some stage, he expressed a wish to learn Arabic; he realized how useful a knowledge of the language would be in meeting local people who, he felt, enjoyed discussing moral and religious matters. But learning Arabic remained an unfulfilled ideal.

However indirect it may have been, Teilhard's first contact was with Islam rather than with any other eastern religion. It is impossible to assess whether or not, during his stay in Egypt, he learnt about Islamic religious beliefs and practices in any depth and whether, for example, he would have been aware of the existence of Sufi brotherhoods and their teaching. During his entire stay in Egypt, his life remained relatively removed from the life of the indigenous population. Teilhard not only belonged to a Jesuit mission, but his social contacts were largely restricted to the expatriate colonial milieu existing in Egypt at the beginning of twentieth century. His scientific interests also reinforced his connections with French scientists and savants working in Egypt at that time. The later experience of China was, to some extent, also mediated through a similar colonial milieu, although it contained less of the missionary element. The inherent limitations of his social milieu were an effective barrier to exploring indigenous religious beliefs.

Teilhard never again lived for so long in a predominantly Islamic country. This raises the question of how far the relative unimportance given to Islam in his religious thinking, and the negative evaluation of Islam's vitality in the modern world, reflected in some remarks in his later essays, may largely be due to his experience of a situation of political, social, and cultural dependence he found in Egypt at the beginning of the twentieth century.

Teilhard's stay in Egypt also provided an opportunity to encounter several aspects of the Christian heritage represented by Orthodox, Coptic, Maronite, and Catholic groups. Several friends who knew him well have confirmed that Teilhard had a good knowledge of eastern Christianity. Whether it stemmed from this time, or from earlier reading in connection with his brother's interest in Byzantium, is difficult to say. Teilhard certainly assisted at different Christian rites and visited early Christian remains in Egypt. The shrine of the Holy Family near Cairo, mentioned several times in his letters, reminded him of the flight of Mary and Joseph to Egypt, and his excursions into the desert made him think of the early desert fathers.

The lasting influence of the desert on Teilhard's thought has already been mentioned. The desert later came to symbolize for him a particular aspect of the religious quest. Analyzing the importance of the desert experience for the growth of Teilhard's "mystic self," Hugh Cairns has written:

> In the desert...Teilhard returned to memorable psychic experience. In the towns of Egypt he had found the people, the colorful and bustling streets and the atmosphere exotic and exhilarating. Now in the fossil-strewn wastes under the harsh sun and desolate darkness he consciously felt in danger, the psychic danger of a "vast doubt," a "night of the soul" and a "pantheism" in which he felt himself being "diffused" in the vastness of Nature.[5]

If this is correct, then the experience of Egypt was of crucial importance for Teilhard's inner development. But it was only during the years to come that he was able to evaluate this experience in a wider context and relate it to his interpretation of mysticism.

More Eastern Connections and More Reading

On his return from Egypt, Teilhard continued with his studies. He first spent several years reading theology at the Jesuit scholasticate at Ore Place in Hastings (1908–12),[6] and, after deciding on a research career in science, he pursued paleontological studies in Paris (1912–14). From the letters written during this period,[7] it is evident that he found Egypt difficult to forget. However beautiful the countryside around Hastings, it was quite unlike what he had experienced in North Africa. Even after his first year in England, he still felt that he left part of his heart in the mountains near the Red Sea.

After his ordination in Hastings in 1911, his whole ambition was to return to Egypt.[8] Although his contact with the Middle East was now indirect, it was no less lively. Teilhard corresponded with pupils in Cairo, received occasional visitors from Egypt, and kept in touch with the research and expeditions of his former friends who were still living there.

Through other Jesuits at Hastings Teilhard also received regular news about the Jesuit missions in China. There was a continual flow of Jesuit teachers and students either going to, or returning from, China. Shanghai was almost a "known place" to Teilhard since he had met many of the Jesuits who now worked there, among them some of his best friends.[9] The contact with China became closer still when his sister Françoise left for Shanghai in 1909. The letters to her parents contain many references to their older brother Albéric, his earlier visit to Shanghai, the people he met, and the deep impression he left on everybody. Similarly, Françoise frequently refers to her brother Pierre, with whom she shared a special bond through their common vocation to the religious life, for "there was a great spiritual intimacy between brother and sister."[10]

Teilhard's letters to his sister have unfortunately not survived. The family was deeply grieved when Françoise died prematurely of smallpox in 1911, after working for only two years in China. Unlike Teilhard later on, Françoise so immersed herself in the Chinese milieu that she became fluent in the language. It is important to remember, though, that she went to China as a missionary, while Teilhard's reason for his later stay in the Far East was primarily scientific. However, the influence of Françoise's example was deep and lasting; Teilhard always remembered her. Comparing himself with his sister, he later wrote that while the unique importance that the reality of God had assumed in their lives made them fundamentally alike, the difference in their approach to religion was that Françoise "was following a road where the realities of this world were much more effaced or left behind"[11] than was the case with himself.

Apart from learning about China, Teilhard also gleaned information about India from a friend who had traveled all over the Indian subcontinent. However, references to these conversations in Teilhard's letters are largely restricted to natural history, scientific contacts in Bombay, and the Jesuit missions in North and South India.[12] More important for his personal development was the meeting with a Jesuit colleague, Father Maréchal, in Louvain in 1910. Not much older than Teilhard, Maréchal combined a similar interest in science and religion as Teilhard and, from 1908 onward, had begun to publish articles on the psychology of the mystics. Teilhard consulted Maréchal several times and always took much notice of his advice. It is quite likely that at that time he read Maréchal's study "On the Feeling of Presence in Mystics and Non-Mystics," published in 1908–9.[13] This article discusses among others Hindu, Buddhist, and Sufi mysticism. It also refers to William James's *The Varieties of Religious Experience* and deals with Bucke's "cosmic consciousness." It is probably through Maréchal's work that Teilhard first came across the term "cosmic consciousness," which so well describes his own experience of nature mysticism in Egypt and elsewhere.

Teilhard's own mystical experiences made him enquire into those of others. Probably from 1908 onward, he became interested in reading about the mystics. The prime motivation for most of this reading was to nourish and develop his own ideas rather than to be merely informed. His inquiry into the nature of mysticism was predominantly a personal and existential rather than a scholarly quest, born from the need to explicate and communicate an inner vision. It is very difficult, however, to retrace his development during this time in detail. Maréchal's article on mystical experience may well have been an early influence in shaping Teilhard's thought on mysticism. We know that even many years later, in 1945, he consulted Maréchal's work on mysticism and made notes on it.[14]

What other sources of information about the comparative study of mysticism and the world's mystical heritage were accessible to Teilhard at the beginning of the twentieth century? It is impossible to point to any single influence with certainty but, given the kind of milieu he lived and studied in, one can make conjectures about possible contacts and readings. Teilhard's theological training at Hastings seems to have included a certain amount of teaching on the history of religions.[15] This had probably been introduced on the initiative of Father Léonce de Grandmaison, later director of the Jesuit review *Études* in Paris. Even though Father de Grandmaison left Hastings soon after Teilhard's arrival, the two men kept in touch, and Grandmaison's influence in drawing Teilhard's attention toward other religious traditions must not be underestimated. As Henri de Lubac has stated:

> In the Catholicism of the first half of the twentieth century, Père Teilhard was one of the rare thinkers to be deeply interested in the great spiritual systems that divide the world between them. In this we can no doubt see something of the influence of Père Léonce de Grandmaison, but it is even more due to reflection on his mystical sense, sharpened by his contacts with the East.[16]

What the history of religions course at the Jesuit house of studies in Hastings included is unknown. However, at the beginning of the twentieth century important developments occurred in the history of religions as a discipline. Its lively controversies were not only found in scholarly journals, but a wider interest in eastern religions was reflected in French periodicals such as the *Revue des Deux Mondes*,[17] *Le Correspondant*, and *Relations d'Orient*, which Teilhard saw regularly.

Father Léonce de Grandmaison influenced several Jesuits in becoming actively involved in the study of the history of religions. It was due to his initiative that, in 1910, the Jesuits founded a new journal, *Recherches de Science Religieuse*, devoted to research in the comparative study of religions, and still in existence today. One of Teilhard's fellow students, Father Rousselot, became closely associated with this journal, while another of his friends, Father Huby, edited a textbook on the history of religions, *Christus: Manuel d'Histoire des Religions*, which continues to be in print.[18] First published in Paris in 1913, this book was being planned while Teilhard was still a student at Hastings and, according to Henri de Lubac, he "certainly knew the book *Christus* some of whose main authors were his companions and friends."[19]

Another of Teilhard's teachers at Hastings, Father Bouvier, attended the International History of Religions Congress at Oxford in 1908; in 1912 he founded, together with W. Schmidt, *La Semaine d'Ethnologie Religieuse* at Louvain,[20] which became an annual event. Its idea may originally also have been one of Grandmaison's suggestions. At Bouvier's invitation, Teilhard went to Louvain to attend the first meeting of this conference on religious ethnology during the summer of 1912. The study week was mainly organized for missionaries in order to acquaint them, according to Teilhard's report, with "the problems and methods of the history of religions."[21] Its major themes focused on totemism and on questions about the origin and evolution of religion. Émile Durkheim's famous book, *The Elementary Forms of Religious Life*, was published in 1912. Ideas about religion and magic held by Durkheim as well as James Frazer, R. R. Marett, Edward B. Tylor, and Father Wilhelm Schmidt were intensely debated at the conference. Teilhard, who had already been introduced to Durkheim's ideas through one of his professors at Hastings, reported on the conference for the paper *Le Correspondant.*[22]

The information gathered about Teilhard's early milieu reveals a multiplicity of contacts, a widening of interests, even a certain awareness about discussions on the origin of religion, and about studies in eastern religions. What is more important, however, certain formative experiences occurred during this early period that permanently affected the direction of his thought. These experiences were shaped by both his religious and scientific activities. His advanced studies in both fields were transformed through the exciting discovery of the meaning of evolution, mentioned in the previous chapter, a discovery that proved to have a lifelong impact on his new, dynamic understanding of the Christian faith. In the opinion of Father René d'Ouince, one of the superiors who knew Teilhard well in later years, it may well be that Teilhard's major ideas first emerged during his last years of study at Hastings rather than in the following period of his life, where most commentators place them.[23]

In his autobiographical essay, "The Heart of Matter," Teilhard speaks of this fundamental transformation:

I had experienced a complete reversal of my Sense of Plenitude, and since those days I have constantly searched and progressed in that new direction....

Until that time my education and my religion had always led me obediently to accept...a fundamental heterogeneity between Matter and Spirit, between Body and Soul, between Unconscious and Conscious. These were to me two "substances" that differed in nature, two "species" of Being....You can well imagine...how strong was my inner feeling of release and expansion when I took my first steps into an "evolutive" Universe, and saw that the dualism in which I had hitherto been enclosed was disappearing like the mist before the rising sun. Matter and Spirit: these were no longer two things, but two *states* or two aspects of one and the same cosmic Stuff....

It was to take me a whole lifetime to appreciate...the unendingly constructive and at the same time revolutionary effect this transposition of value (this change in the very notion of Spirit) produced upon my understanding, upon my prayer and action.[24]

A Mystical Seer Turns Writer

It is evident from Teilhard's own comments that the years between 1910 and 1923—the date he left for China—were central for his development. This period included his years of theological study in Hastings, his scientific studies in Paris, the experience of the First World War, and the emergence of his literary activity. However, in relation to his contacts with the East, this period represents an intermediate stage between the earlier years in Egypt and the much longer, later stay in the Far East.

The formative experience of Egypt echoes through all the war writings, but it is blended with a new experience, that of the Front. Teilhard worked as a medical orderly in a mixed infantry regiment, consisting largely of Tunisians and Kabyle tribesmen from Algeria, the "Zouaves." These French colonial troops certainly reminded him of his earlier years in North Africa, although it is impossible to know whether an element of personal choice was involved in being part of this regiment. Whether the soldiers knew about his stay in Egypt or not, they certainly expressed their admiration for Teilhard by affectionately calling him "Sidi Marabout." Whereas *Sidi* refers to a North African settled in France, *Marabout* is the French rendering of the Arabic *murābit*, a man bound to God, sanctified by asceticism, and blessed with divine favor. In fact, according to anthropologist Clifford Geertz, *Marabout* describes someone

> tied, bound, fastened to God, like a camel to a post, a ship to a pier, a prisoner to a wall; or more appropriately...like a monk to a monastery...in some almost intangible sense, attached, bound, tied—perhaps the best word is shackled—to God.[25]

When Teilhard first joined this regiment, he spoke of his situation as being "*in partibus infidelium*," although there was "no lack of Christians."[26] Looking after the wounded, he sometimes felt helpless because of the differences in language and mentality. At other times, he described the colorful sights with much delight, as when he mentioned in one of his letters a performance given to the troops:

> One would have to have lost the capacity to be astonished by anything not to be moved by such a scene...an audience of Senegalese, Martiniquans, Somalis, Annamites, Tunisians and French....I brought back from it the very definite conviction that, among other results of the war, will be that of mixing and welding together the peoples of the earth in a way that nothing else, perhaps, could have done.[27]

It was amid this mingling of races and the violent military action of the First World War that Teilhard's vision of the human community as profoundly one in both an organic and spiritual sense began to take shape. He seemed to perceive a closely interconnected layer of thought around the globe and an interrelated web of action covering the entire planet Earth. It was this reality, first experienced in the trenches, that he later called the "noosphere." This extraordinary vision and difficult new concept are of central importance in his understanding of human society and its further development, but its detailed discussion has to be deferred until later.

While surrounded by all the fighting and clamor of the troops, he could still find occasions to recall the entrancing beauty of nature and dream of the Egyptian desert and its solitude. This is what the visionary, the mystic, seeks: to live apart from the multitude, to be lulled by passivity, to awaken to cosmic consciousness. But Teilhard recognized this intoxication of the seeker with his own isolation as a "temptation of matter," described in his essay "Cosmic Life" (1916) in autobiographical form:

> One day, I was looking out over the dreary expanse of the desert. As far as the eye could see, the purple steps of the uplands rose up in a series, towards horizons of exotic wildness; again, as I watched the empty, bottomless ocean whose waves were ceaselessly moving in their "unnumbered laughter"; or, buried in a forest whose life-laden shadows seemed to seek to absorb me in their deep, warm folds—on such occasions, maybe, I have been possessed by a great yearning to go and find, far from men and far from toil the place where dwell the vast forces that cradle us and possess us, where my over-tense activity might indefinitely become ever more relaxed....And then all my sensibility became alert, as though at the approach of a god of easy-won happiness and intoxication; for there lay matter, and matter was calling me. To me in my turn, as to all the sons of man, it was speaking as every generation hears it speak; it was begging me to surrender myself unreservedly to it, and to worship it.[28]

This passage recalls the overwhelming impressions left by his earlier mystic experiences, linked to the desert in Egypt, the sea in

43

Jersey, and the woods of Sussex, to which references can be found in other parts of his work.[29] Teilhard always interpreted these experiences in terms of a pantheistic monism that he repudiated. Strict monism makes human beings resolutely cling to the Absolute by rejecting all plurality as merely superficial and ultimately unreal appearances. He characterized his monistic experience as "the eastern vision of the blue Lotus,"[30] a term recalling a French journal of theosophy, which might have influenced him in his usage.

Teilhard's understanding of monism is examined later, but it is important to know that from the beginning of his writing we can find negative references to eastern thought. Teilhard always viewed the monistic experience as succumbing to the "temptation of matter," as a return to an original source, where matter is felt to be "eternal, immense, infinitely fertile." This is "the God from below," "pagan, Hindu pantheism," characterized by a distaste for other human beings because one wants to be alone with nature. It is, therefore, an attitude adverse to society.[31]

Elsewhere the same experience is compared to the Buddhist goal of Nirvana: "Looked at in one way, nature is a drug, lulling us to sleep in the cradle of nirvana and all the ancient pantheisms."[32] Another passage describes the experience of cosmic feeling, sometimes evoked through the encounter with music or poetry, as leading the soul either "to lose itself in the lower Nirvana" or "to unite itself ardently with the great effort towards the higher spheres."[33]

These higher spheres are linked to the search for true mysticism, or what Teilhard then called the "mystical milieu."[34] While he attempted to spell out its characteristics, he continued to pursue comparative reading on different spiritualities and mysticisms, as can be seen from his correspondence and even more his journal. Although not a complete guide to his reading, these references point to some of the literary sources that influenced his writing on mysticism.

Reflections on Mysticism

In late 1917, Teilhard read William James's *The Varieties of Religious Experience*.[35] When he wrote the essay "The Soul of the

World" shortly afterward, he explicitly quoted James as supporting the view that "the current of 'pantheist' (cosmic) mysticism is
no stranger to Christianity."[36] There is more evidence, however,
for the influence of another book by William James, his lectures
on *Pragmatism*,[37] which Teilhard must have read in early 1918.

It is interesting that between 1916, when Teilhard was working on "Cosmic Life," and early 1918, the time of completing
"The Soul of the World," his essays contain no references to
either Hindu or Buddhist terms. However, in January 1918, when
writing about mysticism, Teilhard mentions again the "Hindu
pantheist path," referring explicitly to William James's book,
Pragmatism. The diary entry for January 26, 1918, reads:

> I see more and more that I must live and realize my
> mysticism, —plunge myself into the divine Milieu, and
> develop it around me. By and large, there are three
> paths for arriving at an homogeneous Absolute:[38]
>
> a) the Hindu pantheist path *which annihilates all dif-
> ferences* and experiential differentiations (cf. W. James,
> *Pragmatism*);
>
> b) the Christian path which declares *all earthly dif-
> ferentiations to be in vain*, and discovers a milieu of
> effort and homogeneous personalization in the *merito-
> rious*, in grace;
>
> c) the Christian path (which I prefer) which seeks to
> bring together (and to constitute the Homogeneous) by
> pushing forward the work of heterogeneization *along
> the entire line....*
>
> Through reading the *Pragmatism* of W. James, I was
> struck once again by the necessity to adopt path c....[39]

As William James is quoted with reference to the "Hindu
pantheist path," it may be mentioned that, in one of his lectures,[40]
James speaks at length about the Hindu missionary Vivekananda,
who had visited the United States and Europe in the 1890s.
Commenting on this "paragon of all monistic systems," James
states, "Observe how radical the character of monism here is.
Separation is not simply overcome by the One, it is denied to

exist."[41] Elsewhere, he speaks of "Vivekananda's mystic One"[42] and "Vivekananda's Atman."[43] In his concluding lecture on "Pragmatism and Religion," William James has this to say:

> Nirvana means safety from this everlasting round of adventures of which the world of sense consists. The hindoo and the buddhist, for this is essentially their attitude, are simply afraid, afraid of more experience, afraid of life.[44]

This negative and rather vague impression of Hinduism and Buddhism is not unlike Teilhard's. One wonders how far the latter's conception of Hindu monism may not primarily be due to the discussions found in William James's *Pragmatism* and *The Varieties of Religious Experience*. It was only many years later, after reading more about Indian religions, especially Vedanta, that Teilhard realized the rich diversity of the Indian religious heritage, of which monism represents only one aspect.

There are more than a dozen references to William James in Teilhard's *Journal*, and, in spite of criticisms, he recognized James's position as being somewhat akin to his own.[45] Several times Teilhard used James's distinction of monism, pluralism, and pragmatism as three basic attitudes to the world.[46] He also discussed James's treatment of attitudes to salvation and "the tough-minded in religion."[47]

It is clear that in particular James's book *Pragmatism* made a deep impression on Teilhard by providing a confirmation of his views on different mystical orientations. Teilhard counted James, together with other writers such as Maurice Maeterlinck, Henri Bergson, and Herbert Wells, among the "sincere and passionate spirits" of his age. In their books, one could discern "the religion of a near-by, progressive and universal God" who appealed far more to his contemporaries than the traditional Christian ideal.[48]

In 1918 Teilhard's cousin, who was aware of his strong interest in mysticism, sent him the then-popular book by Édouard Schuré, *Les Grands Initiés*,[49] which deals with various figures of western and eastern mysticism. A rather eclectic work, it describes the mysticism of Rama, Krishna, Hermes, Orpheus, and Pythagoras, together with the teachings of Moses, Plato, and Jesus. This somewhat motley collection emphasizes the essential affinity of eastern and western religions but presents them as a progressive revelation culminating in the teaching of Jesus. The book criticizes the existing opposition between science and religion and concludes with the hope that a transformation of Christianity, and a regeneration of the eastern traditions, may furnish the religious basis for the reconciliation of Asia and Europe.

Teilhard first read this book with great enthusiasm but soon found it rather unreal and out of date. To him the author was at least as interesting as his "initiates" for, once again, Teilhard found his own experiences confirmed here. He wrote to his cousin:

> I've been able to get back to Schuré, from whom I've had a great, but rather complex, pleasure: the joy of finding a mind extremely sympathetic to my own, —the spiritual excitement of making contact with a soul full of enthusiasm for the world, —the satisfaction of realizing that the questions I'm concerned with are indeed those that have animated the deep-rooted life of humanity, —the pleasure of seeing that my attempts at a solution agree perfectly, on the whole, with those of the "great initiates" without doing any violence to dogma, and (because of the integration of the Christian idea) have at the same time their own very special and original slant. You can readily appreciate that it's a great pleasure and encouragement to me to see so clearly what I can use, and what on the other hand is artificial or unsatisfactory, in Schuré's vision: it makes me twice as strong.[50]

It would be erroneous to regard Schuré's book as a major influence on Teilhard's thought,[51] yet the references to this work confirm that his reflections on mysticism at this time included the consideration of certain comparative data. The letter to his cousin also speaks of "the mistake of false mystical systems that, confusing the levels, look for mystery at the phenomenal level." Schuré's treatment was found to be too narrow and incomplete.

It made Teilhard decide "to write something on 'mystical science', to defend from such abuses and place in its real light (glimpsed by Schuré, but with serious errors in perspective), this science of sciences which is also the supreme art and the supreme work."[52]

In his book *Evolution in Religion*, R. C. Zaehner describes Teilhard as "a pantheist by nature" and says that, throughout the First World War, he "seems to have lived in an almost permanent state of 'cosmic consciousness.'"[53] However, Zaehner himself did not look into the way in which this experience was gradually articulated and redefined, nor did he enquire into the literary sources of this "cosmic consciousness." Although the influence of Édouard Schuré has been noted before,[54] nobody seems to have examined the contact with William James nor the possible influence of Joseph Maréchal on Teilhard's understanding of mysticism. Both these authors discuss the nature of cosmic consciousness and thus may have helped Teilhard to formulate his own views more clearly.

In addition to James, Maréchal, and Schuré, Teilhard read other authors such as Ralph Emerson, Herbert Wells, Maurice Maeterlinck, and Robert Hugh Benson.[55] At the same time, he studied the Christian mystics, especially Tauler and Eckhardt.[56] He must also have been aware of Henri Bremond's famous *Histoire littéraire du sentiment religieux*. First published in 1916, this work revealed "to French readers innumerable hitherto unknown mystics."[57] Father Bremond had been Teilhard's teacher in his school days in France. He had earlier guided him to the reading of John Henry Newman, whose influence on Teilhard was as great as was Bergson's. At least in 1923, if not before, Teilhard consulted Bremond's work about the mystics.[58] An essay of the same year refers again to the many people who have experienced "cosmic consciousness" and speaks of "the long procession of initiates given to the vision and worship of the All."[59]

From Teilhard's reading and writing of this period, it is abundantly clear that he felt a strong attraction to pantheistic monism, vividly described as the appeal of matter/earth/cosmos, or as "pagan," as "nature mysticism." This attraction remained constant throughout his life, but it was held in tension and found its fulfillment in a mysticism suffused with personal love. Eventually, he became firmly convinced that mysticism did not lead into isolation, out of the world, but more fully into it.

During the years following the First World War, Teilhard pursued the discussion on pantheism and mysticism mainly with his friend, Father Valensin, who introduced him to the philosopher Maurice Blondel. In 1919, Teilhard and Blondel exchanged several notes relating to their understanding of mysticism to which I refer later.[60] Other philosophically stimulating contacts were the friendships with the philosopher Édouard Le Roy (1870–1954)[61] at the College de France, and with the pioneer woman philosopher, Léontine Zanta (1872–1942).[62] Teilhard maintained a correspondence with both of them over many years. These philosophical contacts, together with the religious and scientific milieu in which Teilhard worked, contributed much to the early dissemination of his ideas. When he was given the chair of geology at the Institut Catholique in 1922—a position previously held by one of his teachers killed during the war—he possessed a public platform from which he could expound his vision and speak about both science and religion from a new perspective.

The attraction of the East was still much in his mind, though, as can be seen from the following reaction to his appointment at the Institut Catholique: "Rather than this academic post, I should of course have preferred research work in Beyrouth or Shanghai or Trichinopoly,"[63] he wrote to a friend. Soon an unexpected possibility offered itself to realize this wish. In 1923, he was invited to join Father Émile Licent, SJ, as collaborator in an expedition to North China and Mongolia, sponsored by the Musée de l'Homme and the Institut Catholique in Paris.

It would be quite wrong to consider this first visit to China already as an act of exile, imposed on Teilhard for philosophically and theologically unacceptable views.[64] The invitation provided a welcome opportunity to fulfill the desire to see more of the East and to visit some of the places forever connected with the memory of a dearly loved brother and sister. The expedition opened up new fields of scientific research that were to win him international acclaim in later years.

Teilhard had several times expressed the wish to return to Egypt. Although he visited other parts of North Africa in later years,[65] he never saw Egypt again but journeyed much further East instead. Yet it was Egypt that provided his first introduction to eastern life and thought, and his stay there permanently influenced his attitude toward the East. One of his biographers has assessed the importance of this experience by saying:

> The Orient meant for Teilhard the East as a world opposed to the West and, the lure of the exotic once exorcized, the challenge to effect the meeting of these two worlds. This dialogue with the East, more specifically with India and China, was to continue during the whole of Teilhard's life.[66]

Without this experience of the Far East, Teilhard's vision would not have encompassed such breadth and universality, and he would not have felt the same compelling need to seek a new road for contemporary spirituality. What form this dialogue with the East took over the next twenty-three years will now have to be seen.

EAST AND WEST

The Spirit of One Earth

Teilhard's long stay in the Far East can be divided into two peri-ods: the first lasted from 1923 to 1931, the second from 1932 to 1946. During the first period, his main base was the Chinese city of Tientsin, today known as Tianjin. During the second period, he lived in Peking, now called Beijing.[1] Until the outbreak of the Second World War, his stay in China was frequently inter-rupted by expeditions and travels in both East and West. This alternating rhythm of living and working with people of different countries, cultures, and creeds had a deep effect on his way of thinking. He watched a new world being born that, amid all its turmoil, was crying out for a new path to the spirit. Few contem-poraries have lived such an intensive spiritual and mystic life while pursuing a scientific career and feeling at the same time so passionately about the modern world.

In terms of his literary production, the years in the Far East mark a new phase; he now wrote with vigor and self-assurance. Two of his important spiritual writings, "The Mass on the World" (1923) and *The Divine Milieu* (1927), were produced during his early years in China. Yet paradoxically, this first period was also the time of his deepest inner crisis, when he "doubted both his religious and scientific vocation."[2] Few essays of this time refer directly to his experience of the East, but many com-ments are found in Teilhard's letters and, during the later period, in his unpublished diaries and in the notes made on his reading.[3]

Without Père Émile Licent, SJ, Teilhard would probably

never have set foot in China. It was due to Licent's invitation to join him on an expedition that Teilhard first went to China, and he owed much of his subsequent scientific success in the first instance to Licent. Almost contemporaries, the two Jesuits had first met in early 1914, just before Licent left for China. They were in correspondence since at least 1921. Teilhard expressed great admiration for Licent's work in his letters and indicated his interest in collaborating with him, should circumstances permit.[4] The opportunity to do so came in 1923, and Teilhard seized it eagerly.

He left France in April 1923 and joined Father Licent in the following month in Tientsin to assist with excavations in central China. Teilhard's boat journey from Marseilles to Shanghai included brief stops in Port Said, Colombo, Penang, Malacca, Saigon, and Hong Kong. On arrival in Shanghai, Teilhard spent some time visiting the city and getting acquainted with the various Jesuit educational and missionary institutions about which he had heard so much. They included an orphanage, several schools, the university, and the famous Siccawei Observatory, built by Jesuit missionaries in 1872 and renowned as China's first modern astronomical observatory.[5]

First Impressions of China

The details of Teilhard's journey to the Far East are picturesquely described in *Letters from a Traveller*. His overall inner impression is perhaps best summed up by his statement that a journey to the Far East represents a "temptation of the multiple."[6] This is more fully spelled out in a letter:

> My strongest impression at the moment is a confused one that the human world...is a huge and disparate thing, just about as coherent, at the moment, as the surface of a rough sea. I still believe, for reasons imbued with mysticism and metaphysics, that this incoherence is the prelude to a unification....The fact remains, however, that the multiplicity of human elements and human points of view revealed by a journey in the Far

East is so "overwhelming" that one cannot conceive of
a religious life, a religious organism, assimilating such a
mass without being profoundly modified and enriched
by it....[7]

This passage, written shortly after arriving in the Far East,
expresses something of his approach to religion in China. While
always considering Christianity as the major "axis" of development for religion, he also inquired what eastern religions might
contribute to the renewal of Christianity. This is evident from
another letter of the same period:

I feel, more strongly than ever, the need of freeing our
religion from everything about it that is specifically
Mediterranean. I do not believe...that the majority of
oriental thought-patterns are anything but outmoded
and obsolescent....But I do say that by taking these
forms, decayed though they be, into account, we discover such a wealth of "potentialities" in philosophy, in
mysticism, and in the study of human conduct that it
becomes scarcely possible to be satisfied with an image
of a mankind entirely and definitely enveloped in the
narrow network of precepts and dogmas in which some
people think they have displayed the whole amplitude
of Christianity.[8]

However, the initial reaction to China seems to have been one of
disappointment, possibly due to the unfavorable impressions
gained from the deserted regions through which he traveled during his first expeditions and the experience of living in the city of
Tientsin. Later, when he encountered the scientific and intellectual
circles of Peking, these opinions were considerably modified.

The name of Tientsin means "the ford of heaven." It was one
of the important treaty ports among the coastal cities of China,
Japan, and Korea, which had been opened to foreign trade by
treaties imposed by western naval powers in the late nineteenth
century. Nationals of different countries had been granted extra-
territorial rights to live in these cities in "concession districts."

Like other cities in the East, Tientsin was thus a dual city, consisting of two separate settlements, one indigenous Chinese and the other foreign, at about two miles distance from the native city. By 1920, there were seven different national "concessions" in Tientsin housing a foreign population of more than eleven thousand (Europeans, Americans, Japanese, Russians), compared with a Chinese population of 837,000. The Jesuits were housed at the southern end of the British concession. By 1922, a museum had been built for the natural history collections gathered by Father Licent. In 1923, the Jesuits opened the High Institute of Commercial and Industrial Arts "to give the young men of China a serious training in technical subjects which the economic development of the country renders necessary."[9]

The cosmopolitan life of western expatriates living in Tientsin in the pre-Communist China of the 1920s is brilliantly evoked in a memoir by Brian Power, who grew up there, knew the Jesuits and also their "Institut des Hautes Études Commerciales," as it was referred to by the French. He was familiar with Licent's museum, and he also met Teilhard.[10]

Soon after Teilhard's arrival in Tientsin, he and Licent set out for western Mongolia, especially the Ordos Desert. For many weeks, they wandered "on mule-back across mountains and deserts,"[11] making important geological and paleontological finds. The work was so successful that Teilhard unexpectedly extended his first visit to China until September the following year. This gave him the opportunity for several other excursions, especially a major expedition to eastern Mongolia in spring 1924.

These expeditions led him into isolated regions marked by ancient features in terms of their geography and populations. Mongolia struck him "as a 'museum' of antique specimens...a slice of the past," giving the impression "of an empty reservoir."[12] When not camping in their tent, the two scientists stayed in Chinese inns, Buddhist lamaseries, and occasionally Christian mission stations. During these travels, they met Mongols, Tibetans, and Chinese Muslims.

The first debt that Teilhard owes to the Far East is "its revelation of the immensity of the earth and of mankind."[13] The new contact with China, especially the experience of the Ordos Desert, had a decisive impact on him. However, there is no break, no new incision in his inner vision brought about by this first stay in China. There is, rather, a deep continuity, an expansion of growth, with new experiences complementing and extending previous insights. The relative isolation of the Ordos Desert stood in stark contrast to the intensity of the war experience; instead of human masses in action, it meant a life of solitude and the absence of intensive activity. The letters of this time compare the stay in the Ordos with the earlier experience of Egypt as well as that of the war. This is well expressed in the lines written to Léontine Zanta in August 1923:

> Though I have less leisure than during the war, and perhaps less freshness too…, in the last two months I have found myself in similar isolation and confronted with realities equally vast. And both these conditions are eminently favorable for meditating on the great All. Now, in the vast solitudes of Mongolia (which, from the human point of view, are a static and dead region), I see the same thing as I saw long ago at the "front" (which from the human point of view, was the most alive region that existed): one single operation is in process of happening in the world, and it alone can justify our action: the emergence of some spiritual Reality, through and across the efforts of life.[14]

Reflections by a Pilgrim of the Future

The 1923 expedition to Mongolia lasted four months. During this time, he increasingly realized that "historical and geographical research is, in itself, empty and deceptive, the true science being that of the future as gradually disclosed by life itself." He wished to develop this idea in a "literary fantasy" of his "impressions of Mongolia."[15] Written while traveling by boat and later entitled "Choses Mongoles," their most often-quoted phrase is probably the succinct sentence with which Teilhard summarized his experience: "I am a pilgrim of the future on my way back from a journey made entirely in the past."[16]

55

After relating the external events of the expedition, Teilhard reflected at a deeper level on what he brought back from four months' travel in Mongolia: "What gain has there been to my innermost being during this long pilgrimage in China? Has the great continent of Asia any profound message for me?" He had come with great hopes, but he was disappointed:

When I landed in China, there was one hope I still retained. If...the only true knowledge of things lies in foreseeing and building up the future as life gradually brings it into being, then what better opportunity to associate myself with the building-up of the future could I hope for than to go and lose myself for weeks on end in the fermenting mass of the peoples of Asia? There I could count on meeting the new currents of thought and mysticism in process of formation, which were preparing to rejuvenate and fertilize our European world.

But this was a naive assumption comparable to the expectation of "those simple people of the past who thought that the gods inhabit the hidden places of the world and that long ago they used to reveal themselves to men." Instead, he found "nothing but absence of thought, senile thought, or infantile thought.... Mongolia seemed to me asleep—perhaps dead."[17] The same idea is expressed in his comment on a stay in a Buddhist lamasery:

Like all monks everywhere and always, lamas have an infallible instinct in choosing the setting for their dwelling-places, so that it is always a delight for the eye to come upon one of their monasteries suddenly, deep in a most unexpected recess. Gilded flagstaffs glistened in the sun over the geometrical group of red and white rectangular buildings. Now and again a monk went past, in a purple or yellow robe—a sight which delighted the eye and filled the heart with peace. But to admire the lamas and their lamaseries one has, unfortunately, to see them from a distance. As soon as one draws near, the gleaming façade is seen to be tarnished and the vivid garments dirty and torn. The people who first created these desert retreats were doubtless really great men, prophets who discovered something of great beauty in the world, and beyond the world. Today one scrutinizes the dull faces of their successors in vain to find the most fleeting trace of that long-faded vision.[18]

Teilhard was aware, however, that he was not in a good position to gain a completely balanced picture. Overall, the Christian missionaries he met during his travels reinforced rather than counteracted his negative impressions. One exception was Father Schram, a missionary from Tibet who, on his return from the Himalayan border, assured Teilhard

> that out there still survived…two or three solitaries who nourish their interior life by contemplating the cosmic cycles and the eternal re-birth of Buddha. But a chance passer-by like myself is not in a position to recognize these infrequent heirs of a venerable tradition of thought whose fruit is reserved for some new season. For myself, I have seen nothing in Mongolia to awaken the "other life" within me.[19]

Distressed at finding nothing "but the traces of a vanished world," Teilhard finished his impressions on a rather triumphant note about the rise of the West. From the whole of sleeping Asia, it seemed to him, "there rose a voice which whispered, 'Now, my brothers of the West, it is your turn.'" However, there is also a faint hint of mutual give and take present, as when he states:

> Our turn. Yes, sleep on, ancient Asia; your people are as weary as your soil is ravaged. By now your night has fallen and the light has passed into other hands. But it was you who kindled this light, you who gave it to us. Have no fear: we shall not allow it to die….So long, too, as a few wise men still have your life (your own life—not a life we would seek to impose on you) in safe-

keeping, it is not extinguished. Tomorrow perhaps it will shine once more over your ravaged plateaux.[20]

This can be taken as a pointer that "within all this shift of civilizations" and "beneath the universal turmoil of living beings" where "something is being made" at present, Asia may have its own insights to contribute. This note of hope was to grow and become more positive in later years, at least occasionally.

It would be inappropriate to judge Teilhard's views on China from these first impressions alone. "Choses Mongoles" is of no great literary importance among his works; yet it clearly shows that the unfavorable comparison between East and West was present from his first encounter with the Far East. A similar perspective still underlies his explicitly comparative essay "The Road of the West" (1932), written nine years later, when Teilhard's knowledge of China had greatly increased. As this essay is of greater significance in his work, it is important to know that some of its ideas were already foreshadowed in the relatively minor reflections on "Choses Mongoles," noted down during the first months in China.

The editors of his Mongolian reflections, included in the book *Letters from a Traveller*, have rightly commented on the ambivalence of this text:

It must be borne in mind that these pages were written on Père Teilhard's first contact with China, the China of steppe and desert. His outlook was to undergo a profound change in the years to follow. In close contact with intellectual movements in Peking, he frequently expressed his certainty that a real awakening of Chinese national consciousness was taking place behind the confused political crises that shook the whole Far East. The evolution seemed to him inevitable though what form it would take might still be uncertain. Of one thing he was sure: "Sooner or later the unification of the human race is bound to come, and if the world wishes to survive, there must be an end to racial conflict. For its maturity the earth needs every drop of blood."[21]

It is true that Teilhard's attitude to China always remained ambivalent. On one hand, we find a mixture of negative disapproval and rejection; on the other, there appears the more positive search for enrichment and convergence, as expressed in an early letter from the Ordos Desert:

> When I came to China I hoped to find a reservoir of thought and mysticism that would bring fresh youth to your West.
>
> "blocked"
>
> I now have the impression that the reservoir is
>
> emptied.
>
> The Chinese are primitive people (beneath their varnish of modernity or Confucianism); the Mongols are in gradual process of disappearance, and their lamas are coarse and dirty monks. The fact remains that in time gone by these people *saw something*, but that they allowed this light to be lost—and that we can rediscover it. I was positively moved by the serenity and majesty of a Buddha in Peking: we have no finer representation of the Divinity!...Could we not enrich our spirit a little with the heavy sap circulating in their veins, while at the same time bringing them the wherewithal to make them live? Could we not try to complete ourselves by converting them? I haven't noticed that the missionaries have the faintest idea of this.[22]

These are first impressions. As such, they must not be given the same importance as Teilhard's more mature literary compositions. The enriching, exuberant aspects of the first encounter with China are enshrined in "The Mass on the World" (1923), a beautiful, symbolic offering of the world "in the steppes of Asia."[23]

One of the finest expressions of Teilhard's mystical vision, this prose poem has attracted comparisons of which he himself would have been unaware. Mircea Eliade, the well-known history of religions scholar, sees "The Mass on the World" as proclaiming the possibility that cosmic matter as such is susceptible of being sanctified in its totality. He writes:

When Teilhard speaks of the penetration of the galaxies by the cosmic Logos, even the most fantastic exaltation of the bodhisattvas seems modest and unimaginative by comparison—because for Teilhard the galaxies in which Christ will be preached millions of years hence are *real*, are living matter. They are not illusory and not even ephemeral.

Thus, in Eliade's view, Teilhard is "revealing the ultimate sacrality of nature and of life."[24]

Another commentator, Lama Anandagarika Govinda, has pointed out that the Ordos Desert lies in an area that has been under the cultural influence of Tibetan Buddhism for centuries. For this reason Govinda has explored similarities between "The Mass on the World" and the mystical meaning of the Tibetan mantra *"Om mani padme hum,"* and with certain ideas of the seventh-century Buddhist poem *Bodhicharyavatara*. These works place a similar emphasis on the spiritual transformation of matter, human beings, and the world, when offered up in an act of religious surrender.[25]

Complementary Riches of East and West

In 1924, while still in China, Teilhard had occasion to extend his knowledge of the country through further expeditions, especially to eastern Mongolia, and through visits to Peking. Earlier impressions were confirmed, and new ones gathered. Reports on his travels are interspersed with observations such as:

The Mongolia of the Gobi is every bit as wild as Central Africa, and the inhabitants are just as primitive. At long intervals you come across a lamasery, and on every prominent rocky peak you find a heap of stones called an obo—at once altar and a landmark—to which the devout Mongol adds a stone as he passes.

Teilhard was truly sensitive to the numinous quality of these tokens of an ancient faith. One of the obos has a dozen cairns, each with a branch stuck on top which the wind from the West has blown sideways like the flame of a torch. In these silent symbols, these ever-lonely altars, scattered over the wilderness, there is something really mysterious, really wild and impressive. The nights, when ours is the only caravan encamped by the well, take on a wonderful color and majesty....It's Whitsun week, and I like to think that "the spirit of Christ has filled the earth."[26]

In Peking, Teilhard encountered the Chinese Geological Survey, where he became especially acquainted with its founder-director, Dr. V. K. Ting (known under his Chinese name Ding Wenjiang). He seemed to be closely in touch with the contemporary intellectual leaders of China. During a discussion on Chinese philosophy and the Chinese religious temperament, Dr. Ting stated that the country was undergoing an antireligious phase. The ancient traditions had been severed, and the influence of western teachers was still too dominant.[27] Teilhard concluded:

Unquestionably the average Chinese is extremely earth-bound, and one may well ask oneself in what corner of his soul, or under what unexpected forms, the forces of religion and mysticism lie hidden in him. Even Dr Ting seemed to me to have envisaged the search for a religion in terms of a vast scientific enterprise, whereas the Absolute, as it is only too clear, cannot *"be taken* by force" but should manifest itself/"give itself" to the spirits that await it. What is certain is that if it is to attract the attention, and then the sympathy, of the Far Easterners, Christianity must present itself in a form...which amplifies (not minimizes!) the mystery, grandeur, interest and problems of the tangible universe.[28]

Yet in spite of seeing China from a predominantly western, and especially Christian, point of view, Teilhard did not share the perspective of most Christian missionaries. He was aware that through his scientific expeditions he penetrated into distant parts of the country, "so completely beyond the reach of any mission-ary,"[29] while he felt that missionaries were generally too cut off from the contemporary scientific milieu, and from wider social movements, to be able to understand his own worldview. To explain his vision was perhaps only possible in a particular European setting, and for this reason he sometimes longed to return to France. After having experienced "at close quarters just what a missionary's life is like, not in the big settlements, but in the remote country parts,"[30] he concluded that Europeans in China were often out of touch with the world at large.

Thus, he was initially glad to go back to Europe at the end of 1924. But it was not long before he wrote to a friend, "I am homesick for China."[31] He then realized that he preferred staying in Tientsin to being at the Institut Catholique in Paris. This change of attitude was mainly due to personal difficulties experienced with his superiors.

Given these difficulties, a return to China seemed to be the easiest solution. Teilhard left France before it was decided that his connection with the Institut Catholique would be permanently severed. At first, the return to the Far East was perhaps planned to last for one year, but it soon became permanent.

This turn of events led to much questioning. During the difficult years of 1926–27, strong anti-church tendencies are expressed in his writings, especially in the letters. A later superior has said of those critical years that Teilhard

> was leaving France under a cloud for an indefinite time, and he saw the momentum of his influence broken just as it was beginning to prove fruitful. The penalty imposed on him seemed unjustified. It was hard for him to "bend". He obeyed in a spirit of faith, but without understanding.[32]

His cousin Marguerite, fully aware of Teilhard's attraction to Asia, has judged the same events in retrospect more positively:

In the life of the Far East his mind found a new freedom. The grandeur of nature in a vast new continent, the multiplicity of human types he met on his travels and in the cosmopolitan society of Peking, gave depth and richness to his thought....His observation of the great ferment of societies and races, alternated with strict solitude, meditation, and concentration on God.

The trenches of the 1914 war had been for him what the cell is to the monk....Père Teilhard now became the wandering hermit of the Asian deserts, a background that facilitated the ascent of his powerful spirit and gave full scope to an outstanding personality and an outstanding destiny.[33]

After his return to Tientsin, in the midst of his deepest personal crisis, Teilhard wrote *The Divine Milieu* (1927), a spiritual masterpiece wherein he explores a specific approach to Christian mysticism and asceticism. *The Divine Milieu* elaborates the themes on mysticism already familiar from "The Mass on the World." The attributes of the "divine milieu" may externally resemble "the errors of a pagan naturalism," "the excesses of quietism and illuminism,"[34] but in reality they are at the antipodes of any false pantheism:

Pantheism seduces us by its vistas of perfect universal union. But ultimately, if it were true, it would give us only fusion and unconsciousness; for, at the end of the evolution it claims to reveal, the elements of the world vanish in the God they create or by which they are absorbed.

Christianity alone...saves...the essential aspiration of all mysticism: *to be united* (that is, to become the other) *while remaining oneself....*

We can only lose ourselves in God by prolonging the most individual characteristics of beings far beyond themselves: that is the fundamental rule by which we can always distinguish the true mystic from his counterfeits.

To sum up, one may say that, in relation to all the main historical forms assumed by the human religious spirit, Christian mysticism extracts *all* that is sweetest and strongest circulating in all the human mysticisms, though without absorbing their evil or suspect elements. It shows an astonishing equilibrium between the active and the passive, between possession of the world and its renunciation, between a taste for things and an indifference to them.[35]

Teilhard always hoped for the publication of *The Divine Milieu*. Official censures from his religious superiors prevented the book from appearing during his lifetime in spite of several revisions,[36] and repeated efforts by his friend, Father Charles in Louvain,[37] to get Teilhard's manuscripts published. When *The Divine Milieu* was finally published in France in 1957, two years after Teilhard's death, it still raised considerable controversy. Since then, several authors have studied the vicissitudes that have affected the understanding of this great spiritual work.[38] Siôn Cowell has provided a new translation of *The Divine Milieu* in English, prefaced by a fine explanatory essay written by Thomas M. King.[39] More recently, Louis M. Savary has written a most helpful commentary on this "revolutionary book of Christian spirituality."[40] But none of these writers relates Teilhard's spiritual vision to the concrete Chinese context of his writing, or to some of the eastern influences that pervade the perception of the divine milieu in the world, so that Teilhard's new, transformed, and even "revolutionary" understanding of spirituality remains still locked into exclusively western categories.

However disappointing it was for Teilhard not to see *The Divine Milieu* published after its completion in 1927, he did have the satisfaction of seeing his professional scientific services as geologist and paleontologist increasingly recognized, especially by the Chinese. Instead of working primarily for the French Musée de l'Homme, as at the beginning of his stay in China, he was very happy to work more and more for the Chinese Geological Survey and to collaborate with the Chinese University in Peking. He was convinced of the necessity of "going over to the Chinese,"[41] and he commented very positively on the intellectual attitudes of modern China, but this attitude was not shared by all foreigners.[42] Teilhard preferred to work in an open milieu that would place at his disposal "the double and complementary riches of East and West."[43] The inherent contrast and tension of this situation was summed up in his remark to his cousin in 1926: "*Old China, new China—dead religion, religion being born.*"[44]

Early in 1927, Teilhard wrote about this new China: "There is going on here, at this very moment, a human development of almost geological dimensions; to participate in it would be a rare chance indeed."[45] This realization made him perhaps less regretful that he was not returning to Paris. He enjoyed a considerable reputation with the Chinese; they referred to him as "the smiling scientist," and gave him the name "Father Daybreak Virtue." Unconventional though this name was, "to the Chinese it stood for the man, and was more prophetic than his unknown donor guessed."[46]

Teilhard's letters of this period also contain references to the communist movement. During his expeditions, he saw much of "Chinese China"; he deplored the scourge of militarism and the extent of suffering imposed on the people by the warlords. He welcomed the communist awakening, but writing to his friend Léontine Zanta in May 1927, he criticized the communists in the Far East for their "internationalization *through hatred*" rather than through sympathy and mutual assistance.[47] However, he set much hope on the young intellectuals:

> One feels that the country's intellectual elite is rapidly casting its skin. In a century the change will have happened. What will it give? A China capable of helping the West in its research, or merely an imitative China? Who can say?...[48]

This expresses quite a different attitude from his earlier appraisal of China. His second stay, unlike the first, made him well aware that a social movement and upheaval were taking place, giving birth to a new China, in fact, to a new Asia, that "the English forces will not prevent."[49] He felt that "nobody knows what will be left of the European establishments (notably the missions) in China in a year, short of very considerable foreign intervention....What happens...is the modern individualization of Asia."[50] Watching the awakening of Chinese national consciousness, Teilhard was already convinced in 1931 that the Chinese possessed the self-awareness of a modern nation.[51]

At that time, he was friendly with Hu Shih (1891–1962), "the young well-read philosopher who has behind him the whole of the Chinese undergraduate world."[52] Often referred to as "Father of the Literary Renaissance" in China, Hu Shih was well known for his achievements as a writer. He gave Teilhard his autobiography to read, that contained the *Credo* Hu Shih was offering to his fellow intellectuals. Hu Shih had undertaken graduate studies in the United States, especially under the philosopher John Dewey, whom he translated into Chinese. Later, Hu Shih chaired the philosophy department at Peking University and became leader of a language reform group. In his numerous writings, he formulated a "religion of social immortality" to replace traditional Chinese beliefs. His "creed" was strongly influenced by modern scientific concepts. Originally published in 1923, it provoked a public controversy in which every leading thinker in China took part. Stated in ten propositions, this creed was called "Hu Shih's New Decalogue" by some Christian missionaries. In 1931, Hu Shih republished the creed with an account of his own development, entitled *My Credo and Its Evolution*, which is the autobiography referred to by Teilhard.[53]

It proposed "a framework for a new philosophy of the universe and life" that Teilhard described as "faith in the world but in a world conceived in a childishly immature and imprecise way....[Hu Shih] doesn't see that the cosmos holds together not by matter but by spirit."[54] While criticizing Hu Shih's *Credo*, Teilhard was nevertheless deeply interested "to see even Chinese thought, in its own way, taking the same direction as my own and that of my friends."[55] He recognized an affinity here.

Earlier, Teilhard had expressed the desire to write "a book of the earth." This seemed preferable to writing a book on China alone, for which, in any case, he did not possess "the knowledge of the language and the past that would open the hidden treasure."

Yet one question clearly fascinated him in relating his Chinese experience to a global perspective. This was

> to discover the new spirit that is struggling to emerge from the ruins of the old crenellated towns and the old pagodas; to recognize and reveal that specific and essential element which the East must bring to the West so that the Earth will be complete.

Over the years, he became increasingly convinced that the social and political turmoil, and the awakening of the new China, might be of great importance for the future development of humankind, much more so than, for example, the contemporary events in India.

It was above all in China that Teilhard experienced the vastness of the Earth and its peoples. He compared this experience to a voice or song murmuring in him,

> not of me, but of the World in me. I would like to express the thoughts of a man who, having finally penetrated the partitions and ceilings of little countries, little coteries, little sects, rises above all these categories and finds himself a child and citizen of the Earth.[56]

He called this "the Note of China, the Note of the All, joyous and magnificent." It was a note of universality as well as an indication of the complementarity between East and West. Speaking about his personal experience, he could say that in China "the West fascinates me: but once west of Turkestan. I...dream of the East."[57] At a deeper level, he always looked out for indications "as to the possibility of a frank spiritual collaboration between East and West."[58] It is this note of complementarity and universality that reverberates through the essay "The Spirit of the Earth" (1931),[59] written to overcome racial, national, and religious barriers, and received with enthusiasm by his friends.

The Decisive Encounter with Peking Man

The Far East was now, during the second part of his stay (1932–46), his permanent home. Outwardly involved in expeditions and research, he still found time for writing philosophical and religious essays. These were read by a large circle of friends in China, France, the United States, and elsewhere. The years 1931–32 are an important watershed. They not only mark his participation in an important expedition but also provide a dividing line between the Tientsin period and the subsequent stay in Peking.

The Chinese reaction toward Teilhard's enlightened attitude on collaboration between East and West was to invite him in 1929 to become an official scientific adviser to their Geological Survey. Teilhard was delighted. Teilhard's friend and colleague, George Barbour, reveals that it was Father Ernest Gherzi, the director of the Siccawei Observatory in Shanghai, who "suggested his friend's name to the head of the Chinese Geological Survey when the latter was looking for an expert adviser."[60] Gherzi and Teilhard had been students together at the Jesuit theological house in Hastings, where they used to go fossil hunting together.

Teilhard thought highly of the Chinese Geological Survey, founded by several Chinese scientists in 1916 after their return from studying in Europe. Their work found further support through that of the Chinese Geological Society, which, in the mid-1920s, counted more than two hundred members and already had a spacious building, a splendid museum, laboratories, and a fine library at their disposal. The West was no longer the only center of scientific research; Peking, with some assistance from the West, was growing increasingly important.

When Teilhard had first arrived in China in 1923, he was supported by the French national museum, the Musée de l'Homme in Paris, where he had studied under its then director, Marcellin Boule. During the early years of his stay in China, the fossils collected by Teilhard and Licent were sent back to the Paris museum. Boule expected this arrangement to be permanent and hoped that Teilhard would eventually work at the museum in Paris and perhaps become its director. He was therefore opposed to Teilhard's fuller integration into a Chinese organization, whereas Teilhard was averse to a separatist attitude. He decided "to go over to the Chinese" and wrote already to one of his friends on February 2, 1927:

> Boule has lately written to tell me that he is cutting off my funds for this year....I have learned from a reliable source...that Boule is dissatisfied: (1) because I left France against his advice (as if it were any of my doing!) and (2) I can now see that everything I have been telling him about my finds here (they are more valuable to Peking and geology in general than to his show-cases) has only served to annoy him. I feel a really filial affection for him as I always shall—so when I answered I did what I could to pacify him.[61]

The Chinese Geological Service was then mainly concerned with the investigation of the paleontological site at Chou-Kou-Tien (now known as Zhoukoudian), some thirty miles southwest of Peking and about a day's mule trip away from the city. At the edge of the Western Hills, this was an area long known for its abundant limestone, where locals had for centuries gathered bones for medicinal purposes, a practice that attracted the attention of paleontologists. Systematic excavations of the Chou-Kou-Tien caves began in 1922, and from the late 1920s onward, Teilhard became increasingly associated with the geological and paleontological aspects of this work. On December 2, 1929, the Chinese scientist Pei discovered the first complete skullcap. Teilhard was assigned the task of determining the age of the formations in which the skull, which came to be known as "Peking Man" (*Sinanthropus pekinensis*) had been found.[62] It was a significant breakthrough that stimulated much scientific discussion about human origins and led to further excavations and finds in the same area. Celebrated as an important Chinese discovery in prehistory, the extensive finds were of great significance for scientific research. Zhoukoudian is today designated as a "World Culture Heritage" site, where Chinese scientists continue to work, but it also contains an impressive, well-kept museum and a memorial garden with stone tablets and photographs of all the scientists associated with *Sinanthropus*, including Teilhard.[63]

Teilhard's association with the work on Peking Man brought him worldwide scientific recognition and contacts.[64] In a subsequently written, short summary of his career, expressed in the third person, he describes the research on Peking Man as

> the most decisive event of his career—by which we mean his share (in his capacity of adviser to the Geological Survey of China) in the quite unexpected discovery of the famous Peking Man (Sinanthropus). Correct dating and interpretation of this sensationally new fossil Man called for a thorough and up-to-date stratigraphic, physiographic and palaeontological examination of the whole Quaternary in the Far East. It was to this central problem that Père Teilhard decided to devote the full maturity of his experience for the last fifteen years of his time in the Far East; and...its ramifications were to take him in turn to India, to Burma and Java.[65]

Jia Lanpo, a young scientist who took part in the excavations as Teilhard's assistant, and later one of China's foremost paleoanthropologists, wrote a detailed history of the Zhoukoudian excavations and the many important discoveries made by the international team of scientists.[66] His account also includes the description of the loss of the fossils of Peking Man after the Second World War. This is a great mystery that has never been explained, and speculations continue to this day. Most recently, this story has been brought to life in a thrilling historical novel by Amir D. Aczel, *The Jesuit and the Skull: Teilhard de Chardin, Evolution, and the Search for Peking Man*.[67] This imaginative reconstruction highlights an important stage in Teilhard's scientific career and portrays the historical search for human origins within a global setting.

When living in Peking during the 1930s, Teilhard was at the height of his career. He spent more time on research and scientific papers at that time than on writing philosophical essays. But in 1939, this situation became reversed through changing political circumstances. From 1939 to 1946, it was practically impossible to pursue any scientific work outside Peking because of the city's occupation by the Japanese. Teilhard lived in considerable isolation, and consequently he devoted most of those years to creative writing and intensive reading. Before 1932, East–West comparisons are mainly found in letters, but after that time several essays are explicitly devoted to comparisons. The first of these was written after returning from a long expedition to Central Asia. Several encounters during this journey left a deep impression on Teilhard and stimulated him to reflect again, and more deeply, on the place of religion and mysticism in the modern world.

The Yellow Expedition across Central Asia

In the early 1930s, the French motor vehicle firm Citroën organized a large-scale expedition across Central Asia known as the "Yellow Expedition" or *Croisière Jaune*,[68] following two earlier successful crossings of the Sahara and the African continent. These rallies were organized to test Citroën automobiles on difficult terrain and make publicity for the French enterprise. In addition, they provided new opportunities for scientific research. The Yellow Expedition was intended to retrace by car the ancient route known as the "Silk Road" that had joined the West and Asian continents since the time of Cyrus the Great, but it also offered possibilities for investigations in geology, anthropology, and even art history.

Consisting of several French engineers and mechanics, some scientists and doctors, an American photographer from the National Geographic Society, film and radio specialists, a painter, an archaeologist, and support personnel, the Yellow Expedition numbered more than forty people. Teilhard had been appointed as the official geologist. The expedition was divided into two groups: the first traveled from China westward across the Gobi Desert to Sinkiang (modern Xinjiang) in Chinese East Turkestan;[69] the second group started in the West and traveled eastward via Syria, Persia, Afghanistan, and India over the Hindu Kush and Pamir Mountains into Central Asia. It was planned that the two groups should meet at the foot of the Pamir Mountains in the old oasis city of Kashgar, at the western end of the Tarim basin, at the crossroads of the southern and northern branches of the ancient Silk Road.

However, due to the difficult political situation in China at that time, these plans could not be fully carried out. The expedition lasted for almost a year, from April 1931 to February 1932. The route of the group of engineers and scientists traveling from Peking westward covered the breadth of northern China, and their journey included many colorful and dangerous adventures, fully reported in the official expedition history written by Georges Le Fèvre.[70] In the words of the expedition leader, Georges-Marie Haardt, it was an "extraordinary journey across the most inaccessible parts of China at a time when the most terrible chaos prevailed and there was no law but the law of the strongest."[71]

In addition to Frenchmen, Teilhard's group included an official contingent of Chinese scientists. Apparently, some of these were political agents. One of the eight Chinese representatives was a member of the central committee of the Kuomintang and also a minister of General Chiang Kai-shek's government.[72] It is a reflection on Teilhard's standing that he was often asked to act as a mediator during the repeated disputes among the Chinese delegation. On arrival at the border of Sinkiang, the province's governor refused the expedition entry into his territory until the Chinese delegation had been sent home. But even after that, the French were held prisoner for three months outside Urumchi, the capital of Sinkiang. Through various clandestine communications, they eventually learned that the other half of the expedition, traveling from West to East, had arrived in Kashgar. They pressed for permission to meet up with this second group, and, after prolonged negotiations, a small contingent was allowed to establish contact between the two expedition teams by traveling further westward, but not as far as Kashgar. This small liaison group consisted exclusively of technical personnel except for Teilhard, who, thanks "to his official position in China,"[73] was the only scientist granted permission to travel further westward.

It was a similar sign of trust that he was later also chosen to accompany a specially selected group led by Joseph Hackin,[74] the director of the Paris museum of eastern art, the Musée Guimet, to return from Sinkiang via a different route to study ancient Buddhist remains. Even from among this group, only a small party was permitted to visit the actual Buddhist sites in the Gobi Desert. Besides Hackin, Teilhard, and a mechanic, this party included a photographer and a painter who copied many Buddhist murals. Although they were allowed to take photos of the Buddhist ruins, they were explicitly forbidden to photograph any of the indigenous population. But the painter could record where the camera could not. Alexander Jacovleff, official artist to the expedition, created a beautiful set of color studies of the various ethnic types encountered during their travels, of which copies still exist.[75]

Teilhard's report on the results of the expedition[76] explicitly mentions the ancient caves cut into rocks by Manichean and Buddhist monks and emphasizes that he closely followed Hackin's comparative work on religious iconography. Teilhard's account includes illustrations of a Buddhist divinity, painted in Tibetan-Mongolian style on a large boulder, and also of a Buddhist lamasery where the group stayed. Hackin also invited Teilhard to accompany him on a study tour of Japan during the following year,[77] but this project did not materialize.

The official maps, later published by the expedition, not only list geographical, geological, and botanical information but also the location of Mongol camps, numerous obo-cairns en route and some eighteen Buddhist lamaseries. In contrast, only one Chinese temple is shown on the entire itinerary. Most of the lamaseries were met at the beginning of their journey, before the expedition reached the Gobi Desert.[78]

Besides camping, the expedition stayed en route in large Buddhist lamaseries, sometimes in Chinese inns, or occasionally, closer to Peking, in Christian mission stations. They encountered Chinese Buddhists and Muslims, talked to Taoist priests, Buddhist lamas, and various Muslim dignitaries. Unfortunately, they also got caught in a major battle at Hami in the aftermath of the Chinese Muslim revolt of the 1930s.[79]

The details of the political struggles in China witnessed by the members of this French expedition make fascinating reading but are outside the scope of this book. Of greater interest in the present context is the expedition members' stay at the Buddhist monastery, Pei Ling Miao. They had the opportunity to witness there a long religious ceremony and engage in discussion with a learned lama, an envoy of the Panchen Lama (the second highest ranking Tibetan lama after the Dalai Lama). At first the lamas promised to perform one of the famous Tibetan demon dances, but for some reason this later proved to be impossible. However, a day's journey further on, something more exciting happened. It was the Chinese New Year, and a local prince invited the expedition members to a solemn ceremony where, in the presence of all the dignitaries of the region, the Panchen Lama himself officiated and gave his blessings.[80] It seems surprising that we have no description of these details, either from Teilhard or others. He was present, though, as we know from a discussion between Teilhard and Hackin on the significance of one of the monastery's wall paintings showing a *Bhavachakra* or wheel of life. Teilhard was impressed by the quality of the Buddhist liturgy, which he considered as public worship of the first order.[81]

Yet no reference to these experiences has been found in Teilhard's own writings. This may be due to several reasons. In the first place, the tumultuous political situation and general lack of communication did not permit regular correspondence, which is why the Yellow Expedition is documented by relatively few letters or other reports. Moreover, all Teilhard's diaries from China were later to be lost in the general upheaval following the end of the Second World War.

By February 1932, Teilhard was back in Peking after an expedition of ten months. He felt the after-effects of the sheer physical strain of this journey and regretted the missed opportunities for research, lost through the political situation. The expedition had endured extremes of heat and cold, a harsh winter in the desert with temperatures of −20 to −30 degrees Celsius, imprisonment, attacks, and robbery.[82] Although the scientific results were not as rich as had been expected,[83] Teilhard had almost doubled his knowledge of the Asian continent and its peoples. He sometimes alluded to their great ethnic variety and, in the heart of Chinese Turkestan, he felt that it is a shock to find yourself among people who remind you more of the Near East than the Far East: a negligible minority of Chinese, and a predominance of Arab, Turkish and Persian types. They are practically all Moslems; you see mosques and minarets and hear the muezzin. The men are dignified, grave and bearded.

And further West he wrote:

There are no Chinese any more apart from the administrators and a few merchants. The men bearded and turbanned, trotting on their asses; the women strictly and becomingly veiled;...the loud chant of the muezzins calling to evening prayer at every corner of little villages. You begin to see Afghans, Persians and Hindus; it's no longer the Far East.[84]

In the midst of the enforced stay at the capital of Sinkiang, Teilhard also mentioned in a letter that two particular themes preoccupied him, the nature of a "personalistic universe" and a work on "The Conversion of the World" intended as "a review of the present state of the various religions."[85] He was fully aware that these plans for new essays could only be realized later. But such reflections show that the long journey through Central Asia raised for him many questions as to the religious significance of his rich and varied experiences. During the Yellow Expedition, he came into contact with different peoples, cultures, and religions of the East. In addition, he was also part of a secular western "lay milieu," represented by the French expedition members, several of whom had completely abandoned religious beliefs and practices. Numerous discussions on religious questions with other expedition members reinforced Teilhard's view that Christianity lacked the necessary openness to contemporary forms of thought and experience. Thus, he increasingly realized the need for a new approach to spirituality and for what he later called "a new mysticism." It is from this perspective that he attempted to present Christianity to the modern world and to formulate some kind of a new "apologetic," which he outlined in several essays written in the late 1930s. There he stressed that Christians must above all "re-think" their own religion.[86]

Another writing project was realized more immediately. Shortly after his return to Peking, Teilhard announced that he was going to write something on "the fundamental metaphysical and religious question" of the One and the Many, to which he saw an "eastern solution" and a "western solution."[87] This theme was fully worked out during the following months in "The Road of the West: To a New Mysticism" (1932),[88] written when traveling on the boat from China to France and completed at Penang on September 8, 1932. Scientific reports apart, this is the first major essay after the Yellow Expedition, and it is also the first explicitly concerned with a particular comparison between East and West. Thus, it may be seen in some way as the outcome of Teilhard's reflections during that long journey across China. I discuss the major ideas of this essay in chapter 6.

From 1932 on, Peking became Teilhard's permanent residence and primary place of work. He made new contacts and friendships among Chinese and western scientists and many international expatriates and visitors to the city. Most important from a personal point of view was his deep love for the American sculptor Lucile Swan who, with her great warmth and hospitality, gave him much inspiration as well as emotional and practical support. She not only created a fine bust of Teilhard but also translated many of his writings into English so that they could be distributed among his English-speaking friends. The rich correspondence between the two during the years 1932–55 was only published in 1993, long after Teilhard's works had become widely known. They give deep insights into his feelings and personal relationships, his way of life in Peking, the development of his thought, and his scientific work and travels.[89]

During the 1930s, Teilhard took part in several expeditions to other parts of the country, especially to southern China, western Honan, and up the Yangtze River. The discovery of the Chinese South in particular was a new experience about which he wrote, "Every moment showed me a China more Chinese than the north. The pagodas are more brilliant and more mannered, hats are wider and more pointed, the whole countryside more like the China we know in books."[90]

Again, we possess only occasional references to the impressions left on him by these various expeditions. A more detailed account of some journeys, shared with George Barbour, are found in the latter's book *In the Field with Teilhard de Chardin*.[91] There he reports some of the discussions he had with Teilhard during their expeditions. At the end of day, when their scientific work was done, Teilhard would launch

> on an analysis of the various religions which developed one after the other throughout history; he sought to discern what contribution each might have made towards a better understanding of the structure of the universe and towards a deeper comprehension of God.[92]

This is only a brief reference, but it proves again that the abstract ideas of Teilhard's essays are but the distillations of his lived experience that supplied the raw material for all his reflections. This experience was further enlarged through contacts with eastern countries outside China, particularly through visits to India, Indonesia, and Burma.

Travels to India, Indonesia, Burma, and Japan

In 1935, Teilhard was invited to visit both India and Indonesia. At first, he was not too enthusiastic about the idea of going to India, where he was to join for some months the Yale-Cambridge expedition led by the German scientist Helmut de Terra. Yet afterward he admitted that he had spent "four really exciting months"[93] and that he "was delighted with India."[94] The main reason for this journey was again scientific; in retrospect, the experience proved a great addition to his knowledge of prehistory and yet, at a deeper level, it gave him "only moderate satisfaction." He summed up this contrast in a letter to his brother:

> As a purpose in life, my science (to which I owe so much) seems to me to be less and less worthwhile. For

77

a long time now, my chief interest in life has lain in
some sort of effort towards a plainer disclosing of God
in the world. It's a more killing task but it's my only
true vocation and nothing can turn me from it.[95]

Teilhard arrived in Bombay in September 1935. He spent a
few days in the city, then went by train to Rawalpindi, now in
Pakistan. From there he traveled by car to Srinagar in Kashmir,
accompanied by the British scientist T. T. Patterson.[96] They joined
de Terra on a houseboat and spent a week on field work in
Kashmir. Subsequently, they moved to western Punjab, living in
Rawalpindi and elsewhere. Together they visited the prehistoric
drawings in the Indus Valley and the excavations at Mohenjo
Daro, which left a deep impression on Teilhard. They also had an
opportunity to visit the regions of Sind and Baluchistan. Later,
their search for prehistoric material took them for a fortnight to
the Narbada valley in central India. Teilhard ended his three
months' stay in India with a week in Calcutta, and from there he
embarked for Java.

Traveling by camel or car in the Salt Range of western
Punjab, now part of Pakistan, the semi-desert country reminded
him of Egypt, and also of Ethiopia, which he had visited a few
years before. This is not only expressed in *Letters from a
Traveller*,[97] but also in Helmut de Terra's vivid account of their
shared visit to India. In his book *Memories of Teilhard de
Chardin* he mentions that the landscape of the Sind Desert

> reminded Teilhard so vividly of the Nile Valley and of
> Cairo where he had worked as a teacher, that he felt as
> though he had been suddenly transported to Egypt.
> Here, as there, rivers threaded the desert with the luxu-
> riant valley pastures to which the ancient civilizations
> had owed their wealth—yet how different had been
> their respective fates![98]

Reflecting on the desert as a place of religious experience, which
has stimulated "the spiritual and visionary sides" of "men of destiny," de Terra particularly remarks that Teilhard "fitted so well

into the wilderness."[99] He loved the "wonderful luminosity" of the north Indian countryside, but he commented more harshly on its population.[100]

It must be remembered that Teilhard's first and most extensive contact with Indians was mainly with Muslims, whom he considered backward in their customs. About Hindus, he wrote:

> So far as I have been able to form an opinion of them, the Hindus have been a disappointment to me. In them, too, the creative power seems in a pretty poor way, and you have to go to India to realize the numbing and deadening effect of a religion obsessed by material forms and ritualism.[101]

However, when he met the Hindu upper classes in Lahore and Calcutta, he found them "highly civilized." He thought Indians charming as individuals, but he judged the country as a whole still incapable of self-government. He was fully aware, though, of the general dislike of the English among the local inhabitants who "want independence at all costs."[102]

Teilhard also observed some Indian religious customs. According to de Terra, they watched a Hindu village festival in honor of Shiva in central India. People danced and chanted all night, offering *puja* and floating little oil lamps on the river:

> With its groups of palms and venerable mango trees, the whole place seemed to have been transformed into a setting for some oriental "Midsummer Night's Dream."...Apparently, the god had visited their fields a few days ago in the guise of a flood, leaving behind numerous symbols of his procreative power in the shape of some longish pebbles, which were regarded as an especial mark of divine favour. From the temple, where festivities were in full swing, came the sound of flutes and drums and the nasal incantations of the priest....The whole village seemed to be involved in the festival. In several houses we glimpsed old men seated by candle-light, holding their hands before their fore-

heads in prayer...and chanting continuously from books with such devotion that for a moment we felt ourselves carried back in time to the far-off days when the Vedic hymns still formed part of daily worship.[103]

Teilhard's more negative impression of Hinduism may be related to other experiences, such as the following, again described by de Terra:

Then there were the fakirs squatting beneath the broad branches of mango trees, their naked torsos smeared with ash and their long matted hair piled turban-like atop their ascetic faces—hideous caricatures of human beings whom Teilhard regarded with compassion, likening them to "spirits of the underworld". Just as the fakirs reminded him of the human bondage caused by religious fanaticism, so he was disgusted by the caste-mark tradition.[104]

It was de Terra's opinion that if there were any foreigner "who could have roused ancient India to new life, it was Teilhard. In this superstition-ridden Indian world, he seemed like a new species of human being."[105] Yet it has also been remarked that, unlike other visitors to the country, Teilhard was neither impressed by the religious fervor of the people nor did he appreciate the Hindu assertion "of a cosmic unity, which was in many ways analogous to his own ideas,"[106] at least he did not realize it then. Closer comparisons reveal a certain affinity between the Hindu sense of unity and some of Teilhard's ideas about oneness, as Beatrice Bruteau has shown in a detailed study comparing his thought with central aspects of the Hindu tradition.[107]

After leaving India, Teilhard paid a brief visit to Rangoon in Burma (now Myanmar), where he spent Christmas 1935. He returned to this city again for a longer period two years later. After his stay in Rangoon, he traveled for about a month all over Java. His scientific work kept him too occupied then to visit any of the famous sites. But he was proud to have lived "in the Javanese kampongs among the gentle and graceful natives."

Although it was the rainy season, conditions were favorable, and he "revelled in the exoticism of this marvellous country."

However, Java was overpopulated; apart from its high peaks and some remnants of jungle, "it is nothing but one immense village; but the huts are so small, so scattered and so lost in the vast sea of green, that all you see is a forest of palms enclosing rice-fields, the whole dominated by a series of volcanoes, each as big as Etna."[108]

On his return journey to China, he wrote down his travel notes, but these do not seem to have survived. Few details are known about this or the subsequent visit to Java, undertaken in April 1938. The scientific work of the second visit has been described at some length by Helmut de Terra, from whom one can also gather that they visited the island's interior and saw some of Java's splendid attractions:

> From Bandung we travelled to Surakarta, ancient seat of the Javanese princes, where we watched dancers rehearsing for a performance in the palace. It was like some old oriental fairy-tale, with young dancing-girls in heavy brocaded costumes gliding beneath the mango trees in the palace courtyard to the strains of a game-lang orchestra....[109]

Unfortunately, neither this nor any other sightseeing was recorded by Teilhard. Slightly more information is available on his subsequent visit to Burma, lasting from December 1937 to March 1938.[110] He stayed as long in Burma as in India, but he took more to this Buddhist country than to Hindu India. He commented with delight on Burmese life and wrote from Pagan, the old temple city:

> I overlook the Irrawaddy, fringed by low mountains and held in a ribbon of green, exactly like the Nile in Upper Egypt....The surroundings are simply one great forest of pagodas....The population is very much of a mixture. First the Burmese, all grace and beaming smiles...dressed in dazzling colours, with an extraordinary proportion of orange-robed monks. Towards the Arakan-Yoma you meet the "Chins", small men, with

moustaches, almost Mongol. To the east the black-turbanned Shans and a chequer-board of small groups of strange ethnic types....A few days ago we were at Pagan, the ancient capital...of the Burmese kings. Now it is simply a village lost in palms, banyans, mangoes and mimosa, but surrounded by over a hundred pagodas, some of them in ruins that may well date back to the twelfth century. Nothing really artistic or grand (all brick-built) but about the whole, particularly when the sun is setting, there is something most fantastic and unreal. I am becoming very fond of this radiant country, three quarters covered with bush or jungle, in which the most insignificant inhabitant is as graceful and colourful as a flower.[111]

According to Helmut de Terra, Teilhard's host and colleague during this expedition, it was hard to finally take leave of Burma with its "idyllic river landscape, the wild expanses of tropical mountain forest, the Buddhist traditions of the country's graceful inhabitants, the colorful splendor of village festivals."[112] In the wilderness of the jungle, de Terra also noted that he "could always sense, in Teilhard's company, something of the mystical empathy with Nature."[113]

On their return boat journey, they called at various ports, including Malacca, on the Malayan coast, halfway between India and China, and well known for its Jesuit missionary associations. Long ago, Saint Francis Xavier regarded the Malacca mission as a springboard for the conversion of China and Japan to Christianity. This vision of a religious conquest of Asia has been described as "a Napoleonic idea in religious terms."[114] Teilhard considered it as something well belonging to the past.

Other journeys to and from China provided an opportunity to get acquainted with places en route such as Ceylon, Penang, Singapore, Saigon, Hanoi, Hong Kong, and Hawaii. Here again, little detailed information is available except for brief descriptions in Teilhard's correspondence, particularly the *Letters from a Traveller*.

Even less known are the details of his three brief stops in

Japan during 1931, 1937, and 1938. Apart from the industrial center of Kobe, Teilhard visited at least the ancient cities of Kyoto and Nara, well known for their famous Buddhist and Shinto temples. In Kyoto, he saw "a whole series of classical temples, more somber in color than the Chinese but very clean, built of a most magnificent wood and nestling in such a wonderful green background of tall dark-foliaged trees." To his regret, he had a missionary as guide so that he could not linger on as long as he would have liked "in front of the gilded altars, *without* idols."[115] Father Leroy, who accompanied Teilhard on one of his subsequent visits to Japan, has said that, on seeing these temples, they both realized the vitality of Japanese religious life in comparison to that of China.[116] The activity in Japanese temples stood in stark contrast to the neglected Confucian temples in China, for example. In view of this difference, it seems surprising that Teilhard himself never commented on this experience.

De Terra found it equally surprising that, given "the grandeur of Teilhard's ideas," he never assumed "the role of preacher or prophet." Instead, his primary concern was with the study of the human being in all its aspects, seeking an all-embracing, universal perspective that, he felt, science had so far left out of its purview. In the opinion of this fellow scientist, Teilhard was wittingly or unwittingly "the founder of a new kind of anthropology, although he would have been hard put to find it a home in existing academic institutions."[117] This comment is as true today as it was then.

Teilhard's new anthropological and universalist perspective found expression in numerous essays, but particularly in his major work, written in Peking between 1938 and 1940. In its English translation it later became known as *The Phenomenon of Man*, but a more accurate rendering of the French original, *Le phénomène humain*, is the more recently adopted title, *The Human Phenomenon*, based on a thoroughly revised and more exact new translation of Teilhard's magnum opus.[118] Although written in a relatively brief time, when he was forced to stay in Peking due to the war, Teilhard considered this work to be a synthesis of forty years of studies, experience, and reflections. Yet in spite of multiple revisions, this book suffered the same fate as *The*

Divine Milieu earlier: permission to publish it was withheld during his lifetime. However, cyclostyled copies of the book were soon circulating among a number of personal friends and scientists.

The Human Phenomenon, primarily addressed to fellow scientists, carries few explicit references to religion except for its epilogue on "The Christian Phenomenon."[119] After dealing with the emergence of pre-life and life, the third section of the book discusses the birth of thought and the emergence of the modern world, which includes a short part on "the rise of the West"[120] that is of special interest. In a very general manner, Teilhard considers here the gradual "confluence" of civilizations. He sees the movement of history as a rhythm of conflict and harmonization between dominant "currents," summarily illustrated by five major civilizations of the past including, among others, Chinese and Indian civilization. Whereas ancient China remained static and unchanged, early India was drawn into metaphysics:

> India—the region par excellence of high philosophic and religious pressures: we can never make too much of our indebtedness to the mystic influences which have come down to each and all of us in the past from this "anticyclone."[121]

Here as elsewhere in Teilhard's work, there is an explicit recognition of India's central position in the development of mysticism. However, this took place in the faraway past, and Teilhard goes on to point out shortcomings:

> But however efficacious these currents for ventilating and illuminating the atmosphere of mankind, we have to recognize that, with their excessive passivity and detachment, they were incapable of building the world. The primitive soul of India arose in its hour like a great wind but, like a great wind also, again in its hour, it passed away. How indeed could it have been otherwise? Phenomena regarded as an illusion (Maya) and their connections as a chain (Karma), what was left in those

doctrines to animate and direct human evolution? A simple mistake was made—but it was enough—in the definition of the spirit and in the appreciation of the bonds which attach it to the sublimation of matter.

Then step by step we are driven nearer to the more western zones of the world—to the Euphrates, the Nile, the Mediterranean—where an exceptional concurrence of places and peoples was, in the course of a few thousand years, to produce that happy blend, thanks to which reason could be harnessed to facts and religion to action.

...We would be allowing sentiment to falsify the facts if we failed to recognize that during historic time the principal axis of anthropogenesis has passed through the West. It is in this ardent zone of growth and universal recasting that all that goes to make man today has been discovered, or at any rate *must have been rediscovered*....

In truth, a neo-humanity has been germinating round the Mediterranean during the last six thousand years....

From one end of the world to the other, all the peoples, to remain human or to become more so, are inexorably led to formulate the hopes and problems of the modern earth in the very same terms in which the West has formulated them.[122]

Although one may agree with Joseph Needham[123] in judging Teilhard's history to be out of focus here, it would be a mistake to regard these paragraphs as merely an ethnocentric statement, based on the naive assumption of western supremacy in all developments of life. However unsatisfactorily presented, this particular passage, as well as *The Human Phenomenon* as a whole, is concerned with a problem of historical genesis: How and where did our modern world originate in its present form, as we know it today?[124] This is followed by a consideration of the collective issue regarding humanity's survival, its further evolution, and the unity of the human family, requiring "the confluence of thought" and a "convergent spirit" among humankind.

In the area of religion and mysticism, this implies that the West is not only indebted to the East for the origin of certain mystical insights, but, what is more, without a "confluence" and a mutual interaction of the different religious traditions from now on, a full understanding of the human phenomenon as a whole cannot emerge. Such a convergent perspective applies to the whole Earth and not to West or East in isolation. The human community, though deeply torn apart, is increasingly feeling the need to think of itself as interdependent and one.[125] It was the Chinese milieu that provided the background for the emergence of this universalist perspective of the spirit of one Earth. Let us, therefore, briefly consider some further encounters of Teilhard in Peking and Shanghai.

Experiences in Peking and Shanghai

In Peking, Teilhard was more in touch with an international scientific, artistic, and diplomatic milieu than with traditional Chinese circles. He knew the intellectual elite of the country, that is to say, leading Chinese scientists and intellectuals rather than the political class. Yet through his wide and varied contacts, he was informed about what was happening elsewhere.[126] Here only two incidents, generally little known, are mentioned since they illustrate Teilhard's awareness of certain political and religious developments at that time.

Between 1933 and 1936, Teilhard counted among his friends Edgar Snow, the journalist and famous author of *Red Star over China*.[127] According to Helen Snow, Teilhard was one of the first westerners to learn about the experience on which this book is based, namely Snow's visit to Mao Tse-Tung and the Chinese communist movement in 1936. Supporting evidence for this comes from another member of Teilhard's Peking circle of friends, Lucile Swan, who writes that Edgar Snow, on his return from visiting the communist headquarters in Yenan, in western China,

> brought photographs and information about the life and conditions there. As he was one of the first journalists to visit the Communists his reports were of the

greatest value, and Père Teilhard questioned him from every angle as this new phenomenon was of much interest to him, as were all large manifestations of human energy.[128]

Apparently, Teilhard read *Red Star over China* with great fascination. Together with the Snows "they discussed the new controversial subjects—fascism, Marxism, socialism, communism, and isms for which we had not even any common language then." Through Mao Tse-Tung's Marxism, an element of western thought and ethics reached for the first time the majority of Chinese villagers never before touched by western missionary influence. In Helen Snow's opinion, Mao Tse-Tung's influence and presence, more than anything else, were an example of Teilhard's thesis of human evolution. Apparently, Mrs. Snow told Mao personally in 1937 about Teilhard's own vision and thought.[129]

Whether this actually happened or not, the story illustrates that Teilhard knew more about the rising forces of communism in China than one would generally suspect. He had been aware for a long time of the compelling attraction of Marxism,[130] and many of his essays refer to the inner strength and activating power of the Marxist belief in the development of human society and the world. He shared this belief to a great extent, but he criticized Marxism for its lack of transcendence.

The longest account of Teilhard's later years in Peking comes from Claude Rivière, who headed the French radio station in Shanghai during the war. In her book *En Chine avec Teilhard de Chardin*,[131] she describes their long discussions on Chinese religion and society. Amid the indescribable misery and suffering of China, where the extremes of poverty, hunger, and cold exceeded anything ever seen in India, Teilhard could maintain an attitude of hope and unparalleled dynamism. Rivière thinks this was only possible because of the strength of his inner vision, which she describes as a deeply mystical one: "To convince oneself of the authenticity of the mystical...nature of [his] faith..., words were unnecessary. It was enough to see him...at the end of a retreat or after his Mass with a transfigured face, suffused with radiant joy."[132] She also mentions that Teilhard left the contemporary world the irreplaceable contribution of a "sense of the Divine which all the great mystics have," and "a visionary intuition of the sacred,"[133] which radiates through his entire work.

With regard to Teilhard's encounter of eastern religions, Claude Rivière reports one incident not documented elsewhere. At the end of 1942, Teilhard and his friend, Father Leroy, visited Claude Rivière in Shanghai. At that moment, a conference of leading Buddhists from all over Asia was taking place in order to discuss the spiritual influence of Buddhism in the Far East. The participants included two well-known "living Buddhas," Lama Lo-Song from Outer Mongolia and Lama Awangishi from Tibet.

Claude Rivière, in her capacity as broadcaster, interviewed the two lamas in the Temple of the Great Jade Buddha in Shanghai when Teilhard was present. She mentions that he specifically asked the lamas about the current state of Buddhism, and also about its foreseeable future. After a lengthy discussion, the Tibetan lama is reported to have ended by saying that Teilhard was a great "living Jesus" of the West. One day he would be famous, and many people would be nourished by his message.[134]

These encounters initiated long discussions about the state of religion in China among Teilhard and his friends. Generally speaking, Chinese Buddhism was at a low ebb during Teilhard's time, although a growing movement of renewal was then spreading through the country.[135] During his expeditions, Teilhard frequently stayed in or near various Buddhist temples; yet he had had little opportunity to get closely acquainted with the great monasteries, where ancient Buddhist and Taoist traditions were still alive. The beautiful old temples in the Western Hills near Peking, which he knew well, had so few pilgrims that "the priests rented some of the courtyards and rooms to foreigners who used them as country retreats" or gave parties there.[136] Teilhard's encounter with Buddhist monks, his earlier meeting with the Panchen Lama, and his experience of Buddhist liturgy are only a few examples that show that he came into contact with some aspects of living Buddhism at a time when, apart from scholarly specialists, relatively few western people had the opportunity to do so. Not all commentators will realize this since Teilhard's essays do not allude to these experiences.

During the years 1939–46, largely marked by the destructive campaigns of the Second World War, travel in China and outside it became virtually impossible. Apart from the one visit to Shanghai, Teilhard remained wholly confined to Peking and its immediate neighborhood. In 1940, Teilhard and Leroy founded the "Institut de Géobiologie," from where they published a bulletin and various scientific papers with the idea of launching a new perspective in anthropological studies. The realization of this ambition was greatly curtailed, however, through the circumstances of the war.[137]

The enforced leisure of these war years made Teilhard write more than ever before, so that many philosophical and religious essays date from this time.[138] His ideas were mainly expressed in writing, but much less in personal communication. Father Leroy, who was in daily contact with him, knew little of Teilhard's innermost thoughts; in fact, he did not realize their full thrust until much later on.[139] This must have applied to a number of Teilhard's friends in Peking. While Teilhard mixed easily with people socially, he is also known to have been a solitary thinker. It is not surprising that he experienced serious nervous depressions during 1939–40, and also later, in 1947–48.[140] Thus the popular conception that some people hold of Teilhard as an overoptimistic and untroubled thinker is far from the truth. On the contrary, a close study of his life and works reveals the depth of suffering and pain experienced again and again at various stages of his life.[141] Apart from the opportunity for regular writing, the war period in Peking also provided him with time for intensive reading and study. This is well documented through the careful notes and comments found in his *carnets de lecture* and diary entries.[142] These contain material of particular interest in relation to his knowledge of eastern religions and, therefore, deserve special mention.

Teilhard's reading during the last years in China covers a wide range of works from such different fields as philosophy, theology, literature, archaeology, biology, physics, sociology, and anthropology.[143] Books on religious topics include titles on ancient Greek religion, Zoroastrianism, Christian thought (especially the theologians Ernst Troeltsch and Karl Barth),[144] mysticism, and Indian religions.

The notes on mysticism are proof of Teilhard's continued interest in a topic central to his thought since his early days of writing. The closer study of Indian religions, however, is more surprising, as we do not know about such detailed reading in earlier years. Of particular interest are the notes he made on Joseph Maréchal's book *Études sur la Psychologie des Mystiques* and on Pierre Johanns's two-volume study *Vers le Christ par le Vedanta*.[145] The five pages of notes on Maréchal's work are concerned with pantheistic monism and include comments on the difference between monistic and theistic forms of mysticism. The distinction between different forms of mysticism is a permanent concern of Teilhard's writings. Maréchal deals with this in a general manner, whereas Johanns's study pursues the comparative theme in great detail. He deals in depth with Indian religious thought, expounding the different forms of Vedanta and comparing the ideas of the great Vedanta theologians about God, the human being, and the world with those of Christianity. Teilhard's ten pages of notes include his own criticisms of both Indian and Christian ideas, in the form presented by Johanns.

Although Teilhard often equated Hinduism with Vedanta monism, the comments on Johanns's book show that, at least since reading this work, if not before, he became aware of the internal differences and complexity of the Hindu religious tradition. He realized that Christianity was by no means unique in its worship of a personal God and that such personal devotion was an important strand in Indian religious thought.

His interest in other aspects of Indian culture is apparent from the brief references to Dravidian India, a mention of the Indian god Shiva and the great goddess Kali, comments on contemporary political developments in the Indian subcontinent,[146] and a diary entry quoting Rabindranath Tagore's famous work *Gitanjali*. Further reading on Indian history and religion was pursued in later years, after Teilhard had returned to the West.

During the last year in Peking, he also studied Aldous Huxley's *Perennial Philosophy*,[147] published in 1945. Teilhard must have got hold of a copy soon after the book's publication, which indicates how keen he was to read in this area. He was well acquainted with Huxley's literary works but, usually, these are simply listed by their titles in his notes. For this work, however, he added some brief but significant excerpts. He noted down Huxley's concern with three issues: human beings require a faith as a basis for their life; the ultimate reality is not a personal God but a spiritual Absolute, a "God-without-form"; union with the One is conceived as a return of the many to the One. Thus, the final state of deliverance does not incorporate any increase or achievement on the part of human beings. As seen later, these are precisely the themes that occupied Teilhard and with which he takes issue in his interpretation of mysticism.

Other notes criticize Roger Bastide's book *Le Problème de la Vie Mystique*,[148] which, in Teilhard's view, presents mysticism quite wrongly as an isolated and exceptional phenomenon. It thereby overlooks the extraordinary importance of mysticism for people today. This was a theme of primary interest to Teilhard. He listed other titles on mysticism for further consultation,[149] presumably in order to clarify his own ideas.

Teilhard's *carnets de lecture* and diary entries express a continual search for additional insight, gained in critical dialogue with other works. Seen from this perspective, his philosophical and religious essays appear as the final product of a long process of assimilation and reflection, based on a wide range of experience and consultation of sources to which he seldom explicitly refers. Thus, his work presents a tremendous synthesis without disclosing the myriad elements employed in its making.

In 1946, after seven years' confinement, Teilhard's Peking period came to an end. Earlier in 1943, a clandestine BBC broadcast had wrongly announced that he had been killed by bandits on the Chinese-Tibetan border.[150] His life was not to end in China, although he still died in exile elsewhere. The stay in the East came to an end when he returned to France in 1946. However, he continued to maintain an interest in reading, reflecting, and writing about eastern religions, especially in relation to the role of mysticism and spirituality in the contemporary world. If anything, these themes gained further prominence throughout the following years.

4

THE ONGOING QUEST

Teilhard's last years were spent in the West. Even when he lived in the Far East, the West was always with him; throughout all the years of exile it remained his true intellectual and spiritual home. After being back in France for several years, he publicly admitted in an interview, however, that a good part of his heart had been left in China, and that he would return to work there should conditions allow.[1] Without the experience of the East, it is certain that his thought would not have developed in the way it did. It would never have reached the same perspectives of unity, universality, and convergence, searching for a spirit of one Earth that ultimately transcends both East and West.

Teilhard's Last Years in the West

The last period of Teilhard's life is divided between the years spent in Paris (1946–51) and those in New York City (1951–55), interrupted by two study tours to South Africa (1951 and 1953) and brief visits to Argentina, Brazil, and Trinidad.

After returning to the West, Teilhard's life was characterized by as much uncertainty and misunderstanding as during his earlier years in China. Some people think that these last years added nothing new to his work and that the essays written during this period repeat only what he had already said earlier. But only a superficial reading can lead to this impression. If his works are studied in their chronological sequence, the reader is struck by the fundamental thrust of his vision and the immense coherence of his central themes expressed between 1916 and 1955. New questions were still being asked, new insights added, and the creative surge forward being continued until the day of his death on Easter Sunday 1955.

Teilhard's mind remained open to new ideas right to the end. He was interested in the latest developments in science, psychology, sociology, and religion and was forever questioning both scientific and religious orthodoxies. On one hand, he upheld the highest demands for exact standards in scientific research, pressing for further advances in the human effort to seek knowledge and understanding, but, on the other, he saw this as part of the same fundamental quest for ultimate unity that elsewhere found expression in spirituality and mysticism. Science, religion, and mysticism are part of the same longing in the hearts and minds of human beings. To see this, Teilhard felt, it is necessary to break the boundaries of a narrowly understood science and to remove the fetters of outworn religious creeds.

This is forcefully expressed throughout the last years of his life, particularly in his unpublished diaries[2] and in letters.[3] The pages of Teilhard's diary are the most convincing proof of the versatility, range, and depth of a mind that remained vigorous, creative, and open to the last. They never relate external events or personal occurrences but, up to three days before his death, are packed with ideas and critical reflections. This last period was also one of intense literary activity; in terms of the sheer quantity of titles, it outnumbers any other,[4] although the essays of this time tend to be shorter than before.

Further Growth and Disappointments

In Paris, Teilhard was at home with the capital's intellectual and social elite.[5] He found a congenial milieu meeting philosophers, scientists, artists, scholars of eastern religions and thought. It was particularly the contact with this last group that gave him an opportunity to discuss his experience of the East, reflect on its significance, and extend his reading on eastern religions.

Yet Teilhard was also in a very sensitive personal position. The Jesuit order did not wish to draw further attention to his thought, nor did they wish to incur its official censure by higher authorities of the Catholic Church. For these reasons, they asked him not to write or speak publicly on any philosophical or religious topic but to restrict himself exclusively to scientific activities. In deference to this request, Teilhard expressed his ideas only when talking to close friends or to small informal groups that met privately. It was on occasions like these, or when writing letters, that he voiced his deep disappointment. Thus, he mentioned to one correspondent how humiliating it was not to be allowed to lecture publicly about his new understanding of Christian mysticism at a time when an Indian Swami was provided with an important public platform at the Sorbonne in order to diffuse what Teilhard considered a rather "nebulous" form of mysticism.[6]

But even his scientific activities were curtailed. In 1948, the suggestion was made to elect Teilhard to the prestigious Collège de France in Paris as a national recognition of his scientific achievements. To seek the necessary permission from the relevant religious authorities, Teilhard made his first and only visit to Rome. Unfortunately, permission to go ahead with the election was withheld, and none of the restrictions on publishing his work was lifted. Thus, the visit was hardly a happy one. Describing his impressions, he wrote home:

> Rome has not given me nor will it give me, I feel, any shock, either aesthetic or spiritual. I was expecting this. So far as the past is concerned, I am immunized; and as for the picturesque, there is nothing more to surprise me after the great East.[7]

Suffering deeply from the lack of recognition of his thought and ideas, and the restricted opportunities he had for work, he remembered with regret that, before 1940, "it was so convenient...to be able to return for some time to China in order to be forgotten...."[8]

Commitment to the World Congress of Faiths

During his years in Paris Teilhard maintained close contact with the French branch of the World Congress of Faiths, the *Union des Croyants*. His work for this movement is little known,[9] but it provides evidence of his continued interest in eastern religions and, even more, his support for the closer coming together of different faiths by belonging to a small group of people who pioneered interfaith dialogue in postwar Paris.

The World Congress of Faiths was founded by Sir Francis Younghusband in London in 1936 and still exists today. From the beginning, several French religion scholars showed an interest in this movement, which aims to build bridges between members of different faiths and is a pioneer of what today is called interreligious dialogue. For various reasons, especially the outbreak of the Second World War, a French branch did not come into existence until 1947. Before that, a group of French people had informally followed the activities of the World Congress of Faiths in England and, according to one of the founders of the French branch, after the war this small group mainly regained its vitality "thanks to the presence of Teilhard," who, as guest and adviser, stimulated the members with his enthusiasm.[10]

Teilhard certainly knew of Sir Francis Younghusband because he refers to him in an essay of 1929;[11] whether he was aware of his subsequent interfaith activities it is difficult to say. Interesting enough, one of the diary entries of the Peking period already mentions a "congress of religions" in 1945: "True structure of a congress of religions: to proceed through selected groups, composed of people who are *already converging* in the religion and mysticism of evolution— = nucleus of the religion *foreseen* for tomorrow."[12] Shortly after his return to Paris, another diary entry of 1946 mentions the suggestion of "an association for the sympathy and synergy of religions," built on a mutually shared concern for contemporary issues.[13] The French branch of the World Congress of Faiths, first called *Le Congrès Universel des Croyants* and subsequently *Union des Croyants*, was founded in 1947 by René Grousset, Louis Massignon, Georges Salles, Charles Puech, Paul Masson-Oursel, and Dr. Loriot. The philosophers Édouard Le Roy, Etienne Gilson, and Gabriel Marcel also gave their support.[14] Teilhard was asked to provide the inaugural address for the first meeting of the movement. As he himself was not permitted to speak publicly, this address on "Faith in Man" (1947)[15] was read out in his absence by René Grousset, the well-known historian of Asia and the Near East.

"Faith in Man" is seen as a necessary "elementary, primordial faith," providing the basis from where one must begin to work toward the summit of the spirit. Such a commonly shared basis is required as "the general atmosphere in which the higher, more elaborated forms of faith which we all hold in one form or another may best (indeed can only) come together."[16] Looking at the development of the French branch of the World Congress of Faiths fifteen years later, Louis Massignon called this address in retrospect "an outstanding text"[17] that, from the start, gave a definite direction to the work of this interfaith movement in France.

Teilhard was also personally present at some smaller meetings during the following years. This is evident from a long discussion on religion and mysticism with Louis Massignon, René Grousset, Aldous Huxley, and Gabriel Marcel.[18] During 1949 and 1950, he also gave three talks to small groups of the movement that met privately in members' houses. In addition, he drafted two pages stating the aims of the French branch of the World Congress of Faiths.[19]

In Teilhard's understanding it was not the object of the World Congress of Faiths to proclaim the essential sameness of all religions, nor should it reject out of hand any purely humanistic creed. Rather, the movement should attempt to bring more closely together all those who believe in a future for human beings and the world. The possibility of such a future depends now on the union of all individuals, races, and nations. Although conditioned by technical and social progress, this union can ultimately only be achieved through sharing a common vision: a supreme center of attraction and personalization is required. The different type of scientific thought and religious faith have to be in much closer contact; only then can a convergent vision emerge. Religions on their own cannot achieve human unity, but they have an essential contribution to make. Without the central insights of the great religious traditions, human efforts toward creating greater sympathy, understanding, and union cannot find their true focus.[20]

Because of his officially precarious position of not being allowed to speak about religious topics in public, Teilhard was never a visibly prominent member of the French branch of the World Congress of Faiths. Yet it is known that he took an active part in many committee meetings.[21] Among the adherents of other faiths present on the committee were an Iranian Sufi, a Confucian, and Swami Siddheswarananda from the Ramakrishna Mission, with whom Teilhard had discussions on yoga and meditation.[22] Swami Siddheswarananda, who had been in Paris since 1937, was particularly interested in the comparison between the mysticism of Saint John of the Cross and Vedanta. Although Teilhard did not agree with his interpretation, the two men seem to have had much sympathy and understanding for each other. This is confirmed by a comment from Swami Siddheswarananda's successor, who wrote that the Swami

> met Père Teilhard de Chardin and was impressed by the personality of the man. In a private letter he commented on de Chardin's capacity of listening to the other; and how Swami Siddheswarananda felt that he himself should acquire the same trait.[23]

Teilhard was particularly friendly with the secretary of *Le Congrès Universel des Croyants*, Madame Solange Lemaître, with whom he remained in close contact until his death. His correspondence with her represents an important exchange of ideas bearing on many aspects of religion and mysticism.[24] It is probably through her that he first learned about the plan for founding a French branch of the World Congress of Faiths.

Solange Lemaître was then working at the museum of eastern art in Paris, the Musée Guimet,[25] in close collaboration with René Grousset. Earlier, she had worked for many years for the association *Amis de l'Orient*. The study of eastern religions was her particular interest; she had published in this field and, in subsequent years, she became well known through her three-volume anthology *Textes mystiques d'Orient et d'Occident*.[26] This selection of mystical texts through the ages from both East and West was discussed in detail with Teilhard when she was working on the book. His ideas are to some extent reflected in this work as are those of the Orientalists Jacques Bacot and Louis Massignon.[27] The contemporary section of the anthology includes an extract from Teilhard's essay "The Mass on the World" (1923), published here before it was available anywhere else. It is prefaced by a short introduction on Teilhard known to have been written by Teilhard himself.[28]

Even after he had left France, he maintained a continuous interest in the work of the French branch of the World Congress of Faiths, as can be seen from his correspondence. In 1952, he wrote that the work of this movement, however modest, might be important in bringing about the transformation of religious thought, if "it is not dominated by too 'oriental' a notion of the relations between matter and spirit."[29] In his last letter to Solange Lemaître, written one month before his death, he mentions that the required religious and mystical transformation may be stimulated by the work of the *Union des Croyants*.[30] Although he personally still understood this transformation too narrowly as occurring within a predominantly Christian framework, these references express a greater awareness of the need for religious unity and a global ecumenism on Teilhard's part than is generally recognized. Mme. Lemaître confirms this in one of her later writings where she relates that, on his last visit to Paris in 1954, Teilhard especially told her to look after the *Union des Croyants*, because it would be "the summit movement of tomorrow."[31]

More Reading about the East

On his return from China, Teilhard developed a close friendship with another member of the *Union des Croyants*, the scholar René Grousset, a specialist on eastern history and thought.[32] Their conversations stimulated further reading on Teilhard's part and to some extent helped him modify his approach to eastern religions.

According to Cuénot, Teilhard "spent some time studying Far Eastern art and philosophy at the Musée Guimet," although it is impossible to obtain any precise information about this.[33] The close contact between Teilhard and French scholars on eastern thought—at that time still uncritically referred to as "orientalists"—as well as his intensive reading during this last stay in Paris, provided an opportunity for Teilhard to reflect on his rich experiences of the East. At the same time, they helped him to appreciate more deeply than before the specific insights of eastern religions. This more nuanced attitude found its reflection in the writing of an essay on "The Spiritual Contribution of the Far East" (1947),[34] the only one among his works referring to the East in its title.

It seems that before writing this essay, Teilhard clarified certain details about eastern metaphysics in discussions with his friend René Grousset.[35] The latter's influence is also evident from Teilhard's diary. It contains several references to Grousset's book *Le Bilan de l'Histoire* (1946), which includes two chapters on "The Contribution of Asia" and "The Contribution of India" to the history of human civilization. Thus the book may well have suggested to Teilhard the choice of his own essay title "The Spiritual Contribution of the Far East," written during the following year. His diary includes extracts and comments from Grousset's book, dealing with aspects of Hinduism, Amida and Zen Buddhism as well as Taoism.

The continuing interest in eastern religions is also documented by other titles. Olivier Lacombe's book *L'Absolu selon le Vedanta*,[36] which deals with the great Hindu theologian Ramanuja, is quoted by Teilhard as evidence that Hindu thought freed itself from extreme monism and comes close to theism.

During 1947 he read through the unpublished letters of the writer Romain Rolland to Mademoiselle Jeanne Mortier.[37] These deal with several aspects of Indian thought, especially the comparison between Indian and western mysticism. The letters cover more than twenty years, including the time when Romain Rolland was working on his well-known biographies of Ramakrishna and Vivekananda. They also refer to Rolland's correspondence with Rudolf Otto and to Otto's work in the comparative study of mysticism. It was planned to publish this correspondence between Romain Rolland and Mlle. Mortier, for which Teilhard wrote a brief introduction, but, together with the letters, it remains unpublished so far.

In his biography, Cuénot notes that Teilhard attended the Orientalists' Congress in 1948 without mentioning any further details.[38] This certainly came about through Teilhard's close contact with French orientalist scholars, especially with René Grousset. The XXI International Orientalists' Congress took place in Paris, with Jacques Bacot as president and René Grousset as general secretary. Teilhard is listed in the published proceedings as a member of the honorary Congress Committee.[39]

More intriguing is the fact that during the autumn of the same year, 1948, while on his visit to Rome, Teilhard was reading about Indian history and religion. The Rome diary quotes extracts from George Dunbar's two-volume work on the *History of India*,[40] dealing with the main developments of Indian civilization. Teilhard's notes refer to the Indus Valley civilization, Aryan and Dravidian elements in Indian culture, classical Hindu scriptures, the development of the major divinities, and the caste system. They also deal with Buddhism and Jainism, the expansion of Buddhism overseas and its extinction in India; the rise of Islam and the Moghuls, especially Akbar; and the coming of the early western explorers and of the Jesuits to India. While Dunbar's work is primarily a political history, it obviously refers to events of general cultural and religious importance. It is interesting to see that Teilhard's notes deal mainly with this last aspect, the development of religion in India. He also criticizes Dunbar for his mistaken view about the late appearance in India of *bhakti*, the movement of fervent religious devotion to a personal God. Teilhard rightly points out that Dunbar fails to recognize the early origin of this movement in ancient India as well as its influence on certain developments in Buddhism.[41]

More important still, at the very heart of western Christendom and at a time when Teilhard was drafting the first plan for his spiritual autobiography, "The Heart of Matter,"[42] he explicitly refers to Radhakrishnan's book *The Hindu View of Life*, noting down in English, "A *central Reality* which is one with *the deeper self* of Man." This is obviously a short reference or a quotation from Radhakrishnan found in Dunbar's work. Teilhard added to it a comment in French that says, "That is the whole question: to define the central self: identification or union." In brackets he noted "Essence: Road of the East." A second comment reads:

= The whole question (is):

where to place *this Centre*: of convergence through tension of relaxation.[43]

At the beginning of the following year Teilhard inquired from his friend, Solange Lemaître, whether she could advise him on the best book on Taoism for the nonspecialized reader, and where to find information about Chu Hsi, the Chinese "Spencer."[44] Again, there exists no information about the reply of his correspondent, nor is it known whether Teilhard followed up these references or for what purpose they were required.

It is in any case impossible to reconstruct Teilhard's entire reading for this, or any other, period of his life. References to books occur at random, but they cannot all be mentioned here. I return to some more references later, when I discuss Teilhard's interpretation of eastern religions and mysticism. For the moment, it is sufficient to note that these references reveal a greater interest and familiarity with certain aspects of eastern thought than one would expect from reading only Teilhard's published essays. Yet at the same time, it must be stressed that he never studied eastern religions in their own right, as presented from within, by their own adherents. In fact, he did not read the scholarly literature on eastern thought primarily from a perspective of scholarly inquiry, but mainly from one of a deep personal commitment. Thus it is not surprising that his attention was often drawn to specific works through particular friendships or in search for confirmation of his own thought.

It was through such a personal contact that Teilhard first learnt about Sri Aurobindo's great work, *The Life Divine*, which Jacques Masui,[45] editor of a journal on comparative spirituality and of a series of eastern religious texts in translation, lent him in either 1953 or 1954. Teilhard understood Sri Aurobindo mainly as a "modernist" and, after reading some chapters, he apparently returned *The Life Divine* to Masui with the comment, "This is comparable to my own work, but for the Indian tradition."[46] Such a remark no doubt refers to Aurobindo's and Teilhard's shared attempt to integrate a modern evolutionary perspective with the traditional insights of their faith and to provide an evolutionary reinterpretation of their respective religions.

Other titles read during these last years deal with wider aspects of religion and culture. As examples may be mentioned E. Brunner, *Christianity and Civilizations*; M. Eliade, *Le Mythe de l'Éternel Retour*; J. Huxley, *Religion without Revelation*; C. Jung, *Modern Man in Search of a Soul*;[47] J. Needham, *Order and Life*, and *Time: The Refreshing River*; F. C. Northrop, *The Meeting of East and West*.[48]

All these works indicate Teilhard's wide-ranging interests. From his essays and letters, it is clear that he emphasized above all the importance of central Christian insights for the contemporary world. At the same time, he stressed the present need for a transformation of Christianity. However, he also thought that such a transformation could not come about without a movement of convergence that must include the contribution of eastern religions. However, these ideas were hardly worked out in any systematic form.

An Open Religious Quest

When Teilhard came across J. Casserley's book, *The Retreat of Christianity from the Modern World*,[49] he felt almost jealous about the author's reference to a "Christianity which surpasses itself." It so coincided with his own perspective that he wished he had found this "perfect expression" himself. The book convinced him that

> in the non-Roman branches of Christianity a spirit of religious invention is finally manifesting itself which is the sole possible agent of a true ecumenism: not the sterile and conservative ecumenism of a "common ground", but the creative ecumenism of a "convergence…on to a common ideal."[50]

However, he had also been convinced for some time that "the great theologians of Rome" did not facilitate a "convergence of religions," nor did they grasp what such a phenomenon implied.[51] Although Teilhard himself did not fully map out the implications of such an approach, he sensed the importance of certain insights from the East.

Among the many tentative suggestions in his diary, one of the most puzzling and least expected is the reference to the Indian god

Shiva and to "Christ-Omega/Shiva" in 1948.[52] Most intriguing is an extract from a letter to "Mg."[53] After referring to the overpowering forces of the cosmos, which can neither be tamed nor appeased, he says that "it is not enough to refuse or ridicule Shiva: for *he exists*. What is necessary, is to christify him. Christ would not be complete if he did not integrate Shiva (as a component), while transforming him."[54] Not only the immense organic structure of the universe, but also its apparent indifference to human suffering and the blind inhumanity of its forces of destruction may illuminate certain aspects of the Divine for us. According to Teilhard, these must be integrated into our image of God.

Teilhard's reflections occur within the context of further quotations from René Grousset's book *Le Bilan de L'Histoire*, mentioned earlier. The earlier extracts, dating from 1946, also refer to Shiva's cosmic dance and to the contradictory aspects associated with his nature.[55] Grousset depicts the great Indian god Shiva as a figure embodying the untamed forces of nature; he represents the powers of destruction as well as those of periodic renewal, for in him are integrated the forces of joy, suffering, and energy that pulsate through the universe. This ambivalence of Shiva appealed to Teilhard, who saw the cosmos as animated by divine energy, filled and alive with "christic" elements, and it is precisely this cosmic dimension of God which, in his view, traditional Christianity has never fully explored.[56]

Here again, as so often, Teilhard briefly perceived, but never explored in depth, an enriching eastern insight that might transform and enlarge the Christian concept and experience of the Divine. However, whereas his vision of the cosmos and his increasingly ecumenical view of humanity made him "most anxious to integrate eastern thought,"[57] his emphasis on the unique nature of personhood inclined him also to repudiate certain aspects of eastern religions. Several times, he emphatically underlined the difference of his vision from that of Hinduism, for example—so much so that he has been accused of a deep misunderstanding of the rich strands of this religious tradition. For him, the Christian view of a person's relation to God cannot be expressed in Hindu terms, at least not in those of Vedanta monism. Thus, he wrote to a correspondent, "If you only knew how much I mistrust Hindu mysticism—it is based not on union, which generates love, but on identification, which excludes love."[58]

It is quite surprising, therefore, that one of the earliest books on Teilhard's thought, published during his lifetime, placed his views among those of "the existentialists and Hinduisers." In contrast to this opinion, Teilhard was at pains to point out that these two groups were in fact his "bêtes noires."[59] He felt so concerned about this criticism that, on the one occasion when he stated his intellectual position in public by giving a newspaper interview, he strongly repudiated the false interpretations of his thought as either "totalitarianism" or "hinduising pantheism," which seeks the spiritual in the direction "of an identification of beings with an underlying common ground."[60]

At the same time, he became aware of the growing interest in Indian religions in the West, largely due to the spiritual emptiness left by the Second World War. In the intellectual climate of the postwar period, some people embraced atheism or existentialism, while others turned to eastern gurus for direction. Teilhard learned about the teachings of these gurus through some of his friends who became closely involved with Indian religions. For example, his diary refers to the guru of one of his former acquaintances from China, Ella Maillart, with whom he shared the knowledge and love of Chinese Turkestan.[61] He noted down what Ella Maillart's guru had to say about the nature of the true self, and he commented again on the necessary distinction of whether the higher self is found through identification or convergence.[62]

Two other friends in New York, Lucile Swan and Malvina Hoffman, belonged to a group directed by a Hindu Swami. Teilhard described the spirituality of this circle as "terribly vague,"[63] just as the mysticism preached by another Swami appeared to him to be "infra-western."[64] When Lucile Swan planned to visit India in 1950, he wrote to her:

> I wonder what is going to be, at the end, your final reaction to India,—to its mixture of decaying splendor and swarming population. Looking from outside, I feel more and more convinced that, for a long time, the East

may bring its tremendous mass, but will not act as a "moteur" (engine) in the development of the world.[65]

However, he was also prepared to admit that, for many western people, Indian religions may hold the answer to their spiritual quest for, at present, it is so difficult to pierce through the hardened forms of religion that Christian theologians propound as "orthodoxy."[66] Too often, their teaching presents a "religion without mystery," where "everything is clear, everything certain, everything 'revealed.'"[67] Some of the best western minds may be religiously uprooted not for a lack, but for an excess, of religious desire, a thirst that remains unquenched.[68] The dynamic forces that animate neo-Hindu, neo-Buddhist, and, even more, neo-humanist movements, make traditional Christianity appear tame and "underdeveloped" at times. It is from this spirit of dissatisfaction and the growing realization of the need for renewal that Teilhard increasingly searched not only for a Christian, but a "trans-Christian" God whose image corresponds to a growing need for adoration. As this need is no longer fully met in Christianity, people in the West join centers and groups *where the religious quest is still open.*"[69]

Although Teilhard expressed such views only in private, and not in public, his influence was nevertheless judged as too great in France. In 1951, the offer of a research post in anthropology from the Wenner-Gren Foundation in New York led to his final residence in the United States. From 1951 until his death in 1955, he lived in Manhattan with the Jesuit fathers at St. Ignatius Church on Park Avenue. Once more he was practically in exile.[70] The stimulating experience of different intellectual horizons, a renewed contact with field work in South Africa, as well as a brief return to France in 1954 could not compensate for the fact that these last years were extremely difficult and lonely. Teilhard's isolation and depression were enhanced by the feeling of being misunderstood by his own order, his "beloved family," which contained some of his closest friends.[71] Father Leroy has described the difficulties of these last years with much sensitivity, emphasizing Teilhard's suffering and "inner martyrdom." This agony and struggle unto the last has also been well brought out in the biography by Mary and Ellen Lukas.[72]

It is all the more extraordinary and moving that the two great essays "The Heart of Matter" (1950) and "The Christic" (1955) were produced during these last years. As fundamental affirmations of Teilhard's deep faith and hope, they bear permanent witness to the compelling force of a lifelong inner vision and provide a vivid proof of the tremendous psychic energy and profound faith that sustained him in the face of all opposition.

Father Leroy has depicted his friend as frequently silent and withdrawn during the last months of his life. However, one of the surprising utterances reported from this period is Teilhard's avowal, "I now live permanently in the presence of God."[73] It is precisely this experience of living in God's presence that radiates so strongly through the last pages of his work, especially "The Christic." Written with a fervor and intensity found only in his earliest writings from the First World War, this essay is a final testimony of his creative power and his lifelong, passionate dedication to a mystical vision at once profoundly personal and universal.

Throughout his life, Teilhard was a wanderer between different worlds. His life and thought are interwoven like the parts of an immense symphony with ever-new variations on a basic theme. This theme is the supreme adventure of the ascent to the spirit and the continuous breakthrough of God's presence in the world of matter and flesh. Teilhard's vision, like that of other seers before him, was one of consuming fire, kindled by the radiant powers of love. It was a mystical vision deeply Christian in origin and orientation; yet it broke through traditional boundaries and grew into a vision global in intent.

In this process of growth and expansion, the experience of the East, its peoples, cultures, and religions, played an indispensable part. As he himself admitted, the invitation to come to China in 1923 proved to be "the decisive event of his destiny," for until then, he had profoundly sensed "the attraction of the Earth," without really understanding "the grandeur of either the Earth, or of the phenomena of the Earth."[74]

His vision of convergence, of the complementary religious insights of East and West, and of the need for a new understanding of Christianity emerged in full in China. It impressed itself upon his mind with even greater force and urgency on his return to the West. Today, the attraction of Indian religions to many westerners is much greater than it was during Teilhard's time. The questions that he asked then are even more important now, although they may have to be asked in a different way. Nevertheless, in spite of differences in detail, the basic orientation of his search and the open-endedness of his quest, particularly in later years, may well point beyond Christianity as we know it. At a time when few western contemporaries were aware of, and alive to, the problems of spirituality in the modern context of an evolutionary world, Teilhard was already seeking complementary insights in the East while stressing the central importance of mysticism for religion today.

I have traced some of the formative events, personal encounters, and significant reading that influenced Teilhard's approach to eastern religions. I next examine some central texts that reveal his comparative evaluation of eastern and western religions, always undertaken from the perspective of a mystical quest. More than that, these texts express an ongoing search for a new approach to mysticism in a new era of human consciousness.

II
EASTERN AND WESTERN RELIGIONS IN A CONVERGING WORLD

The revival of inwardness may prove to be a revolutionary act in relation to the objectified world; it may prove to be a revolt against determinism or, in other words, a spiritual permeation of the world in order to inspire and transfigure it.

Nikolai Berdyaev

I believe the mystical is less different, less separated from the rational than one says, but I also believe that the whole problem which the world, and we in particular, are presently facing, is a problem of faith.

Pierre Teilhard de Chardin

5

THE SEARCH FOR UNITY

From Monistic Pantheism to Mysticism

In the formulation of his religious thought, Teilhard came to distinguish gradually, but early, between monistic pantheism and mysticism. This distinction is absolutely fundamental in his approach to eastern religions. For Teilhard, pantheism and mysticism are distinct but not unrelated. Their different characteristics were mainly elaborated in the early writings, during those years that have been called "the mystical period."

It must be borne in mind that Teilhard's interpretation of mysticism was not primarily theoretical or speculative but proceeded from the experiential basis of a personal vision. The pattern of this inner realization unfolds clearly when one reads his works diachronically, in the order in which they were created. The early war essays, written after the formative experience of Egypt but before his contact with the Far East, introduce an important distinction between different forms of mysticism, which in essence was maintained throughout his later writings. However, with the stay in the Far East further references to this distinction usually include comparisons with eastern religions, especially in the essays written after 1932.

Teilhard's Method

Before examining these texts, it may be helpful to comment briefly on Teilhard's method. As already mentioned, his thinking

111

was always rooted in a primary layer of religious experience. This must be understood in the widest sense, for it includes certain "peak experiences" as well as his continuous adherence to the Christian faith and its religious practices, such as daily prayer, celebration of the Mass, regular retreats, and so on. It would be wrong, however, to consider this religious experience in isolation from his total life experience and especially to separate it from his experience of scientific work in biology, geology, and paleontology. Teilhard's reflection on the entire range of this experience led him to formulate certain key ideas that recur like leitmotifs throughout his work. Prolonged scientific training and research deeply influenced his expressions, and his ideas and vocabulary are strongly marked by biological patterns of thought. This is particularly true of the generalized use of evolutionary categories, including such themes as organic growth, complexity, and synthesis.[1]

Already at an early stage, Teilhard was conscious that he had a method of his own, a way of thinking that linked the particular to the universal, the cosmic-natural-scientific dimension to the universal-personal-religious sphere, and the immanent to the transcendent.[2] Apart from the transference of scientific terms to philosophical and religious thought, his method also includes the use of typology, particularly when interpreting historical data.

This typological approach to history means that "Teilhard understands every phase of history in terms of an overarching paradigmatic pattern."[3] This pattern is often represented by the metaphor of a spiral, a synthesis of the circle and the straight line. A cyclical interpretation of history implies a fundamental recurrence of events, whereas a linear interpretation leaves room for novelty. Through the image of the spiral, history is interpreted in terms of ascending levels, in which patterns recur, accompanied by elements of novelty. This typological method of interpretation is evident in Teilhard's approach to the development of human societies and civilizations. It is also apparent in his approach to religions, where specific "types" of development are singled out and compared. At the neglect of a wealth of historical detail, these types tend to emphasize certain patterns and key developments.

When reading Teilhard's essays, one must keep this scientific and typological orientation in mind but also remember the general nature of his writings. It is important to distinguish between the frequently revised, final versions of the books and essays destined for publication and his many briefer notes, which he left as summaries or lecture outlines. The shorter essays are often only variations of a theme more extensively dealt with in other writings, whereas the major essays were always carefully planned and only written down after considerable reflection. A particular piece of writing may thus have taken several months, or even years, to reach its final form.

Teilhard was a prolific writer. Apart from the many volumes of scientific, philosophical, and religious writings, he maintained an enormous correspondence. He also kept a diary for forty years. This is not a diary in the ordinary sense of the word, but rather a record consisting of a series of notes, jotted down in exercise books that contain, in the words of Father Leroy,

> any comment of a philosophical, scientific or religious nature he thought worth preserving. These notes…with no apparent connecting thread, will enable students of Père Teilhard's thought to follow day by day the workings of a ceaselessly active mind.[4]

When one compares the entries in Teilhard's diary—where he first noted down the idea of a new essay, followed later by its detailed plan and title—with the letters and essays of the same period, one can follow the unfolding of his ideas systematically. Thus, one discovers how his thought emerged, grew, and matured, until it found its definite expression in a specific essay.

To understand Teilhard's thought on a particular theme and assess its full meaning, it is necessary to compare all available texts on the same theme and to study his writings in their chronological order. This, however, is an especially difficult task, as the published volumes of his writings do not follow each other chronologically. With the exception of a few titles, each book represents a selection of essays chosen from the entire span of his life. This manner of publication, perhaps the only one possible at the time, can easily give a misleading impression of Teilhard's thought and has in no way facilitated the understanding of a notoriously complex and subtle thinker.[5]

Monistic Pantheism in His Early Writings

Most of Teilhard's early essays are found in the book entitled *Writings in the Time of War*. This is generally much less well known than his later works. These essays include discussions of pantheism, monism, and mysticism.[6] I look in particular at two essays of special significance, "Cosmic Life" (1916)[7] and "The Mystical Milieu" (1917),[8] read in parallel, along with contemporaneous entries in his *Journal*, and with the important later essay "Pantheism and Christianity" (1923).[9]

The particular attraction of pantheism lies in the fact that it represents an all-embracing, unitary experience, for it implies the fundamental oneness of all phenomena. For Teilhard, this experience is closely linked with our response to nature. The natural world that surrounds humans is both infinitely attractive and repellent; with the variety and immensity of its phenomena, it seems so much greater than the human being itself. The experience of nature may produce states of anxiety and alienation in some people, but it can lead others to an awareness of "cosmic consciousness," that is, a feeling of expansion and fusion. Teilhard wrote in "Cosmic Life" that the first impulse in this experience of cosmic consciousness is for a human being "*to allow himself to be rocked* like a child by the great mother in whose arms he has just woken"[10] and feel cradled in deepest security. Nature's attraction lies particularly in the great and mysterious unity of her phenomena, "les grands homogènes," as Teilhard called them:

> Entranced by those great homogeneous systems—ocean, air, desert—the human being, poised over emptiness and silence, locked up within, envies the intimate fusion of the drops of water in the sea, of the molecules in the atmosphere; and he glimpses the bliss there would be in becoming continually more intermingled with Another, in sinking deeper and deeper into it, like smoke that vanishes, like the sound that dies away in

space, like the stone that slips gently down to the bottom of the sea.[11]

This is a strictly monistic experience, typical of all forms of pantheism that remain naturalistic, and immanent, leading different people in quite different contexts to worship the divine around them. Teilhard asked himself:

And why, indeed, should I not worship it, the stable, the great, the rich, the mother, the divine? Is not matter, in its own way, eternal and immense? Is it not matter whose absence our imagination refuses to conceive....Is it not the absolutely fertile generatrix, the *Terra Mater*, that carries within her the seeds of all life and the sustenance of all joy? Is it not at once the common origin of beings and the only end we could dream of, the primordial and indestructible essence from which all emerged and into which all returns....All the attributes which a philosophy of the spirit posits as lying outside the universe, do they not in fact lie at the opposite pole? Are they not realized and are they not to be attained in the depths of the world, in divine matter?[12]

This appeal of matter, of the Divine in nature, is everlasting. On one hand, Teilhard emphasized our intimate relation to nature, to cosmic life, and recognized the appeal of a monistic pantheism; on the other hand, he also outlined the possibility of a different kind of pantheism, leaving room for transcendence beyond nature. Thus, he distinguished "non-Christian pantheisms" and "paganism," that allow only a "communion with earth," from a possible Christian pantheism, based on a "communion with God through earth." For a naturalistic, immanent pantheism, everything in the universe is uniformly true and valuable: so much so that the fusion of the individual must be effected with all, *without distinction and without qualification*. Everything that is active, that moves or breathes, every physical, astral, or animate energy, every fragment of force, every spark of life, is equally sacred; for, in the humblest atom and the most brilliant star, in the lowest insect and the finest intelligence, there is the radiant smile and thrill of the *same Absolute*.[13]

This fundamental equivalence without distinction of everything that exists, "at the expense of conscious and personal life, for the benefit of the rudimentary and diffuse modes of being," is for Teilhard the basic characteristic of what he first called the "eastern vision of the blue Lotus." From his sources, and later characterizations, it is clear that he identified this form of experience with eastern, and especially Hindu, monism. This monistic pantheism is a very basic and powerful experience; it constitutes the permanent "temptation of matter," consisting of a search for fusion and identity with an initial source. He equated such an attitude with effortless enjoyment, inertia, and "the tendency to follow the line of least resistance."[14]

In his *Journal*, this experience is described as "*pagan, naive pantheism*...which envisages only the fusion with the original All: thus, there are no real grades in being, no progress...*no failures*." For Teilhard, however, this powerful experience had to be prolonged and ultimately transcended.

The human quest for the All, the passion for unity, cannot be adequately satisfied through fusion with a common ground or nostalgia for the past. To seek return, whether to primal matter or the time of origin, proves a futile quest. The more the seeker advances, the more he realizes, "'*The world is empty*,' that is to say, by remaining on the mere level of experience, one goes around the world without penetrating it...." Teilhard asked himself, "Why does the pantheistic feeling so often take its origin from emptiness (sea, desert, stellar spaces, the past...)?" In his experience, these phenomena did not possess the fullness he sought: "The past and the far-away are empty and give access to nothing." This remark shows that the magic spell of the cosmos was already shattered for him; the fulfillment of nature's promise had to be found elsewhere.

"Where do we seek the secret?—in the desert? In the far-away past? In secret matter? It is to be found in the future and its increase (*unforeseeable* because not open to experience yet...)."[15] The ultimate goal is to be reached through a maximum of energy and effort; it is a union to come, a goal in the future. Through it alone will the pantheistic yearning for oneness be stilled.

Teilhard's powerful nature experiences, together with his theistic faith, and the realization of the fundamental importance of personal and social worlds, made him search for a synthesis between the immanent and transcendent aspirations of the mystical quest. Early in 1916, he noted in his diary:

> If I write anything, if I become intellectually active, it must be, it seems to me, *in order* to bring together, to reconcile (in a sense) God and the world, that is to say, to show that God eminently fulfils our immanent and pantheistic aspirations (i.e. God and matter; "the divine matter" (= amazing realization of this in our Lord Jesus Christ).[16]

This intention was put into practice in "Cosmic Life," written soon afterward. The essay is preceded by the words: "There is a communion with God, and a communion with earth, and a communion with God through earth."[17] The mere "communion with earth" refers to the experience of monistic pantheism, while "communion with God" stands for an excessively otherworldly attitude, linked to a view of God and religion as separate from the world. The exclusive concern for the transcendent, often regarded as the main characteristic of a religious quest, does not place enough importance on the value of human effort and the development of the world.

These two attitudes—communion with earth, and communion with God—are regarded as incomplete; only the synthesis of both is acceptable. This synthesis of "communion with God through earth" is not simply a combination of two different attractions, but something of a new order altogether. The initial experience of "cosmic consciousness," the love of the earth and all its realities, is prolonged and transformed through the experience of God as both an immanent and transcendent presence. Strictly speaking, therefore, one cannot say that Teilhard rejects monistic pantheism, although, linguistically, expressions of rejection are found. Rather, this form of pantheism is judged insufficient; it finds its fulfillment only in a fully developed theistic mysticism. The latter, in turn, is not exclusively spiritual but assumes unto itself, in an ascending order, the various levels of reality, material as well as spiritual. Unlike R. C. Zaehner in his book *Mysticism Sacred and Profane*,[18] Teilhard does not see a break between "sacred" and "profane" mysticism. On the contrary, the former is a continuation of the latter.

Teilhard referred to himself as a "naturally pantheistic soul."[19] He initially experienced the appeal of the Absolute through the contact with nature, whose unity and homogeneity appeared to contrast starkly with the plurality of human beings and their scandalous "heterogeneity." The presence of another person seems to interrupt the unity of the world, to pluralize it for the seeker of ultimate unity. Teilhard acutely felt the problematic aspect of interpersonal relationships, especially when he described the "other" as an intruder, as someone who breaks the unity and coherence of the mystic's inner vision, and disturbs his solitude. He wrote in his diary, "Who says person, says contingent, artificial, fragmentary...,"[20] and his intrinsic difficulty with "others" is more forcefully expressed in the much later written book *The Divine Milieu*:

> But "others," my God—by which I do not mean "the poor, the halt, the lame and the sick," but "others" quite simply as "others," those who seem to exist independently of me because their universe seems closed to mine, and who seem to shatter the unity and the silence of the world for me—would I be sincere if I did not confess that my instinctive reaction is to rebuff them? and that the mere thought of entering into spiritual communication with them disgusts me?[21]

Thus, the realm of the personal appeared at first problematic to Teilhard. He realized this particularly through the profoundly disturbing experience of the war. At the same time, the close friendship with his cousin Marguerite made him see the great enrichment found in personal relationships. Ultimately, the mystic quest must lead to a reality that embraces the cosmic as well as the personal, the human, and the Divine. For Teilhard, the only reality that answers to this is the vision of Christ, which brings together the universal and the personal.

Pantheism Prolonged and Transcended

Teilhard's movement from monistic pantheism or nature mysticism to a person-centered mysticism is fully described in the essay "The Mystical Milieu" (1917). Written more than one year after "Cosmic Life," it presents the progress of mystical experience in a series of expanding circles, an approach that has been compared to that of Saint Teresa's *Interior Castle*. The first three circles are seen as those of presence, consistence, and energy; they stand for the homogeneity of the universe, for its fundamental oneness. Teilhard describes the "seer"—another name for the "mystic"—as

> immersed in a *universal Milieu*, higher than that which contains the restlessness of ordinary, sensibly apprehended life: a Milieu *that knows no change*, immune to the surge of superficial vicissitudes—a *homogeneous* Milieu in which contrasts and differences are toned down.

But this experience may lead him to "be lost in naturalistic mysticism, or take the degraded form of godless pantheism."[22]

Nevertheless, the passion for unity and universality remains the most basic mystic intuition. The mystic finds the incorruptible principle of the universe, and this extends everywhere: "*The world is filled* and filled with the Absolute. To see this is to be made free." But the mystical effort to see must give way to "*the effort to feel and to surrender.*"[23] The vision must lead to a communion with the essence of the universe, which is creative action, pulsating energy: "The mystic was looking for the devouring fire which he could identify with the Divine that summons him from all sides: science points it out to him. *See, the universe is ablaze!*"[24]

The reference to science may seem odd here at first. Yet in Teilhard's view, it is through the evolutionary insights of science that the universe comes more alive than ever before. That science can stimulate a mystical quest and vision has been demonstrated by Fritjof Capra, among others, in his exciting exploration of the parallels between modern physics and eastern mysticism in his book *The Tao of Physics*.[25] For Teilhard, the mystic is plunged into an "ocean of energy," from which he draws "undiluted joy":

> In very truth, it is God, and God alone whose Spirit stirs up the whole mass of the universe in ferment....
>
> ....
>
> The fact is that creation has never stopped. The creative act is one huge continual gesture, drawn out over the totality of time. It is still going on.[26]

The circle of energy is a transitional phase leading into the "Heterogeneous," the "circle of the spirit," and, at its summit, the "circle of the person." This dialectical development stands in contrast to the first three circles. There, the mystic was immersed in some universal Divine and lived in "a sort of *higher dream* in which the distinctions of practical life seem of minor importance and are blurred."[27]

In the two succeeding circles, the experience of the Divine as merely immanent is surpassed. Now the seer turns from his own interiority to the multitude of other beings, that, at first, had seemed "an infliction hard to bear."[28] The Divine itself is experienced as both transcendent to the cosmos and yet interwoven with it at all levels. The seer realizes that action and communion are neither situated in the divine nor the created sphere,

> but in a special reality born of their mutual interaction. The mystical milieu *is not a completed zone* in which beings, once they have succeeded in entering it, remain immobilized. It is a *complex* element, made up of *divinized created being*....We cannot give it precisely the name of God: it is his Kingdom. Nor can we say that it is: it is in the process of *becoming*.[29]

The mystic now becomes the "supreme *realist*," who fights the battle for the light, who moves forward to the real by searching to know, to love, and to fulfill it. For Teilhard, the mystical milieu gradually assumes a form at once divine and human, which for him culminates in the person of Jesus.

Thus, the last part of this essay invokes the name of Jesus after each paragraph. It reads like a Jesus-prayer. The end of "The Mystical Milieu" also states that this is only an introduction to mysticism, for Teilhard did not feel qualified to describe the most sublime mystical states but only wished to emphasize their natural and cosmic roots, without which no mystical experience can grow and be nourished. He recognized the need for contact with matter in the widest sense in order to sharpen human sensibility; he spoke of "the vast cosmic realities that give God his tangible and palpable being here below." In his view, the great Christian mystics cannot even be understood unless one realizes "the full depth of the truth that *Jesus must be loved as a world*."[30]

The aspirations of a naturalistic pantheism thus find their culmination in a rightly understood Christian pantheism. In this vision, a transcendent reality over and above the universe is acknowledged, but at the same time, the Divine is experienced as the most intimate, and universally present, element of all realities in the cosmos. This "universal element" is, by virtue of the incarnation, found in Christ.[31] It is the "christic element" present everywhere, but eminently so at the level of personal life and interpersonal encounter. The monistic experience of cosmic life and consciousness is crowned by this vision of the cosmic and universal Christ in whom all beings converge.[32] It is the same powerful and unitive experience that made the poet Gerard Manley Hopkins say that "the world is charged with the grandeur of God," and that "Christ plays in ten thousand places, lovely in limbs, and lovely in eyes not his to the Father through the features of men's faces."[33]

Teilhard elaborated this unifying vision of mystical experience into a philosophical theory of "creative union" that represents his answer to the much-discussed classical problem of the one and the many.[34] For him, union always implies both unification and differentiation. This theory is fundamental for his approach to all spiritual and material realities, for his understanding of personal relationships, and for his concept of God. Although Teilhard's vision of unity has been described as that of a "christomonist,"[35] he himself preferred to speak of "pan-Christism," a term taken from Maurice Blondel, or of "'pan-Christic' monism," and "'pan-Christic' mysticism."[36]

The deeply coherent vision of a union between God and the world found poetic expression in the titles of other war essays, such as "The Soul of the World" (1918)[37] and "The Great Monad" (1918).[38] The "mystical milieu" was later simply renamed "divine milieu": a milieu suffused and charged with divine presence, a center that draws human beings into intimate union and communion with God. At its roots, the mystical experience is always embedded in natural and cosmic dimensions, but this is animated throughout by divine elements. The world has an activating center from where all life and energy radiates.

The permanent value of the experience of pantheism lies in the fact that it may progressively lead into deeper forms of mysticism. There can be a progression from naturalistic, monistic pantheism to theistic and pan-christic mysticism. Rightly understood, pantheism can be seen as close, and even necessary, to Christianity. For Teilhard, this was the "true pantheism," to be distinguished from any form of "false pantheism."

The difference between pantheism and mysticism was a fundamental one and permanently influenced Teilhard's approach to eastern religions. He arrived at this distinction through reflection on his own monistic experiences, but one must not forget that these mainly occurred in Egypt. It is for this reason that his descriptions of pantheism frequently include references to the desert.

The Spiritual Power of Matter

Teilhard's approach to pantheism and mysticism can be further illustrated through his written exchanges with his friend, Father Auguste Valensin, and the philosopher Maurice Blondel.[39] During the summer of 1925, Teilhard returned to the island of Jersey, where he had lived as a young Jesuit from 1901 to 1905. He met up with his old friend, Auguste Valensin, who was then working on an article about pantheism. Teilhard criticized his work "for dismissing too summarily 'living pantheism,'" and for understanding it in a too purely negative way. He tried to persuade

Valensin "to go beyond the refutation of pantheistic thought-systems by incorporating a second, constructive study" that would present a synthesis of the Christian faith. Valensin seems to have followed his friend's advice to some extent by revising his work. Yet in Teilhard's judgment, Valensin's approach to pantheism resulted more from the desire to construct a philosophy than from the need to revere an omnipresence in the universe.[40]

The extraordinary experience of this omnipresence rings vividly through Teilhard's own composition, "The Spiritual Power of Matter" (1919),[41] written in Jersey during the summer of 1919. It culminates in the stirring "Hymn to Matter," whose stark realism and radical concreteness can be easily misunderstood:

> Blessed be you, harsh matter, barren soil, stubborn rock: you who yield only to violence, you who force us to work if we would eat.
>
> Blessed be you, perilous matter, violent sea, untameable passion: you who unless we fetter you will devour us.
>
> Blessed be you, mighty matter, irresistible march of evolution, reality ever new-born....
>
> Blessed be you, universal matter, immeasurable time...:
>
> you who by overflowing and dissolving our narrow standards of measurement reveal to us the dimensions of God.
>
> Blessed be you, impenetrable matter: you, who, interposed between our minds and the world of essences, cause us to languish with the desire to pierce through the seamless veil of phenomena.
>
> ....
>
> I bless you, matter, and you I acclaim: not as the pontiffs of science or the moralizing preachers depict you, debased, disfigured—a mass of brute forces and base appetites—but as you reveal yourself to me today, *in your totality and your true nature.*
>
> ....

> I acclaim you as the divine *milieu*, charged with cre-
> ative power, as the ocean stirred by the Spirit, as the clay
> moulded and infused with life by the incarnate Word....[42]

This hymn is the culmination of an allegorical story that
describes a man walking in the desert. He encounters there the
vision of an immense, living heart, moving palpably beneath the
surface of things, a spiritual reality shining through the life of
matter, nature, the Earth. This image expresses Teilhard's passionate conviction that matter has a "heart," a center. Since this
early text of August 1919 expresses some of his own deepest
experience, it is no coincidence that, more than thirty years later,
Teilhard chose to append the text of "The Spiritual Power of
Matter" and its stirring "Hymn to Matter" to his autobiographical essay "The Heart of Matter."[43]

When the philosopher Blondel read this, and later also the
two versions of "My Universe" (1918 and 1924)[44] and the essay
"Pantheism and Christianity" (1923),[45] he objected to some of the
details and argued that it was necessary "to detach oneself from
the illusory realism of the intellect and the senses." According to
Blondel, a clear distinction must be made:

> True pan-Christism sharply disassociates itself from
> anything having to do with physicism and pantheism.
> This means that it is important not to be a "visionary,"
> and the real seer is one who, contemplating in darkness,
> has the sense of the infinite richness of the mystery, one
> who never stops, as required by the masters of the mys-
> tical life, even at visions which are truly supernatural in
> character—less still, at symbols of his own invention.[46]

Although Teilhard had earlier written to his cousin
Marguerite that "the Church's mystical practice" was "the basic
foundation" of his thinking,[47] he felt nevertheless that Blondel's
approach to mysticism was "more traditional" and "orthodox"
than his own and regretted that the philosopher lacked a certain
"cosmic sense."[48] Whereas Blondel thought that the experience of
the world was a phase to be left behind, and that Teilhard perhaps

misrepresented the Christian mystics, especially Saint John of the Cross, Teilhard, on his part, expressed the view that he had already gone beyond the stage where Blondel was now. The "communion with God through earth," which he had proposed in "Cosmic Life," did not exclude the mystical journey through "the night" but rather introduced and justified it.[49]

Blondel, as others after him, may have been shocked by the realism of Teilhard's pantheism. He did not appreciate the full implications of a simultaneous love of the world and love of God. Whereas most theologians and spiritual writers interpret the word *mystical* in a minimalist sense, implying little organic or physical meaning, Teilhard argued against a presentation of the spiritual as "an attenuation of the material." For him the spiritual is in fact "the material carried beyond itself: it is super-material."[50] The fundamental passion for the All, and the deeply unifying experience of the cosmos, represents a "natural mysticism of which Christian mysticism can only be the sublimation and crowning peak."[51]

To reveal the Christian soul of pantheism, or the pantheistic aspect of Christianity, is the stated aim of "Pantheism and Christianity" (1923). This essay, written a few months before Teilhard's first visit to the Far East, discusses pantheism in general terms, without explicit reference to eastern monism. Teilhard argues that there have always been naturally pantheistic souls who experienced cosmic consciousness, but this sense of the All, this "passion for the Whole" seems at present "to be going through a real crisis of awakening" and is highly peculiar to our own time.[52] The "worship of the world" that "dominates modern religious history" has developed on a scale unknown before, because of the newly discovered dimensions and complexity of the universe: "The present religious crisis derives from the antagonism between the God of supernatural revelation on one side and the great mysterious figure of the universe on the other."[53] And yet, looking at the sources of the Christian tradition, "Has any evolutionist pantheism, in fact, ever spoken more magnificently of the All than St. Paul did in the words he addressed to the first Christians?"[54]

The religion of the All has hitherto been primarily expressed in terms of paganism and anti-Christianity. Discussing the reasons for this, Teilhard wrote:

Whether because the Christian God seemed useless and distant,...in comparison with the powerful evolution immanent in things—or whether because philosophic thought believed that it found its perfect expression in a monism which united beings to a degree at which all distinction was lost—the fact remains that the great mass of those who follow the religion of the All have abandoned Christianity.[55]

The human need for worship is seeking new forms of expression, and this accounts for "the present proliferation of neo-Buddhism, of theosophies, of spiritualistic doctrines." Few Christians would have admitted this in the 1920s, and probably even fewer would have stressed the need for a "Christian transposition of the fundamental pantheist tendency." In Teilhard's view, Christianity "must directly confront the spellbinding grandeur that is revealing itself—overcome it, take possession of it, and assimilate it." Only by adopting such an attitude can Christianity satisfy the legitimate pantheistic aspirations of people and, at the same time, provide the necessary environment wherein "Christian dogma and mysticism...can develop freely."[56]

Teilhard's primary concern was with such a development of Christian mysticism. But from the beginning of his reflections, he was also acutely aware of introducing a new element into the understanding of mysticism not seen by spiritual writers of the past. There is perhaps no more insightful discussion of Teilhard's Christian mysticism than in the works of Henri de Lubac, especially his study *The Religion of Teilhard de Chardin*.[57] De Lubac has stated more than once that anything Teilhard ever wrote about the "mystical milieu" and the "divine milieu" makes sense only in the context of the Christian faith. However, it is possible to understand this in a minimalist sense—the Christian faith as traditionally practiced—or, alternatively, in a much more open-ended way, where it acquires a more searching meaning. The comparative aspects of Teilhard's understanding of mysticism have so far been little explored, but they add a new dimension related to his experience of the East.

The True Meaning of Pantheism

Although pantheism was much debated and criticized by his friends, Teilhard had no doubt that there exists a genuine Christian pantheism, a cosmic sense, and an experience of God as "all in all," as expressed in 1 Corinthians 15:28 and frequently quoted by Teilhard in its original Greek form *"en pasi panta theos."* Throughout his works, Teilhard maintained the possibility of a "true pantheism," which he distinguished from all "false pantheisms." According to de Lubac, Teilhard is hardly ever prepared to condemn pantheism as such "without any exact qualification," of which he lists as examples "ancient pantheism," "common pantheism," "the Hindu type of pantheism," "the pantheisms of East and West," as well as "humanitarian neo-pantheisms."[58]

In his lexical study of Teilhard's language, Claude Cuénot has found twenty-eight contexts in which the term *pantheism* is used, each qualified by a different adjective or noun.[59] Basically, however, this wide-ranging usage relates to only two major types, of which the second one can be further subdivided:

I *Pantheism of diffusion*   II *Pantheism of convergence*
    a) pantheism of unification
    b) pantheism of union

The first type implies the loss of consciousness and the dissolution of the person at a lower level. Its major synonyms in Teilhard's works are pantheism of expansion, dissolution, or identification. This form of pantheism is also equated with the lower forms of monism or with ancient and false forms of pantheism.

The second type is by its very nature a more complex form. The Absolute is here perceived as a center, formed through the gathering up of all beings into itself, maintaining their difference while uniting them. This implies a higher degree of consciousness, and a progressive personalization. This form of pantheism represents a continuum, ranging from a merely external unification of all elements (IIa) to the deepest personal union, effected through love (IIb). In Teilhard's writings, the major synonyms for this form (IIb) are pantheism of love, tension, or differentiation. The

127

latter is ultimately identified with Christian, or what he called true pantheism.

These two major types represent two antipodal forms whose fundamental difference Teilhard always maintained. In a conversation, recorded as late as 1954, he expressed this difference rather schematically as follows:[60]

I	Pantheism of diffusion identification	attitude *without* love	God is All
II	Pantheism of convergence differentiation	essentially effect of love	God is All in all (St. Paul)

It would be wrong to see these two types as exclusively opposed to each other. From Teilhard's early writings onward, it is evident that there is continuity as well as discontinuity between these forms: monistic pantheism finds its prolongation and true fulfillment in a person-centered, theistic mysticism based on love. The human search for ultimate unity can proceed along many different paths, which Teilhard grouped into two major types with not too sharp a break between them. Mysticism is seen as different and more complex than monistic pantheism. Yet at the same time, it must not be forgotten that the mystic experience remains always rooted in a cosmic matrix and, what is more, that it may develop toward new dimensions. The search for ultimate unity may well lead to the discovery of new forms of religious experience.

As is shown later, not only the presence of love, but also its dynamic, transforming capacity is, for Teilhard, the truly differentiating factor between pantheism and mysticism, as well as between different "types" of mysticism.

Could Teilhard have avoided being misunderstood in his vigorous defense of pantheism? If one examines his thought closely, it becomes clear that he argues less for a one-dimensional, simple pantheism than for what contemporary theologians and process philosophers more appropriately call *panentheism*, an expression pointing to the vivid presence of the Divine that reverberates through all realities and experiences. Although this word already existed during Teilhard's lifetime, it was little known and not in general use; it would have probably been even more suspect than pantheism and been rejected as a "modern" invention. Although Teilhard was always looking for more adequate expressions to communicate his spiritual vision, he unfortunately never spoke of *panentheism*,[61] yet this term so well corresponds to his views.

Besides the polarity between two existing "types" of pantheism, Teilhard also refers to yet another polarity, summarized by the expressions "road of the East" and "road of the West." These rather unsatisfactory terms, first formulated after living for considerable time in the Far East, are Teilhard's way of distinguishing between two fundamental religious orientations, probably not found anywhere in pure form, whether West or East. Since much of Teilhard's search for ultimate unity is discussed with reference to these two "roads," they now invite closer analysis and critical examination.

6

TWO ROADS TO UNITY
"Road of the East" and
"Road of the West"

Soon after arriving in the Far East in 1923, Teilhard wrote that he hoped to find there "a reservoir of thought and mysticism that would bring fresh youth to our West."[1] From the beginning of his stay in China, he compared the East with the West, particularly in his letters, in comments, and in reflections sent to his friends. A more systematic comparison of eastern and western mysticism occurs only several years later in his writings. It is in fact an essay of 1932 that refers for the first time to both the "road of the East" and the "road of the West." These expressions seem to have been formulated by Teilhard himself, and one wonders whether he would ever have chosen them had he not lived in the East for so long.

The comparison between two different "roads" is dealt with at length in an essay entitled "The Road of the West: To a New Mysticism" (1932),[2] which I discuss at length here because of its importance in voicing Teilhard's understanding of mysticism. The main theme of this essay was subsequently expressed in a variety of ways, and specific comparisons between eastern and western religions, although generally brief, are found in many later essays.[3]

The idea of two different roads for achieving ultimate unity is directly associated with the difference between monism and mysticism, but it expresses this earlier distinction in a different, more accentuated manner. After 1932, references to the two roads are present in many essay and diary entries, with a marked preponderance of the "road of the West." Since Teilhard's understanding of eastern religions is nearly always linked to this fundamental dichotomy, several questions arise: Why did he emphasize the existence of two "roads"? What did he mean by them? What was the reason for linking the "road of the West" with the idea of a "new mysticism"?

Two Fundamental Orientations in Mysticism

The theme of the essay, "The Road of the West," was first announced in a letter of March 1932. It was written after Teilhard's return from the Yellow Expedition that had left such a deep impression on him:

> At the first possible opportunity, I propose to write something new on the fundamental metaphysical and religious question: "What is the Multiple, and how can it be reduced to Unity?" (the eastern solution, and the western solution).[4]

The opportunity to deal with this question came soon, for the essay was completed at the beginning of September 1932. From then on, the dichotomy between the "road of the East" and the "road of the West" was used intermittently as a metaphor to refer to two different types of spirituality, represented by two opposing ways of the human search for the Absolute. Although their contrast may on occasion have been forced, Teilhard took great pains to explain what he meant by this dichotomy in order to reduce or exclude misleading interpretations. He also used more general and less geographically dependent terms to express the fundamental difference that he perceived in the overall orientation of the human religious quest.

The comparison between the two different roads or paths relates primarily to the understanding of mysticism, for, in Teilhard's view, the phenomenon of mysticism, and the relentless quest for absolute oneness or unity underlying it, represents the central core of all religion: "Without mysticism, there can be no successful religion: and there can be no well-founded mysticism apart from faith in some unification of the universe."[5] While many traditional mystics may be described as being primarily either soul- or God-centered, Teilhard's approach to mysticism is intrinsically related to the world surrounding us, to the experience of multiplicity and organic complexity found in both nature and society. In this sense, his view may be characterized as an "extrovert" rather than "introvertive" mysticism. The threefold, interdependent relationship among humans, the world, and the Absolute introduces a different degree of complexity into the understanding of mysticism, and much of Teilhard's interpretation hinges on this pivotal difference.

"The Road of the West: To a New Mysticism" discusses what sort of unity is sought in different types of mysticism. The essay intends

> to show how, in continuity with (and at the same time in opposition to) ancient forms of mysticism (particularly eastern), humanity today, the child of western science, is even now—for all its appearance of skeptical positivism—pursuing along a new road the persistent effort which since time began seems to have been driving life towards some plenifying unity.[6]

This intention should be borne in mind when one reads some of the subsequent characterizations of the "road of the East" and the "road of the West."

In general, the passage just quoted already implies four themes that are more fully developed in the remaining part of the essay:

1. The ancient origin of eastern mysticism from which western mysticism itself was initially derived.
2. The interrelatedness of eastern and western mysticism can be expressed in terms of both continuity and partial opposition.
3. The development of modern science, too, is an expression of the continuous human search for unity.

4. Contemporary people pursue this search in a new situation, on a "new road" or path, leading to a new form of mysticism that will ultimately transcend previous forms of mysticism.

The Ancient "Road of the East"

Before the meaning of this "new road," leading to a new mysticism, can be fully understood, it is important to inquire into what is really meant by the "ancient forms of mysticism" that Teilhard associates particularly with the East. In other words, what does he mean by the "road of the East"?

He was the first to admit that he was speaking in "over-simplified terms" when he briefly sketched the characteristics of the "road of the East" or described the "eastern solution" to the human quest for ultimate oneness. The search for meaning underneath the manifold reality of experience has led throughout history to various conceptions of unity and absolutes. In Teilhard's thought, the "road of the East" stands for a path whereby the ultimate One is totally opposed to the many. Unity can only be achieved by a return to the One, that is to say, through the suppression or negation of the multiple. This is a "unity by impoverishment" rather than enrichment, a unity of simplicity, and not of complexity. The most important practical consequence of such an absolute religious and philosophical attitude is the implicit denial that the achievements of human life have an intrinsic value of their own. It is the "total death of constructive activity: the fundamental emptiness of the experiential universe."[7]

Which eastern religions did Teilhard associate with this schematic characterization of the "road of the East"? He assumed that a search for ultimate unity achieved through release or return, through identification with an underlying ground rather than union with a higher center, was typical of both Buddhist and Brahmin thought: it was an attitude that, at one time, affected all Asian mentality right up to Japan.

These sweeping generalizations can and must be criticized for their negativity toward the East and for their lack of differentiation regarding historical developments and the existence of different types of eastern religiosity. However, it would be a mistake to judge these assessments in isolation, without paying due regard to the wider context relating to Teilhard's thought on religion and mysticism as a whole. He was emphatic to point out that the incomparable greatness of the religions of the East lies in their being second to none in vibrating with a passion for ultimate unity. The mystical search for oneness in eastern—especially Indian—religions is historically primary in the sense that it was the first type of mysticism to appear in historical time and in that various features of eastern mysticism found their way to the West and influenced certain religious developments there. One can say that the characteristics of the "road of the East" are not only Indian, but equally neo-Platonic, and through the writing of Pseudo-Dionysius impressed their lasting stamp on much of Christian mysticism.

Although Teilhard later acknowledged the "extreme poly-morphism" of Indian religious thought, he always equated the essence of Indian spirituality with a very particular conception of unity, which, in his opinion, gives even Hindu theism "in what-ever form it may be expressed, a coloring and flavor that are immediately recognizable."[8] This emphasis on a particular under-standing of unity seems to derive mainly from his acquaintance with Indian monistic views, especially as found in Vedanta.

Elsewhere, it becomes even more apparent that the "road of the East" is mainly equated with certain forms of Hindu monism. What Teilhard finds especially unacceptable in this road is the exaggerated feeling of the final unreality of all phenomena, the teaching that the world is ultimately illusion, *maya*. The "road of the East" implies for him the denial of the existence of matter; it characterizes an attempt to escape from matter and its confusing multiplicity, encountered in both the natural and social world. The appeal of this road can be summarized as "renounce the earth, its passions and cares, and the effort it demands." Logically, this is "a doctrine of passivity, of relaxation of tension, of withdrawal from things," in order to achieve an identification or fusion with an ultimate One. Expressed in theistic rather than impersonal terms, it would mean that God is arrived at by a nega-tion of the world rather than by its completion and fulfilment.[9]

This fundamental religious orientation understands the pri-

mary task of human beings as one of renunciation and detachment from the world. The goal of religious activity is considered
to be contemplation rather than action. Such contemplation or
even absorption leads to a "mysticism of identification" with the
Absolute or, to use Indian terminology, an identification of *Atman*
with *Brahman*. For Teilhard, such a spirituality implies "simplification"; it incurs the risk of evading the responsibilities of human
life. Perfection or salvation is sought by a person's direct vertical
rise to the Absolute, without a corresponding horizontal connection with the surrounding social milieu or the wider context of the
world. Comparable to his earlier characterization of naturalistic,
or monistic, pantheism, the "road of the East" is seen to lead to
a fusion of the individual—without distinction or qualification—
with an original All, leaving no room for either human progress
or failure: "In strict logic, the Indian sage cannot concern himself
with anything the life of the world has been, is, or will be."[10]

Teilhard reacted negatively to such a road of one-sided,
exclusive detachment. In fact, he criticized all exclusively contemplative life, whether in East or West. The "road of the East" was
seen as one of "dehumanizing spirituality," leading to a "dissolution of personality" rather than to its perfection and fulfillment.
Such statements, however, must not be understood as applying literally to eastern religions as known and practiced today. Other
passages show that Teilhard was to some extent aware of the
reformist tendencies in contemporary Hinduism and Buddhism.
He referred to the modern "renaissance" of eastern religions that
has so much influenced certain people in Europe that some have
even suggested "that the monist serenity of the East might well
convert the confused pluralism of the West,"[11] a statement written
in 1932 but perhaps even more relevant today.

Yet it is obvious that Teilhard did not share the opinion,
much more common since then, that the difficulties and especially
the materialism of the West might find a ready remedy in the spirituality of the East. European disciples of eastern religions may
well be subject to "a vast misunderstanding" here. In his view,
they are neither aware of the logical implications of an extreme
monism, nor do they realize its practical consequences, which
reveal themselves only to someone who has had a prolonged per-

sonal contact with eastern societies. This is more forcefully expressed in another essay:

> We turn to the imposing mass of Hindu and eastern mystical systems. The East, the first shrine, and, we are assured, the ever-living dwelling place of the Spirit. The East, where so many from the West still dream of finding shelter for their faith in life....Let us take a closer look at those mighty constructions; and, without even venturing into the temple to savor what sort of incense still burns within it, let us, not as archaeologists or poets, but as architects of the future, examine the solidity of its walls. The very moment we came into fundamental contact with Asia there can be no question of doubt. Those impressive columns are utterly incapable of supporting the drive of our world in these days.[12]

In Teilhard's opinion, western followers of eastern religions may be a long way from realizing the full implications of certain forms of traditional eastern thought. However, the societies and religions of the East have been in close contact and interaction with western thought for over two centuries now. This has led to a revival and new vigor of eastern religions, revealing their important contribution to the contemporary search of an appropriate spirituality for the modern world.

Seen in this light, the discussion about the "road of the East" is of a largely theoretical nature. The characteristics of this road are not to be understood as descriptions of an empirical state of affairs. Teilhard's statements about this road are hedged in by a number of qualifications[13] that must not be overlooked. The frequent use of quotation marks for the "road of the East" also point to a nonliteral understanding of this term. It is emphasized that the "eastern" solution certainly exists *in theory*, but it is only put forward "to make plain the exact nature and originality of western neo-mysticism." The latter is a new kind of mysticism emerging only now "in a diametrically opposite direction" to the "road of the East."[14]

The New "Road of the West"

Although seen as more important, the characteristics of this new "road of the West" are sketched in equally brief form. The western road is mainly seen as opposed to the "road of the East" because of its different attitude to the world. In terms of the mystical quest, this means that unity is achieved through unification, union, and ultimate convergence of the many in the One. Thus, the One is not opposed to the multiple, but it is partially born from it.

Such a view presupposes that the universe is considered as an organic whole, formed of interlinked elements that are always in the process of coming more closely together. Unity or oneness is created through the union of all elements effected over time. The multiple is no longer reduced to an underlying common ground, but, on the contrary, a new, higher form of unity is emerging through the gradual transformation and convergence of multiple elements. All parts of reality, whether impersonal or personal, are transformed and united into a higher center. Instead of escape from, there is transformation of matter. At the same time, transcendence is gained through effort rather than release. Instead of emptiness, this "road" is characterized by fullness. The world itself is being experienced as filled with the divine Absolute. Its omnipresence radiates through all levels of reality and, therefore, each element possesses an intrinsic value of its own.

Religiously speaking, this means "heaven is not opposed to the earth but it is born from the conquest and transformation of the earth." Expressed in theistic terms, "God is reached, not by draining away of self, but by sublimation."[15] It is this effort to reach *beyond* and *not below* consciousness, to seek a higher form of personalization rather than to dissolve personality in general cosmic consciousness that Teilhard saw as the most distinctive feature of the "road of the West."

However, one must not look for an "explicit formulation of this doctrine" or make the mistake of equating the "road of the West" with Christianity. Teilhard repeated over and over again that the "road of the West" is a *new* road, representing the "great religious discovery" of modern times. This road consists for him in a

137

new synthesis of two traditionally exclusive concerns, namely the human search for the One and the relation to the many. One could also say that it represents a combination of "other-worldly" and "this-worldly" attitudes, a synthesis already partly hinted at in the maxim of "Cosmic Life" (1916) that states that there is "communion with God through earth." This new orientation affects "all the living branches of modern religions"; it will transform traditional Christianity just as much as "the new forms of Islam and Buddhism."[16] The impact of the modern world is so universal that it will effect a transformation of the traditional religious outlook that will, in fact, bring the different religions more closely together.

New forms of asceticism and mysticism are being developed today, due to a new historical situation wherein people's consciousness of their own becoming has been tremendously expanded, even revolutionized. Spirituality is being closely related in an entirely new way to the development of the tangible world and needs to be even more integrally connected to it. In the past, religious teachings were primarily linked to individual needs and hopes or to national and racial movements. Today, humanity is experiencing itself as one, as belonging together in a sense unknown before. However, to realize the oneness of the human community and promote the necessary action to bring about world unity requires a common focus. Human beings need to be inspired by the vision of one world with a single soul. This point was not only made by Teilhard, but it was equally stressed by several Indian thinkers, for example, Sri Aurobindo and Radhakrishnan.

The new "road of the West" encourages a dynamic attitude toward a world deeply affected by vast social changes and by complex developments in science and technology. But why does Teilhard link the characteristics of this new road specifically to the West?

Two reasons can be given for this. On one hand, modern science and technology, however much influenced by earlier ideas from both East and West, historically emerged in the West. On the other hand, Christianity, with its teaching on the incarnation of the Divine in matter, has frequently encouraged a positive attitude to the world. For these reasons, Teilhard considered the "road of the West" as especially growing out of the central stem of the western religious tradition. Unfortunately, he did not recognize that eastern religions, particularly Taoism but also certain aspects of Hinduism and Buddhism, possess their own world-affirming orientations.

It is also apparent that Christianity has not always actively promoted a dynamic attitude toward the world. Many negative aspects can be found in the history of Christian spirituality. In the past, the two roads of world negation and world affirmation were often held in tension. Originally, western mysticism was influenced by the East, as can be seen, for example, in the ideal of renunciation and perfection that inspired the desert fathers. Teilhard looked upon the entire history of western mysticism as a long-drawn-out effort to separate these two spiritualities: the oriental way, which suppresses matter, and the occidental way, which sublimates it. These are not simply two components that can be harmonized into one spirituality, as is sometimes thought; for him, they are "two incompatible attitudes," yet attitudes that, on closer examination, can be found in both East and West.

For Teilhard, these two incompatible attitudes are at present still intermingled in Christianity to some extent. Yet there is an increasing need for distinguishing between these two roads. Humanity has now arrived at an important bifurcation in its development: its path divides between the old "road of the East" and the new "road of the West," where, considering all earthly values, ultimate unity is found through the unification of the world rather than its abandonment.

By recommending this new "road," Teilhard was far from encouraging any form of "naturalism," "hedonism," or "pantheism." On the contrary, he wished to lead Christianity back to the central essence of its own tradition:

> If Christianity is to remain true to itself..., only one condition, and that is an essential one, must be fulfilled: to the maintenance of the primacy of the *spirit* over matter (which...brings with it the renunciation of possession), must be added the primacy in the spiritual of the *personal*, which brings together at the same time the maximum differentiation of the elements and their

maximum union. In short...if Christianity is to remain itself, it must come to the rescue of western mysticism, and in so doing take it to itself.[17]

This passage shows clearly that Teilhard considered mysticism to be of major importance for contemporary spirituality. The two forms of mysticism—the "road of the East" and the "road of the West"—were not only two alternative orientations that he had personally experienced, but they represented two possible options for humanity at the crossroads:

> Humankind has now reached such a degree of concentration and moral tension that it can no longer postpone taking the spiritual step which will give it a soul. Agnosticism and pluralism are either dead or impotent. It is only a renewed faith in some unity to be born of the world that can preserve our zest for life. And at this precise point we come to the parting of the ways....[18]

This parting of the ways is understood as a separation between the ancient "road of the East" and the new "road of the West," each of which leads to a different goal: an ultimate unity of "impoverishment" or "simplicity" is contrasted with a unity of "richness" or "complexity." For Teilhard, there could be no hesitation about which road to take. Indeed, he thought that the choice had already "to all intents and purposes, been made," for both history and experience seem to indicate that life is advancing on the "road of the West."

Early Criticisms of Teilhard's Comparisons

The essay "The Road of the West" was not without its critics. Nevertheless, in spite of early criticisms of Teilhard's comparisons, he vigorously defended and continued to use the idea of two "roads" in relation to two different types of mysticism. This is significant, for it shows that, however inadequate, this dichotomy expresses a fundamental orientation of his thought.

Shortly after writing "The Road of the West" (1932), he

restated its main ideas again in a lecture on "Orient et Occident—la Mystique de la Personnalité," given in early 1933 to a student society in Paris. Only the notes taken down by two listeners have survived from this lecture.[19] These reflect certain nuances in Teilhard's position that may reflect his response to early criticisms. The notes include statements such as "The opposition between a contemplative Orient and an Occident immersed in life is a questionable one; we are attributing our own qualities to the Orient." And: "This opposition is not right, not distinct enough; one must show that we carry the virtues of the East within us and we may try to bring them to light."

With reference to the Buddhist teaching on emptiness, Teilhard is reported to have said:

> Perhaps this *Void* is nothing other but what we call the *Ineffable*, perhaps this is a question of words. But what we can say is that their mysticism does not authorize them toward a positive attitude which makes them seek modern science and western ideas. This gesture by which they try to catch up with us, seems to be condemned by eastern mysticism. Given the conditions of the present world, it is the western conception which tends to become universal.[20]

The term "road of the West" is only used once in these notes, emphasizing again the newness of this "road." This newness presents perhaps less of a difficulty for most readers than Teilhard's all too summary treatment of the "road of the East." It was soon severely criticized by two of Teilhard's friends, both of whom were particularly interested in eastern religions.

One was the fellow Jesuit Father Henri de Lubac who, from 1931 onward, taught a course in the history of religions in the Faculty of Theology at the Jesuit study house in Lyons. He developed a special interest in Buddhism, on which he published several books during the 1950s.[21] Teilhard had known de Lubac since 1922 and had corresponded with him regularly from 1930 onward. After reading "The Road of the West," of which Teilhard must have given him a copy, de Lubac immediately criticized the essay and possibly wrote to Teilhard suggesting something like "Is there not a Christian detachment, and can it be maintained that Buddhistic renunciation is void of all moral validity?"[22] In a letter to de Lubac, written on October 8, 1933, Teilhard replied:

> I was most interested in your friendly criticisms of "The Road of the West." But if I am not mistaken, they prove precisely the importance of what I tried to show (not clearly enough, no doubt). I fully admit the alternation of detachment and attachment (cf. *Milieu Divin*). But I believe that it is in the particular, *specific* nature of Buddhist detachment that there lies the weakness and the (at least logical) danger of eastern religions. The Buddhist *denies* himself in order to kill desire (he *does not believe* in the value of being). The authentic Christian also denies himself but *by excess* of desire and of faith in the value of being. This is one of those cases where the same appearances cover contrary realities. It seems to me highly important to unmask the ambiguity here. This is not to say, of course, that, vitally speaking, Buddhist renunciation has no moral validity. But it is expressed in a false theory (as in the case of so many other pantheisms).[23]

Another criticism came from Abbé Jules Monchanin, an authority on eastern religions and today considered a pioneer of Christian-Hindu dialogue. Monchanin had first met Teilhard in 1925, and he greatly admired some of his privately circulated writings.[24] Deeply attracted by Indian spirituality, Monchanin went to live in India in 1939. He first worked there as a parish priest, then lived in a South Indian ashram. In 1950, he founded with Dom Henri le Saux, later known as Swami Abhishiktananda, the Shantivanam Ashram, also in South India. This subsequently became known worldwide through its association with Father Bede Griffiths.

Transmitted through their mutual friend, Father de Lubac, Monchanin had received a copy of Teilhard's essay, "The Road of the West," and had criticized it at length. Well versed in Indian mystical thought, Monchanin found in Teilhard's views "a certain pragmatist emphasis and a too exclusively western presentation."[25] Were the religions of India in fact as negative as Teilhard believed? In a long letter to Father de Lubac, Teilhard took up several of Monchanin's points, as evident from the following passage:

> I was very touched by the trouble taken by M. Monchanin over reading and criticizing me. His observations lead me to make the following counter-observations:
>
> 1. Basically, if the religions of India are less negative than I said, that does not essentially affect my thesis, the purpose of which is above all to distinguish "two essential types" of possible mysticisms. It would be quite extraordinary, I admit, for either of these types to be met anywhere in the *pure state*. I therefore took especially eastern mysticism as an example that is as close as possible to negativism. Given these reservations..., I still believe that, *logically*, eastern religions and contemplation kill action....
>
> 2. It is impossible for me to admit the formula that mysticism "is ultimately not meant to perfect the world but to allow the *praise of God*." For years, my entire effort has precisely been to criticize these juridical and vague terms, and to find an organic and ontological meaning for them. What does it mean "to praise God"?...Nothing, in my view, is *more spiritual* than the consummation of the universe. Any spirituality pursued at the periphery of this effort is verbalism, attenuation, abstraction—the dreary piety of churches and convents. I fear that M. Monchanin has not really "caught" anything of what I try to express—or that we are at antipodes of each other. In any case, he does not seem to have "understood the world."[26]

This passage expresses more clearly than any other that the "road of the East" and the "road of the West" are essentially *two distinct types.* They represent a theoretical distinction and are, so to speak, a heuristic device to investigate and interpret fundamental orientations to reality. This does not imply that either of these two types exists as such in practice in any individual adherent of a particular religion. The roads are perhaps best likened to signposts that send people mainly into one direction or the other.

The harshness of expression characteristic of "The Road of the West" (1932) is somewhat modified by the more sympathetic and detailed treatment of eastern religions in Teilhard's later essay "The Spiritual Contribution of the Far East" (1947).[27] There the term "road of the East" is abandoned in favor of a more differentiated discussion of Asian spirituality, to which I return later.

The interrelationship and difference of the two roads is also discussed in "My Fundamental Vision" (1948).[28] Quoting Aldous Huxley's *Perennial Philosophy,* Teilhard refers to the apparently complete agreement of the mystics of all religions and times regarding their search for spiritual perfection. Their perennial quest seems to be characterized by "an effort to escape spiritually, through universalization, into the Ineffable." Yet contrary to Aldous Huxley and many others, Teilhard was convinced that this is only a "superficial unanimity," disguising "a serious opposition (or even fundamental incompatibility) which originates in a confusion between two symmetrical but 'antipodal' approaches to the understanding, and hence to the pursuit, of the unity of the spirit."[29]

The two different approaches—either initial identification or ultimate differentiation and convergence—are equated with the two roads. The first road conceives spiritual unification to be a "return to a common 'divine' basis *underlying* and *more real than*, all the sensibly perceptible determinants of the universe." Teilhard calls this road, for convenience, as he qualifies, the "road of the East." From the perspective of the "road of the West," the "common basis" of the eastern road is mere illusion. Given contemporary physics and an adequate metaphysics related to modern science, "the only homogeneous form of spiritualization, the only viable mysticism, must be...a positive act not of relaxation, but of active convergence and concentration."[30]

As should be apparent by now, a central part of Teilhard's

argument concerns the possible differences in understanding the nature of the spirit itself and the divergent ways in which human beings can find ultimate unity.

The distinction between two essential types of mysticism is also expressed in two brief notes, whose very title reflects Teilhard's attempt to clarify his insights for himself and others: "A Clarification: Reflections on Two Converse Forms of the Spirit" (1950)[31] distinguishes between "unity through relaxation, or the search for a common foundation," and "unity through tension, or the road to the universal center." Ultimate unity may thus be found either at the base through the elimination of all opposites between things, or at the apex, through ultra-differentiation.

Another short text, "Some Notes on the Mystical Sense: An Attempt at Clarification" (1951),[32] speaks of the "two principal ways" tried by the mystics. The "road of the East" and the "road of the West" are here replaced by a more neutral terminology. The difference in mystical orientation is simply presented in terms of "two ways," or rather, "two components, that have hitherto to all intents and purposes been merged into one."[33] However, the distinguishing characteristic of these two paths is now mainly perceived to consist in the absence or presence of love, ultimately centered on an ultra-personal God rather than an impersonal, common ground.

These examples show that the "road of the East" and the "road of the West" must not be understood literally, nor can they be properly assessed without considering them within a wider context. Teilhard also uses many other words to express the same contrast and dichotomy in the mystic quest for unity. Representative examples of such dichotomous classifications are best listed in a table. (See next page.)

CHRONOLOGICAL LIST OF DICHOTOMOUS CLASSIFICATIONS USED BY TEILHARD

YEAR	DICHOTOMY		SOURCE
1931	*Two solutions to the problem of the One and the Many*		LI, 223
	"Eastern" solution	"Western" solution	LZ, 108
1932	*Two roads to unity*		
	"Road of the East"	"Road of the West"	TF, 42 ff.
	Two roads of spiritualization		
	Eastern: suppression	Western: sublimation	TF, 52
1937	*Two entirely opposite forms of union*		
	Union of dissolution	Union by differentiation or Union of concentration (the *only* true union)	HE, 103 f.
1939	*Two kinds of pantheism*		
	The unity of the whole is born from the fusion of the elements	The elements are *fulfilled* by entering a deeper center	CE, 136
1945	*Two ways of mysticism (often confused, though opposed)*		
	The way of simplification ("road of the East")	The way of synthesis (new "road of the West")	
	Unity through fusion	Unity through unification	SC, 183 f.
1948	*Two ineffables*		
	Eastern "ineffable of relaxation"	Christian "ineffable of tension"	TF, 194
1950	*Two converse forms or "isotopes" of the spirit*		
	Spirit of identification or fusion	Spirit of unification or of "amorization"	
	Pantheism of identification at the opposite pole from love	Pantheism of unification, beyond love	AE, 218 AE, 223
1951	*Two principal ways tried by the mystics (or two components hitherto merged into one)*		
	To become one with a common ground; this leads to an identification, an ineffable of de-differentiation and de-personalization. This is a mysticism WITHOUT LOVE.	To become one with all by access to the center—unification of the elements within a *common focus*, the specific effect of LOVE.	TF, 209 f.

Relating the Two "Roads" to Past and Present

A look at the table listing "the dichotomous classifications used by Teilhard" shows clearly that the contrast between the "road of the East" and the "road of the West" forms part of a wider group of comparisons, present throughout many of Teilhard's writings. In one form or another, they all express two distinctive spiritual orientations in the search for the Absolute, or two possible forms of conceiving ultimate unity. They also relate to two basic types of mysticism. Thus, the dichotomy of two roads continues and further accentuates the difference between the two types of pantheism to which Teilhard refers mainly in his earlier writings.

The major problem in interpreting the meaning of two different roads or paths is Teilhard's changing vocabulary, with its resulting lack of definition and clarity. It is perhaps less in terms of exact philosophical analysis than in terms of a basic intuition that they must be interpreted and evaluated. Seen from within a wider context, it would be quite wrong, for example, to equate the "road of the East" with the great variety of religions existing in the East. However, there is the difficulty that Teilhard's approach to eastern religions is mainly expressed through this comparison of abstract types and rarely relates to more concrete historical detail.

He emphasized more than once that the two roads resemble two spiritual "currents"; they are basically "two essential types."[34] Thus their characterization must not be taken too literally. The two roads represent a schematized comparison that requires a typological interpretation relating to other aspects of Teilhard's thought rather than to ideas introduced from outside his work.

The choice of the word *road* itself is indicative here. Its meaning implies the existence of a path as well as a certain direction and goal. Different roads lead into different directions, and crossroads in particular stand for definite alternatives among which individuals must choose. Teilhard not only emphasizes the existence of a choice between contrasting "roads" in religion and mysticism, but many aspects of contemporary society and culture imply the necessity of making a choice. The entire situation of humankind today is one of being at the crossroads. At present, the necessity to opt for one road rather than another is particularly urgent with regard to humanity's power of choosing and shaping its own future. In Teilhard's view, such a choice cannot really be made without an adequate religious perspective, without the animating and sustaining powers of a rightly understood faith. This is the "heart of the problem": to choose the right "road" in a situation where the future of humankind involves a "grand option."[35]

Teilhard has an overriding concern with the future and the dynamics of time. Time possesses a great evolutionary and historical importance; its role is different now from that in the past.[36] This applies also to the understanding of spirituality, although one can point to the Christian idea of the *kairos* here, which is a God-given, crucial moment in time, specifically appointed, and calling for significant choice and an existential decision on the part of the human subject.

The time factor is certainly an essential element in the dichotomy between the two roads, or "types," of spirituality. I would suggest that the "road of the East" and the "road of the West" are not simply opposites on the same plane, existing simultaneously in time. As Teilhard wrote at the beginning of his essay, the "road of the West" exists "in continuity with," and "in opposition to," the ancient "road of the East." One can understand this to mean that the "road of the East" typifies a road of the past; it stands for a stage of the human religious quest that once existed to a greater or lesser degree in all religions. It is associated with passivity, world negation, asceticism, and an excessive otherworldliness. In other words, the mystic search for ultimate unity is predominantly associated with world rejection in one form or another, characteristic of all the great historical religions.

However, this ancient "road," dominant for so long, represents an outdated spirituality now, for it is based on an inadequate understanding of the nature of the spirit as well as the nature of an evolutionary world. Although distinct from the temporal, the spiritual is not sharply separated from it but grows out of and beyond it. The next stage to be gained, or the road to be taken, is a *new* road, linked to a clearer perception of the importance of temporal realities, of the growth of this world in the present and future. This is what Teilhard calls the "road of the West" and, in his view, Christianity contains in its essence the most powerful potential to chart this new road. Ultimately, however, this new "road of the West" represents, at least in the formulation of his later years, "a hitherto unknown form of religion,"[37] that requires a new, but as yet unformulated, mysticism.

Thus, the "road of the West" must not be identified with Christianity as we know it, or as it exists at present, containing a mixture of both eastern and western elements. In fact, neither the "road of the East" nor the "road of the West" can be fully equated with any particular religious tradition; each indicates a major spiritual orientation present in both eastern and western religions.

These two types of spirituality might be compared with Max Weber's distinction between "world-rejecting asceticism" and "inner-worldly asceticism" as two fundamental attitudes toward the world. Weber, too, relates these two different religious orientations to the contrast between oriental and occidental religiosity.[38] Yet it must be stressed that, in terms of their relation to time, Weber's "ideal-types" are also past-oriented. They oppose two existing attitudes and typify what has been. One of Teilhard's ideal types, however, the "road of the West," attempts to express *what is not yet*. It points to what is emerging now and anticipates what may develop in the future. The incorporation of the time process introduces, therefore, a different dynamic into his typological distinction. Taking into account the progressive developments over time, one could say that the "road of the East" is the road of the past, in some form or another present in all religious traditions, whereas the "road of the West" is the road of the future.

The general, ideal type function of the two roads, expressing two possible types of spirituality, must not be confused with specific, historical-empirical examples. However, such confusion does occasionally occur in Teilhard's own writings. It is easily made, especially when the distinction of the two basic types is linked to the descriptive geographical references of East and West.

Although some of Teilhard's commentators infer an implicit attitude of superiority from his expression, "road of the West," this seems to have been far from Teilhard's own intention. As Cuénot has pointed out, his "criticism of eastern thought did not arise from

TWO FORMS OF UNITY

"Road of the East"   *"Road of the West"*
(both continuity and partial opposition)[*]

"Road of the East"	"Road of the West"
Return to primordial unity	Progress to ultimate unity, achieved through convergence
Detachment	Alternation detachment-attachment
Simplification	Complexity
Identification	Unification and differentiation
Vertical orientation (human-Absolute)	Diagonal orientation [synthesis of vertical (human-Absolute) with horizontal (human-world) orientation = via tertia]
Exclusive stress on contemplation	Alternation action-contemplation
Dehumanizing spirituality	Progressive spiritual transformation of matter
Emptiness	Fulfillment
Mysticism of identification with a common ground	Mysticism of union with a higher center

TIME—PROCESS

Past ⟶ Present ⟶ Future

Historically first	Slowly emerging now
Ancient	New
Now outdated	Still incomplete
Stage to be transcended	New stage to be gained

[*] The curved line indicates that the distinction between the two "roads" is a fluid one: the two forms of unity are not clearly divided from one another.

any belief that radically the westerner is superior to the oriental."[39] In a new historical situation, Teilhard wished to draw attention to an increasingly important distinction, implying the choice of a new road not available in the past. This choice has only arisen with the growing differentiation of the world, and of human consciousness, in recent times. In a more neutral way, the two roads may be seen as two different paths toward greater unity or oneness. Their main characteristics can be outlined in a diagram that shows the contrast as well as the continuity between these two paths. (See table at left.)

The difference between the "road of the East" and the "road of the West" thus expresses a fundamental alternative in religious and mystical orientation. Theoretically, the two opposite roads exist together; yet, at the empirical level, the two alternatives both overlap and succeed each other in time. The complexity of the "road of the West" is also linguistically apparent, for it is usually characterized by more than one word. The "road of the West" points to a synthesis that, in this form, is new but incorporates certain features of the "road of the East."

One can therefore conclude that there exists a double dialectic in Teilhard's thought with regard to the two roads toward ultimate unity or oneness. On one hand, the two roads are historically somehow connected, and yet they are fundamentally opposed: the "road of the East" is linked to certain forms of spirituality, which may have been sufficient for the past but differ from those needed for the present and future. On the other hand, it must be pointed out that the characterizations of these two ways or roads rest on entirely different premises. Teilhard always remained an outsider to the "road of the East," if one understands the latter literally. Unlike Monchanin, and others since, he never acquired a deep personal knowledge of eastern religions in spite of the many years spent in the East. He lived there primarily as a working research scientist and as a member of an international scientific elite that included a large number of western expatriates.

His criticisms of eastern religions are therefore still those of a cultural and religious outsider. They remain necessarily superficial, whereas he could criticize Christianity with much greater subtlety and sophistication because he knew it so closely from the inside. The comparison between two different roads is also held in tension by the fact that Teilhard often speaks of a coming together, or convergence, of roads. That the "road of the East" and the "road of the West" should meet, he judged a distinct possibility; indeed, he considered it a necessity if a truly new mysticism is to emerge.

I next reflect on Teilhard's far too summary and inadequate assessment of eastern religions and examine how his understanding of religious diversity relates to the larger idea of a convergence of roads. What does such a movement of convergence mean for the understanding and practice of contemporary spirituality?

7

THE CONVERGENCE OF ROADS

The idea of convergence relates to a meeting point, a focus that gathers in lines from different directions, a center where they can meet and be grouped together. Other words associated with convergence are *intersection, conflux, conjunction*, even *union*. This idea of convergence, of meeting together, of dialoguing, sharing, and working for a common aim, is central to Teilhard's vision of unity.

Convergence is a movement or process observable in many areas of human activity, today often referred to as a "process of globalization." The development of the modern world is related to a profound change of age and direction affecting all aspects of contemporary culture, including religion. As early as 1923, Teilhard wrote, "We are standing, at the present moment, not only at a change of century and civilization, but at a *change of epoch*!"[1] He described the convergence of humanity upon itself as a process of "planetization."[2]

The contemporary world is marked by striking paradoxes, however, and almost unbearably tense opposites. It seems deeply torn apart, filled with violence and wars, with suffering, injustice, religious and racial hatred, and bloodshed. Nevertheless, in spite of so much divergence and disunity, innumerable movements have come into existence that are working for a greater economic, political, and cultural unity of humankind. In fact, the past offers no parallel to the way in which the contemporary world is coming to be centered upon the belief that humanity ultimately forms one community and that human rights and dignity pertain to all members of the human species. Never before in human history have so many been aware of the oneness of humankind, a oneness pertaining to a common origin, a shared development, and a unity of purpose. However, this is not a oneness actually given, but it exists as an ideal, a deeply felt wish and desire, a profound aspiration and dream that may come true one day if we strive for its realization.

This general movement of convergence in contemporary culture has far-reaching effects on the world's religions. Teilhard asked the important question of whether the active "currents of faith,"[3] or the truly "living branches of modern religions"[4] can give meaning to this tremendous change of epoch. Will they be able to respond creatively to a historically new situation?

He believed that the living religions themselves are moving closer together and that they have a valuable contribution to make to the epoch-making process of human convergence in a global world. Indeed, a greater unity of the world's religions is indispensable if the full convergence of humanity is to come about.

How does Teilhard describe the active currents of faith, the living branches of religion? It is important to remember that, largely, his approach to the world's religious heritage rarely included historical and factual descriptions. It remained primarily typological and evaluative, especially with regard to the critical situation facing the world today, a situation that demands decisive commitment and the choice of a specific "road." Is such a road open to us?

The idea of a convergence of roads suggests an altogether new path, a synthesis that will overcome the opposition between different spiritualities of the past, particularly those of East and West. Teilhard's conception of an ultimate unity of convergence is inspiring. It is also extraordinary, however, if one considers his rather brief and frequently negative assessment of eastern religions, due perhaps more to a lack of knowledge than of sympathy. Although he obviously knew far more about Christianity than about eastern thought, he emphasized the importance of the central insights of all religions but judged their value mainly from the perspective of the modern world and its future development. What are, in brief, some of his comments on eastern religions?

Teilhard's Assessment of Eastern Religions

The first non-Christian religion that Teilhard encountered during his early years in Egypt was Islam. However, his few direct references to this great religious tradition are mainly critical. Most of his statements on eastern religions relate to Hinduism and Buddhism, followed by Confucianism and Taoism. None of these religious traditions was ever assessed from within and according to its own criteria. Yet mostly, Teilhard did not make his comparisons from a narrowly dogmatic point of view. His comments are based on a largely universalistic perspective, concerned with seeking a richer, more adequate spirituality for humankind today. In fact, this universalistic perspective is the very reason why he often judged existing religions so critically.

Certain descriptions of Hinduism and Buddhism have already been quoted. Here, brief mention may be made of Teilhard's few and rather harsh comments on Islam. He described Islam most inadequately as "no more than a backward-looking revival of Judaism,"[5] a "residual Judaism" that "in spite of the number of its adherents and its continual progress...contributes no special solution to the modern religious problem."[6] Although only made in passing, these remarks are not based on total ignorance. One must remember that Teilhard lived for three years in a predominantly Islamic country and knew several Islam scholars, some of whom he counted as his friends. During his extensive travels, he also occasionally had the opportunity to discuss religious questions with educated, devout Muslims. This makes the brevity of his remarks and the obvious lack of understanding even more disconcerting, especially for us today when there exists much more information and awareness regarding the wealth of social, religious, scientific, and historical developments in Islamic countries.

Teilhard's works contain a few more positive references to Islam. Among them is a curt acknowledgment of the insights of medieval Islamic philosophy into the close interrelationship between humans and nature. Also mentioned with approval is the recognition of the organic nature of society found in the works of some Islamic thinkers.[7] Several references to the mysticism of the Sufis are also present in Teilhard's writings. The cosmic sense of "oneness" experienced by the Sufi is, in his view, similar to that of the Hindu and Christian mystic,[8] and yet it belongs to a "mysticism of the monist or pantheist type."[9]

Writing from a comparative perspective in 1933, Teilhard thought that Islam, like other religious beliefs, faced serious difficulties in the modern world. He commented:

> Islam has retained the idea of the existence and the greatness of God. That, it is true, is the seed from which everything may one day be born again; but at the same time Islam has achieved the extraordinary feat of making this God as ineffective and sterile as a non-being for all that concerns the knowledge and betterment of the world. After destroying a great deal and creating locally an ephemeral beauty, Islam offers itself today as a principle of fixation and stagnation.[10]

To some extent, Teilhard also recognized that contemporary Islam was showing signs of renewal. He spoke of "high-minded" Islamic thinkers who were "alive to modern requirements."[11] An Islamic "renascence" may therefore be well conceivable. Yet he also asked whether it is really the spirit of the Koran that fires the enthusiasm of young Muslims, or whether it is not some kind of "new religion" that, he thought, had been influenced by Christian ideas.[12]

It is easier to witness the dynamic activity of the Islamic world in the twenty-first century than it was during the 1930s. Teilhard's severe judgment of Islam is basically because his evolutionary thought "represents the exact opposite of Islam" with its immobilist position based on the Koran.[13] Thus, it is mainly the ideas of Islamic modernists and reformers that appealed to him. It is not surprising, therefore, that his thought is sometimes compared with the universalistic and evolutionary perspective of the Islamic reformer Muhammed Iqbal,[14] now so highly revered and influential in Pakistan. According to a French commentator, Teilhardian ideas are also said to have found an extraordinary response "in certain Islamic milieux of Morocco."[15]

Besides Islam, the historical riches of Confucianism and Taoism were also largely ignored. To Teilhard, it appeared that no one who has been deeply influenced by modern culture and the knowledge that goes with it can sincerely be a Confucian, a Buddhist or Muslim (unless he is prepared to live a double interior life, or profoundly to modify for his own use the terms of his religion).[16]

This statement, written down in 1933 in Peking, indicates the very limited scope of Teilhard's assessment of eastern religious traditions. As John Grim and Mary Evelyn Tucker have commented in a brief biographical account, Teilhard's major interest during his years of travel in China

was primarily in the natural terrain. Although he interacted with innumerable ethnic groups he rarely entered into their cultures more than was necessary for expediting his business or satisfying a general interest. One of the ironies of his career is that the Confucian tradition and its concern for realization of the cosmic identity of heaven, earth and man remained outside of Teilhard's concerns. Similarly tribal peoples and their earth-centered spirituality were regarded by Teilhard as simply an earlier stage in the evolutionary development of the Christian revelation."[17]

It was Indian monistic thought that always held a particular fascination for Teilhard, although he encountered Hinduism only briefly and rather late in life, and he then did not feel attracted to its rich forms of religiosity. Moreover, in the judgment of his friend, Henri de Lubac, who knew him well, Teilhard "always seems to have sympathized more with certain aspects of Buddhism" than with Hinduism.[18] It was particularly the universalist and cosmic, rather than the contemplative, perspectives of Buddhism that appealed to him. During his first visit to the Far Fast, he expressed the hope that Christianity might be renewed through the contact with Buddhism.[19] Later, however, he judged Buddhism dead in China,[20] although he was aware of the existence of Buddhist forces of renewal. Yet the "varieties of neo-Buddhism" that could be observed in China and elsewhere were quite rightly seen by him as developments linked to western influences.[21]

Teilhard's approach to eastern religious thought must be criticized for its all-too-summary assessment and for his undifferentiated use of the term "eastern religions." Like certain earlier western scholars, he often subsumed both Buddhism and Hinduism under this term without distinguishing their specific beliefs and practices. For example, when speaking about the great appeal of eastern religions, he writes, "Let us, to put a name to them, say Buddhism." But then he goes on to talk about India, and especially Indian monism, which contrasts most sharply with his own understanding of the spirit:

> For the Hindu sage, spirit is the homogeneous unity in which the complete adept is lost to self, all individual features and values being suppressed. All quest for knowledge, all personalization, all earthly progress are so many diseases of the soul. *Matter is dead weight and illusion.* By contrast, spirit is for me...the unity by synthesis in which the saint realizes his full being, carrying to the furthest possible point what differentiates its nature, and the particular resources it possesses....*Matter is heavily loaded, throughout, with sublime possibilities.*[22]

The "venerable cosmogonies of Asia" did not reveal to Teilhard a God who is "a savior of man's work." In earlier years, he thought that he might be able to discern such a God in the East but, by the beginning of the 1930s, he became firmly convinced that a new path to mysticism was emerging on the "road of the West." Although this new way implies "a contagious faith in an ideal to which human life can be given,"[23] it is far from being a clearly signposted road. In fact, at present it may be conceived as a road pointing toward several possible directions, among which a choice has still to be made.

Teilhard was always looking for a faith that could take up, sustain, and further animate the dynamism of the modern world. But where is there such a faith—a faith that can grow and expand, rather than one that regresses by simply reaffirming a distant, deadly past against a living present? This tension between the present and the past has caused a state of crisis affecting all religions, whether in the East or West. The recognition of this crisis led Teilhard to a general critique of the state of religions in the modern world. This is more comprehensive in scope than his assessment of eastern religions but equally brief in its formulation.

Religions in a State of Crisis

The experience of the long Yellow Expedition to Inner Mongolia during the years 1931–32 made Teilhard particularly sensitive to the question of what meaning religion has for the contemporary world. During this expedition, which lasted for almost a year, a group of men from widely different backgrounds lived and worked together as a closely knit team. Many of them had no religious faith at all. With the help of new half-track automobiles (*autochenilles*) developed by the French car manufacturer, Citroën, the two groups of the expedition set out to cross Central Asia from both the West and the East, hoping to discover the ancient Silk Road while simultaneously testing the qualities of Citroën equipment.

Teilhard had been invited to take part as a geologist. He belonged to the "China group," which started from Peking and crossed China by traversing the Gobi Desert, experiencing many hair-raising adventures en route. They penetrated into remote and hostile areas of the globe, characterized by many ancient features, not least the religious customs and practices of their inhabitants. The contrast between old and new worlds was particularly apparent here.

During this period of intensive travel across Central Asia, Teilhard became acutely aware of the need for a new approach in presenting religion in the modern world. After returning from the expedition, he not only developed the idea of two different "roads," but two of his subsequently written essays, "Christianity in the World" (1933)[24] and "How I Believe" (1934),[25] include an explicit discussion of the contemporary situation of the world's religions. He described this situation as one of trial, for the great religions are being "put to the test."[26]

159

According to Teilhard, all religions are facing a crisis that has primarily come about through the rise of modernity. The development of the modern world does not only imply scientific and technological advances accompanied by deep social and cultural changes, but it means even more a change in the nature of knowledge itself. This, in turn, has led to a profound alteration in people's vision of the world and in the perception of their own consciousness. The historical roots of this transformation have often been analyzed by Teilhard.[27] The following passage can stand for many others that express the nature of this change:

> Among the most disquieting aspects of the modern world is its general and growing dissatisfaction in religious matters....There is no present sign anywhere of Faith *in a state of expansion*: there are only, here and there, *creeds* that at the best are holding their own, where they are not positively retrogressing....Any effort to understand what is now taking place in human consciousness must of necessity proceed from the fundamental change of perspective which since the sixteenth century has shattered and rendered movable to our experience what, until then, had always seemed to be the ultimate in stability: the world itself. To our clearer vision the universe is no longer a State but a Process. The cosmos has become a Cosmogenesis....
>
> ...And now we find that man in his turn is identified with an anthropogenesis. This is a major event which must lead, as we shall see, to the profound modification of the whole structure not only of our Thought but of our Beliefs.[28]

In Teilhard's view, humanity's deepest beliefs, that is, the search for an Absolute and the experience of God, are in need of new forms of expression. For him, like for other modern thinkers, the human being has "become adult,"[29] responsible for the making of his own future. Yet at the same time, we face ever-greater problems. Thus, a situation of turmoil has arisen. Our contemporaries experience a loss of equilibrium and often lack a sense of purpose. Reflecting on the search for a goal of life, Teilhard wrote a passage in 1933 that rings even truer today:

> Lack of employment. This phrase defines, in its most immediately apparent and most tangible aspect, the crisis the world is passing through at this moment. Humanity began to be without occupation...from the first moment when its new-born mind was released from perception and immediate action, to wander in the domain of things that are distant or possible.... There are many symptoms to indicate that it is now without occupation, and that it may well continue to become increasingly so, now that the balance has finally been upset between material needs and powers of production, so that, in theory, all people have to do is to allow the machine that emancipated them to run on, and fold their arms. The present crisis is much more than a difficult interval accidentally encountered by a particular type of civilization....It expresses the inevitable result of the loss of equilibrium brought about in animal life by the appearance of thought. People no longer know today how to occupy their physical powers: but what is more serious, they do not know towards what universal and final end they should direct the driving force of their souls. It has already been said, though without sufficiently deep appreciation of the words: the present crisis is a spiritual crisis....Humanity today is undecided, and distressed, at the very peak of its power, because it has not defined its spiritual pole. It lacks religion.[30]

What particular conditions must be fulfilled for religions to point a way out of this crisis, to reveal a road leading to meaning? In Teilhard's view, religions that merely uphold the ideal of an established order and are static in their approach to human beings and the world cannot make sense of the newly discovered "dimensions and forward momentum of the universe." If religions *"are to appeal to us, and save us, they must be dynamic."*[31]

They must be able to inspire human action here and now, sustain our zest for living, and relate human life to an ultimate goal.

These are, briefly stated, the premises from which Teilhard examined existing religions. His intuitions can be inspiring, for they can spark off further creative reflections. But the lack of concrete detail is most unsatisfactory and can at times be truly misleading. It was not his aim, however, to develop a comprehensive sociology or theology of religions but rather to emphasize what is at the center of all true religion. Behind all the intellectual constructions, the many new words, the groping attempts to express what he had seen, felt, and experienced, his thought most emphatically points to the fire of that living flame whose continuity alone ensures that human beings are truly alive.

The religious crisis has two major aspects according to Teilhard. On one hand, many people are undergoing an almost permanent crisis of identity and meaning that requires spiritual answers. However, anyone sensitive to current spiritual needs also realizes the inadequacy of past religious answers to the difficult questions of the present. On the other hand, there is the critical situation of the world religions themselves, unable to supply such answers in adequate form. For Teilhard, a modern person is not "a-religious" but revolts against the narrowness of certain religious teachings. It is not atheism, but an "unsatisfied theism," from which the world suffers.[32] The existence of atheism and the whole process of secularization contain signs of a metamorphosis of the religious sense in human beings, pointing toward the development of new forms of religiousness.

Teilhard hints at the possibility of such new forms when he refers to "the religion of tomorrow"[33] or speaks of a "convergence of religions."[34] The idea of convergence, or the closer coming together of the world's religions, implies a movement from diversity toward greater unity. Such a movement of convergence cannot just happen in the West but is ultimately global, and inconceivable without a substantial contribution of the "road of the East." The importance of convergence led Teilhard to re-examine his understanding of the "road of the East."

Different Types of Eastern Spiritualities

A vigorous process of reinterpreting the traditional religious heritage of the world has been taking place in both East and West. A growing interest in the teachings of the great world religions, especially those of the East, can be observed in many quarters. This is far more obvious today than it was during Teilhard's lifetime. Even then, there were a considerable number of people already interested in eastern religions. One only needs to think of the early western adherents of Theosophy and Vedanta from the late nineteenth century onward, or of the more recent followers of different schools of Hinduism or Buddhism, such as the Hare Krishna movement, Zen meditation, or other groups from the East that have been active in Europe and America for many decades now.

Teilhard tended to disagree with western contemporaries who were overenthusiastic and uncritical admirers of the East. He felt that nothing could be more unjust than the judgment of those who "designate western civilization as materialist."[35] Yet he recognized that at present, in a time of tremendous turmoil, when humankind is in search of a soul, many people turn for enlightenment toward the East. To them, "the East stands for spirit, the West for matter."[36] For Teilhard, this is not only an oversimplified dichotomy, but spirit and matter cannot be opposed in this way. His own position was almost at the opposite pole: for him it is the West that "has set in motion a powerful mysticism."[37] However, this must not be seen in isolation, for certain elements of eastern spirituality are of great importance in the development of contemporary religious life.

This idea is especially discussed in "The Spiritual Contribution of the Far East" (1947),[38] written after Teilhard's final return from China to the West. It is his only essay with a reference to the East in its title, and it is important for its more nuanced, reflective approach, backed by detailed reading and discussions with what were then called "orientalist scholars," referring to those studying eastern religions and cultures.

Teilhard explicitly admits that he presents his own reflections without being able to claim any "special competence in the history of Asiatic thought." Yet based on his considerable experience of the Far East, he wants to offer some personal reflections to those who, under the influence of popular writings, have formed a vague and rather uniform impression of eastern spirituality. He distinguishes three types of eastern spirituality found in India, China, and Japan. In his view, India mainly represents an extraordinary sense of the one and divine, expressed through both pantheistic and theistic attitudes. However, for the Indian, in contrast to the westerner,

> the world is in some way less clear than God: so much so, that it is the world and not God whose existence presents difficulty to the intelligence and needs to be justified. The invisible is more real than the visible: that is the fundamental religious experience—initially diffuse in the poetry of the Upanishads, and gradually condensed later in the commentaries of the Vedanta— which, right up to the present day, has continually sought embodiment in a complex series of monist philosophies: while at the same time, through an accompanying exaggeration of the feeling of the "unreality of phenomena," Buddhism was being born, causing a large proportion of mystical energies to evaporate in "the intoxication of emptiness."[39]

China, by contrast, is fundamentally naturalistic and humanist in its basic orientation. Chinese thought was dominated throughout its history "by an ever-present sense of the *primacy of the tangible* in relation to the invisible." This predominant orientation is not only found in Taoism and Confucianism. Teilhard rightly points out that this attitude is so intrinsic to the Chinese that it also transformed Buddhism on its arrival in the Far East by substituting for Nirvana "the attractive, compassionate, and so human figure of Amida."[40]

Japan's particular form of humanism, in contrast to China's, is a "heroic sense of the collective." Teilhard characterizes these three different eastern spiritualities as predominantly expressing a "mysticism of God," a "mysticism of the individual confronted with the world," and a "social mysticism." They are seen to be mutually exclusive rather than complementary types, at least in their present forms.

If India is characterized by "an atmosphere of the transcendent and divine," China has always been "a focus of material and human aspirations." But it is perhaps more the *"appreciation* of man" than what Teilhard calls the *"faith* in man" and his possibilities that belongs to ancient China. To preserve the harmony of an established order, to seek equilibrium rather than conquest, such is Chinese wisdom that comes to terms with the world.[41] Japanese spirituality lacks neither dynamic movement nor the spirit of conquest but there exists no adequate structure to utilize "this magnificent source of energy." The practical spirit of service and sacrifice found in Japan has remained within the narrow boundaries of a racial mentality, centered on a common origin, giving rise to "an exclusive, closed mysticism."[42]

"God and his transcendence; the world and its value; the individual and the importance of the person: mankind and social requirements"—each of these problems has found a particular solution in eastern spiritualities, but no overall synthesis has been attempted. It is precisely the search for such an integrated approach, that Teilhard saw as "the problem of the spirit, taken in its complete totality."[43] The East has not solved this problem yet; nor, one might add, has the West.

Teilhard thought that a *new* solution, never tried before, might ultimately be found on the new "road of the West." This is described as "an advance, a general breakthrough" of the spirit, a drive of "all reflective consciousness in the direction of an increasing unity," a convergence still to be achieved.[44] This new type of spirituality is a hitherto untried synthesis that places a supreme value on all human efforts, including the most material activities. Far from having found its clear expression yet, Teilhard saw this spirituality as the basic "note," or orientation, underlying the "creative fever of the West." Combined with it, "there is a true mystical ferment...a young mysticism, original and powerful, still perhaps clumsily constructed and ill-expressed in its theory, but perfectly defined in its main lines...." This mysticism is animated by love as "the supreme spiritual energy" and is centered on "the irreplaceable and incommunicable essence" of the human person.[45] While Europe is looking to Asia for wisdom, Asia is turning to the West for its science and technology.

Teilhard asked, with some justification, Are there not also signs that the East is joining up "not only technologically but mystically too, with the road of the West"? If such a juncture between the two roads is to occur in the future, what will be the contribution, the specific "note" of the East? Against the naive conception of a unitary form of eastern spirituality, easily assumed by many westerners, Teilhard briefly points out that the East has developed several types of spirituality that are incompatible with each other in their present forms. These different types have not yet found their common meeting point. Nor has the West, after surging ahead in certain developments, been able to determine the possible and necessary "confluence of East and West,"[46] understood as the future meeting of eastern and western spiritualities and cultures. The eastern "currents" will contribute "greater vigor" and provide a "qualitative enrichment" to the new "road of the West." Taken together, these two roads may lead to the development of a new spirituality for humanity.

Teilhard did not envisage this meeting of the two roads to occur like the merging of "two complementary blocs," or "two conflicting principles," into one. Instead, he likened their confluence and convergence to the way several rivers come together to cut a breach through a barrier common to them all. The breakthrough is first achieved through widening out an opening initially cut by one of the rivers. For complex historical reasons, the opening of such a road, connected with "a new surge of human consciousness," occurred in the West. Ultimately, both East and West will contribute to the shape and direction that this road is going to take. For example, Teilhard saw signs of a spiritual rapprochement in the influence that western thought has had on contemporary Indian thinkers such as Tagore and on recent developments in China and Japan.[47]

With human consciousness at the threshold of a new stage of development, the real battle for the spirit is only beginning now, according to Teilhard. All available forces, whether from East or West, have to be brought into action to win this battle:

For a long time now, the eastern soul (Hindu, Chinese, or Japanese), each following its own specially favored line and its own special way, has had the answer to the religious aspirations whose pole of convergence and whose laws we, in the West, are now engaged in determining more exactly: that answer is no doubt less clear than ours and less of a synthesis, but it has, possibly, a deeper innate foundation, and greater vigor. And what results may we not expect when the confluence is at last effected? In the first place, there will be the quantitative influx of a vast human flood now waiting to be used; but what is even more valuable, there will be the qualitative enrichment produced by the coming together of different psychic essences and different temperaments.[48]

In the religious as in the scientific domain, it is only in union with all other people "that each individual can hope to reach what is most ultimate and profound in his own being." The spiritual contribution of the Far East does not so much lie in "a higher form of spirit" that, some mistakenly think, the East may give to the West, but, rather, the new "mystical note rising from the West" will be enlarged and enriched by the deepest insights of the East. What is meant by this?

Contributions from East and West

Why does Teilhard believe in a new "mystical note" rising from the West? He thought that the new mysticism of the "road of the West" is not only rooted in the western religious tradition; it is also closely linked with new forms of humanism, and with the whole experience of modernity, that first emerged in the West. In a globalized world, this is now becoming universalized.

In some way, we can compare this with the development of modern science as universal and global. It is well known that western science, during antiquity and medieval times, absorbed many ideas and inventions from the East, but the breakthrough to truly modern science first occurred in the West. Joseph Needham speaks about the "fusion point" of eastern and western scientific ideas that has occurred in most sciences but not in all. It has brought about what he calls the "oecumenogenesis" of modern science, but this process of "fusion" or convergence affects different sciences at a different rate and thus can be faster or slower: "The more 'biological' the science, the more organic its subject-matter, the longer the process seems to take; and in the most difficult field of all, the study of the human and animal body in health and disease, the process is as yet far from accomplished."[49] If one transfers this argument to other disciplines, one can say that a "fusion point" of eastern and western ideas in the more abstract areas of philosophy and religion is even further away. Yet such a "confluence" of thought is necessary if a truly universal civilization and a new realm of religious and mystical experience are to emerge.

Thus, as with the emergence of modern science, Teilhard thought that the creative religious effort required for the present would initially come from the West. In other words, it will develop in the general direction that the West has begun to take already, but it is a process far from complete. It not only implies the transformation of the West's own religious heritage but an ultimate "confluence" or "convergence" of religions. Teilhard was thinking of a new type of spirituality when he referred, rather misleadingly, to the "road of the West," as if it existed already and had already reached its mature form of development. At other times, however, he described this new spirituality much more suitably as a "new mysticism of convergence."

Interreligious encounter and dialogue, as we know it in the present, more open climate of thought, was practiced less during Teilhard's days. Yet many of his ideas are favorable to a meeting of religions in a convergent perspective. For him this implied the search for a differentiated unity still to be achieved rather than the claim that an essential, reductionist unity already exists. The meeting of religions cannot be found in "the sterile and conservative ecumenism of a 'common ground' but [in] the creative ecumenism of a 'convergence' on a common ideal."[50] This is not to be understood as syncretism. Teilhard clearly perceived both the diversity and complementarity of the "active currents of faith." Religious diversity is here to stay, just as social, cultural, and racial diversity have to be acknowledged and lived with. Rightly understood, they offer tremendous resources for mutual enrichment. Besides, underneath the outward diversity, convergent lines of development can be perceived. One may wonder how far the different religious traditions today are not in the process of developing a unitary and differentiated, though not uniform, belief system that is becoming increasingly similar.

R. E. Whitson has fruitfully explored the potential of a convergent perspective for the encounter of religions. In his book *The Coming Convergence of World Religions*[51] he writes:

> As with general cultural convergence, religious convergence is unitive yet diversified. It excludes reduction and substitution as emerging from the unitive process, expecting, rather, some form of unitive pluralism. Religious convergence is not syncretism...[nor does it] consist in the emergence of one tradition as simply dominant and absorbing the others.
>
> ...The religious traditions have developed separately and now will continue their development together. They have a *further meaning together* which we had not even suspected. It is not that we will discover that all along they really were all the same. On the contrary, we must expect to find that their differences...are actually meaningful together, contribute to each other and constitute the new unity out of their diversity.[52]

In Teilhardian terms, convergent lines toward a creative religious effort are appearing on the horizon. They hold the promise for a future of religion, but a religion unlike that of the past. It is a religion that sees the world as one and, through a continuous and dynamic development, seeks a new synthesis beyond the past dichotomies of the religious and secular, sacred and profane, spiritual and material, heavenly and worldly. It is in this sense that Teilhard wrote that the era not of religions "but of *religion* has by no means been left behind: it is quite certainly only beginning."[53]

Religions will come closer together through a concurrent process of differentiation and unification, and not through reduction and syncretism. It is not in terms of institutional forms and power but, rather, in the essential, activating force of what traditionally is called "spirituality" that Teilhard saw the increasing influence of religion and, even more, of a rightly understood mysticism. From 1933 onward, he referred to the "convergence of religions." However, it was only in later years that he expressed more clearly what this might imply. He then saw the tension between religious "alternatives" less in terms of East and West than between opposing types of belief. What is most urgently required is the integration of the perennial insights of the world's religions with the new insights of the modern world in evolution.

For him the convergence of roads had to occur around a "religion of action,"[54] a premise not necessarily accepted by all religious thinkers today. The image of different rivers using a breach first cut by one of them as well as the concept of convergence imply an overall orientation, not an indiscriminate fusion. Convergence occurs around a principal "axis." The essential insights of the Christian tradition, together with certain developments of the modern world, are seen as such an axis, whose positive characteristics lie in its world-affirming and world-transforming capacity and its potential for a mysticism of action.

The Role of Christianity

Teilhard understood Christianity itself less and less as a particular set of doctrines than as a specific *axis* of development, important for the future of religion, acting as some sort of catalyst for the development of modern spirituality. The *new* road of spirituality that he envisaged is "amplified by a long living tradition" of what is most essential to Christianity.[55] Many past rituals and beliefs may well be irrelevant at present. Thus, one might well ask, What will remain of Christianity many years later?[56]

A merely backward-looking revival would be inadequate for any religious tradition; it would indicate the absence of true religious creativity. Christianity may have served as "the matrix of western civilization," and "Everyone is prepared to admit the importance of Christianity *in the past*; but what about the present? and still more about the future?"[57]

Teilhard's writings include a detailed critique of certain Christian beliefs, and more than once he suggested new lines of interpretation. This reinterpretation of Christianity for the modern world must be recognized as one of the major purposes of Teilhard's work, but it can only be briefly touched upon here. In 1927, when speaking of the possibility of a spiritual collaboration between East and West, he wrote:

> Look: we just can't breathe in our different compartments, our closed categories. Without destroying our more limited organisms, we must fuse them together, synthesize them....The fact is, one sometimes gets the impression that our little churches hide the earth from us. I've just remembered a thought I first had over ten years ago. There are some who want to identify Christian orthodoxy with "integrism," that is to say with respect for the tiniest wheels of a little microcosm constructed centuries ago. In reality, the true Christian ideal is "integralism," namely the extension of the Christian directives to all the resources contained in the world. Integralism or integrism, dogma-as-axis or dogma-as-framework, there we have the struggle that has been going on in the Church for more than a century. Integrism is simple and convenient, both for the faithful and the authorities. But it implicitly excludes from God's Kingdom (or denies on principle) the huge potentialities whirling around us in social and moral questions, in philosophy, science, etc....[58]

Later, he stated in his important essay "How I Believe" (1934), written as "a personal confession,"[59] what he considered this "dogma-as-axis" to be. While Christianity "is eminently the religion of the imperishable and the personal," whose God "thinks, loves, speaks, punishes, rewards, in the same way as *a person* does," much of the Christian road has been too other-worldly in the past: "Christianity gives the impression of not believing in human progress. It has never developed *the sense of the earth*, or it has allowed that sense to lie dormant in it." It is precisely the encounter between Christianity and the development of the modern world—the sense of the Earth in all its aspects—that make a new synthesis, a convergent road, possible and necessary.

The axis and center of the Christian tradition relate to the figure of Christ, reinterpreted by Teilhard on a cosmic scale as the universal Christ who combines the personal with the universal. This mystery of the Divine incarnate in matter and flesh answers both monistic and theistic aspirations. Its powerful vision was for Teilhard the fulfillment of "the very hopes which neither the pantheisms of the East nor those of the West could satisfy."

As a synthesis of Christ and the universe in evolution, the universal Christ represents a figure that can give "meaning and direction to the world."[60] The "essence of Christianity is neither more nor less than a belief in the unification of the world in God by the Incarnation."[61] Without the reality of the incarnation, Christianity loses all its splendor and power of attraction, its distinctive dynamic. Abandoning this mystery would mean to lose sight of the true heart of reality. Teilhard would therefore have had little sympathy with some contemporary christological debates denying the reality of the incarnation. He emphasized, by contrast, its central role and referred to the "infinite possibilities which the 'universalization' of Christ opens up for religious thought."[62] It was in this context that he first spoke of

> a general convergence of religions upon a universal Christ who fundamentally satisfies them all: that seems to me the only possible conversion of the world, and the only form in which a religion of the future can be conceived.[63]

It would be wrong to conclude from this that Christianity represents the fulfillment of all religions. Teilhard's symbol of the "universal Christ" is by no means identical with Christianity but far transcends its limits. The central axis around which a convergence of religions might occur is not identical with Christianity as we know it but, rather, with *Christianity faithfully extended to its utmost limit.*[64] First expressed in 1933, he later modified this view and "universalized" it further, when he recognized more clearly the implications of convergence for the contemporary situation of the world's religions.

The Meaning of the "Convergence of Roads"

Teilhard sometimes compared the different religions with the "living branches" of a plant, growing from its central stem. He also likened them to "rivers" joining a stream, or "currents" within the one great river of humankind. At present, these currents are still at cross-purposes, but they can be seen as "coming to run together."[65] Thus expressed, one might think of a simple fusion of all religions. This impression is also gained when he refers to "confluence," which merely means the flowing together of various rivers, without any indication of the direction of the flow. Thus, he speaks about the "confluence" as well as the "convergence," of religions, but one has to point out that there exists a subtle, but very important, difference between these two terms.

Teilhard applied the idea of *confluence* to a number of interrelated phenomena. In subtitles he referred to "The Confluence of Religions" (1939),[66] "The Confluence of Human Branches" (1939),[67] "The Confluence of Thought" (1940),[68] and "The Confluence of East and West" (1947).[69] These expressions all point to the idea that there is a movement toward greater unification at work in human life and thought, a movement that also affects the world's religions. Nothing is implied about the direction of this movement, however.

That there is such a direction and selection, rather than an indiscriminate random gathering, is definitely expressed by the term *convergence*. It connotes a certain definite orientation, indicated by three aspects: convergence occurs around a central axis; the movement of convergence leads toward a "summit," where the different currents truly converge; convergence also implies a certain irreversibility of movement. The most frequent similes used by Teilhard to describe this movement are either the spiral, which, unlike the simple coil, is truly centered, or the cone, which has an apex.[70]

Like *confluence*, the term *convergence* is applied to the whole of humanity, to human thought and civilization in general.

In fact, the convergence of religions is understood by Teilhard as a special case of the more general convergence of humankind that can be clearly observed today. Through external conditions, humankind is being drawn closer together to form one world, and ultimately one civilization, marked by a complex unity-in-diversity rather than being reduced to sameness. However, external forces alone cannot bring about such complex and diversified, real unity. They can only produce what has been called "a mechanistic unity";[71] they do not create a truly organic unity between people. To bring about unanimity and transform the disparate fragments of humankind into a new humanity, the spiritual energies of inner bonds of love and fellowship are required. For this reason, Teilhard particularly stressed the importance of the convergence of religions for the development of such unity.

Confluence and *convergence* are sometimes used interchangeably in Teilhard's writings, but where this occurs, the first term tends to imply the directionality of the second. An exception is the explicit distinction between the two concepts found in a letter of 1953:

> I insist on the possible difference…between human "confluence" and "convergence": the first would come to an end with the formation of a "pool"…,—the second leaves open the possibility (or even the probability) of a critical point of Reflection…ahead.[72]

Convergence always occurs around a specific axis that denotes the overall direction of future developments. In the evolutionary framework of Teilhard's thought, the "stability of essences," characteristic of the static philosophies of being, has been replaced by the "permanence of axes." However, Teilhard's dynamic vision is not a philosophy of pure becoming in the Heraclitean sense of the ancient Greeks, where everything is simply in flux. Nor is it like the Buddhist view of impermanence and change. Instead of being an undifferentiated movement and constant flux, change occurs as "convergent genesis," bringing about the birth of some new mutation or synthesis, both at a higher level and in the forward move of time.[73]

To articulate this idea even more clearly, Teilhard uses another notion from the life sciences and applies it to the development of religion. This is the concept of *phylum*. The *phyla* are the major lines or branches of the evolutionary series of living forms, the "natural units" of the world. In *The Human Phenomenon*, Teilhard describes the phylum in the context of the expansion of life.[74] It is a living "bundle" that develops on its own, autonomously; it is also a collective reality of many forms, bound together through a specific structure and characterized by a dynamic nature that can only be seen properly in movement. By analogy, the term is used for religion. Christianity is said to be a *phylum* in the development of religions, but so is "the religion of tomorrow":

> Religion, like science or civilization, has (if I may use the term) an "onto-genesis" co-extensive with the history of humankind. Thus, true religion (by which I mean the form of religion at which the general groping of reflective action on earth will one day arrive), like every other reality of the "planetary" order, partakes of the nature of a "phylum."[75]

The use of such terms as *axis* and *phylum* indicates that when Teilhard sees the different religions as branches, he does not mean this at all in the sense in which, for example, Ramakrishna and Gandhi speak about all religions being branches of the same tree. The latter imply by this image the undifferentiated unity of all religions, what one might call their "common ground." Their idea proceeds from the assumption of an "essential unity" of all religions and points to the relative nature of all formulated creeds. In this sense, unity is perceived as an already existing basis or essence; it is not a summit still to be achieved.

A unity of convergence, by contrast, represents a synthesis that integrates and transcends, rather than reduces, the multiplicity of existing religions. Seen in this perspective, Hindu universalism toward other religions is comparable to its monistic pattern in mysticism. Thus, two incompatible attitudes are apparent in the notion of the convergence of religions, so long as it is not decided whether such convergence "must be effected between lines of equal value (syncretism) or along a privileged central axis."[76]

For Teilhard, unity is not pre-given, not reducible to something already in existence. Like all living things, unity has to grow and take shape over time. The different branches of a tree are not alike; they differ in form and importance. The growth of a tree advances mainly through a central stem—a trunk—and individual branches have their points of growth too. There is both differentiation and unity, and there are major lines of development. In this perspective, the convergence of roads is not a simple coming together, a mere random confluence. It implies neither a reduction in what is essential nor an artificial syncretism. Particular elements of growth in the religious traditions of East and West favor convergence around a specific axis. Nevertheless, such an axis must integrate several components from different sources.

The idea of convergence is a very fruitful and powerful one. It first took shape in Teilhard's mind through the convergent nature of his own experiences in West and East, in science and religion. But the idea of convergence has a great potential for further development,[77] going well beyond the use Teilhard himself made of this concept. It is without doubt that the distinctions between the "road of the East" and the "road of the West" are redundant from a contemporary global perspective. They had already receded into the background during the last years of Teilhard's own life when they were subsumed, or rather overtaken, by his far more compelling and attractive vision of a "convergence of roads." More than the convergence of roads, or the confluence of East and West, the emphasis on the "convergence of religions" presents a thought of seminal importance today, at least for people who prefer planetary to ethnocentric thinking and are working for greater unity in the world.

A convergent encounter of the world religions has vital consequences for the understanding and practice of spirituality. More and more signs point to the growing influence of spirituality in all areas of life today. For more than any institution, ritual, or creed, it is the realm of the spiritual that is coming to be seen as the essential area of religion. The exploration of this field is gaining increasing interest, and more people than ever before are attracted to venture on hitherto uncharted roads into a territory of great promise.

The idea of a new spirituality born from the experience of convergent interreligious and intercultural encounter belongs into a wider context, namely, that of the close relationship between religion and the general dynamic of human, cultural, and social evolution. The interdependence of evolution and religion is as decisive for understanding Teilhard's approach to religions in West and East as it is for his reinterpretation of Christianity. Only when considering this crucial aspect of his thought can one understand why it is important to distinguish between different types of spirituality and mysticism, and why, in spite of the existing global religious diversity, a more complex and comprehensive unity of convergence can be envisaged among the different religions.

8

RELIGION AND EVOLUTION

We often simply understand the word *evolution* to refer to biological evolution, or to the emergence and development of living forms, as outlined by Charles Darwin and other scientists. Nevertheless, let us not forget that the word *evolution* itself evolved, and that Darwin was not the first to use it. Social and historical thinkers before him had already applied this concept to the development of the human mind and to that of different societies. Only subsequently was the idea introduced into biology. Already during the eighteenth century, French philosophers like Montesquieu, Diderot, Rousseau, and Voltaire thought about evolutionary development and contributed ideas that would eventually lead to new thinking about the mutability of species. Such new thought departed from the belief held since antiquity, and reflected in the stories of the Bible, that the chain of beings is fixed, not changing and evolving. It was in fact the suggestions of his predecessors that inspired Darwin to adopt and develop the theory of evolution in order to explain the observations on animals and plants he had collected during his famous voyage to South America on HMS *Beagle*.

A great deal of interest in Darwin and his theory of evolution was generated in 2009 through the celebration of the 200th anniversary of his birth (February 12, 1809), and the 150th anniversary of the publication of his most famous work, *On the Origin of Species* (published on November 12, 1859). The great international attention given to Darwin's achievements during that year produced innumerable debates and publications about the contemporary understanding of evolution. Since Darwin's days the scientific understanding of the working, or what is sometimes called the "mechanism," of evolution has been greatly expanded and modified. Several scientists have also proposed interpretations of the *wider* meaning of evolution, for it is without doubt that the social importance of evolution is enormous, not only for understanding the past but for providing insights or even guidelines for the future.

The fact of the evolution of our planet Earth and of the organic evolution of all life is one of the most fundamental perspectives for understanding the world in which we live. But how does this basic fact relate to the way we think and act? So far, the conscious thinking of many individuals has been little affected by the discovery of evolution. The life of their inner worlds has taken little cognizance of the dynamics of the outer world. However, the recognition of evolution as a unifying perspective and process affecting all aspects of the modern world has also had revolutionary consequences for human thinking. Few religious thinkers have taken the trouble of wrestling with this challenging issue; few have reflected on the crucial importance of evolution for religious thought and practice.

Teilhard is one of the few modern thinkers on religion for whom evolution provided the dominant note of his entire work. As he wrote in his best-known book, *The Human Phenomenon*, evolution was to him much more than "a theory, a system or a hypothesis." On the contrary, he considered it to be "a general condition to which all theories, all hypotheses, all systems must bow....Evolution is a light illuminating all facts, a curve that all lines must follow."[1] From early on he was conscious of the importance of evolution for contemporary religion, and much of his search for a new spirituality commensurate with the modern world revolves around the attempt to bring together mystic-religious insights with evolutionary understanding.

The basic structure of an evolutionary perspective underlies all his thought on religion; it shaped his critical comments on particular religions and provoked certain general reflections on the place of religion in the modern world. Already in 1916, he wrote:

> Religion and evolution should neither be confused nor divorced. They are destined to form one single contin-

uous organism, in which their respective lives prolong, are dependent on, and complete one another, without being identified or lost....Since it is in our age that the duality has become so markedly apparent, it is for us to effect the synthesis.[2]

This synthesis he saw as his lifelong task and, in one way or another, all his essays touch upon religion and evolution. Nevertheless, three main themes can be singled out in particular: the recognition of the historical evolution of religions in the past; the evolutionary role of religion for humanity's present and future development; and the further evolution of religion itself.

Historical Evolution of Religions in the Past

In the past, religions developed for the most part independently of each other. Like the great civilizations, they grew "in patches," in separate geographical and historical contexts. When they came into contact at all, it was frequently in a situation of contrast and opposition, where one religion tended to dominate, strongly influence, or even supplant another. Today, in a post-colonial world, all societies are economically, technically, and scientifically closely interdependent; they need to cooperate if they want to survive. With more direct, much faster means of communication, and many more sources of information, we also have many more opportunities to gain greater knowledge and experience of each other's religious traditions. This new situation calls for a new understanding of religion that will make more people comprehend each other's religious differences, so that they can speak about them in a mutually meaningful way rather than in terms of exclusive opposition.

Reflecting on religion from a historical and evolutionary perspective, Teilhard was convinced that the historical evolution of the great religions cannot provide the full answer as to the nature and meaning of religion itself. The quest for the origin of religion in the history and prehistory of humankind has proved as elusive as the search for the absolute origin of human beings themselves. Nineteenth-century scholars committed a "genetic fallacy" when they assumed that the beginning or genesis of religion could be fully traced and analyzed or, alternatively, that a recovery of the absolute beginnings of each tradition would provide the ultimate touchstone by which existing religions could be assessed. Teilhard often expressed the view that the full meaning of a particular religion, as of anything else, does not manifest itself at its moment of origin, just as we cannot discern a fully grown adult in a newborn baby but recognize that there exists a great difference between them.

He therefore did not share the views of those who nostalgically preached an eternal return to the origins of religion, to a golden age, when humans were supposedly at unity with nature and themselves. Nor did he side with progressive thinkers who took religion to be an outdated stage of earlier human development, now surpassed. The knowledge of evolution may have led some to think

> that nothing of our past beliefs remained. Indeed there have been a great number of systems in which the fact of religion was interpreted as a psychological phenomenon linked with the childhood of humanity. At its greatest, at the origins of civilization, it had gradually to decline and give place to more positive theories from which God (a personal and transcendent God above all) must be excluded. This was a pure illusion.[3]

Most of all it is necessary to combat a narrow understanding of religion based on the assumption that "science has made God and religions superfluous." In the past, religions encompassed a complex variety of beliefs and practical skills from which, through increasing differentiation over a long period of time, separate disciplines with their own methods and results emerged. However, this does not mean that "the need for an Absolute," on which, according to Teilhard, all religions are based, disappeared in the course of that differentiation. In fact, this need is becoming more apparent in the modern world than ever before. It is precisely the function of religion to provide a "dominating principle of order, and an axis of movement." More than anything else, religion gives human beings "something of supreme value, to create, to hold in awe, or to love."

In certain cases, religion may well be "opium," as Karl Marx maintained, or simply a wish fulfillment providing humans with solace and escape, as Sigmund Freud thought; yet this is not the true role of religion. At the critical stage of our present development, the nature of religion is coming into sharper focus too and may be recognized with greater clarity than in the past. For Teilhard, "the phenomenon of religion cannot be regarded as the manifestation of a transitory stage which is destined to grow weaker and disappear with the growth of mankind." Rather, religion "must of itself grow greater and more clearly defined," to the same extent that humanity becomes more adult.[4] Teilhard was fond of quoting Julian Huxley's idea that in the human being evolution has now become conscious of itself, "dangerously and critically so—conscious and perfected to the point of being able to control its own driving forces and to rebound upon itself."[5]

Nevertheless, despite—or, in fact, because of—a tremendous drive toward human unity, "we are passing through a critical phase of individualism" when a "kind of rebellious independence becomes the ideal moral attitude. Intellectually, this dispersion of past efforts and thoughts takes the form of agnosticism."[6] Teilhard thinks it possible, and likely, that humankind is at the threshold of higher forms of consciousness at both a personal and social level. The responsibility for further self-evolution lies now with humans themselves rather than with external factors. Rightly understood, a higher social integration of humankind, so necessary for the survival of the human species, is linked to a fuller development of the inner resources of the human person. The development of both individual and community, therefore, are not seen as mutually exclusive but as interdependent.[7] Teilhard emphasizes at the same time the personal and social dimension of religious beliefs, and this has practical implications for both religion and politics.

The immense evolutionary process is seen as progressing toward a summit. This summit is understood as both spiritual and personal. Because of the importance assigned to the personal, Teilhard considered theistic forms of belief as the highest expression of religious consciousness so far developed. However, this is precisely the form of belief that is experiencing its most acute crisis. The awakening of "the sense of the human being" and "the spirit of the earth," rather than the spirit of God, has led to the emergence of a powerful faith in the human being and the world unknown before. Religious consciousness itself is undergoing a radical transformation, not comparable to the previous emergence and development of any particular religion: "The present event is much more massive than the coming of Buddhism or Islam...." People are beginning to understand that in the future the only religion possible "is the religion which will teach them, *in the very first place*, to recognize, love, and serve with passion the universe of which we form a part."[8]

Christian monotheism is more explicitly affected by this metamorphosis than any other religious tradition. However, the increasing impact of the modern world, or what others would call the growing forces of secularization, will eventually be felt by all religions.[9] During a voyage across the Indian Ocean in 1929, while reflecting on the growing sense of the human in the modern world and the rise of indifference to Christianity, Teilhard wrote:

> Faith in the world is irresistibly establishing itself at the heart of a civilization which is still dominated by, or which at any rate was formed by, faith in Christ. Inevitably, an extremely grave organic conflict is being produced between these two principles. If we appreciate the depth of this dramatic struggle, we have a perfectly clear explanation of the troubles which, for the last century, have been disturbing the world of established religions in the West.[10]

To Teilhard, the image of God especially needed urgent redefinition. Modern people have not yet found the God they can adore, a God commensurate with the newly discovered dimensions of the universe. In 1950, he noted in his diary, "God is not dead—but HE CHANGES."[11] In a letter to a friend, he speaks of "the transformation...of the 'God of the Gospel' into the 'God of Evolution'—a transformation without deformation." This dynamic approach to the concept of God and the relation of the Divine to the world is, in fact, central to modern process theology.[12] However, a new religious vision cannot develop in cultural isolation. In Teilhard's view, it requires the coming together of experiences drawn from different religious traditions. This is nowhere more apparent than in his emphasis on the evolutionary role and function of religious insights in the general development of humankind.

Evolutionary Role of Religion in the Present and Future

To some people the process of evolution appears to be so multidirectional and multifaceted that no clear pattern is discernible. Others believe evolution either occurs randomly or moves toward greater divergence. Teilhard considers the evolutionary process to be of a convergent rather than divergent nature, pointing to the possibility of an increasingly greater unity. As expressed in a brief "profession of faith"[13] drafted in 1933, Teilhard saw this unity as gradually growing through human efforts and the ongoing work in the world. Ultimately, it is a unity of a spiritual kind, with "spirit being understood, not as an exclusion, but as the transformation or a sublimation, or a climax of matter." Seen from this perspective,

> the substantial joy of life is found in the consciousness or feeling, that by *everything* we enjoy, create, overcome, discover, or suffer, in ourselves or in the others, in any possible line of life or death (organic, biological, social, artistic, scientific, etc.) we are gradually increasing (and we are gradually incorporated into) the growing Soul or Spirit of the world.[14]

Teilhard wrote this brief "profession of faith" while he was traveling by boat to the United States to attend the 1933 Pan-Pacific Congress of Geology in Washington. He summarizes his position in three points that deserve to be quoted in full:

1. The evolution or birth of the universe is of a *convergent, not* of a divergent, nature—towards a final unity.

2. This unity (gradually built by the work of the World) is of a *spiritual* nature (spirit being understood, not as an exclusion, but as a transformation or a sublimation, or a climax of matter).

3. The centre of this spiritualized Matter, spiritual whole, therefore, has to be supremely *conscious and personal*. The Ocean collecting all the spiritual streams of the universe is not only something but somebody. He has got Itself, a face and a heart.

If one admits those three points, the entire life (including the death) becomes for each of us a continuous discovery and conquest of a divine and overwhelming Presence.[15]

This passage expresses clearly that evolution is not an impersonal, automatic process occurring outside us, completely independently from any human involvement. On the contrary, human choices and efforts have a decisive role to play in influencing the direction of evolution. To further a spiritually transforming evolutionary process toward something "supremely conscious and personal" is, to Teilhard, our most noble task, a task in which we are helped, sustained, and guided by religion.

From his earliest days, Teilhard regarded religion as the most important motivating force of the psychic, mental, and spiritual energy required for human action. As early as 1915, he wrote to his cousin:

One of the surest marks of the truth of religion, in itself and in an individual soul, is to note to what extent it brings into action, that is, causes to rise up from sources deep within each one of us a certain maximum of energy and effort. Action and sanctification go hand in hand, each supporting the other.[16]

If religion is presented here as a source of energy for the individual, the dynamic and "energizing" aspects of religion were later predominantly expressed with reference to the human group. For example, in the essay "The Phenomenon of Man" (1930), the achievement of greater human unity is seen as interlinked with morality and religion, which assume a strictly energizing and structural value over the complete Earth, and both are "closely concerned with the true conservation and progress of the universe."[17]

In "The Spirit of the Earth" (1931) the true function of religion, not always clearly perceived in the past, is "*to sustain and spur on the progress of life*." Thus, the "religious function" increases in the same direction and to the same extent as "hominization," the emergence and growth of the human. Religion grows "continuously with the human being itself" by taking on a new and more closely determined form with each new phase of humankind.[18] As stated elsewhere, religion is biologically "the necessary counterpart to the release of the earth's spiritual energy." It was "born to animate and control this overflow of spirit" and "must itself grow greater and more clearly defined in step with it and in the same degree."[19] The "phenomenon of the spirit" consists of "interiorization" or "concentration."[20] It is the "biological role" of religion not only to lead to such inner concentration but also to be an "animator" of human action in the widest sense by giving "a form to the free psychic energy of the world"[21] and sustaining the human zest for life.

Teilhard develops this theme more fully in "The Zest for Living" (1950),[22] originally a lecture given to the French branch of the World Congress of Faiths. There Teilhard explains that the mainspring for humankind's further self-evolution lies in the maintenance of a vigorous "taste for life" and for action. The greatest enemy for human beings is a *taedium vitae*, that is to say, a sense of inner boredom and indifference, a lack of meaning and ultimate value. In his view, the most essential requirement in furthering evolution consists in the provision of the necessary spiritual energy. This is "*entrusted* to the expert knowledge and skill of *religions*." Religions have an "evolutionary role" in animating human beings; they alone can give what is most vitally necessary: "a faith—and a great faith and ever more faith." Yet in the present situation, this role of maintaining the zest for living is dependent on "the combined effort of religions."[23]

Teilhard inquired into the spiritual energy resources available to the world and points to a striking contrast that applies even more forcefully to our own energy-conscious days:

> All over the earth the attention of thousands of engineers and economists is concentrated on the problem of world resources of coal, oil or uranium—and yet nobody, on the other hand, bothers to carry out a survey of the zest for life: to take its "temperature," to feed it, to look after it, and (why not, indeed?) to increase it.[24]

For him all energy is "psychic in nature," defined as "a capacity for action or, more exactly, for interaction."[25] Scientists are rightly concerned with the material energy resources of humankind; it is equally necessary, however, to take stock of our inner resources, which continually feed and shape fundamental attitudes to life and action.

Some years earlier, in 1947, he had expressed this idea already in an essay on "The Human Rebound of Evolution and its Consequences."[26] One of the themes treated there is "The Spiritual Nourishment of Human Endeavour," where he says that if

> we accept the idea of a reflective rebounding of evolution, it is not enough to reckon the future of the world in terms of reserves of mechanical energy and food supplies, or the probable longevity of the earth....the evolutionary vigor of humankind can wither away although it be surrounded by mountains of coal, oceans of petroleum and limitless stocks of corn; it can do so as surely as in a desert of ice, if the human being should lose his impulse, or worse, develop a distaste for ever-increased growth "in complexity and consciousness". With all respects to the materialist school, which still refuses to examine *human* biology, it is undeniable that in the human being the external drive of Life tends to be transformed and turn inward to become an *ardour*

187

of Life....So, if Evolution is to continue, it is this impetus which must be maintained at the heart of the human being and encouraged at all costs. Failing that upward current, almost nothing will move.[27]

Evolution in the sense of continuing development, growth, and change will also affect the "reserves of faith." For Teilhard, the quantity and quality of the religious sense available in our world must continually increase. This view is very much dependent on his overall perspective of evolution. Others might argue with equal persuasion that the forces of religion are decreasing rather than growing at present, that religion is on the retreat. However, Teilhard did not share this position; he saw the growth of religion linked to the development of increasing convergence that includes a specific direction: "a sifting and general convergence of religions, governed by and based on their value as evolutionary stimulus" for the whole of humankind.[28]

In other words, Teilhard argued for an interdependent development of evolution and religion. In his view, religions in the past were largely concerned with individual salvation, but they must now also be able to provide an ideal for the human community. Yet the various creeds have so far not fulfilled this function: "However universal their promises and visions of the beyond might be, they did not explicitly...allow any room to a global and controlled transformation of the whole of life and thought" on earth here and now. The different religions grew up at a time when truly universal perspectives did not really exist, and the need for a greater human unity was not yet realized. What is most needed today is

> no longer simply a religion of individuals and of heaven, but a religion of humankind and of the earth....In these circumstances, we are forced to recognize that nothing can subsist tomorrow...except those mystical currents which are able, through a synthesis of the traditional faith in the above and our generation's newborn faith in some opening toward the ahead....[29]

Already in 1934, Teilhard expressed the view that, since the nineteenth century, humanity has seen "the birth and establishment of a new faith: the religion of evolution." This "youthful form of religion," represented by various neohumanist and Marxist movements, is a "contagious faith in an ideal to which a human life can be given." Contemporary collective and social movements embody a powerful vision whose force of inspiration Teilhard often admired. Such movements possess a vivid "sense of the earth," a dynamic vigor and deep commitment to the development of the world that older religions often lack.

Contemporary social and political movements are based on a concern for social action and justice, and their sense of urgency contrasts sharply with the dreary piety of many religious bodies. However, ultimately, neohumanism and Marxism leave us with a "feeling of insecurity" and "incompleteness" through their inability to point toward a transcendence beyond the human being. Although vitally concerned with the raising of consciousness, many contemporary movements do not understand the true nature of the spirit as "endowed with immortality and personality."[30]

If the developments of modern society are really so truly novel, one might well ask, Why not "regroup the whole of the earth's religious power directly and *a novo* upon some 'evolutionary sense' or 'sense of the human being'—and pay no attention to the ancient creeds?" Why not, in fact, have "a completely fresh faith, rather than a rejuvenation and confluence" of the old religions?[31]

Teilhard posed these questions deliberately. He may have asked them especially with reference to Julian Huxley's attempt to create a new religion under the name of "evolutionary humanism." It is known that Teilhard greatly admired Huxley's work and recognized the similarity of its direction and intent to his own; this was acknowledged by Huxley too. The latter stated in his introduction to *The Phenomenon of Man*, "He and I were on the same quest, and had been pursuing parallel roads ever since we were young men in our twenties."[32]

Elsewhere, Huxley wrote about meeting Teilhard, "I realized that I had found not only a friend, but a partner in the intellectual and spiritual adventure."[33] In the judgment of a fellow scientist, George Gaylord Simpson, who knew Teilhard well:

> Huxley and Teilhard could hardly differ more as regards theories of evolution, attitudes towards science, and conclusions as to theology, but they both have proposed systems in which, in quite different ways and proportions, science and mysticism are involved.[34]

In 1941, after reading Huxley's *The Uniqueness of Man,* Teilhard noted, "In a way so parallel to my own ideas (though without integrating God as the term of the series) that I feel greatly cheered." Referring to his own work, he expressed at the same time the regret that "there is nothing being published to give a constructive, dynamically Christian interpretation of what's happening."[35]

Teilhard and Huxley had personal contacts from 1946 onward. In 1951, the latter asked for a contribution to a book, and Teilhard wrote "The Transformation and Continuation in Man of the Mechanism of Evolution,"[36] dedicated to Huxley. However, the contribution was not accepted, since it did not fit in with "the tone of the other communications" that Huxley was editing.[37]

Although in sympathy with Huxley's aim to construct a suitable "ideology" for evolution by creating a faith that relates to our contemporary situation, Teilhard considered this "human faith," religiously speaking, a "little elementary." Thus, he judged it a "hazy and inefficient *Weltanschauung.*" In his opinion, Huxley's endeavor "to establish a new religion" cannot be successful because it lacks a divine pole and does not include the expectation of some "Ultra-human."[38]

In a personal letter to Julian Huxley, Teilhard stated his conviction that evolution cannot continue without a "faith" to maintain its élan, and that "such a faith (in some Ultra-human) is from now on a necessary ingredient for any form of religion (and for Christianity in particular)." Evolution has grown conscious of itself. This, as well as the phenomenon of human convergence, requires an irreversible center, both "lovable and loving."

Christianity discovered this empirically, and this gives it an irreplaceable hold "as long as one has not found anything better in the same direction."[39]

However, in his subsequent essay "The Christic" (1955), Teilhard doubted whether human consciousness, left to itself, could—even in an effort of planetary co-reflection—ever found a new religion, "the sort of religion that has been foretold with such warmth and brilliance by my friend Julian Huxley: to which he has given the name of 'evolutionary humanism.'"[40] Neohumanism may be a dynamic, and even spiritualizing, force, but it cannot provide human beings with the transcendent focus disclosed by divine revelation. In fact, it is over this issue of revealed transcendence, and the central message of the traditional religions, that Teilhard differed most markedly from Huxley's understanding of the relationship between religion and evolution.[41]

Further Evolution of Religion

In "The Zest for Living" (1950), Teilhard listed two reasons why the existing religions are of vital importance for the further evolution of human beings, and why they cannot be replaced by a completely new faith:

> First of all, there can be no doubt that, in each of the great religious branches that cover the world at this moment, a certain spiritual attitude and vision which have been produced by centuries of experience are preserved and continued; these are as indispensable and irreplaceable for the integrity of a total terrestrial religious consciousness as the various "racial" components...may well be for the looked-for perfecting of a final human zoological type.

But it is not only the "irreplaceable elements of a certain complete image of the universe" that the various currents of faith, "still active on earth, working in their incommunicable core," are handing down:

191

Very much more even than *fragments of vision*, it is *experiences of contact* with a supreme Inexpressible which they preserve and pass on. It is as though, from the final goal which evolution demands and toward which it hastens, a certain influx came down to illuminate and give warmth to our lives....

To preserve and increase on earth the "pressure of evolution" it is vitally important...that through the mutual buttressing provided by the reflection of religious ideas a progressively more real and more magnetic God be seen by us to stand out at the higher pole of hominization.[42]

The great religions all point to the revelation of a transcendent level and focus that somehow is related to the realms of human experience. But through the encounter and the closer coming together of the different religious traditions, religious discovery and experience will be greatly enhanced. For Teilhard, it is in a higher divine focus and center that humans will find the deepest source of energy and action, a center that animates all evolution and provides its culmination. We can best contribute to the world's development if "sustained and guided by the tradition of the great human mystical systems along the road of contemplation and prayer, we succeed in entering directly into receptive communication with the very source of all inner drive."[43]

It is from this source that humans, in the depth of their being, can receive love "as an effect of 'grace' and 'revelation'." Thus, the human "taste for life"—of the *goût de vivre*[44]—not only relates to a sense of survival but also beyond that includes an aspiration toward a higher form of life, a life of the spirit animated by the great insights of the religious traditions. The closer contact between the world's religions today may perhaps initiate a new level of reflection, a higher form of consciousness among human beings. The essay ends with the words, "The zest for life: the central and favored ligament, indeed, in which can be seen, within the economy of a supremely organic universe, a supremely intimate bond between mysticism, research, and biology." Then he added a note to his manuscript:

A different ending?
    Religious "contact" = Initiation of the 3rd *reflection*...
    = *neo-zest made explicit: Love* (higher form of zest!!).[45]

Closer contacts between individuals, and between religious groups, may help to create bonds of love that provide a more compelling focus for human unity than merely external forces of unification. Indeed, it was Teilhard's firm conviction that the further evolution of humanity toward greater unity "will never materialize unless we fully develop within ourselves the exceptionally strong unifying powers exerted by inter-human sympathy and religious forces."[46] He saw the encounter of religions as full of promise for the future of religion, and he was anxious to encourage all efforts toward greater unity.

Today we can perceive even greater pressure toward more collaboration, and even convergence, among different representatives of the world's religions, but this development has not yet gained its full momentum. In fact, a further convergence of the historically diverse religious traditions appeared to Teilhard to be a structurally necessary requirement for the higher evolution of humankind itself. However, such convergence is not an individual but a collective phenomenon. Religion is not "a strictly personal matter," as some might think. Teilhard condemned any individualist claim of this kind, and stated from his "spiritual-evolutionary point of view" that

> the religious phenomenon, taken as a whole, is simply the reaction of the Universe as such, of collective consciousness and human action in process of development....Religion, born of the earth's need for the disclosing of a god, is related to and co-extensive with, not the individual but the whole of humankind. In religion, as in science, is accumulated...an infinity of human enquiries. How could I fail to associate myself with that accumulation...? I would not be so foolish as to seek to build up science by my own unaided efforts. Similarly, my own effort to reach faith can succeed only when contained within a total human experience and

prolonged by it. I must therefore plunge resolutely into the great river of religions into which the rivulet of my own private enquiries has just flowed. Yet when I look around me, I see the waters are disturbed; the eddies are whirling in so many different directions. From so many quarters I can hear the summons of this or that divine revelation. To which of these apparently opposed currents am I to surrender myself, if the stream is to carry me to the ocean?[47]

In Teilhard's later years, these "opposed currents" were not so much seen by him in terms of eastern and western religions than as "rival mysticisms," cutting across the existing religions rather than opposing one group of religions to another. There exists a general tension between modern science and traditional religions; more specifically, many people experience a polarization between a "faith in God" and "faith in the world."[48] Humanity today is divided into two profoundly separated categories of "believers":

a) Those whose hopes are directed toward a spiritual state or an absolute finality situated beyond and outside this world;
b) Those who hope for the perfection of the tangible Universe within itself.[49]

For Teilhard, each of these hopes provides human beings with "a source of a magnificent spiritual impulse," but they must be brought together. They must also give equal room to both personality and transcendence. To combine in a unified gesture of worship the passionate desire to conquer the world, and the passionate longing to transcend it and be united with God, is the required vital religious act, "specifically new, corresponding to a new age in the history of the Earth."[50]

These thoughts were further elaborated in the important address "Faith in Man" (1947),[51] given at the inauguration of the French branch of the World Congress of Faiths. Another participant read the text, since Teilhard had been forbidden to speak on religious matters in public. It stresses the possibility that people

194

from different religious backgrounds can initially come together and cooperate through a commonly shared "faith in the human being," defined as "the more or less active and fervent conviction that Humankind as an organic and organized whole possesses a future" that, beyond mere survival, implies some form of higher life. Such a faith in the potential of human beings and in the future of humanity is the necessary foundation for a "basic ecumenism." Without this, an ultimate ecumenical encounter of the world's religions "at the summit" is impossible.[52] This "faith in the human being" can be a "uniting force" in the contemporary world:

> Present-day Humankind, as it becomes increasingly aware of its unity—not only past unity in the blood, but future unity in progress—is experiencing a vital need to close in upon itself. A tendency toward unification is everywhere manifest, and especially in the different branches of religion. We are looking for something that will draw us together, below or above the level of that which divides.[53]

But this "faith in the human being" has to be combined with both a "sense of the earth," and a sense of the transcendent. To achieve unity, it is necessary to share a common view of humanity and divinity. What is needed for the evolution of religion, and for a mutually enriching encounter of religions,

> is the clear perception of a sharply defined (and real) "type" of God, and an equally sharply defined "type" of humanity. —If each group retains *its own* type of God and *its own* type of humanity (and if those types are heterogeneous) then no agreement can have serious value: it will be based only on ambiguities or pure sentimentality.[54]

For Teilhard, a more sharply defined "type" of God is found in the "universal Christ," a figure "incommensurable with any prophet or any Buddha." This particular concept of God is seen as "a privileged central axis," around which a convergence of religions might occur. Yet he also says that our image of God is not complete; the human discovery of the Divine is an ongoing process. In this sense, he speaks of a "Christic nucleus,"[55] or what he calls in his diary "Christ—the 'spearhead' of monotheism."[56] On the margin of the same diary entry one can find an additional comment, "Christ-Shiva." As mentioned before, some months earlier Teilhard had noted down that our understanding of Christ must also contain those aspects of the Divine that are expressed by the Indian god Shiva.[57] It is especially the Shiva of the cosmic dance, the universal divine energy pulsating through the universe, manifesting itself at times as the blind forces of nature that, he felt, have not been integrated into the Christian notion of God.

These ideas were never fully developed. They indicate a search for a richer understanding of the concept of God and suggest the need for a cross-fertilization of different theological ways of thinking. Teilhard was aware that the necessary reinterpretation of Christianity could not take place without certain insights from other religious traditions. The most important reorientation, however, has to occur with regard to evolution itself. In the past, all great religions have "succeeded in determining certain definite axes of justice and holiness" but at present, "a disturbing gap is constantly widening between our moral life and the new conditions created by the progress of the world." One can maintain, therefore, that "however admirable and progressive these codes of interior perfection may be, they generally have the defect of having been developed, and of being kept alive, outside the perspectives of a universe in evolution."[58] Faced with contemporary problems, "it would be useless and even wrong-headed to look to the saints of the past for explicit approval or condemnation of the new attitudes suggested since the problem of human progress (as we understand it today) *did not arise* for them."[59]

Teilhard's view of the interrelationship between religion and evolution is linked to the fundamental conviction that "from the depths of Matter to the highest peak of the Spirit there is only *one evolution.*"[60] Religions have an indispensable role to play in furthering the evolutionary advance toward the spirit. But there is the difficulty that no past religious teachings can fully cope with the many new aspects of humanity's present development at the species level. What is needed most is a creative religious effort. What is urgently required is "a whole new philosophy of life, a whole new ethical system, and a whole new mysticism."[61]

It is of crucial importance today to find out whether religions can, in fact, animate, sustain, and further advance human progress. Teilhard always maintained that the convergence of religions would occur around those elements in each religious tradition that are best suited for activating human energy and effort. Not all religious teachings are of equal value in this respect, nor do all religions have the same inner strength to animate human beings' forward search and their effort of building the earth. Teilhard associated "true religion" with the "main axis of spiritualization," closely related to the understanding of personhood and transcendence.[62] Although the different religious traditions are to some extent complementary, it is important to discern a central "axis" that can provide maximum activation for human evolution toward the spirit. In this sense, the evolutionary value of different religions, their dynamic qualities to activate and advance the human desire for progressive spiritualization, differ considerably.

Teilhard distinguished among three possible attitudes toward religion and evolution. First, the evolutionary perspective may be so completely embraced that all traditional religions are rejected. Second, traditional religious teachings may be upheld in their entirety, so that all evolutionary insights are excluded. Third, religion may be reinterpreted in the light of evolutionary understanding, so that some religious teachings are maintained, whereas others have to be reformulated or even rejected. In other words, these three possibilities offer a choice among

1. the complete acceptance of evolution, while rejecting all religion;
2. the complete acceptance of religion as traditionally understood, while rejecting evolution; and
3. the acceptance of both religion and evolution, as closely interrelated, where religion is reinterpreted from an evolutionary perspective, and the process of evolution opens up fresh spiritual developments within the human community.

It is in the last sense that Teilhard foresaw a further evolution of religion as necessary, leading to a new breakthrough in spirituality. However, only the future can tell whether such a creative religious breakthrough will in fact occur. His critique of eastern religions closely relates to particular religious values that he thought were incompatible with a modern, evolutionary understanding of human beings and the world. That evolution is such a decisive criterion for his evaluation of religion is apparent from the following remark, made to a friend in Peking:

> There are two general attitudes with regard to evolution: either one denies or admits it. Those *who admit* it can serve it (that is the humanitarian movement), and love it (that is Christianity); those *who deny it*, condemn the process. I mean Hinduism and Buddhism.[63]

Different Understandings of Evolution in Hinduism

The preceding statement can be taken as yet another expression of his frequently negative attitude to Indian religions. Yet it is perhaps in no other religious tradition that the issue of evolution has been so much debated, especially in modern times. Several Hindu reformers see the ultimate meaning of the human being and the cosmos in terms of a spiritual evolution. Teilhard primarily understood Indian thought to contain a certain antithesis to his own ideas through its particular understanding of unity in terms of monism. But it is equally clear that he saw yet another important difference in their respective approaches to evolution.

On closer comparison, it can be maintained "that there are many points of similarity between Teilhard's thought and the structure developed over the centuries by Hindu religious thinkers," as Beatrice Bruteau has convincingly argued and well demonstrated in her comparative study on Teilhard de Chardin and the Hindu traditions.[64] However, this similarity does not really apply to the understanding of evolution, as Teilhard himself was first to admit. The right understanding and appropriate recognition of evolution is for him part of the real difference between Christianity and Hinduism, although he also pointed out that Christianity has not sufficiently considered evolution either. He wrote in his *carnet de lecture*:

> Real critical dividing line between
> Hinduism =   1. Unity of synthesis in God.
> Christianity =   2. Cosmos in evolution.[65]

The same difference is brought out in his critical comments on the teachings of the great Hindu theologians of the Middle Ages, Shankara and Ramanuja. It would be just as anachronistic, of course, to expect modern evolutionary insights from these thinkers as from medieval Christian theologians. However elevating the thought of medieval thinkers is in many respects, to Teilhard it was inadequate when looked at from the contemporary perspective of an ongoing process of evolution.

He stressed in particular that the Hindu understanding of evolution is primarily one of prior involution or emanation of the Divine, not unlike the emanationist philosophy of Plotinus. The process of evolution is here only a "self-analysis of God" in the cosmos, and not a true synthesis, which implies that the development of the human being, and of the world, really achieves something of ultimate value and significance.[66] Teilhard's idea of the process of "evolutionary creation" is not the self-making of an always preexisting divinity. He objected to the "semi-pantheistic theories" of India, which assume "the evolution of man out of God"; this is, in fact, "involution." However, in spite of these differences, he also expressed the view that if modern Vedanta were to incorporate new evolutionary insights it might coincide much more closely with a reinterpreted form of Christianity.[67]

It can be argued that a modern synthesis of Indian and evolutionary ideas has been realized in the important work of Sri Aurobindo. His "integral yoga" presents itself as a reinterpretation of Advaita Vedanta in the light of modern evolution. Although Teilhard was unfamiliar with Sri Aurobindo's writings, he may have recognized at the end of his life that Sri Aurobindo's great book, *The Life Divine*, is marked by a similar thrust and orientation as his own work. Yet there are fundamental differences, too, not only with regard to their respective understandings of the ultimate goal of evolution, and the role of individual and collective efforts in the process of further spiritualization, as was pointed out early on by Father Monchanin,[68] but also in their respective concepts of evolution and involution.

Teilhard also uses the term *involution*, but it describes a rather different process from what it means in Aurobindo's thought. For both thinkers involution is the fundamental law of evolution, but in an almost opposite sense.[69] When Teilhard speaks of a universe in process of involution, he refers to its increase in both external and internal complexity. The turning-in upon itself, or involution, of the evolutionary process is what he calls "the great law of *complexity and consciousness," a law that itself implies that the world has a psychically convergent structure and curvature.*[70] Stated briefly, it indicates that at all levels of life a direct correlation exists between an increased complexity of matter and a corresponding growth of interiority and consciousness.

For Teilhard, involution is part of the very process of evolution itself. For Aurobindo, however, evolution always presupposes prior involution; the latter is a condition of the former. Involution in the Aurobindian sense means "that the Absolute, *before* evolving out of matter, first involved itself into it."[71] Evolution is therefore understood as the gradual manifestation of what existed already—the divine life. There is nothing new, no new being, and no real growth.

For Teilhard, "evolution is a discovery which does not generate its term," whereas for Aurobindo the same process is "a rediscovery of itself by the original term." Consequently, the Absolute "literally re-generates itself through evolution out of involution."[72] If this is so, then Teilhard's objection that Hindu thought does not recognize newness and progressive growth as part of evolution but merely equates evolutionary development with the involution of spirit in matter applies also to Aurobindo's reinterpretation of Hinduism. I cannot discuss this difficult issue further here, but it is certain that Teilhard clearly distinguished between his own understanding of the evolutionary process and the Indian approach to evolution in terms of involution.[73] He also related this difference to a fundamentally different religious orientation toward the human being and the world. Such differences in interpreting the process of evolution are of paramount importance, since evolution, besides providing an explanation for the organic development of the past, has now a special importance for understanding our present situation and for shaping our attitudes toward the future.

A New Dynamic: The Evolution of Mysticism

Scientists greatly vary in their interpretation of evolution. A number of competing theories have been proposed to explain the evolutionary emergence of matter, life, and thought.[74] They disagree as to the overall direction and precise mechanism of evolution and even more about its meaning for us. Some mock, ridicule, and criticize what they consider Teilhard's grand evolutionary speculations. However, this is not unlike the late eighteenth and early nineteenth centuries, when the scientists of the day mocked the idea of evolution itself. What Teilhard glimpsed and hinted at when he spoke of the further evolution of humankind, and of religion and mysticism, may still prove to possess more substance than many dare to expect or dream.

Already Darwin noted with wonder the stupendous dimensions of one world in his diary written on HMS *Beagle*. Since then many scientists have both experienced, and commented upon, the exhilarating sense of discovery and enrichment accompanying their research ventures. Today the number of people who long to free science from its narrow materialistic and empirical presuppositions is growing. Although the company may not be large yet, Teilhard would no longer be alone in seeing the insights of science as closely related to those of mysticism.

What meaning has the development of religions throughout human history? Scholars of religion have asked this question, and so have sociologists. One of them, Robert Bellah, has even proposed a detailed scheme of "religious evolution" correlating different types of religious symbols with religious action, organization, and social meanings.[75] Teilhard's ideas were never systematized in this manner; his reflections remain fluid, his vocabulary changing.

He spoke of the evolution of religion not simply in terms of recurring religious experience, but in the sense of a growing religious awareness. Several types of religious and mystical experience have developed in the past, but the religious sense in human beings is still growing. It is becoming more unified and intensive as time advances.

In spite of its past and present diversity, religion is ultimately a unitary phenomenon. Like science it is one, universal and global, but it embraces many different aspects. Like human beings and human culture in general, religion is subject to further evolution; it will undergo mutation and transformation. This perspective of a further evolution of religion is an integral part of Teilhard's attempt to combine the insights of religion and science. He may have pointed toward a way for their eventual reconciliation, which, in the words of Julian Huxley,

> will come when the religiously minded understand that theology needs a scientific foundation, and grasp the fact that religion itself evolves, and when the scientifically minded accept the equally basic fact that religion is part of the evolutionary process and an important element in its psychological phase, of human history.[76]

The complex developments of the contemporary world affecting both individual and social life have a critical effect on human religious awareness. Since the onset of modernity, people experience an acute tension between the developments of secular life and the appeal of traditional religious precepts. Not only does the individual person seek ultimate meaning and value, but also the whole of humankind is in need of a goal of life. Teilhard's critical attitude toward eastern religions may be related to the fact that, during his lifetime, there existed less awareness about the necessary transformation of religion in the East than in the West. In the East, religions were more closely identified with the dominant culture and were difficult to distinguish from traditional ways of life. However, at present major social changes are taking place on a revolutionary scale, particularly in China, but also in Japan and, more recently, in Cambodia and Vietnam and in other

Asian, African, and Latin American countries. Many political movements and events now challenge traditional beliefs and they are often vehemently antireligious. This trenchant critique of established religions, whose values were taken for granted rather than deliberately chosen in the past, will necessitate a reflection on what is essential to a particular religion and what is not.

In some notes written in 1953, Teilhard indicated two general conditions for the future evolution of "the religious," summarized as follows:

> 1) If humans are to reach the natural term of their development, it is essential that the religious "temperature" rise higher and higher in humankind as it proceeds towards greater unification.
>
> 2) Of all the forms of faith tried out as possibilities in the course of time by the rising forces of religion, only that form is destined to survive which will prove capable of stimulating or "activating" to their maximum the forces of self-evolution in the human being.[77]

The importance of religions is here again related to their dynamic capacity of providing energy for individual and social action. In the last years of his life, Teilhard was particularly concerned with reflecting on the "ethic-mystical consequences of evolution"[78] and with developing a "science of human energetics."[79] He understood this as a systematic study of the energy required for the further self-evolution of human beings,[80] but the central role of religion and mysticism for this "energetics" has been little explored. He referred to the necessary encounter of "physics" and "mysticism" within "the area of (evolutionary) energetics." Such a new "energetics" is alone capable of defining the necessary conditions of culture, morality, and religion.

However, he was aware of the difficulty of such a project when he asked the rhetorical question, "But how to speak of all this...without being repudiated by both scientists and theologians?"[81] To Teilhard, according to his own words, written down in English, it had become clear "that human progress cannot go further on without developing a Mysticism of its own, a Mysticism based on a *faith* in the value and 'infallibility' of Evolution."[82] Whereas he presented Christianity in his earlier years as "the very religion of evolution,"[83] he later increasingly stressed the need for a deep transformation of his own religious tradition:

> Christianity has only a chance to survive...if it shows itself capable...to activate to a maximum in the human being "the energy of self-evolution", i.e. if it is success-ful...not only in 'amorizing' the world but in valuing it more highly than any other form of religion."[84]

What is needed is no longer simply a "Christianity faithfully extended to its utmost limit,"[85] but a "Christianity which sur-passes itself,"[86] the emergence of something "trans-Christian" in theology and mysticism.[87]

It was in this sense that he talked about "the urgent need for the formulation of a mysticism of the West," a "new mysticism, at once fully human and fully Christian," that could be the source of a new energy for which "we have as yet *no name.*"[88] These formu-lations are suggestive, not definitive, formulations; they point to possible explorations in need of further development. Approached in a spirit of encounter and convergence, they leave room for important insights from eastern religions, although Teilhard himself did not think that the major breakthrough in the future evolution of religion would occur in the East. However critical his remarks, his letters and diaries show that his thought on eastern religions was characterized by what Paul Tillich has called "a dialectical union of acceptance and rejection."[89] Speaking from an evolution-ary perspective, Teilhard emphasized the need to take full cog-nizance of the rich and diverse religious experience of humankind, so that a truly global religious consciousness will develop.

Elsewhere he referred to the possibility of a "mystical evolu-tion"[90] for he did not regard mysticism as something of merely historical interest but, on the contrary, of the greatest contempo-rary importance, decisive for the continuity of religion in both East and West. This emphasis on a new understanding of mysti-cism is closely linked to Teilhard's attempt at seeking an integra-tion of the worldviews of both science and religion, which he considers part of the same deep human quest to find ultimate unity. In this sense, science itself, in its ongoing quest and research, becomes tinged with mysticism.

This does not mean that Teilhard suggested a naive concordance between science and religion. His entire endeavor was devoted to seeking an ultimate coherence of our manifold experience, to convey a convergent vision greater than what either traditional religion or science offer on their own. Religion and mysticism are seen as an expression of the human search for ultimate union and communion with God, but *via* the process of the unification of the world. All human efforts, whether religious or scientific, whether action or contemplation, must finally lead to worship, adoration, and ecstasy.

One can argue that he underestimated the capacity of eastern religions to adapt themselves to an evolutionary and scientific understanding of the world. Also, the difficulty about evolution is perhaps less great with regard to the compatibility of religion with scientific teachings about the organic evolution of life in the past than with attitudes regarding evolution now, and with the decisions required to shape the direction of evolutionary developments in the present and future.

Traditional religious teachings of the East may however contain more "mystical reserves" for animating human action than Teilhard as an outsider was able to perceive. The growing convergence of world religions is particularly important in this respect. Without being tied to the traditional boundaries of religious institutions, the mutually enriching encounter of people from different faiths may itself be a decisive influence on the further evolution of religion.

An interesting discussion of the mutual interaction of religion and evolution is found in the work of the geneticist Theodosius Dobzhansky. In his book *The Biology of Ultimate Concern*,[91] he, like Teilhard, points out that human evolution has left its earlier stage of

> happy spiritual childhood far in the past. Modern man must raise his sights above the simple biological joys of survival and procreation. He needs nothing less than a

religious synthesis. This synthesis cannot be simply a revival of any one of the existing religions, and it need not be a new religion. The synthesis may be grounded in one of the world's great religions, or in all of them together.

By education and upbringing, Dobzhansky favors, again like Teilhard, Christianity as the framework for this synthesis. Nevertheless, he admits that the possibility of other frameworks cannot be excluded. He is equally adamant in stating that it must be a true synthesis that integrates the rational and evolutionary views of science as much as those of religion.[92]

There is no going back in time to the religion of the past, only a going forward within the dynamic of an evolutionary perspective. Traditional spirituality has thus arrived at important crossroads: either a new religious vision will emerge, or religion will stagnate and die if we cannot separate the ossified from the living tradition. For Teilhard, the direction to take, the path to follow, is the road of a "new mysticism," for it is the realm of the mystical that represents the most living element in religion. The phenomenon of mysticism is still growing, and the intensity of its flame can best feed our common endeavor to create a better, more united world for humankind on earth.

9

TOWARD A NEW MYSTICISM

What is the nature of mysticism? Which major features characterize the mysticisms of the past? How far are these still relevant or perhaps redundant for contemporary spiritual practice? These are some of the questions underlying Teilhard's inquiry into mysticism. They also provide the dominant perspective for his approach to eastern religions. He frequently used the words *mystical* and *mysticism*, but he always objected to their narrow definition. Writing about Christian theology, for example, he said that it has the tendency "to give the word 'mystical' (in mystical body, mystical union) a minimum of organic or physical meaning." This is due to "the very common mistake of regarding the spiritual as an attenuation of the material, whereas it is in fact the material carried beyond itself: it is super-material."[1]

Besides numerous references to mysticism throughout his work, some major essays and books are entirely devoted to this theme, especially "The Mystical Milieu" (1917), "The Mass on the World" (1923), "My Universe" (1924), his book *The Divine Milieu* (1927), "How I Believe" (1934), "The Phenomenon of Spirituality" (1937), "My Fundamental Vision"(1948), "The Heart of Matter" (1950), and "The Christic" (1955). Written over a lifetime, and often presented in autobiographical form, apparent even from their titles, they confirm the view that his understanding of mysticism is closely related to his own experience. Given the need to interpret this experience to himself and others, he inquired at random into the presence of mysticism inside and outside Christianity. His comparisons were thus initially personally motivated and undertaken to illuminate his own experience. This helps to explain their particular orientation and accounts for some inherent limitations of his views on eastern and western mysticism.

Although many of his religious writings have a mystical matrix, they are mostly not concerned with descriptive reports of individual experiences, as is the case with so many other mystics. Many passages transcend the concerns of personal mystical experience through their reflections on the role of mysticism in contemporary society and culture and on the spiritual evolution of humanity.

The mystical quest of Teilhard's life found a moving expression and climax in his final essays, "The Heart of Matter" and "The Christic." Many commentators have recognized the importance of mysticism in his work,[2] but most have examined his Christ-centered mysticism and its place in contemporary Christian theology. His comparisons with eastern religions, his distinction of different paths and goals in mysticism, as well as the central role of mysticism in the future evolution of religion, have received comparatively less attention.

The study of the history of mysticism, with its rich store of mystical literature, has attracted increasing attention over the past decades.[3] Every religion possesses its great mystics, and the accounts of their different experiences have been examined from many points of view. Modern studies on mysticism are mostly concerned with rigorous analysis and classification in an attempt to account more systematically for the diversity of mystical experience in the religious history of humankind.[4]

It is easy to see that Teilhard's reflections are not of this kind. His was not an academic writing *about* mysticism; on the contrary, his prime interest was practice rather than theory, especially the *practice* of spirituality in the modern world as an indispensable source of life-giving energy and love. Yet references to Teilhard's thought in contemporary works on mysticism are practically nonexistent, except for the works of some Catholic authors. Nevertheless, his reflections supply important data that ought to be taken into account when scholars construct their classifications and discuss different theories about mysticism.

The Newness of Teilhard's Mysticism

As with the experience of other mystics, Teilhard's vision entails claims about the nature of reality that require close examination. What is more, his emphasis on the need to go beyond merely historical studies and strive toward a new form of mysticism deserves serious consideration. At present, this is perhaps more recognized by people working in the natural sciences, especially science and religion, than by those working only in the area of religion.

From the beginning of his reflections, Teilhard claimed an element of newness in his understanding of mysticism, distinct from that of earlier mystics.[5] What is this new mysticism of which he spoke so much in the last years of his life? He searched for a new approach, a mysticism of evolution and convergence, that he described as a new road in spirituality. He thought that this road had begun to open up in the West but could not develop in a truly convergent manner without the contribution of the East and its religions. What is the meaning of this mysticism? What is its newness? And what is its importance for religion today?

All Teilhard's comparisons between western and eastern mysticism are undertaken from the premise that the spiritual quest is not perennially the same. A change in human consciousness and self-understanding, linked to new historical and social developments, has brought about a situation in which human spiritual needs have come into sharper focus. The protagonists of an essential unity of all religions, of a common mystical core, uphold an eternal timelessness of spirituality that leaves no room for further development.[6] Teilhard disagrees with this most emphatically. He does not think that all mysticism is and always has been the same, or that it always will be. What is ultimately at issue is the question of what pertains to spirituality today; the answer to this question may well lead to a parting of ways.

New developments in contemporary culture urgently call for a new approach to the understanding and practice of spirituality. It is this need, born from a historically new situation, that Teilhard saw and felt with extraordinary depth and intensity like few others. Based on formative mystical experiences and a lifelong reflection on the meaning of mysticism in the modern world, he put forward a particular interpretation that diverges from that of other writers in several respects.

Mysticism is usually taken to refer to extraordinary states of contemplation, inner visions, trances, stages of illumination, and so on. In this sense, it means an experience of inwardness without correlating it to outwardness, to the external world, and the multiple concerns of society. Traditional mysticism has, par excellence, been understood as an individual quest, often in tension with official religious institutions. Teilhard, by contrast, does not restrict mysticism to contemplative states or extraordinary experiences of the individual alone but gives the "phenomenon of mysticism" a more comprehensive meaning. Even when talking about mysticism primarily in relation to the individual, he links it to a continuum of progressively more centered experiences, ranging from pantheistic and monistic to theistic forms.

However, the word *mysticism* also stands for the goal of *all* spiritual life. It then refers to the most powerful and activating center of human spirituality that can only be reached by correlating and integrating outer activities with the inner life.

If an exclusively introvertive and individual quest for contemplation and spiritual union was the predominant ideal of the past, it is no longer adequate for the present and future. The time vector is essential here for—in Teilhard's view—the integration and perfection of one's inner life, as well as the search for an Absolute, do not occur independently from time. The acceptance of an extended meaning of evolution implies development and growth, the existence of different, organically related levels of development, and the directionality of time and history. The evolutionary process has not only shaped the history of the cosmos, of the world, and human beings; it also affects all human thought and culture, including religion, and the understanding of the spirit itself. Not all writers on mysticism would agree with these premises, which may be mainly western in origin but are not without parallels in certain forms of eastern thought.

Given modern developments, an adequate religious worldview for the present and future cannot be entirely modeled on the patterns of the past. To seek ultimate unity implies at the same time a changed relationship between human beings and all other phenomena in the world; thus, it must be accompanied by a process of unification. Consequently, the interpretation of mysticism is closely linked to a new emphasis on the importance of human action. It is, in fact, in and through action that the spirit unfolds and that spirituality grows. Spirituality is no longer simply a problem of inwardness, as in the past. On the contrary, the problem of human action, together with the choice of the right values and beliefs on which to base such action, is the major problem of the spirit today.

Ultimately, Teilhard sees the vast process of human evolution as one of expanding interiorization and spiritualization through the progressive integration and unification of human experiences and action. Mysticism is therefore not only of individual, but also of great social importance. It acquires significance for humanity as a whole, and for the future of religion itself. Seen from this perspective, Teilhard's understanding of mysticism overlaps with but is not entirely contained by traditional categories usually associated with mysticism. His "new mysticism" is neither primarily a nature-, soul-, or God-mysticism, but rather, if such a formulation were permitted, a personal-universal world-in-evolution mysticism, implying a dynamic process of convergence.[7]

Two Basic Types of Mysticism

Although not a specialist in these matters, Teilhard was always aware of "the vast and polymorphous domain of mysticism."[8] He recognized that a great variety of experiences has been described by the word *mysticism* at different times and places. Unlike the English scholar R. C. Zaehner and other writers on mysticism, he did not argue for a sharp break between natural pantheism and religious mysticism of a monistic or theistic kind at the experiential level.[9] He saw these different experiences as continuous and organically related, although each also possesses a distinctive element of its own. Structurally and ontologically, he always distinguished two basic types of mysticism as fundamental alternatives, or even opposites, but this does not imply that the individual experiences them as such psychologically.

211

Different types of mysticism are often distinguished based on whether fundamentally unitive experiences of the soul are described in terms of human absorption into, or union with, God. Teilhard, however, hinges his distinction of two basic types on the process of *unification*. The very choice of this word indicates that mysticism does not simply imply the union of two given terms, that is, the human being and God, but it means an ongoing process of successive "centering." It involves the inner unification of the self, as well as the outer unification of what surrounds it, that is to say, other people as well as work and nature. This process of unification has such a central importance in Teilhard's worldview that it is sharply set off from any mysticism of *identification*, which, in his opinion, was traditionally mainly prevalent in the East and is referred to by him—summarily and quite wrongly—as the "road of the East." However, on closer examination it becomes clear that the characterization of this "road" is primarily dependent on what he knew of the various monistic trends in Indian thought. His typological method misled him into thinking of eastern religions as far too unitary, without sufficiently taking into account the historical diversity and pluralism of the great religions of the East. This may be partly because he neither possessed the close contacts, nor pursued the necessary study, to gain a deep insight into eastern mystical thought, whereas his background, training, and personal commitment gave him much fuller access to the wide range of Christian mysticism.

Many essays express the fundamental distinction between two basic types of mysticism without reference to either eastern or western religions. I use one of the latest, "Some Notes on the Mystical Sense: An Attempt at Clarification" (1951),[10] since it presents Teilhard's ideas about two types of mysticism, worked out over a lifetime, in such succinct, notelike form. In fact, this "Note" of two pages may be considered a brief summary of a longer essay written several months earlier, "A Clarification: Reflections on Two Converse Forms of the Spirit" (July 1950).[11] On one hand, the note describes the human mystical sense as a presentiment of the total, final unity of the world or, alternatively, as a cosmic sense of "oneness." Yet on the other hand, it emphasizes that there are two principal ways, or roads, through which this oneness is realized. Teilhard even wondered whether there may be more than two ways; perhaps a rhetorical question, yet evidence for his acknowledgment of the diversity of mystical experience at the empirical level, not to be confused with the theoretical distinction between two basic or pure types.

The first type is characterized by *identification* with an undifferentiated common ground. It means the fusion or dissolution of human specificity, represented by personal consciousness, with an Ineffable "of de-differentiation and de-personalization." Because of the negation of the central core of personhood, both in the Absolute, and in one's experience of It, and of oneself, this is "both by definition and by structure" a "mysticism WITHOUT LOVE."

The second road or type, by contrast, is marked by *unification*. Instead of dissolution and fusion, it is the concentration and unification of each and all "through a peak of intensity arrived at by what is most incommunicable in each element." Although not specifically mentioned, personhood and its ultimate fulfillment in a higher personal center are central to this second type, as the context clearly shows. This type of mysticism represents "an ultra-personalizing, ultra-determining, and ultra-differentiating UNIFICATION of the elements within a *common focus*; the specific effect of LOVE."

The first type of experience relates to an impersonal "God," if that is not a contradiction in terms, as *all*. By contrast, the second type of experience sees God as "all in all," to use Saint Paul's phrase. This is "an ultra-personal," a "centric" God—expressions that emphasize that God must not be thought of as a person in an anthropomorphic sense.

The main difference, then, between a mysticism of identification and a mysticism of unification is the absence or presence of personal love, itself dependent on a particular understanding of the personal nature of the human being and of ultimate reality. This basic typology must not be understood to reiterate the common distinction between a monistic and theistic type of mysticism. The presence of personal love here does not only mean a loving relationship between human beings and God. It implies more than a simple coming together and union, for it is linked to a complex, and increasingly convergent, process of unification.

Thus, the meaning of love itself is being transformed and understood in a much more dynamic sense. Even when Teilhard refers elsewhere simply to "union" or "unity," he still associates a process of unification with these terms.

The second type of mysticism—that of unification—is not strictly identical with theistic forms of mysticism either. Instead, it is "a road not yet described in any 'book' (?!)...the true path 'toward and for' oneness." It is said to be the new "road of the West," a path of unification that has only become possible through the contact of Christianity with the modern world. There is no reference to the "road of the East" here. Overall, these short "Notes on the Mystical Sense" favor the more neutral terminology of two basic "ways" of mysticism, distinguished by the absence or presence of love in an *ultra-personal* God.

The first type, then, is an essentially monistic mysticism, the second a *trans-theistic* mysticism toward which Christianity tends but that has not yet been fully developed. Structurally through its theology, and practically through the emphasis given to love and charity, Christianity belongs to this second type. Yet its mysticism showed a certain "lack of richness" in the past: it was "not sufficiently universalist and cosmic," because oneness was too exclusively sought "in singleness, rather than in God's *synthetic power*." God was loved "*above* all things" rather than "*in* and *through* all things."[12]

This passage, like so many others, emphasizes again the difference between the mysticism of the past and what is required for the present. Teilhard's typology, here and elsewhere, is only an "attempt at clarification,"[13] and not a fully worked-out scheme of classification and interpretation. This is also evident from his changing terminology for, in another context, he speaks of two types of pantheism rather than mysticism: "Pantheism of identification, at the opposite pole from love: 'God is all'. And pantheism of unification, beyond love: 'God all in all.'"[14] In each case, the same emphasis is placed on the difference between the process of *identification* and that of *unification*.

R. C. Zaehner understood the text just quoted as a confirmation of his own views, put forward in his book *Mysticism Sacred and Profane*. He considered Teilhard as "one of the very few who draw clear distinctions between different types of mysticism."[15] However, the typologies of these two writers do not completely coincide, since Zaehner overlooks both the time factor and the dynamic complexity in Teilhard's mysticism of unification; similarly, he insists on too sharp a separation between the different types. The fact that Teilhard referred to the types as both "pantheism" and "mysticism" is an indication that he saw the two phenomena as interrelated, as part of a continuum. This is also borne out by his insistence on the possibility of a true, Christian pantheism: the experience of the oneness and unity of the cosmos must become an integral part of the Christian faith.

The New Mysticism as a Third Way

One can gain yet another view of Teilhard's interpretation of mysticism, since some of his texts do not oppose the process of unification to that of identification but express the basic polarity by a predominantly forward or upward orientation. Their inherent tension is transcended through a third direction that represents a new synthesis, sometimes called *via tertia* or "third way" by Teilhard. Diagrammatically, these three different "ways" or directions can be shown as follows:[16]

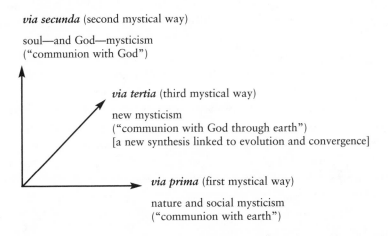

via secunda (second mystical way)

soul—and God—mysticism
("communion with God")

via tertia (third mystical way)

new mysticism
("communion with God through earth")
[a new synthesis linked to evolution and convergence]

via prima (first mystical way)

nature and social mysticism
("communion with earth")

The horizontal line stands for pantheistic nature mysticism and a social mysticism of the collective, represented by various forms of neohumanism. This mysticism of the world is the *via prima*, opposed to the vertical line of the *via secunda*, the way of all traditional mysticism, which seeks to link the human being directly with the Absolute to the exclusion of the world (that is, all forms of either soul- or God-mysticism). The diagonal *via tertia* indicates the emergence of a new kind of mysticism, whereby a person is united with the Absolute *via the unification of the world*. Each of these three lines can in turn be identified with parts of the maxim of Teilhard's first essay, "Cosmic Life" (1916).[17]

At other times, these three lines are described as three "currents." The upward direction is thought of as a predominantly "eastern current" but subsumes under it the otherworldliness of past Christian spirituality. The forward direction is mainly found in the neohumanist and Marxist "world-current," and the diagonal represents a "neo-Christian current," a new synthesis between the essential "axes" of Christian belief and a newborn faith in the world. This example shows once again that Teilhard's thought on mysticism is not confined to a systematically elaborated typology. Rather, it is expressed by different schemata cutting across each other and open to varying interpretations.

Teilhard understood the search for unification via the tangible as primarily a western preoccupation. The concern for the value of the material world is closely linked to the Christian understanding of the incarnation. Yet the full implications of an incarnational approach—the transformation and sanctification of all human and earthly realities—take on an altogether different dimension with the relatively modern discovery and analysis of what these realities in themselves are and how they are always involved in a continuously evolving process of change and transformation. With advancing knowledge, the limits of the real are forever pushed further back; the world surrounding us is expanding its parameter. For Teilhard, the search for a systematically unified knowledge in the area of science is akin to the mystic search for oneness in the area of religion. This interrelated quest for oneness made him seek a new mysticism, where unity is achieved through ultra-differentiation.

However, in spite of his insistence on the unitary quest for oneness, and his conviction that the general awareness of mysticism is growing today, one can say that nobody has ever become a mystic by their own choice. The very gratuitousness of the mystical phenomenon seems to indicate that the initiative for it comes from outside us. For this reason, a receptive state of passivity has traditionally been associated with the mystic. Teilhard does not overlook this. In his book on the interior life, *The Divine Milieu*, he discusses both activity and passivity, attachment and detachment. However, as he frequently emphasizes human activity and choice in a world-affirming manner, in contrast to a traditionally passive and world-negating attitude, some misinterpret his thought as too activist. They forget that although *The Divine Milieu* begins with "the divinization of our activities," it continues with "the divinization of our passivities." Whether this is meant to be an alternative rhythm or an advance by progression may be open to debate.

One commentator, Father Ravier, who from 1951 onward was Teilhard's last religious superior in France and one of his much-appreciated correspondents, is of the opinion that in spite of Teilhard's occasionally severe words against pure contemplatives, he nevertheless acknowledged the path of the mystic to be a particular vocation he himself did not possess. According to Ravier, a true mystic must ultimately pass from the *via tertia* to the *via secunda*, to an intimate soul-God relationship to the exclusion of the world. As the *via secunda* was not given to Teilhard, the *via tertia*, the integration of the love of God with the love of the world, was the only option open to him.[18]

If one accepts this interpretation, then the *via tertia* is merely a compromise, unworthy of being pursued by the genuine mystic. Ravier's remark reaffirms the utter passivity and withdrawal of the mystic state without leaving room for any new development. This seems to do injustice to Teilhard's own position. Furthermore, it is puzzling to learn about another, quite contrary comment made earlier by Father Ravier in a public sermon given in 1965, when he is not only reported to have spoken about his "marvelous friendship" with Teilhard but also about the great influence of Teilhard's "authentically mystical thought."[19]

Teilhard's frequent references to a new "road," a new mysticism, definitely indicate the search for a new synthesis that is more than a compromise. Many passages could be quoted in support of this, especially from the unpublished diaries of the last years, where Teilhard noted down the following reflection, for example:

> Via tertia—distinguish syncretism and synthesis...
>
> My line: to synthesize mysticism and evolution (cosmic effort: detachment and synthesis). Union implies unification, that is to say, an evolutionary mystical union....
>
> THE MYSTICAL ILLUSION = pretends to Union and Presence *independently of Time* and Evolution...as if the contact with God could be achieved without the Evolution of Consciousness—from the beginning....[20]

The idea of a new "mysticism of evolution" and a "mysticism of action" suggests a new vision related to the development of a new world. This understanding of mysticism cannot solely be assessed by reference to the mystics of the past,[21] for Teilhard's interpretation of mysticism is strongly future oriented, and it is evaluative. The mysticism of identification and that of unification are not simple equivalents, but one type is seen as more developed, fuller, richer, and truer.

Many passages indicate an evaluative perspective that—in spite of Teilhard's emphasis on convergence—remained too western oriented. For example, he is reported to have said at a 1948 meeting of the French branch of the World Congress of Faiths in Paris:

> I believe the mystical is less different, less separated from the rational than one says, but I also believe that the whole problem which the world, and we in particular, are presently facing, is a problem of faith....
>
> I have the weakness to believe that the West has a very strong latent mysticism, underlying, not made explicit yet, but at least as strong as eastern mysticism.
>
> If the western group were really able to express in a new manner, or to renew that mysticism of the West of which I once spoke, I think that would be something much more powerful than even dialogue, for it would

make a faith appear within humankind, a mysticism which exists not yet....[22]

Perhaps it is Teilhard's main achievement to have sought a new formulation for a mysticism of the West, that is to say, a mysticism rooted in the Christian doctrines of creation and incarnation but expressed in a new manner. However, the use of the term *via tertia*, the references to a new road, to a not-yet-existing mysticism, all point toward a synthesis going beyond the past distinctions of West and East. The element of newness and the process of convergence associated with the new road indicate that the new mysticism of unification, or union, must ultimately transcend the traditional religious heritage of the West.

Similar reflections are expressed in an earlier essay written in 1941 in Peking, "The Atomism of the Spirit,"[23] where he discusses the evolutionary rise of complexity and consciousness and the search for a higher synthesis that he calls the "Omega point." Referring to the domain of mysticism that combines a sense of the human, a sense of the Earth, and the sense of an Omega, Teilhard is convinced that

> if people's *vision can extend* beyond the immense and the infinitesimal almost into the complex, a way of action opens up for them which has the power to synthesize and transfigure every other form of activity: by that I mean the specific act of experiencing and advancing, in and around themselves—through the whole expanse and the whole depth of the real—the unification of the universe upon its deep-seated center....
>
> Now in the domain of mysticism...ever since human beings, in becoming human, started on their quest for unity, they have constantly oscillated, in their visions, in their asceticism, or in their dreams, between a cult of the spirit which made them jettison matter and a cult of matter which made them deny spirit....Detachment now comes not through a severance but through a traversing and a sublimation; and spiritualization not by negation of the multiple or an escape from it, but by

emergence. This is the *via tertia* that opens up before us as soon as spirit is no longer the opposite extreme but the higher pole of matter in course of super-centration. It is not a cautious and neutral middle course, but the bold, higher road, in which the values of the two other roads are combined and correct one another....

A neo-spirituality for a neo-spirit, in a universe whose convergent nature has been recognized.[24]

This quotation expresses clearly the newness of an evolutionary mysticism, "a bold, higher road" that prolongs and transforms the best of the two different "roads" of the past. Weighing up different texts, particularly those of Teilhard's later years, one realizes therefore the necessary, in fact essential, contribution of eastern religious insights to a newly emerging mysticism. In January 1951, Teilhard wrote from Paris to Ida Treat, one of his friends in the United States:

Actually, as time goes by, I have a curious impression of liberation and simplification: interest in old evidence, and an intensification of this evidence along lines that are so fresh that I feel as if I were discovering a World that is radically enlarged and transformed. For the moment one realizes that the Universe flows (and always has flowed) in the direction of "ever greater order and consciousness," a whole group of values is introduced into things which...give everything an extraordinary savor, warmth, and limpidity: a superior and synthetic form of "mysticism" in which the strengths and seductions of oriental "pantheism" and Christian personalism converge and culminate! Impossible for me not to pursue this vision in a series of essays that keeps getting longer without my yet having managed to grasp exactly and fully what I feel: fortunate situation![25]

This passage brings out the suggestive and exploratory nature of Teilhard's ideas about a new mysticism. These ideas are in need of much further development. The most fruitful approach would be a comparison between the understanding of love and personhood in different religious traditions, for he maintains that a specific form of love is what most separates and distinguishes the two main types of mysticism. It is impossible to explore this here in full, but the emphasis on love has a special bearing on Teilhard's remarks about Indian religions.

Love as Unifying Energy

The emphasis on mutual love between the human being and God is often seen as the most significant characteristic that divides theistic from monistic forms of mysticism. Examples of this can be found in Hindu, Muslim, and Christian religious thought. For Teilhard, too, the presence of love is the most distinctive feature that separates the mysticism of unification from that of identification, and it is for him intimately bound up with certain Christian teachings. However, from a comparative perspective one must ask whether the loving devotion of Hindu *bhakti*, for example, is not the same as Christian love. Teilhard raised this question several times and referred to it even in one of his last essays, "The Christic."[26] Nevertheless, while admitting a close similarity between the two, he nevertheless maintained a distinctive difference, mainly due to a more complex understanding of the nature of love.

He often speaks of love in a traditional manner, but sometimes he also understands it in a new way. For example, he refers to a "neo-love" that combines the love of God with that of a world in evolution. Love is more than a personal attraction between two partners leading to union and communion. It is a unifying energy, in fact, "the supreme spiritual energy" that draws together all elements and persons in their "irreplaceable and incommunicable essence" through a universal process of unification.[27] Love has a central, irreplaceable part in his general "energetics," for it possesses a personal and cosmic dimension and is a creative force in the evolutionary process itself. At the cosmic level, it is an animating energy pulsating through the universe, almost like the *shakti* of Hindu Tantra, which Teilhard does not seem to have known.[28]

The comparability of Teilhard's ideas with certain Tantra teachings relates to his view that one of the ways in which humans partake of this great cosmic force is sexual energy. This is part of the cosmic dynamic and constitutive of being-in-the-world. There are numerous references in his writings to human sexuality as a fundamental force, providing the basis for any other human love, including the love of God, and that form of love that finds expression in charity. It is not the repression of sexuality but, on the contrary, its acceptance and transformation that are necessary for a full flowering of mysticism. The mystical quest for unification has its natural roots in the powers of attraction linked to human sexuality. Thus, the dynamic of sexuality and mysticism are closely interrelated. In 1916, he wrote in his diary "the transformation of love—with sexual roots—into a *cosmic* passion is a *natural* evolution. This rather vague stage gives birth to all mysticisms...."[29] Many years later, he criticized a book on the mystical life by saying that it possessed "no original element. The mystical phenomenon regarded as rather an exception—almost historical." The author

> does not see that it is a universal phenomenon..., linked to the axis of reflective life: sense of the One, cosmic sense, sense of Evolution;—nor does he discern the physico-psychological relation between sexuality and mysticism. In short, he does not see...the evolutionary value of the mystical phenomenon.[30]

Besides the cosmic and sexual dimension, Teilhard emphasizes the personalizing aspect of love as particularly important for mysticism. A human being becomes a person through a process of personalization, that is to say, through a gradual movement of inner centering and unification made possible through being linked to others by love. Teilhard distinguishes three phases in this process: "If a human being is to be fully himself and fully living, he must, (1) be centered upon himself; (2) be 'de-centred' upon 'the other; (3) be super-centered upon a being greater than himself." He calls this also "the happiness of growing greater—of loving—of worshipping."[31]

The unifying force of personal love, its power of centering and integration, is so important that Teilhard speaks of "a mysticism of centration."[32] This mysticism is closely associated with the understanding of personhood as the essence of the human being. More than anything else, it is through this personal center that a human being relates to God, who is a person in a much more eminent sense.

The philosophy of personhood has a long history in Christianity and operates with concepts largely alien to eastern traditions. Many misunderstandings arise from this fundamental difference in approach. People often confuse "person" with the empirical ego, or with a psychological "personality," which true mysticism strives to transcend. Because of the limitation of our empirical personality, and the possible anthropomorphic connotations of the personal, Indian writers often place the impersonal above the personal and define the Absolute as impersonal, in contrast to any theistic conception. In the context of Indian Advaita in particular, the personal is seen as limiting because it is understood to imply duality and circumscribed individuality, which are transcended in the realization of a universal *Atman*.

Teilhard argued so much against Indian monism because he saw it overwhelmingly as a mystical experience of human identification with the One alone, implying the loss of personal consciousness.[33] Similarly, he criticized Aldous Huxley's *Perennial Philosophy*[34] for confusing the impersonal with the universal, and the personal with the anthropomorphic. In Teilhard's view, it is essential to distinguish clearly between the universal and the personal, but also to relate them to each other and see them both in an evolutionary perspective. Only in the Christian understanding of love are all these elements brought together for, in Teilhard's view, no other religious faith in history has ever released "a higher degree of warmth, a more intense dynamism of unification" than Christianity, especially the Christianity of our own day.[35] The essential elements of Christian love find themselves prolonged in what he called "a new mystical orientation," linked to the "love of evolution."[36] In the past, Christian love has not always found

its full expression, since it has often been too "other-worldly."
Instead, a truly dynamic form of Christian love must be concerned with the effort of developing human beings beyond themselves. He therefore referred to "a radical reinterpretation" and
"recasting" of the notion of Christian charity.[37]

Teilhard obviously seemed to think that eastern religions did
not understand love in its highest, personal form, nor as love of
evolution. In his diary, he briefly acknowledged the presence of an
"affective theism" in Indian Vaishnavite and Shaivite *bhakti* and
in Japanese Amida Buddhism. Yet although psychologically very
similar, to him this was not the same as a fully dynamic, person-
centered love. The importance of this difference is evident from
the following remarks:

> The *mystic* (and most fundamental) current which has
> kept running and developing in Christianity...a current
> of love (love of God and love of humankind)—*not* the
> buddhistic "piété", but a personalistic form of love.
> This is important, because...such "love" (of the World
> in its elements and as a whole) is probably the very axis
> of future human progress and evolution.[38]

From these and other passages, it is clear that Teilhard was
obviously unfamiliar with the details of the rich *bhakti* tradition
of Indian theism with its exceptionally wide-ranging theological
reflections on the nature of love between human beings and God.
It is not so much personal love that is absent here but, rather, the
love of evolution with its accompanying dynamic approach.

It is certain, though, that the emphasis on a new kind of mysticism is closely dependent on a particular understanding of love,
as well as on the nature of the human person and the role of theism, all of which are reinterpreted from an evolutionary perspective. One can again point to the dialectical tension in Teilhard's
thought here. On one hand, he assigns a central place to the
Christian "personalistic form of love" in his interpretation of
mysticism, but on the other, he stresses that this love, identified as
the "Christian mystical act" par excellence, has not yet found its

full expression but must grow further and become more universalized.[39]

Comparative Reflections on Mysticism

If one compares Teilhard's understanding of mysticism with
that of others, what similarities and differences emerge? It has
been pointed out more than once that significant parallels to his
thought exist in the traditional mysticism of both western and
eastern Christianity. This is not surprising since he prolongs all
that is most authentic in the Christian mystical tradition. Yet
there is also an additional, and quite new, element present, for
Teilhard's emphasis on the role of mysticism far transcends the
concerns of those who seek a simple reawakening of past
Christian mysticism.

Francis Kelly Nemeck, in his comparative study of the mysticism of Teilhard and Saint John of the Cross,[40] shows that these
two mystics have more in common than one might first assume.
He considers the two to some extent complementary but judges
Teilhard's mysticism "as on the whole better balanced with regard
to the convergence and complementarity of transcendence and
immanence," whereas Saint John penetrates more into the dark-
ness of faith and the "night" of the senses and the spirit.[41]

The comparison between Saint John of the Cross and
Teilhard is of particular interest when taking into account that
the Hindu Swami Siddheswarananda considers Saint John's
understanding of mysticism as akin to Indian teaching on *jnana-
yoga*, *bhakti-yoga*, and *raja-yoga*.[42] As is to be expected from a
Ramakrishna-Mission monk, Swami Siddheswarananda specifically affirms the unity of mystical experience underlying different
religions. At the same time, he emphasizes that mysticism can,
strictly speaking, only be pursued by monks. Even the teachings
of Christ are interpreted by him as being essentially monastic. To
follow the path of mysticism requires a single-minded pursuit of
the spiritual life to the exclusion of everything else. There can be
no realization in and through the world, if one uses Teilhardian
terms; the orientation of the mystic is strongly vertical and individualistic.

Teilhard met Swami Siddheswarananda through their mutual work for the French branch of the World Congress of Faiths and discussed certain questions regarding the interpretation of mystical experience with him.[43] However, he disagreed with the Swami's comparison between the mysticism of Vedanta and Saint John of the Cross. In 1948, when speaking about the two basic types of mysticism, Teilhard wrote in "My Fundamental Vision":

> Surprisingly, it would not appear that a clear distinction has yet been drawn between these two diametrically contrasted attitudes: and this accounts for the confusion which muddles together or identifies the ineffable of the Vedanta and that of, for example, St John of the Cross—and so not only allows any number of excellent souls to become helpless victims of the most pernicious illusions produced in the East, but also (what is more serious) delays a task that is daily becoming more urgent—the individualization and the full flowering of a valid and powerful modern mysticism.

The difference between these two perspectives is further enhanced through an additional note that says:

> When approached by the road of the East (identification) the ineffable is not such that it can be loved. By the road of the West (union) it is attained through a continuation of the direction of love. This very simple criterion makes it possible to distinguish and keep separate, as being antithetical, verbal expressions that are almost identical when used by Christian or Hindu.[44]

Here again Teilhard equates the Hindu position with monism, which gives Indian thought much of its characteristic flavor, without being universal in Hinduism. There are closer parallels than he realized. In particular, his understanding of spirituality as a "detachment by super-attachment"[45] as well as his unifying vision of convergence possess a remarkable affinity with

226

certain teachings of the Bhagavad Gita, especially as understood in modern Hinduism.

Although Teilhard must have encountered a discussion of this much-revered Hindu scripture in his reading, he never refers to it all. The Bhagavad Gita contains a tremendous theophany, disclosing the vision of a supreme personal God who unites all beings within himself. This is a close union of love that is not identity, and it represents a vision of convergence not unlike the ultimate unity of Teilhard's mysticism. At least, this is the view taken by Zaehner.[46] However, one must not forget that the Bhagavad Gita has been subject to widely divergent interpretations, and not everyone sees in it the same vision of convergent union as Zaehner does. Another objection relates to the fact that an evolutionary perspective introduces a new complexity and dynamic that requires a much more subtle notion of convergence than could have been originally intended by the Bhagavad Gita. But admittedly, this scripture lends itself particularly well to modern reinterpretations, and it provides a strong basis for a theistic mysticism.

The most surprising, and in many ways closest, contemporary parallel to Teilhard's understanding of mysticism exists in Sri Aurobindo's work. His reinterpretation of Hinduism, however, is deeply influenced by ideas of western origin. In Zaehner's view, both Aurobindo and Teilhard, in their separate traditions, "represent something totally new in mystical religion."[47] Yet it is of little help in furthering understanding or comparative assessment when some of Aurobindo's disciples maintain that Teilhard has written little that Aurobindo has not expressed much better or claim that the latter has in fact achieved the mystical realization the former only talked about.

In one respect, however, Teilhard and Aurobindo are curiously alike: despite their efforts to find a synthesis of thought between East and West, both remain locked in their own religious and cultural perspectives. Aurobindo emphatically claims that the future development of religion is linked to his reinterpretation of Indian mysticism in the form of "integral yoga," whereas Teilhard conceives of it mainly in terms of a new "road of the West" or a western-based "mysticism of evolution." These positions are opposed to, and exclusive of, each other. To achieve true synthesis and convergence, both need to be transcended. That such a movement of convergence requires a further development of Teilhard's ideas, he himself would have been the first to admit. A thinker who repeatedly emphasized that evolution is an all-encompassing, generalized biological, social, and cultural phenomenon would hardly expect that the process of religious evolution would come to a halt with himself, as Aurobindo seems to have done.

A New Mysticism of Evolution and Action

On comparison, the newness of Teilhard's mystical experience and interpretation is a relative one, due mainly to a change in emphasis, perspective, and scale. Independent parallels exist in Christian mysticism, both ancient and modern,[48] but, unknown to him, examples of a unifying cosmic vision and of world-affirming attitudes can also be found in eastern religions. This is not only true of Hinduism and Buddhism, but even more so of traditional Chinese thinking, as shown particularly by Allerd Stikker's comparison among Taoism, Teilhard, and western thought.[49]

However, there is a real danger of making too facile, and even anachronistic, comparisons that may completely misrepresent Teilhard's intentions. It is always necessary to investigate closely whether particular aspects of different religions and cultures are truly comparable at different times in history and on what assumptions such comparisons are based.

Teilhard's interpretation of mysticism combines in a unique manner the appeal of the transcendent with that of a dynamic, tangible, and evolving world, transformed from within through the immanent presence of the Divine that so allured and beckoned him through all living forms. Although many mystics before him have seen this wonderful "diaphany,"[50] he was aware that their understanding of mysticism in relation to the world has often been very different indeed. This is largely because the problem of the modern world and its progress did not arise for them in the way experienced now.

This problem is assuming increasing urgency today. It is related to the development of science and technology, the expansion of knowledge into ever-new fields, and the increasing differentiation of modern society. Frequently, however, this is misunderstood as a development that is merely external to us, whereas in fact it is closely linked to a fundamental change in human consciousness and self-reflection, individual as well as social.

The negativity that Teilhard often associates with the "road of the East" is linked to the recognition that the underlying structure of eastern spiritualities frequently implies, at least theoretically, a negation of the world. This is especially true of certain aspects of Indian religions: matter is illusory, the world and its phenomena are ultimately unreal. Consequently, there can be no real evolution, no real growth and progress in the world, or in the work of human beings. Ultimately, renunciation is the highest ideal, and all action has to be abandoned to achieve true realization in complete inwardness.

However, this ideal is, in practice, little different from the asceticism, contemplation, and otherworldliness found in much of the western monastic and spiritual tradition. Teilhard argues against any kind of one-sided asceticism; instead, he seeks a harmonious balance between human inwardness and outwardness. The experience of mysticism, of spirituality at the deepest level, becomes centrally linked to the importance of the experiential universe, the world surrounding us. Thus, the mystic is not a dreamer, who escapes the world and its problems but, on the contrary, such a person is a supreme realist. Instead of seeking separate, inner contemplation apart from the world, mystics are the ones to chart a new road *into* the realities of this world. Here, too, the superiority of praxis over theory is emphasized.

The way of mysticism must be integrated with the many-sided aspects of social and practical life here and now. It must provide humankind with a viable spirituality to cope with the problems, responsibilities, and choices of the contemporary world rather than invite individuals to an inward escape from them. Teilhard's emphasis lies not so much on stressing a "this-worldly" as against an "other-worldly" attitude, but on making a fervent plea to develop what has been called a *"changeful orientation to the world."*[51] In other words, his approach to spirituality is closely concerned with our capacity for world-transforming action and decisive moral choices. A new spirituality must combine in an entirely new way a commitment to the rich diversity of the world and human experience with the ongoing search for absolute oneness, transcendence, and divine union.

Teilhard foresaw the rise of a new "mysticism of evolution" that is different from and opposed to an earlier "mysticism of evasion."[52] This "neomysticism" implies not only a "love of evolution," but refers also to the possibility of a further "evolution of mysticism," whereby the mystical sense, the search for ultimate oneness, is assuming planetary dimensions. Teilhard thought that the experience of mysticism, instead of being an isolated phenomenon experienced by only a few outstanding individuals, would become much more widespread than has been the case so far. The "mystical temperature" of humankind is rising to the same extent as human consciousness and self-reflection are growing.

Teilhard's two basic types of mystical orientation may easily be mistaken to repeat simply the well-known distinction of monistic and theistic forms of mysticism. Yet there is a subtle, and very important, difference here: a new element is introduced through the emphasis on a *dynamic typology*. The two different types of mysticism are separated from each other through a process of either identification or unification. This dynamic and processual character is closely related to a critical awareness about the different place of time in modern consciousness, as well as the importance of matter, world, and cosmos for spiritual development.

The fundamental stress on the newness of the present time ultimately overcomes and transcends past divisions of peoples and cultures in space, linked to separate religious developments in East and West. What can the religious teachings of the past, whether eastern or western, contribute to the "building of the earth," to the shaping of the future? Moved by this question, Teilhard looked for the active and animating elements in different religious traditions, for pointers toward a new religious breakthrough, and for a yet unformulated new mysticism. He conceived of this as a synthesis that would integrate in a new way two traditionally separate concerns of human beings: the search for God, and the development of this world.

Mysticism in Teilhard's thought does not refer, therefore, to the traditional, individualistic, exclusively soul- or God-centered spirituality so often associated with the mystical quest. If mysticism is the very heart of religious life, it must provide human beings today with the deepest springs of energy for both action and interaction with others.[53] It cannot merely be an isolated *spirit*uality, but must stand for a *spirit-in-and-through-matter mentality*, for spirit and matter are not seen as separate and opposed, but interdependent.

Human spiritual development and religious experience are thus understood as closely interwoven with, and inseparable from, human experience in general. One might say that, ultimately, Teilhard looked for unity, homogeneity, and a final coherence of the mystical vision in the light of modern science. Although science itself can determine neither our image of the Divine nor the nature of religion, it nevertheless rules out certain representations of God and certain forms of worship "as *not being homogeneous* with the dimensions of the universe known to our experience. This notion of homogeneity is, without doubt, of central importance in intellectual, moral, and mystical life."[54] The mystic "seer," who can perceive the intimate union and interaction between God and all the elements of the world, has overcome the twofold danger of seeking either monistic fusion with the world or spiritualist escape from it into a "beyond." Instead, such a mystic realizes that ultimate unity with God can be found on a third and completely new road in and through the world.[55]

Seen from this perspective, much in the mystical spirituality of the past was criticized by Teilhard, both in East and West. The search for a harmonious balance between the unification of the world and a person's inner life introduces an element of newness into the understanding of mysticism, widening it out to include aspects usually thought of as separate. Closely connected with human attitudes to the natural and social world, and made dynamic through a stress on convergence and unifying action, this "mysticism of action" becomes an experience potentially open to all people. In his comparative study of mysticism, F. C. Happold has described Teilhard's mysticism as springing from the inspiration of a universe seen as moved and compenetrated by God in the totality of its evolution....This is essentially a new type of mysticism, the result of a profound, life-long, reconciling meditation on religious and scientific truth; and it is thus of immense relevance and significance for a scientific age such as ours.[56]

Teilhard's mystical vision was truly that of a "scientist and seer," to quote the subtitle of Charles Raven's early biography of Teilhard.[57] This vision embraced "physics," "metaphysics," and "mysticism," as expressed by him,[58] but with the meaning of each of these words extended in an unusual way. However, Teilhard's approach to mysticism, although linked to a very particular, novel interpretation, was not primarily intellectual. It was above all experiential, existential, and action oriented. Both Teilhard's life and thought bear witness to the dynamic center of all religious life: the ardor of a mystic vision. Here lies the real center of gravity for his entire work. Without seeing this, no interpretation can do full justice to this vision.

To conclude then, Teilhard always looked at religion and mysticism from a universal rather than a particular perspective, but one deeply rooted in personal, mystical experience, as well as in the global context of East-West travel and international scientific research. With varying degrees of clarity, he affirmed throughout his work that in human life and reflection the presence of religion is an essential datum, a basic fact, to be taken into account in any systematic study of the human being, historically as well as theoretically. Religion is an integral part of the "human phenomenon," and at the very heart of religion lies the phenomenon of mysticism, culminating in a radiant center of energy and love linked to a dynamic, evolutionary mysticism of action. Instead of being an exceptional occurrence, mysticism—in particular a dynamic mysticism of action—represents a major axis of human evolution. Mysticism, rightly understood and practiced, is of the greatest evolutionary importance in furthering human self-understanding and future development.

232

This interpretation can be presented in the form of a diagram:

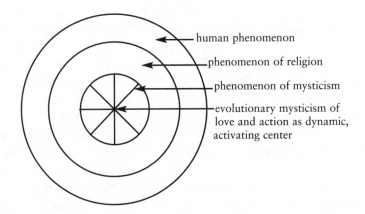

human phenomenon

phenomenon of religion

phenomenon of mysticism

evolutionary mysticism of love and action as dynamic, activating center

Although this evolutionary mysticism of action is deeply grounded in Christian incarnational theology, the full flowering of an active, and activating, spirituality can only emerge in the contemporary world if the different religious traditions meet each other and work more closely together in convergent encounter. To solve the problem of the spirit, the combined effort of the world faiths is needed. The rich resources of eastern spiritualities form an essential part of the human religious quest, and of the global religious heritage of humanity, as Teilhard rightly recognized, although he failed to explore all that this might entail.

The new "mysticism of action" is growing—and is much debated at present, as can be seen from William Johnston's study *The Inner Eye of Love*. Like Teilhard, Johnston emphasizes the universal call to mysticism as well as the central role and unifying force of love, an existential love that is not purely spiritual but has its roots in matter. Johnston writes with great compassion that

> modern people are looking for a new spirituality and a new asceticism which will enable them to benefit from the good points of scientific progress while at the same time developing and training those mystical faculties which lead to enlightenment. This is quite a challenge.[59]

Living in Japan for many years, Johnston has spent his whole life exploring the enriching insights of eastern mysticisms, especially of Zen Buddhism, in a way Teilhard never did nor could have done during his lifetime. Other examples of western religious practitioners who have been transformed by eastern spiritualities are Bede Griffiths from England and Swami Abhishiktananda, originally from France. They were deeply influenced by their long stay in India, whereas Thomas Merton was much inspired by religions from the East while living in the United States.

These are just a few examples showing that, by now, several religious people have gone far beyond Teilhard in discovering a deep complementarity and convergence between East and West. However, this is what he expected. His vision of ultimate unity and coherence lacks the necessary detail; indeed, this is its most serious defect. Yet his reflections on eastern religions and on a new mysticism of action, inspired by the insights of evolution, can provide a stimulating challenge and can act as a catalyst for others. They can be creatively applied in situations of interreligious encounter as well as in the contemporary study of religions.

Teilhard's emphasis on a new mysticism for a new world, shaped by the processes of evolution, change, and transformation, stems from the burning desire to develop an adequate spirituality for today, a spirituality that can give meaning to human lives by pointing to a direction and definite goal. Teilhard insists on the existence of fundamentally different spiritual orientations and, most of all, argues against a mere revival of the mysticisms of the past. Past spirituality is simply not enough for today; the development of a rich, action-oriented spirituality appropriate for life in the contemporary world requires crucial choices. What kind of spirituality is chosen will not only affect the shape of our future, but also be decisive for the place of religion in the twenty-first century. Teilhard's choice lies with a new mysticism, an evolutionary mysticism of action and convergence that, for him, alone holds the promise of a future for religion. Such a new mysticism can only become a reality insofar as others go beyond Teilhard in exploring this new path.

Epilogue

SPIRITUALITY AND MYSTICISM IN AN EVOLUTIONARY WORLD

In our fast-changing global society, ever more people come to realize that the future balance of humanity and the planet will depend on the human community itself. Humanity has to accept full responsibility for its own further self-evolution. This is only possible if the necessary ecological conditions are met, harmony with the complex web of life and its evolutionary processes of becoming is maintained, and a closer collaboration between diverse human groups is more consciously fostered. This requires us to reexamine what it means to be human. We must redefine our understanding of humanity by working for a radical transformation of contemporary consciousness and culture.

In religion and spirituality, as in other areas of human endeavor, humankind is truly at the crossroads, faced with choices that invite revolutionary changes. Early in his scientific career, Pierre Teilhard de Chardin was aware that the impact of evolution implies a profound metamorphosis in religious sensibilities and demands a new religious synthesis. The choice is not simply between the acceptance or rejection of religion, but between two fundamentally different directions—either a past-oriented revival or a forward-looking new religious breakthrough. At present, we need to know which road to explore, which direction to take in order to find active and life-giving, rather than life-negating, spiritualities.

Today, rival spiritualities and mysticisms cut across different religions, for past- and forward-looking movements exist everywhere side by side. To achieve a new spiritual awareness it is not

235

enough to return to the insights of the past, whether they are those of East or West. All religions possess a great spiritual heritage, but this has been developed and kept alive outside the perspectives of a fast-evolving world. It is now essential to relate evolutionary insights in a creative way to our contemporary situation. In the past few decades, a lively interest in the spiritualities of different religious traditions has developed both within and beyond traditional religious institutions and through the rise of many new religious movements. A strong interest in spirituality has also emerged in completely secular settings. At the same time, there exists a growing tendency toward a new interfaith spirituality, sometimes described as "interspirituality," based on convergent insights from different mystical and spiritual traditions.[1]

Teilhard de Chardin recognized the need for a dynamic and creative approach to humanity's global religious heritage earlier than most. From the 1930s onward, he perceived and pursued a definite path toward a new mysticism. It is obvious that this exciting new path was far from clearly signposted; he conceived it as too narrow and too closely bound up with western ways of thinking. For someone wishing to gain a deeper insight into the experiential and spiritual dimension of eastern religions, Teilhard's works are clearly inadequate and marked by typically colonialist and orientalist perspectives that have been severely critiqued by now. We need to go beyond Teilhard by further developing his ideas while trying to understand why and how he arrived at the views he held. We also need to highlight the focal point of his spiritual vision, which, in spite of its shortcomings, possesses a universal scope and dynamic of extraordinary power and attraction.

To sum up my findings on Teilhard's attitudes and experience of eastern, especially Asian religions, I offer several concluding comments. His life and travels in the East brought him into contact with many aspects of eastern religions, yet nonetheless he remained a "chance passer-by," as he first described himself on his arrival in China. He never acquired a detailed knowledge of eastern religious beliefs and practices, and he clearly acknowledged more than once that he was not a specialist on eastern religious thought. However, his general acquaintance with the peoples and cultures of the East was nonetheless greater than is usually acknowledged. Moreover, his reading on Indian religions, different mystics, and diverse forms of mysticism was more extensive than has previously been assumed.

From a contemporary perspective of interreligious encounter and the growing efforts to understand cultural and religious differences in the world, his comments on eastern religions can sometimes make difficult reading. Understood literally rather than typologically, they are often inaccurate, harsh, and unjust. His views about the value of eastern religions in the modern world remain in an oppositional mode of thought instead of being genuinely inclusive and universal. His perspective regarding the East is in many ways closely akin to that of Carl Gustav Jung, who spoke of the "assiduously cultivated credulity of the West in regard to eastern thought," and who affirmed with similar emphasis that "the West will produce its own yoga, and it will be on the basis laid down by Christianity."[2] Teilhard always remained convinced that a new breakthrough in spirituality and mysticism would initially begin in the West.

Other writers today maintain with equal fervor that a spiritual renewal can only come from the East, and from nowhere else. Such a possibility cannot be ruled out a priori, although given present religious interactions, this seems perhaps less likely. Eastern religions have become increasingly important for a reorientation of religion in the West; yet at the same time, western religious ideas are helping to create a new focus for religious self-understanding in the East. There exists now a strong movement of complementary interchange and convergence, at least among those in West and East most alive to the spiritual needs of the contemporary world.

Teilhard de Chardin saw the growing importance of greater collaboration and convergence among the different religions of the world with extraordinary clarity, although he remained almost blind to the great spiritual treasures of eastern religions. What explanations can be suggested for this lack in perception and judgment?

One of the most important reasons is that the major focus of his thought on religion was always contemporary rather than historical. He was mainly concerned with the relevance of religion for *contemporary* humankind confronted with the task of building the future. Thus, many details relating to traditional religious life in the East were of no interest to his world- and action-oriented approach.

Equally important is the fact that his contacts with eastern religions were restricted by the milieu in which he lived. During the 1920s, the foreign concessions in Tientsin and the international diplomatic and scholarly community in Peking before the Second World War were an effective barrier that separated westerners from the indigenous population. This applied perhaps less to Teilhard than to many others, since he had the opportunity to travel across vast areas of China, and elsewhere in Asia, during his expeditions. He worked in close collaboration with Chinese scientists and met some leading intellectuals and activists. Yet he primarily came into contact with western-educated Chinese, or at least with members of a western-oriented, scientific elite, who often were alienated from their own religious and cultural traditions. The opportunities to see eastern religious life in an active and dynamic situation were relatively rare. For this reason, he may well have underestimated the dynamic qualities of eastern religions and not recognized their intrinsic strength in addressing the problems of the modern world. However, judging from contemporary accounts, Chinese religious life was at a very low ebb during Teilhard's stay, so that one wonders whether his views would have been significantly different had he spent a major part of his life in India or Japan rather than in China.

Like an explorer, Teilhard lived much of his life in the open air. Whether on field trips or in the laboratory, his scientific research consisted of teamwork with other people drawn from widely different backgrounds. Given this experience, his approach to religion and mysticism was necessarily very different from that of religious specialists and theologians whose thought often develops only within the confines of their own studies. In fact, it is possible that Teilhard's views on eastern religions were so critical because he lived in the East for so long. Unlike other westerners who, removed from the East, emphasize selective features of eastern spirituality, he experienced the religions of the East in their wider social and cultural context. He therefore did not make the mistake of seeing eastern spiritualities in isolation from their wider social setting. The sociopolitical context was quite different during the first half of the twentieth century from what it is today under radically changed political and economic circumstances.

However, Teilhard's understanding of religion and mysticism was also the result of a particular religious temperament. The blending of mystical experience with scientific thought and practice produced a unique personal-existential synthesis not always matched by an equally satisfactory synthesis at the intellectual and philosophical level. One can ask whether his interpretation of mysticism is not based too exclusively on a unitary model of consciousness, leaving little room for wide psychological and cultural differences or for the immense historical diversity of eastern and western religious traditions.

It is true to say, though, that the fundamental vision he wanted to communicate to others stems less from the desire to construct a philosophy than from the vivid experience of the living God and from the need to affirm and praise God's presence as divine "diaphany" in the world today.

Teilhard's personal synthesis cannot be repeated in the way it was lived, although many aspects of his thought can be taken up and developed further. His understanding of the role of religion in the modern world can inspire others to study and experience the important contributions that ethical and spiritual teachings of different religious traditions can make to the building of a global humanity and world civilization. Teilhard's importance may ultimately lie more in having first explored a particular perspective and asked important questions than in the provision of specific answers.

From the vantage point of a traveler between different worlds—that of East and West, as well as from the recesses of the past to the threshold of the future—Teilhard realized earlier than most the revolutionary impact of contemporary scientific, social, and cultural changes on traditional religious teaching. During his travels, he could observe that, in many respects, humankind already possesses a common global culture in a material sense. With rare acuity, he pointed to the urgent need for sharing common spiritual values that can provide humanity with a coherent view of reality and give meaning and direction to the dynamic developments of contemporary life. He was also one of the first to emphasize that the major issue in the "battle of the spirit" today concerns the confrontation between a religious and a humanistic-atheistic worldview.[3] In other words, beyond the need for more interreligious encounter there exists a pressing task to engage more passionately in dialogue with contemporary culture. That includes a much deeper engagement with an evolutionary worldview, taking cognizance of the immense process of becoming that has opened up new dimensions of time, space, and complexity that have profound repercussions for contemporary consciousness and culture.

Religiously speaking, Teilhard thought that humanity is still living in the faraway past, in the Neolithic age, as it were. For example, he described certain religious beliefs and practices of the West as forms of "paleo-Christianity" that he wished to see replaced by a dynamic "neo-Christianity." Yet no religion is free from fossilized forms. What he rather inadequately referred to as the "road of the East" appears, on closer examination, to point to all past forms of religious "other-worldliness," to any outdated spirituality that is too ascetic and world-rejecting, whether in East or West. The need for a new road or, rather, a new, higher synthesis, exists at present in all religious traditions. Nowadays, major changes are taking place in the world faiths in terms of a new "this-worldly" orientation. This shift accounts for the emergence of new forms of Buddhism, Hinduism, and Islam as well as for new interpretations of Christianity. Thus, the convergent encounter of religions has opened up new possibilities and entered a new evolutionary stage of development.

What mattered most to Teilhard was the necessary transformation of each religious heritage to bring out its central insights and distinctive contributions, its vision of truth and ultimate unity, a vision that can be shared by people from different faiths. When a friend once discussed the possibility of religious conversion with Teilhard, he is reported to have replied:

"One should never, or almost never, change the religion of one's forefathers....One must always try to carry the past with one, but carry it with greater understanding and deeper revelation." Perhaps foolishly I said: "Do you mean if you are a Buddhist or a Hindu you should not become a Christian?" He hesitated. "Well, I really meant if you are a Christian", he said. "But even so, if you were of another religion altogether, it would be better to try to carry its truth with you and transform it if you could, though of course sometimes this might not be possible."[4]

Teilhard traveled to the East both physically and mentally, but in a sense, he did not travel far enough. By now, many others have traveled farther and journeyed more deeply into the religions and cultures of the East. Some can relate this experience of discovery and enrichment in significantly new ways to our western ways of thinking. This marks a new beginning, for we are in need of a global, worldwide ecumenism that is truly inclusive and universal and goes beyond the ecumenism of the Christian churches.

Since Teilhard's time eastern countries have achieved political independence, greater self-determination accompanied by rapid modernization, and have strengthened the awareness of their own cultural and religious traditions. The radically new technological and communication developments, especially through the creation of the World Wide Web, now facilitate a cross-cultural and interreligious dialogue in completely new ways. They provide strong evidence for what Teilhard called "the planetization of humanity," or the global interconnections that are now possible between all parts of the world. The striking pace of change in the different cultures of the globe requires a further evolution of human consciousness and thought, as well as of religions. Interfaith dialogue can make an important contribution to these developments, but frequently such dialogue is still taking place at too superficial a level. Instead of leading to an existential commitment and new religious experience, it remains for many a purely intellectual and verbal exercise. Up to now, personal participation in dialogue-in-depth is still relatively rare, but this experience must grow for a new spiritual dynamic, and for new mystical spiritualities, to emerge.

When Teilhard first learnt about Tibetan Buddhism, he thought that the insights of Tibetan monks might be reserved for "a new season." This season has come since our global world has moved into a new era, manifest in social, political, and economic developments, but also evident from the extraordinary growth of interfaith encounter and the increased dialogue between members of different faiths. Visible proof of this are the many interfaith organizations and publications that have come into existence; there has also been the international Parliament of the World's Religions, held four times since 1993. The most recent of these was convened in Melbourne in December 2009, attracting nearly six thousand participants whose activities and collaboration provided strong evidence for the maturing of the global interreligious movement.

Many monks from Tibet and countless gurus from India and other Asian countries have come to live and teach in the West, whereas western monks such as Thomas Merton, Bede Griffiths, Swami Abhishiktananda, William Johnston, and many other people from the West have been deeply influenced by Indian, Tibetan, and Japanese teachings. An active exchange of ideas and a sharing of experience is now taking place especially between Buddhists and Christians, to name just one example. Western people are perhaps more drawn to Buddhism than to any other eastern religion; the mutual attraction is strongest here, and the encounter most enriching for both sides. Similarly, there are many inspiring examples of Hindu-Christian in-depth dialogue. If their respective understanding and experience of God provides an important unifying focus for believers from different faiths, then the rich Indian heritage of *bhakti* theology and the Hindu vision of the Divine have much to contribute toward the development of a more differentiated, richer image of God.

Teilhard's own thought, characterized by the synthesis of a modern scientific worldview with religious and mystical insights, has aroused considerable interest in the East, especially in India, Sri Lanka, Japan, the Philippines, and now also in China. In the opinion of Father Heinrich Dumoulin, the historian of Zen Buddhism, Teilhard's ideas provide a particularly suitable preparation for the intellectual and religious dialogue of the West with Asia.[5] This mutual dialogue has to grow even more, for a new religious vision cannot develop in cultural isolation. At present, however, too many people in the West still inhabit ethnocentric, cultural, and religious ghettos of the past. It is therefore essential to learn what John Dunne has imaginatively called the "passing over" into other people's lives and cultures. Writing about his encounter with eastern religions, he says, "When you pass over to other lives, and by way of other lives to other cultures and other religions, you come back again with new insight into your own life, and by way of your own life to your own culture and religion."[6]

Western people can learn a great deal from eastern religions; for example, the nondogmatic, experimental approach to the search for truth; the emphasis on finding the true self, a search that requires a recentering of one's inner being, a withdrawal of the senses from overactivity and distraction and, at its best, exploring a dimension of consciousness beyond ordinary consciousness. Regular meditation, as practiced in Hinduism and Buddhism, represents an enriching activity of "cultivated nonactivity" that can achieve inner integration and wisdom and, in certain instances, lead to union and communion with one's fellow beings, and with God.

These aspects are initially beneficial to individuals in order to arrive at peace with themselves. In addition, they can also provide inner resources for developing peaceful relationships with others and thus be beneficial to social life. To live in harmony with nature and society is a theme found in Indian and, even more, Chinese religions, and it is precisely this inner and outer harmony that we need so much.

We are living in the midst of an information explosion: a welter of ideas, images, and sounds constantly confront and assault us. A growing number of people realize that we require not only an outer but also an "inner ecology," a restoration of true inwardness that implies a deliberate restraint in thought, speech, and action, a greater simplicity of life, and a special kind of asceticism to disentangle and reduce the complexity of our needs. Without such a restraint, we will cut ourselves off from the inner springs of spiritual energy and creativity.

It is little surprising that in the current experience of widespread disorientation and alienation there has been a fast-growing interest in the mysticism of all religions in the West. The western inquiry into the varieties of religious experience and different types of mysticism is a comparatively recent phenomenon. It began in the late nineteenth century but took off in a big way during the second part of the twentieth century. Through our global interconnections, this has now become even more complex, revealing an ever-greater awareness of the presence of mystical elements in most, if not all, religious traditions.

Comparisons in this field are difficult, however, and can be misleadingly simplistic. Non-western languages often possess no word that exactly corresponds to the meaning of either "spirituality" or "mysticism" in the West.[7] Instead, eastern religions speak of *moksha, samadhi, nirvana,* and *satori*—words that possess quite different semantic traditions and may have other connotations than "mysticism." Here again more study and dialogue will help us to evolve a new understanding and possibly bring about a more commonly shared focus of vision.

Besides the current western interest in the mystical heritage of the world's religions, there exists another, quite different area of dynamic growth where religious insights are applied to the transformation of the social order. The message of spiritual freedom is related to the liberation of human beings from external structures of oppression, whether expressed in the liberation theology of South America or in socialist reinterpretations of Buddhism in South Asia. In a way, the greatest religious problem today is how to be both a mystic and a militant, as Adam Curle has said.[8] In other words, how to combine the search for an expansion of inner awareness with effective social action, and how to find one's true identity in the synthesis of both.

The necessary return to the center must not only be a journey inward, but it must help to weave new connections to the outer world. Interfaith dialogue that remains a monologue among monks, contemplatives, and a few individual seekers is therefore not enough. The need for a new spirituality, a new mysticism of action, is much greater and universal. The search for an adequate contemporary spirituality is in many ways a lay movement inside and even more outside different religions; it relates to the concerns of all rather than only to those of a social and spiritual elite.

The new religious vision for today cannot be found in an eclectic spiritual syncretism or in a return to simpler states of inwardness and withdrawal based exclusively on eastern forms of meditation. Teilhard saw this clearly and, like Jung, he warned westerners not to seek in the East what they cannot find there: an integral spirituality for the modern world. Spirituality is not meant to be an alternative lifestyle, a road of retreat and escape; it needs to be an active leaven of life, feeding the zest and healing the wounds of life. Seen from an evolutionary perspective, spirituality can help us to grow and make the world advance.

The development of religion and society is always closely interrelated. This applies not only to religious institutions but also to the religious self-understanding and spiritual practice of individuals. With the increasing expansion of knowledge we are also gaining a growing acquaintance with each other's religious heritage. This is more than a merely quantitative development; one should not underestimate the possible qualitative effect of a greater knowledge about the world's religions on religious awareness itself. Taking full cognizance of the religious experience of humanity may produce what has been called a "global religious consciousness." It may bring with it a profound transformation, a mutation, in religious awareness, and a new awakening to what is most central to all faith and genuine spirituality, on a scale unknown in the past. Perhaps this is what Teilhard meant when he said that the era not of religions, but of religion, far from being past, is only beginning. He expressed this with increasing urgency, especially at the end of his life, when he emphasized the need for a new mysticism linked to evolution and transformative action in an ever more globally interrelated world, more conscious of itself. Yet he was also aware that this requires an open religious quest that cuts across major religious, denominational, and cultural differences. These changes are now occurring on an almost global scale, although they seem to pass almost unnoticed in many quarters. Yet they represent a radical, even revolutionary transformation, albeit still a largely "silent revolution" born from the dynamic of an evolutionary world.

The experience of an emerging global society has brought with it the idea that we must develop a new consciousness and identity as world citizens. Similarly, we perhaps need a new kind of "world believer" who can meaningfully relate to the perspectives of more than one religious tradition and thereby find a deep enrichment through what has been called a "double" or even "multiple" religious belonging. This requires the intersection of both a particular and universal dimension: rooted in their own religious and cultural traditions, individuals also need to be open to the worldviews of others to widen their own understandings to a vision of universality. Such a process of convergence and synthesis in understanding different religious and cultural traditions has already started, and the results of mutual consultation and dialogue are evident in the search for a new world ethic, evident in such documents as the "Declaration of a Global Ethic" or "The Earth Charter" or current attempts to formulate a "Charter of Compassion."

Much more information and education are necessary to advance the process of understanding and collaboration. This is most important for the social and ecological balance of contemporary global society. What is more, if in the future more and more people increasingly become freed from the necessity of physical labor and possess more abundant leisure time, reflections on fundamental questions of meaning will become available to an ever-greater number of human beings. It will no longer be solely an elite who can cultivate inwardness and the life of the spirit; a new road of spirituality will become a genuine option for a much greater number of people. Thus one might envisage the practice of religion as less institution and culture bound, while the activating and dynamic elements of spirituality are becoming more universally shared.

Today new modes of thinking, feeling, and being are sought, leading to the experience of new forms of unity and community, both more complex and more differentiated than in the past. A more unifying, convergent approach may eventually overcome the existing separations and oppositions, not least the division between religion and modern science, which has been constructed in such an oppositional way by religious crusaders and dogmatic scientists of our time.

The adventure of discovery and knowledge associated with the modern scientific quest has been one of the most powerful developments in human history. Yet many people are now experiencing a deep disenchantment with science because of the reductionist and empiricist narrowness frequently associated with contemporary scientific practice and with the strong dogmatism of some scientists who preach as emphatically as any religious fundamentalist to convert others to their point of view. No wonder that some people prefer to exchange the realm of science with that of the merely mystical, magical, or occult, but this may mean regressing rather than advancing the evolution of humanity.

For Teilhard and some other scientists the way into the future lies in a new synthesis of the rational and mystical, in a truly integral vision that can animate all areas of human work and endeavor. Teilhard combined the insights of evolutionary science with those of a new mysticism; in fact, he spoke of the mysticism of science itself as well as of the mysticism of research.[9] Others recognized his evolutionary mysticism early, for example his American scientific colleague and friend, George Gaylord Simpson, who described him as a "most mystical evolutionary theologian."[10] Coming from a religious rather than scientific perspective, the Jesuit William Johnston also presents Teilhard as a "mystic of science" in his book *Mystical Theology: The Science of Love*. He concludes, "Teilhard's mysticism was only possible in the twentieth century. After him, mystical theology can never be the same."[11] For Johnston, as for Teilhard, theological reflections on mysticism must engage in dialogue with both science and eastern religions. The "science of love" of today's mystical journey must engage the whole person and lead to transformative social action.

John Grim and Mary Evelyn Tucker have written about Teilhard's mysticism that he "realized a radical re-conceptualization of the mystical journey as an entry into evolution, discovering there an immanental sense of the divine," that his mysticism is activated "in scientific investigation and social commitment to research as well as in comprehensive compassion for all life," and that he "came to profound reflections on the mystical character of science itself in exploring the universe that are among his most original contributions."[12]

Today several leading scientists engage in lively discussions on "Science and the Spiritual Quest."[13] In her book *The Sacred*

Depths of Nature,[14] U.S. cell biologist and former president of the Institute of Religion in an Age of Science Ursula Goodenough writes of the different responses elicited by the Epic of Evolution. Her own response includes the articulation of "a covenant with Mystery" and the formulation of "emergent religious principles" that she believes can serve as a "framework for a global Ethos."[15] She concludes her reflections with the following remarks:

> Humans need stories...that help to orient us in our lives and in the cosmos. The Epic of Evolution is such a story, beautifully suited to anchor our search for planetary consensus, telling us of our nature, our place, our context. Moreover, responses to this story...can yield deep and abiding spiritual experiences. And then, after that, we need other stories as well, human-centered stories, a mythos that embodies our ideals and our passions. This mythos comes to us, often in experiences called revelation, from the sages and artists of past and present times.[16]

These remarks weave together different strands of experience that show what remarkable spiritual resources can be discovered through contemporary scientific and evolutionary understanding. Spirituality is now closely related to both science and faith, to the development of the world and that of knowledge, to the dynamic development of society as well as the spiritual growth of the individual. Moreover, it invites the cultivation of "spiritual literacy," a literacy that goes more deeply than all other literacies by fostering the tremendous inner potential of humans to cultivate insight, wisdom, compassion, and love as well as the zest for life through learning to read the signature of the Spirit within ourselves and the whole universe.

The possibility of a new mysticism provides a powerful focus of attraction: it leads into the world rather than out of it. A mysticism of action closely linked to evolution can inspire the spiritualization of human beings in and through the unification of the world in all areas of becoming. The ascent of humanity is more than an ascent to knowledge. Humankind is called to the height

248

of the Spirit, but none of us can reach this summit by ourselves, in separation from others. The present generation will only follow the call to such an ascent if a dynamic and action-oriented spirituality becomes the true driving force of contemporary society and is nourished by convergent approaches of science, religion, and mysticism that can ensure a harmonious future for all of life and humanity on Earth.

APPENDICES

I

TEILHARD'S YEARS IN THE EAST

COUNTRY	DATE	PLACE OF RESIDENCE (IN ITALICS), VISITS, OR EXPEDITIONS
Egypt	1905–8	*Cairo*, Alexandria, Nile Valley, Memphis, Luxor, Karnak, Upper Egypt.
China	1923–46	
	1923–24	Via Suez, Colombo, Penang, Malacca, Saigon, Hong Kong, Shanghai to *Tientsin*. Expeditions to Ordos Desert and eastern Mongolia.
	1926–27	Via Saigon, Annam, Hanoi to *Tientsin*. Expeditions to eastern Mongolia and Yellow River area (Shensi and Shansi provinces).
	1928–30	After two months in Ethiopia and French Somaliland, via Ceylon to *Tientsin*. Expeditions to Manchuria, Yellow River area, Chou-Kou-Tien, and Gobi Desert.
	1931–32	Via Hawaii and Japan to *Peking*. Yellow Expedition: Gobi Desert, Black Gobi, Hami, Urumchi (Sinkiang), Aksu, Bäzäklik, Liangchow, Pei Ling Miao, Shara Muren, Kalgan, Peking.
	1933–35	Via Ceylon, Penang, Singapore, Port Said, Saigon, Shanghai to *Peking*. Expeditions along Yangtze River and in South China.
	1936–37	After four months in India and Indonesia (1935–36), via Hong Kong and Shanghai to *Peking*.
	1937–38	After four months in Burma and Indonesia, return to *Peking*.
	1939–46	*Peking*, Shanghai.
India	1935	October–December: Via Bombay to Rawalpindi, Kashmir, Punjab: Salt Range, Mohenjo-Daro, Lahore; Sind and Baluchistan; central India: Narbada Valley; Calcutta. Via Rangoon and Singapore to Indonesia.

253

Indonesia	1936	One month (January). Djakarta. Expeditions to the center and south of Java.
	1938	Fortnight (April). Island of Java: Bandung, Surakarta, Trinil, La Solo.
Burma	1935	Visit to Rangoon over Christmas.
	1937–38	December–March: Rangoon, Pagan, Upper Burma, Irrawaddy Valley.
Japan	1931, 1937–38	Three brief visits: Kobe, Kyoto, Nara.

Author's note: The former spellings of place names found in Teilhard's works have been maintained here; the modern spellings are often different.

II

EARLY WRITINGS THAT INCLUDE
A DISCUSSION OF PANTHEISM,
MONISM, AND MYSTICISM

YEAR	TITLE	ENGLISH EDITION	FRENCH EDITION
1916	"Cosmic Life"	WTW, 13–71	vol. 12 17–82
1917	"The Mystical Milieu"	WTW, 115–49	vol. 12 153–92
1917	"The Soul of the World"	WTW, 177–90	vol. 12 243–59
1918	"My Universe"	HM, 196–208	vol. 12 293–307
1918	"Note on the 'Universal Element' of the World"	WTW, 271–76	vol. 12 387–93
1919	"Note on the Presentation of the Gospel in a New Age"	HM, 209–24	vol. 12 395–414
1919	"The Universal Element"	WTW, 289–302	vol. 12 429–45
1923	"Pantheism and Christianity"	CE, 56–75	vol. 10 71–91
1923	"The Mass on the World"	HM, 119–34	vol. 13 139–56
1924	"My Universe"	SC, 37–85	vol. 9 63–114

Author's note: See the List of Abbreviations (in the Notes section) for the English titles, and the Bibliography for the volumes of the French edition.

III

Later Writings That Include Specific Comparisons with Eastern Religions

YEAR	TITLE	ENGLISH EDITION	FRENCH EDITION
1932	"The Road of the West"	TF, 40–59	vol. 11, 45–64
1933	"Christianity in the World"	SC, 98–112	vol. 9, 129–45
1934	"How I Believe"	CE, 96–132	vol. 10, 115–59
1939	"The Grand Option"	FM, 37–60	vol. 5, 57–81
1940	*The Phenomenon of Man*	PM, 209–12	vol. 1, 231–35
1944	"Introduction to the Christian Life"	CE, 151–72	vol. 10, 177–200
1945	"Action and Activation"	SC, 174–86	vol. 9, 219–33
1946	"Ecumenism"	SC, 197–98	vol. 9, 251–55
1947	"The Spiritual Contribution of the Far East"	TF, 134–47	vol. 11, 147–60
1948	"My Fundamental Vision"	TF, 163–208	vol. 11, 177–233
1950	"A Clarification: Reflections on Two Converse Forms of the Spirit"	AE, 215–27	vol. 7, 223–36
1950	"The Heart of the Matter"	HM, 14–79	vol. 13, 19–74

| 1951 | "Some Notes on the Mystical Sense: An Attempt at Clarification" | TF, 209–11 | vol. 11, 225–29 |
| 1955 | "The Christic" | HM, 80–102 | vol. 13, 94–117 |

Author's note: See the List of Abbreviations for the English titles (in the Notes section) and the Bibliography for the volumes of the French edition. Book titles are italicized; all essay titles are set in quotation marks.

IV

TEILHARD'S READING

Comments on Two Books Read in 1945

Teilhard kept a *carnet de lecture*, a notebook on his reading, in which he regularly listed and commented on the books he had read. Unfortunately, it is impossible to reconstruct a comprehensive list of his reading, since only three notebooks have survived, two dating from 1945 and one from after 1952. However incomplete and fragmentary, these notes and comments on particular books provide a valuable insight into the working of Teilhard's mind and his reaction to other people's thought. So far, no full study of the three existing notebooks has been undertaken, but the French text of the second notebook was published in 2007.[1] Where extracts of particular books have been noted down, these can be compared with the original works from which they were taken. Teilhard's comments on his reading can frequently be supplemented by further evidence from his diaries of the same period, which have also remained unpublished so far.

As far as I am aware, only Teilhard's notes on reading Karl Barth have received closer attention up to now.[2] I comment here on some notes from the first and second notebook relating to two works, one a comparative study on mysticism, the other a two-volume work on Indian religions. Teilhard's excerpts from these books consist of brief notes with accompanying comments. They will probably be of most interest to readers with a specialized interest in mysticism and in Indian religions. However, as it is little known that Teilhard read such books at all, and because the

258

notes throw additional light on his attitude toward eastern religions, it is important to present this material and interpret its meaning within a larger context.

Joseph Maréchal

Studies in the Psychology of the Mystics

Teilhard had known Joseph Maréchal and his work since 1910. At an early stage, he may have read Maréchal's essay "On the Feeling of Presence in Mystics and Non-Mystics" (1908–9), but no conclusive evidence exists for this. Much later, however, in 1945, his *carnet de lecture I* gives several pages of extracts from Maréchal's *Études sur la Psychologie des Mystiques*.[3] These provide an interesting example of Teilhard's use of sources and document his continuing interest in mysticism. Maréchal's work includes, among others, a comparative discussion of Hindu and Muslim mysticism, an essay on mystical grace centering on Al Hallaj, and an extensive, annotated bibliography on mysticism.

Apart from a brief reference to Leuba's work in the psychology of religion, Teilhard's notes relate exclusively to one particular essay, entitled "Réflexions sur l'étude comparée des mysticisms."[4] It deals with doctrinal and psychological elements in the study of mysticism and contains sections on Buddhism, Patanjali's Yoga, and the different psychological attitudes of eastern and western mystics. In addition, Muslim and Christian mysticism and asceticism are discussed.

Teilhard's notes are particularly concerned with doctrinal points. After a brief reference to Persian dualism, the Hindu teaching on the immanence of the Divine is described as a position that does not allow "an increase in the mystical movement." This is followed by Maréchal's characterization of Buddhism as "neither a cosmological dualism nor a monism" but a practical agnosticism. The content of liberation ("i.e. Nirvana," Teilhard added) is undetermined ("logically apersonal"), leaving room, however, for a hypothetical transcendence.[5] In brackets, Teilhard noted that it is necessary to explain "the development of Buddhist mysticism (Great vehicle? Amida-Buddhism?)."

Most of the notes are taken from subsection 4 of Maréchal's essay dealing with "Le monisme panthéistique."[6] They are primarily concerned with Indian, that is to say, Upanishadic monism and with western philosophical monism. Teilhard copied a long passage from La Vallé Poussin, used by Maréchal: The Upanishads are the perennial source of idealistic mysticism for both orthodox and unorthodox Indian thinkers, from Buddha to Shankara, from Ramanuja to Rammohun Roy.

Teilhard then summarized Maréchal's discussion of Shankara's Vedanta, dealing with the *Atman-Brahman* identification. The Absolute is absolute nonduality, and all multiple is equated with illusion or *maya*. One does not know Brahman, one simply is Brahman. Teilhard only comments, *"No love!"*

Whereas Hindu monism seems to inspire a mysticism of exclusive inner withdrawal, abandoning the evanescent world and its nothingness, western pantheism, even in its most daring introvertive developments, never completely renounces the idea that an ascent toward the Divine can be achieved through the world. In Maréchal's words, copied by Teilhard, "Renunciation is superior integration rather than simple detachment."[7] This is followed by an emphatic "No!!" For Teilhard, this is not the most fundamental difference between western and Hindu monism; it consists much more in "two antithetical notions of unity" and a "profound difference in the subjective attitude." Both forms of monism share a common aspiration toward the One, but the movement to reach it is different. When Maréchal states that western monism maintains, through analogy, a positive relationship between finite forms and the Absolute, Teilhard adds "road of the West."

One of the primary sources of western philosophical monism are the *Enneads* of Plotinus. Teilhard noted details of Maréchal's discussion, especially on the possible influence of Plotinus on Vedanta, Muslim Sufism, and, through Pseudo-Dionysius, Christian mysticism.

Modern philosophical monism is represented through Fichte, Schelling, and Hegel. Maréchal draws a sharp distinction between "natural" and "supernatural" mysticism, still maintained by certain writers today. Teilhard does not accept this view; for him, the main difference lies in the possibility or impossibility of love.

Maréchal's subsequent section is entitled "Le monothéisme et la possibilité d'une Mystique surnaturelle."[8] Teilhard simply copied this title and commented, "The Christian mystical act has not yet found its metaphysics." This sentence is underlined twice in red and black. With it, the notes on Maréchal's book in the *carnet de lecture* end.

The meaning of this comment becomes more clear when read in conjunction with a contemporary diary entry referring to Maréchal's book. In the diary, the "Christian mystical act" is identified with "love." Its corresponding "metaphysics" has not been adequately expressed yet. It would have to give maximum room to an ultimate unity as well as to the intrinsic value of the cosmos, by which Teilhard means the world in its fullest sense, natural as well as human.[9]

The significance of these notes is twofold. First, they show that in 1945 Teilhard was still interested in the different interpretations of pantheistic monism. Second, the few personal comments prove that, while he admitted an affinity and continuity between various forms of monism, he saw the different types of mysticism as distinguished through their divergent views about the relationship between the manifold and the Absolute. The fundamental question is whether the One is reached through a union of love, including a love for the realities of this world. Such love is not a simple attraction, but it implies a dynamic movement that, through the ultimate convergence of all elements in the One, realizes the highest possible form of union. This particular interpretation led Teilhard to disagree with certain aspects of Maréchal's presentation of Christian mysticism, as he disagreed elsewhere with that of other writers.

The references to Maréchal's work in the *carnet de lecture* and diary show a dialectical tension in Teilhard's thought: considering the monistic and theistic interpretations of mysticism, he accepted certain aspects of each while rejecting other elements in both. It would seem, therefore, that he searched for a new synthesis in the understanding of mysticism not developed so far.

Pierre Johanns

To Christ through the Vedanta

Soon after reading Maréchal's book, Teilhard turned to a more specialized work on Indian thought. The first ten pages of his *carnet de lecture II*, also dating from 1945, deal with a book by Pierre Johanns, *Vers le Christ par le Vedanta*.[10] These extracts are considerably longer and, because of their importance, they deserve detailed comment.

First, the background of the book. In the early part of the twentieth century, Father Johanns[11] was well known among Roman Catholic missionaries for his attempt to bring about a closer encounter between Christianity and Hinduism. He studied Hindu religious thought in depth because he considered it to be an eminent *praeparatio evangelica*, a suitable preparation for the reception of the Christian gospel. Thus, Hinduism was seen as providing the natural foundations for the supernatural revelation of Christianity. Johanns's attitude may be regarded as a Roman Catholic variant of the Protestant "fulfillment school" that dominated missionary circles at the beginning of the twentieth century.

In pursuit of his aim to show that the best of eastern thought finds its completion in Christianity, Father Johanns and Father Dandoy edited a journal called *The Light from the East*.[12] Johanns's own major contribution was a series of 137 articles, published in this journal from 1922 to 1934, under the overall theme "To Christ through the Vedanta." Later published in two volumes in French translation, they became the best known of Johanns's works on Indian religious thought.

The two volumes of *Vers le Christ par le Vedanta* represent a well-referenced scholarly study. In the introduction, Johanns states that there exists no important Catholic doctrine, as formulated by Saint Thomas Aquinas, that cannot also be found in one or the other system of Vedanta philosophy. On one hand, he argues for the complementarity of the various branches of Vedanta philosophy and, on the other, for the affinity of this synthesis with Thomistic doctrine.

One-third of Johanns's first volume is devoted to the great

ninth-century Hindu theologian Shankara, and two-thirds to the eleventh-century theologian Ramanuja. Whereas Ramanuja has a well-developed doctrine of God, the human being, and the world, Shankara gives such an exalted position to the Absolute that the treatment of humans and the world remain secondary in his work. Johanns emphasizes, however, that pantheism is not only foreign to Shankara's doctrine but has been clearly refuted by him. At the same time, Johanns was aware that Shankara's lofty doctrine ought to be supplemented by a fully positive philosophy of the human being, of nature, and an adequate philosophy of religion. Teilhard's comments are along similar lines, but they go beyond Johanns's criticisms by questioning some of the latter's own presuppositions.

Volume 2 of Johanns's work is entirely devoted to the study of Vallabha, a Vedanta theologian of the sixteenth century. The introduction claims that Johanns's volume, published in 1933, is the first exposition of Vallabha's thought in any European language.[13]

Teilhard's extracts and comments on Johanns's two volumes are sufficiently copious to draw certain conclusions as to his interest in reading such a work and his method in assimilating its content. The main body of the notes either summarizes certain ideas about Vedanta, as found in Johanns, or it quotes passages in full. However, these quotations do not always strictly follow the original; they may carry a different orthography, leave out words, or abbreviate them. Although not always literally correct, they always reproduce the correct meaning. In addition, the notes include critical comments from Teilhard, referring either to Vedanta or to Johanns himself. Through a close comparison of the extracts in the *carnet de lecture* with the original text, the personal comments can be clearly discerned from the copied notes. Teilhard's own remarks are mainly found on the margin of his notebook, or they are inserted in brackets following the extracts.

The notes begin with the author and title of the book: *Vers le Christ par le Vedanta*. Above "Vedanta," Teilhard added in brackets, "Late Neo-Vedanta, influenced by Christianity." This may appear surprising if it were meant as an explanatory comment. However, it does not seem to relate directly to the title of Johanns's work but appears to be an afterthought. One can interpret this remark as intended to distinguish the classical Vedanta, dealt with by Johanns, from the modern neo-Vedanta of the nineteenth and twentieth centuries. In the latter, a reinterpretation of classical Vedanta teaching occurred, initially influenced through the contact with western, especially Christian, ideas.

The first page of notes is devoted to Shankara. The date of his death is mentioned, and the fact that, through his defense of brahmanical orthodoxy, he conquered Buddhist heterodoxy. His teaching predominates among educated Hindus but is not universally accepted in India. Shankara had some difficulty in interpreting certain Vedic texts that state that the universe is an evolution from God. Through his exclusive emphasis on the Absolute, the world and the individuality of the soul become pure illusion or *maya*. By concentrating solely on the true nature of Brahman, Shankara so exalts the nature of the Absolute that no internal relationship within it may exist.

Commenting on Johanns's remark that Shankara is led by his own logic to negate the existence of the world, Teilhard noted on the margin, "Logic of the Absolute is exaggerated! Evolution equals zero!" Shankara leaves no room for the world and its development; he cannot explain the manifold in relation to the One.

Teilhard's notes do not reproduce any excerpts from Johanns's detailed chapters on Shankara's analysis of the Upanishadic statement *tat tvam asi*, understood as strict identity between Brahman and Atman. It is difficult to say whether he read these chapters. It is evident that he could not accept an exclusively absolutist position. The relationship between an absolute One and a manifold world, as well as the understanding of evolution, always remained his major interest. This is borne out by the subsequent notes on Ramanuja and Vallabha. The last remark on Shankara mentions that his absolute position, which allows for no synthesis whatsoever, strikes objective as well as subjective pantheism at its roots.

Whereas just over one page of Teilhard's notes are devoted to Shankara, more than two pages deal with Ramanuja, followed by more than three pages on the comparison of the two thinkers. This faithfully reflects the distribution of material in Johanns's first volume.

Teilhard, like most Christians, finds Ramanuja more attractive than Shankara's metaphysical monism. Following Johanns's exposition, he notes that for Ramanuja, God is personal and loves human beings. His concept of God may be philosophically less elevated than Shankara's, but it corresponds more to our religious needs. While Shankara evades any real explanation of the relationship between the world and God, Ramanuja wants to save the reality of the world by seeing it as absolutely within God.

Teilhard noted on the margin of his notebook that this may be identical to his own view of things except that it is "static" and without "center-complexity." However, this statement is preceded by both an exclamation and a question mark. For Teilhard, the great metaphysical discovery of modem times is the principle of evolution rather than *in*volution. Hinduism, like neo-Platonism, does not accept evolution in its true sense, but only emanation. Many of Teilhard's remarks bear on this distinction between evolutionary creation and involution or emanation. A consequence of the latter is the acceptance of matter as evil or illusory. He remarks, "Even for the theist Ramanuja the cosmos equals involution, and matter is an obstacle!"

Other notes are concerned with the nature of the Indian concept of *karma* as an impersonal, objective law, leading to the involvement of the soul with matter. There is no answer to the question where karma comes from. One of the ways to gain liberation from the effects of karma is through *bhakti*, consisting of loving devotion linked to disinterested meditation and asceticism. For Ramanuja, the liberated soul is not annihilated in the fullness of God but becomes wholly conscious while matter falls away. Thus, matter is always seen as the oppressive element. Teilhard added the comment: "Always the road *of the East.*"

This is followed by a reference to Johanns's "fortunate distinction" in saying that God is not the self of the soul, as Ramanuja maintains, but its *"Super-self,"* perhaps better expressed as the higher Self that makes love possible. Teilhard mentions in addition that love requires God to be the higher Self of the cosmos.

The comparisons between Ramanuja and Shankara, found in the second half of Johanns's volume 1 relate to the concept of God, the understanding of the universe, and the relationship between God and the world. Teilhard notes that for Shankara this is a relationship of identity, while Ramanuja maintains the inherence of the world in God. After this, two different understandings of Nirvana are mentioned: Buddhist "emptiness" and Shankara's "positive indetermination," which may be "plenitude."

With reference to Ramanuja's treatment of God as personal, Teilhard wrote, "NB. Christianity is thus not alone in maintaining a personal God." It is important to know that he made such a comment. It shows that at least when reading this book, if not before, he was aware that theism is an integral part of the Hindu religious tradition, and Christianity can claim no uniqueness in this respect. Teilhard asks what is then specifically Christian? It is suggested that this may be a new form of love, linked to the incarnate "Christ-Omega."

In Teilhard's view, neither Ramanuja nor Shankara offer us an ideal that is in any way related to humankind or the world. Rather, they present a pure spirit in a real (Ramanuja) or illusory (Shankara), but nevertheless accidental, relationship to the world of matter. Thus, matter is rejected as illusory, or it is simply juxtaposed to spirit. Such a position is, according to Teilhard, due to a complete disregard for the true nature of evolution, which implies the interdependence of matter and spirit. Whereas for Christianity the idea of salvation involves the notion of progress, the Vedantic concept of self-realization really means a regress, a return to the One, arrived at negatively through silence and meditation.

Teilhard's comments on Johanns's text emphasize that the author does not see that Hindus, in spite of a personal God, fail to recognize an ultimate unity achieved by convergence, nor do they acknowledge the real implications of evolution. That is to say, whenever there is talk of evolution, what really is meant is the involution of spirit in matter.

Ramanuja's system is crowned by *bhakti*—the love of God as both the end and means of human self-realization. Teilhard notes his difficulty here: love may be evasion or negation of the cosmos; alternatively, it may lead the devotee to a fusion, a drowning in God. Ramanuja's love, then, would be a "pseudo-love." Is the entire cosmos only a "play" or, as noted earlier, a "panorama," where the divine light is dimly diffused? Is it not also "a plan to be realized," a "serious work" to be achieved?

Johanns attributes much of the difference between Hinduism and Christianity to a different notion of creation. For him, the Christian doctrine of *creatio ex nihilo* implies the idea of the realization of the self in a way that complements the Indian view of its liberation. Teilhard, however, thinks that the difference between Hinduism and Christianity is less related to the doctrine of creation than to the concept of two different forms of unity. *Creatio ex nihilo* is simply a deus ex machina, a "metaphysical monster," if not related to the idea of a "maximum unity" achieved through the integration of the multiple into the One.

Johanns's second volume is exclusively concerned with Vallabha's teaching, to which Teilhard's notebook devotes two and a half pages. Vallabha's date of death is stated and his system is characterized as some kind of qualified pantheism. His thought attempts a synthesis of the different positions of Shankara and Ramanuja. This is achieved through introducing the threefold distinction among an utterly transcendent God (*nirguna brahman*), a God accessible through his qualities (*saguna brahman*), and a God who appears in the world through Krishna.

For Vallabha, the personality of God is a supreme attribute of the Absolute. The phenomenal world owes its existence to a self-analysis of God. It consists of divine fragments that see themselves only from the outside, not recognizing their true nature. Vallabha's thought raises "the great question" how to reconcile the idea of an unchangeable God with that of the cosmos, understood as God become explicit.

Where Shankara suppresses the cosmos, Ramanuja treats it as the body of the Lord, and Vallabha sees it as an explicit unfolding of what has always been. This means that creation and evolution never add anything new. Teilhard concluded, therefore, that Hindus do not really have creation: it is not a process of *synthesis*, but merely of *analysis*, of involution rather than evolution. This "deforming projection" remains in the realm of the static and identical.

Perhaps written at a later stage, these notes bear an additional comment as follows: "True solution of the problem Hinduism/

Christianity: to christianize/christify/evolution (satisfies the aspirations of Shankara, Ramanuja, Vallabha...)." This is matched by a similar remark made subsequently: "The entire Vedanta would coincide with Neo-Christianity if transposed into evolutionary-unifying matter [*matière evolutif-unitif*]."

This proves that, for Teilhard, an adequate understanding of matter and evolution is a more decisive difference between Christianity and Hinduism than traditional theological doctrines. However, the full implications of a dynamic, evolutionary view have also still to be further integrated into Christianity. This is the reason why he refers to "Neo-Christianity."

Teilhard's further notes include, among others, references to Vallabha's views on such matters as grace (*pushti*), detachment, and *rasa* as a search through suffering; the dance of Krishna that makes the universe vibrate in exaltation, and the importance of the body and the world. While Vallabha's view of detachment is judged as static, Teilhard compares his interpretation of *rasa* with Saint John's dark night of the soul. Then he goes on to emphasize once more the distinction between love in Vedanta and Christianity, dependent on whether unity is achieved through fusion or synthesis. This is followed by a short note on Vallabha's place in the *philosophia perennis*.

For Johanns, not only the doctrine of creation but also of original sin implies a basic difference between Christianity and Hinduism. Teilhard disagrees with this and, consequently, criticizes Johanns for his "paleo-Christianity." The whole concept of "original sin" ought to be changed not "out of a lack of humility, but out of love for God!!!"

In a final remark, Teilhard points to what he considers the real, critical dividing line between Hinduism and Christianity. It relates to two decisive issues, namely, whether there is a unity of synthesis or convergence in God and whether the cosmos is in process of evolution.

Teilhard's ten pages of extracts and comments are important in several respects. First of all, they show that he studied two philosophically demanding works on Indian religious thought that discuss central ideas of classical Vedanta teachings in considerable detail. The extracts also provide evidence of his continued interest in monism, which always exercised a lasting fascination on his mind. The exaltation of the One always raises the inherent philosophical difficulty of how to account for the manifold realities of the world and their evolutionary development.

Furthermore, the notes clearly indicate that Teilhard knew of the theistic strands of Hinduism. He realized their difference from monistic teachings, of which he learned much earlier. This may be because, historically, they were the first to become generally known in the West and, in many people's minds, Hinduism is often still equated with monism.

Last, the comments also include several comparisons between Hinduism and Christianity, emphasizing what are, in Teilhard's view, deficiencies in the Hindu position. Yet at the same time, traditional Christian doctrines are criticized as "paleo-Christianity," in contrast to his own conception of a reinterpreted "neo-Christianity."

These comments underline once again that Teilhard favors a theistic and convergent, rather than a monistic, approach to the Absolute; he sees the cosmos as an ongoing process of evolution toward a higher synthesis. From this perspective, he criticizes both Hinduism and Christianity. Yet he also points to the possibility of a much greater affinity between Vedanta and neo-Christianity, if the former were to incorporate a dynamic evolutionary perspective that understands evolution as more than involution. This is perhaps an indication that, in spite of his criticisms, Teilhard's attitude ultimately implies the complementarity and convergence of the two religious traditions of Hinduism and Christianity.

Notes

Abbreviations

Frequently quoted works of Teilhard de Chardin are abbreviated in the notes to each chapter. For full details and a complete list of his writings see the bibliography.

Books

(Consisting mostly of essays written during different years of Teilhard's life)

AE   *Activation of Energy* (London: Collins, 1970)
CE   *Christianity and Evolution* (London: Collins, 1971)
FM   *The Future of Man* (London: Collins, 1964)
HE   *Human Energy* (London: Collins, 1969)
HM   *The Heart of Matter* (London: Collins, 1978)
HPh   *The Human Phenomenon* (Brighton and Portland, OR: Sussex Academic Press, 1999)
HU   *Hymn of the Universe* (London: Collins, 1965)
MD   *Le Milieu Divin or The Divine Milieu* (London: Collins, 1960)
OSc   *L'Oeuvre Scientifique*, 11 volumes (Olten and Freiburg: Walter, 1971)
PM   *The Phenomenon of Man* (London: Collins, 1959); retranslated as *The Human Phenomenon* (Brighton: Sussex Academic Press, 1999)
SC   *Science and Christ* (London: Collins, 1968)
TF   *Toward the Future* (London: Collins, 1975)
WTW   *Writings in Time of War* (London: Collins, 1968)

271

Letters and Reading Notes

LF   *Lettres Familières de Pierre Teilhard de Chardin Mon Ami 1948–1955* (Paris: Centurion, 1976).

LI   *Lettres Intimes à Auguste Valensin, Bruno de Solages, Henri de Lubac, André Ravier 1919–1955* (Paris: Aubier-Montaigne, 1974).

LT   *Letters from a Traveller* (London: Collins, 1966).

LTF   *Letters to Two Friends 1926–1952* (London: Collins, 1972).

LZ   *Letters to Léontine Zanta* (London: Collins, 1969).

MM   *The Making of a Mind: Letters from a Soldier Priest, 1916–1919* (London: Collins, 1965).

NL   *Notes de Lectures (1945–1947)* (Paris: Médiasèvres, 2007).

TB   *Pierre Teilhard de Chardin–Maurice Blondel Correspondence* (New York: Herder and Herder, 1967). French edition (Paris: Beauchesne, 1965).

LTLS   *The Letters of Teilhard de Chardin and Lucile Swan* (Washington, DC: Georgetown University Press, 1993).

Notes

Introduction

1. I have retained capital letters for *East* and *West* since they are well-established and widely used geographical terms, but the adjectives *eastern* and *western* that are derived from them are given in lower case in order not to essentialize their meaning.

2. Gérard-Henry Baudry, *Teilhard de Chardin et l'appel de l'Orient: La convergence des religions* (Paris: Aubin, 2005), is the only exception. For details see chap. 1, n. 43.

3. The three most significant comparative studies undertaken are R. C. Zaehner, *Evolution in Religion: A Study in Sri Aurobindo and Pierre Teilhard de Chardin* (Oxford: Clarendon, 1971); B. Bruteau, *Evolution toward Divinity: Teilhard de Chardin and the Hindu Traditions* (Wheaton: Theosophical Publishing

House, 1974); M. I. Bergeron, *La Chine et Teilhard* (Paris: Delarge, 1976). Mircea Eliade has suggested that the cultural significance of Teilhard's work, whose literary success has been far greater than that of the most popular philosopher of his generation, Jean Paul Sartre, may well deserve the attention of the historian of religion. See his "Cultural Fashions and the History of Religions" in J. M. Kitagawa, ed., *The History of Religions* (Chicago: University of Chicago Press, 1967), 21–38.

4. CE, 122.

5. *Génèse d'une Pensée* (Paris: Grasset 1961), back cover; my translation.

6. See Thomas Berry, *The Great Work: Our Way into the Future* (New York: Bell Tower, 1999).

Chapter 1

1. Both essays are found in P. Teilhard de Chardin, *The Heart of Matter* (London: Collins, 1978; abbreviated HM). The book represents the English translation of *Le Coeur de la Matière* (Paris: Éditions du Seuil, 1976), vol. 13 of Teilhard's collected works in French, plus some additional material not translated before. For the essay "The Heart of Matter," from which the book takes its title, see HM, 14–79; for "The Christic" see HM, 80–102. "My Fundamental Vision" is found in *Toward the Future* (London: Collins, 1975; abbreviated TF), 163–208.

2. TF, 164. For a fine outline of the major elements of what Teilhard saw consult the article by John A. Grim and Mary Evelyn Tucker, "An Overview of Teilhard's Commitment to 'Seeing' as Expressed in His Phenomenology, Metaphysics, and Mysticism" in C. Deane-Drummond, ed., *Pierre Teilhard de Chardin on People and Planet* (London and Oakville, CT: Equinox, 2006), 55–73.

3. *The Phenomenon of Man* (New York: Harper, 1959; abbreviated PM), 33.

4. PM, 35.

5. *Le Milieu Divin* (Paris: Éditions du Seuil, 1960); also published as *The Divine Milieu* (abbreviated MD), 29.

6. MD, 122.

7. Letter of September 9, 1923, to Abbé Breuil in *Letters from a Traveller* (London: Collins, 1966; abbreviated LT), 87.

8. For a complete list of Teilhard de Chardin's publications, see the Bibliography at the end of this book. A brief summary of the content of each of Teilhard's works, arranged in the chronological order in which they were written (not following the date of their much-later publication) is found in the Italian reference work by Fabio Mantovani, *Dizionario delle Opere di Teilhard de Chardin* (Verona: Gabrielli editori, 2006). For more details about access to Teilhard's digitalized works, contact the Fondation Teilhard de Chardin, Museum National d'Histoire Naturelle, 38, rue Geoffroy Saint-Hilaire, 75005 Paris; e-mail teilhard@mnhn.fr; see also their Website www.mnhn.fr/teilhard.

9. HM, 196–208.

10. See P. Teilhard de Chardin, *Journal* (Paris: Fayard, 1975), 223; my translation.

11. See *Journal*, 49.

12. HM, 25.

13. HM, 25.

14. HM, 25f.

15. Teilhard's vision of Christ is discussed fully in Ch. F. Mooney, *Teilhard de Chardin and the Mystery of Christ* (London: Collins, 1966). Besides the discovery of evolution, Newman's *Essay on the Development of Christian Doctrine* was of decisive importance in influencing Teilhard's reinterpretation of his religious beliefs. The developmental process involved in the emergence of Teilhard's cosmic christic vision has been analyzed with great subtlety by H. C. Cairns, "The Identity and Originality of Teilhard de Chardin," unpublished PhD diss., University of Edinburgh, 1971.

16. First published in 1968, *Writings in Time of War* are now volume 12 of Teilhard's *Collected Works*. Gérard-Henry Baudry has researched in detail where and under what conditions these essays were written between the battles of the First World War. See his article "Ninety Years Ago: Teilhard at Verdun," *Teilhard Newsletter* 26 (March 2009): 7–12 (published online by the British Teilhard Association at www.teilhard.org.uk).

17. See Ursula King, *Spirit of Fire: The Life and Vision of*

Teilhard de Chardin (Maryknoll, NY: Orbis, 1996). Illustrated by many photographs and accompanied by numerous quotations, this biography provides far more information about Teilhard's life and experiences than can be given in this study.

18. See *The Making of a Mind: Letters from a Soldier-Priest 1916–1919* (London: Collins, 1965; abbreviated MM), 26.

19. Quoted in C. Rivière, *Teilhard, Claudel et Mauriac* (Paris: Éditions universitaires, 1963), 52f. My translation.

20. The essays "Cosmic Life," "The Mystical Milieu," "The Soul of the World," and "The Universal Element" are found in P. Teilhard de Chardin, *Writings in Time of War* (London: Collins, 1968; abbreviated WTW). "The Spiritual Power of Matter" was first published in the collection *Hymn of the Universe* (London: Collins, 1965; abbreviated HU); it can also be found in the book *The Heart of Matter* (New York: Harcourt Brace Jovanovich, 1979), 67–77. The English translations of "The Great Monad" and "My Universe" are included in the same book.

21. WTW, 32.

22. MM, 155f.

23. For a comprehensive account of the extraordinary difficulties that Teilhard's manuscripts faced, see the informative study by his former Jesuit Superior in Paris, René d'Ouince, *Un prophète en procès: Teilhard de Chardin dans l'Église de son temps*, 2 vols. (Paris: Aubier-Montaigne, 1970). Some of the misunderstandings and criticisms of Teilhard's work are also discussed in H. de Lubac, *Teilhard Posthume: Réflexions et souvenirs* (Paris: Fayard, 1977).

24. He was awarded the "Prix Visquenel" and the "Prix Gustave Roux." See OSc I, 420 and 423.

25. HM, 47.

26. LT, 83.

27. See W. Grootaers, "When and Where Was the 'Mass on the World' Written?" *Teilhard Review* 12 (1977): 91–94.

28. HM, 132.

29. HM, 133.

30. HM, 125.

31. HM, 126.

32. LT, 105.

33. LT, 87 and 86.

34. Ibid. When an extract of "The Mass on the World" was first published in an anthology, the symbolic passage on the "offering" was chosen because of its universalist perspective; see S. Lemaître, *Anthologie des Textes Mystiques* (Paris: Plon, 1955), 295ff. For an insightful study of "The Mass on the World" see Thomas M. King, *Teilhard's Mass: Approaches to the Mass on the World* (Mahwah, NJ: Paulist, 2005).

35. See "The Mystical Milieu" (1917), WTW, 115–49.

36. MD, 16.

37. HM, 15.

38. HM, 102.

39. HM, 83.

40. HM, 99.

41. Mary and Ellen Lukas, *Teilhard: A Biography* (New York: Doubleday; and London: Collins, 1977).

42. See Henri de Lubac, *The Religion of Teilhard de Chardin* (London: Collins, 1967). For a brief introduction to de Lubac's work see David Grumett, *De Lubac: A Guide for the Perplexed* (London: T & T Clark, 2007). It makes only sparse reference to de Lubac's studies on Teilhard de Chardin.

43. Since the original publication of this book in 1980, the only author who has studied Teilhard's attraction to the East in some detail is Gérard-Henry Baudry, *Teilhard de Chardin et l'appel de l'Orient: La convergence des religions* (Paris: Aubin, 2005), who acknowledges my earlier research (see 98, 104, 140). Baudry's account remains largely descriptive, however, and contains little new information. Of special interest is the section on "Teilhard et la Chine Nouvelle," 121–32. The large, well-researched French biography by Patrice Boudignon, *Pierre Teilhard de Chardin: Sa vie, son oeuvre, sa réflexion* (Paris: Cerf, 2008), includes relatively little about the East. Its main focus is Teilhard's recurring theme of global humanity's forward movement toward greater unity, and some of his female friendships. The shorter, widely read biography by Édith Héronnière, *Teilhard de Chardin* (Paris: Pygmalion/G. Watelet, 1999), rather novel-like in style and not translated into English, does not say much about

the impact of the East on Teilhard's mystical vision and on his overall worldview.

Chapter 2

1. See Françoise Teilhard de Chardin (1879–1911), *Lettres et Témoignages* (Paris: Beauchesne, 1975). This book gives biographical information about her work and family. The letters start with Françoise's entry into a convent in France; about half of them are written from China. Most letters are addressed to her parents, but a few are written to her brother Pierre; one of his letters to her is reproduced on p. 60.

2. Quoted in C. Cuénot, *Teilhard de Chardin* (London: Burns & Oates, 1965), 10, from an article in which Teilhard described his expedition to the El Faiyûm area southwest of Cairo; see his "Huit Jours au Fayoum," originally published in *Relations d'Orient* (December 1907): 276–78, reprinted in Teilhard's *Oeuvres Scientifiques* (published in 13 volumes; abbreviated as OSc). See OSc I, 31–38, where he refers to some of the desert scenes as "very biblical" (35).

3. Quoted in *Teilhard de Chardin Album* (London: Collins, 1966), 36.

4. Henri Lammens (1826–1937), a Belgian Jesuit born in Beirut, published on Islam from 1906 onward. Later he became professor of Arabic at St. Joseph's University, Beirut. Among his many publications is the well-known book *Islam—Beliefs and Institutions* (London: Cass, 1968). More information about Teilhard's years in Egypt can be gleaned from his *Lettres d'Égypte 1905–1908* (Paris: Ed. Montaigne, 1963).

5. H. C. Cairns, "The Identity and Originality of Teilhard de Chardin," (PhD diss., University of Edinburgh, 1971), 121. For references to the desert in Teilhard's early writings see WTW, 29 and 31; *Journal*, 42, 57, 58, 177, 178; MM, 159: "the happy days when I felt the intoxication of the desert."

6. In October 2008 the Borough Council of Hastings unveiled a blue plaque near the former Ore Place to commemorate Teilhard's years of study in Hastings. It reads "Pierre Teilhard de Chardin, 1881–1955, Philosopher, Priest and Author Studied at the

Jesuit Seminary Ore Place 1908–1912." More details and photos can be found in Stephen Retout's article "The Unveiling at Hastings," *Teilhard Newsletter* 26 (March 2009): 3–5 (published online by the British Teilhard Association at www.teilhard.org.uk).

7. See P. Teilhard de Chardin, *Lettres d'Hastings et de Paris 1908–1914* (Paris: Aubier, 1965). The English translation *Letters from Hastings 1908–1912* (New York: Herder & Herder, 1968), covers only his time in Hastings, but not the Paris years.

8. See Françoise Teilhard de Chardin, 173 and 176.

9. *Lettres d'Hastings et de Paris*, 82 and 127. His sister's letters refer to Teilhard's regular correspondence with several Jesuits in Shanghai; they also mention the presence of three Chinese novices at Hastings. See Françoise Teilhard de Chardin, 222 and 237.

10. H. de Lubac, *The Religion of Teilhard de Chardin* (London: Collins, 1967), 367, n. 110.

11. MM, 288. For Teilhard's letters to his parents on the death of his sister, see Françoise Teilhard de Chardin, 263–69. Of the three letters found there, two have been excerpted in H. de Lubac, *The Religion of Teilhard de Chardin*, 256f.

12. See *Lettres d'Hastings et de Paris*, 183, 191, 194.

13. Originally published in *Revue des Questions Scientifiques*, this article was later included in J. Maréchal, *Études sur la Psychologie des Mystiques* (Paris: Alcan, 1924; English translation: London: Burns, Oates & Washburne, 1927). For a reference to Teilhard's meeting with Maréchal, see *Lettres d'Hastings et de Paris*, 182.

14. These notes are discussed in appendix IV on "Teilhard's Reading." Its first part deals with comments on "Joseph Maréchal, *Studies in the Psychology of the Mystics*." Surprisingly, no reference to Maréchal's importance is found in the Teilhard biography by Mary and Ellen Lukas. For a discussion of Maréchal's decisive influence on Teilhard's conceptual development see H. C. Cairns, 126.

15. R. d'Ouince, *Un Prophète en procès*, vol. 1, 52; confirmed in a personal interview with Father d'Ouince, Paris, March 1973.

16. H. de Lubac, *The Religion of Teilhard de Chardin*, 233.

17. Since its foundation in 1829 this was one of the major French journals for the dissemination of eastern thought. See R. Schwab, *La Renaissance Orientale* (Paris: Payot, 1950), 109.

18. See Paris: Beauchesne, 1997. Originally published in Paris, 1913, a second, enlarged version was printed in 1916; in 1952, a Spanish translation was published in Buenos Aires; see J. Huby, ed., *Christus: Manual de Historia de las Religionas.* After an introduction by L. de Grandmaison, the book contains some excellent contributions on ancient and living religions, among others, L. Wieger on Chinese religions, L. de la Vallé Poussin on Buddhism and Indian religions. To some extent, the book was meant to reply to S. Reinach's controversial *Orpheus: Histoire générale des religions* (Paris: Alcide Picard, 1909). See *Christus*, 3, n. 1.

19. Personal communication from Father H. de Lubac. Father d'Ouince relates how the closely knit group of friends at Hastings discussed their future contribution to the renewal of theology. They assigned philosophy to Valensin, the history of religions and theology to Huby, Rousselot, and Charles, and "l'évangélisation des gentils" to Teilhard. See R. d'Ouince, *Un Prophète en procès*, vol. 1, 67.

20. For an account see F. Bouvier, A. Lemonnyer, eds, *Comptes rendus analytiques des Semaines d'Ethnologie religieuse de Louvain 1912–3* (Paris, 1913); B. Emonet, "La Semaine d'Ethnologie Religieuse—Louvain 27.8–4.9.1912" in *Études* 133 (1912): 83–100. In the same journal, Bouvier had reported in 1908 on the History of Religions Congress at Oxford under the title "La Science comparée des Religions comment elle se fait et se défait."

21. OSc I, 75. Besides Teilhard, several of his friends—i.e., the Jesuits Grandmaison, Huby, Charles, Valensin, and Lammens, as well as Pinard de la Boullaye—attended the Louvain conference. The latter was then already working on his famous survey *L'Étude Comparée des Religions.* In preparation since 1910, but first published in 1922, this is considered the most comprehensive survey of the development of the history of religions as a discipline up to that time. According to personal information from H. de Lubac, it is possible and even likely that Teilhard was familiar with this work, although he would not have studied it in detail. Father Pinard de la Boullaye was then teaching at the Jesuit house at Enghien (Belgium), which possessed an excellent library collec-

tion in the history of religions. In 1914, Pinard de la Boullaye was offered the chair in the History of Religions at the Institut Catholique, Paris. The second Louvain conference in 1913 was also attended by the Islamicist Louis Massignon, whom Teilhard knew well in later years.

22. "Pour fixer les traits d'un monde qui s'efface—La semaine d'ethnologie religieuse de Louvain," *Le Correspondant*, 10.11.1912; reprinted in OSc I, 75–82. Ten years later, Teilhard still referred to these scholarly debates when reviewing a book on *Les Religions de la Préhistoire* for an anthropological journal. See OSc, I, 416f.

23. Personal communication from Father René d'Ouince, Paris, March 1973.

24. HM, 26, 28.

25. C. Geertz, *Islam Observed: Religious Developments in Morocco and Indonesia* (New Haven: Yale University Press, 1968), 44.

26. MM, 47.

27. MM, 125. For a similar description see *Journal*, 104.

28. WTW, 29.

29. See especially "Nostalgia for the Front" (1917), and "The Heart of Matter" (1950), both in HM, for comparable passages.

30. The journal *Le Lotus Bleu* was founded by Madame Blavatsky in 1887. Since then, it has regularly appeared in Paris as the joint publication of the theosophical societies of France, Belgium, and Switzerland. From its early days, it has published articles on Hindu mysticism. There exists no conclusive evidence whether Teilhard knew this journal or not.

31. See the footnote in *Journal*, 53.

32. MM, 60.

33. MM, 97.

34. See the essay of this title in WTW, 115–49, written in 1917.

35. Based on William James's Gifford Lectures given at the University of Edinburgh between 1901 and 1902, *Varieties of Religious Experience* was published in London in 1904 and translated into French as *L'expérience religieuse* (Paris: Alcan, 1906).

36. WTW, 189.

37. W. James, *Pragmatism: A New Name for Some Old Ways of Thinking* (London: Longmans, Green, 1907).

38. A footnote in the *Journal*, added by Teilhard, mentions that these three paths equal the three first chapters of his essay "Cosmic Life."

39. *Journal*, 266; my translation.

40. See lecture IV, "The One and the Many."

41. W. James, *Pragmatism*, 151, 153.

42. Ibid., 262.

43. Ibid., 274.

44. Ibid., 292.

45. See *Journal*, 264.

46. See *Journal*, 270, 374; WTW, 301.

47. See *Journal*, 269, 270–72.

48. P. Teilhard de Chardin, *Écrits du temps de la guerre* (Paris: Éditions du Seuil, 1965), 371. The quotation is from an essay whose English translation is only found in the book *The Heart of Matter* (and not in *Writings in Time of War*). See "Note on the Presentation of the Gospel in a New Age" (1919), HM, 209–24.

49. Édouard Schuré, *Les Grands Initiés: Esquisse de l'Histoire Secrète des Religions* (Paris: Perrin, 1889). An English translation first appeared in 1912. The book became immensely popular. By 1920, it had reached its fifty-eighth edition, according to H. Pinard de la Boullaye, *L'Étude Comparée des Religions* (Paris: Beauchesne, 1929), vol. 1, 510, n. 1. He also mentions that, together with R. Reinach's *Orpheus*, Schuré's book popularized the critical stance of B. Bauer. It has been claimed that, since 1889, the book has gone through 220 editions. Even today, Schuré's title can still be found in print in several languages.

50. MM, 267.

51. See *Lettres Intime*, abbrev. LI, 109, n. 20, 12.

52. MM, 268. This remark may point to the essay "Forma Christi" (1918), or even more "The Universal Element" (1919), both in WTW. See this whole letter of December 13, 1918, for Teilhard's discussion of Schuré's work.

53. R. C. Zaehner, *Evolution in Religion* (Oxford: Clarendon Press, 1971), 6.

54. C. Schneider, "P. Teilhard de Chardin et É. Schuré," *Cahiers d'études cathares* 13 (1962), 31–35.

55. Benson's stories on mysticism made such a deep impression on Teilhard that he wrote "Three Stories in the Style of Benson," found in P. Teilhard de Chardin, *Hymn of the Universe*, 39–55. As Teilhard's first degree had been a *licence-ès-lettres* (Caen, 1902), one need hardly be surprised that he was more inclined to seek the inspiration of poets and writers than the guidance of scholars in his reading on mysticism.

56. See *Journal*, 366, 379–81, 386.

57. R. Garric in *Letters to Léontine Zanta*, abbrev. LZ, 9.

58. See letter of Christmas 1923, where Teilhard mentions his reading of Bremond: LI, 149, n. 31, 12.

59. My translation; see CE, 58 and 60. The essay is "Pantheism and Christianity" (1923); the expression recalls the "initiates" of Schuré's book, read in 1918.

60. See P. Teilhard de Chardin—M. Blondel, *Correspondence*, ed. H. de Lubac (New York: Herder & Herder, 1967), discussed in chap. 5.

61. Le Roy had been appointed in 1921 as Bergson's successor on the chair of philosophy at the College de France in Paris. Teilhard's influence can be discerned in several of Le Roy's works. Teilhard's letters to Le Roy have only been published recently; see Teilhard de Chardin, *Lettres à Édouard Le Roy (1921–1946): Maturation d'une pensée*. Introduction de François Euvé, SJ (Paris: Éditions Facultés Jésuites de Paris, 2008).

62. The first French woman to obtain a doctorate of philosophy in 1914, she was noted for her work on Plato. Before 1918, she had stayed for some time in Egypt, and later, she provided a role model for Simone de Beauvoir. Teilhard corresponded with her during his years in China. See Pierre Teilhard de Chardin, *Letters to Léontine Zanta* (London: Collins, 1969), which includes an informative essay by Robert Garric on "Père Teilhard and Mademoiselle Zanta." See also J. Baudry, *Dictionnaire des correspondants de Teilhard de Chardin* (Lille: G.-H. Baudry, 1974), 153–56.

63. Quoted by P. Leroy in his introduction to LT, 26.

64. A point stressed in G. Baudry, *Qui était Teilhard de Chardin?* (Lille: Baudry, 1972), 30.

65. In 1928, he spent two months in Ethiopia, and in what was then French Somaliland; see LT, 144–50.

66. C. Cuénot, 10. For a list of "Teilhard's Years in the East" see appendix I in this book.

Chapter 3

1. I retain the earlier spelling of these two cities as used throughout Teilhard's writings.

2. R. d'Ouince in LTF, 5.

3. See *Letters from a Traveller* (LT) and *Letters to Léontine Zanta* (LZ); both start in 1926; see also *Lettres Intimes* (LI), begun in 1919. For a synopsis of "Teilhard's Years in the East" see appendix I; for some comments on "Teilhard's Reading" see appendix IV.

4. See C. Cuénot, "Le Père Émile Licent S.J., un portrait," *Le ruban rouge* 19 (Paris, 1963): 36–45, and "Le R. P. Émile Licent S.J.," *Bulletin de la Société d'études indochinoises* 1 (Saigon, 1966): 9–83. It was Licent's hope to create a Jesuit educational center for North China in Tientsin, comparable to the one the Jesuits had built in Shanghai. This extraordinary man and his work deserve a separate study.

5. For the origins and early history of the Jesuit mission in China, and the Jesuits' sustained effort to engage with Chinese language and thought, see the impressive study by Liam Matthew Brockey, *Journey to the East: The Jesuit Mission to China, 1579–1724* (Cambridge, MA: Belknap Press, 2007).

6. LI, 104.

7. LT, 73.

8. LI, 104, as translated in Cuénot (1965), 137.

9. See O. D. Rasmussen, *Tientsin: An Illustrated Outline History* (Tientsin: Tientsin Press, 1925), 254; ibid., 256, refers to Teilhard's and Licent's forthcoming publication about their paleontological expeditions to North China and Mongolia.

10. See Brian Power, *The Ford of Heaven* (London: Peter Owen, 1984). A revised version has been published with the sub-

title *A Childhood in Tianjin, China* (Oxford: Signal Books, 2005) (including some photographs), and translated into Chinese. This book has been described as "perhaps the finest of the 'treaty port' memoirs." See Brian Power's obituary, *The Guardian*, August 4, 2008.

11. LZ, 51f.

12. LT, 81.

13. C. Cuénot, *Teilhard de Chardin: A Biographical Study* (London: Burns & Oates, 1965), 116.

14. LZ, 52.

15. LT, 90.

16. LT, 101. Teilhard's reflections, written in October 1923, on his return from Mongolia to Tientsin, are found in LT, 92–103.

17. LT, 99–100, *passim*.

18. LT, 95.

19. LT, 101.

20. LT, 102.

21. LT, 103.

22. LZ, 53; see also LZ, 57f.

23. HM, 119. The literary history of "The Mass on the World" has been researched by Father Grootaers, a Belgian missionary who spent ten years in China where he knew Teilhard, especially since Teilhard was his spiritual director for two years. Later Father Grootaers, a specialist of Chinese and Japanese dialects, taught in Tokyo and made a Japanese translation of "The Mass on the World." This has been prefaced by the essay "When and Where Did Teilhard Write 'The Mass on the World'?" also published in *Teilhard Review* 12 (1977): 91–94. According to Grootaers, it "must have been written on days spent under the tent and inside the Ordos desert (i.e. the region inside the Yellow river bend)." Grootaers considers the essay "The Priest" (1918, see WTW, 203–24) as the first version of the Mass, the main text as the second, to be followed by a third version, announced in a letter from Teilhard in 1929. However, this last project came to nothing.

24. M. Eliade, "Cultural Fashions and the History of Religions," in J. M. Kitagawa, ed., *The History of Religions* (Chicago: University of Chicago Press, 1967), 33f.

25. See Lama Anandagarika Govinda, "Die Weltan-schauung Teilhard de Chardins im Spiegel des östlichen Denkens," in H. de Terra, ed., *Perspektiven Teilhard de Chardins* (Munich: Beck, 1966), 124–53.

26. LT, 116f.

27. See LZ, 64f.; also LT, 108f.

28. LZ, 65.

29. LT, 119.

30. LT, 110.

31. LI, 126.

32. R. d'Ouince in LTF, 5.

33. LT, 122.

34. MD, 107.

35. MD, 103f, 106, 107f.

36. See LI, 471–82: "Les Revisions du Milieu Divin." Further material is found in the letters after 1927, and in R. d'Ouince, *Un Prophète en Procès*; ibid., vol. 1, 207ff. describes the polemic after the publication of *Le Milieu Divin* in 1957.

37. A close friend of Teilhard's since their student days in Hastings. In 1925, Teilhard wrote about Charles that "eastern questions fascinate him clearly more and more. His hobbyhorse (excellent in my view) is that Hindu philosophies can be much more Christianized than that of Aristotle" (LI, 128f.). After visiting Ceylon in the early 1930s, Father Charles published a monograph on the Buddhist monks of Ceylon that was read and criticized by Teilhard. See LI, 251.

38. More details about the revisions and the polemic surrounding *The Divine Milieu* are found in Hain-Yan Wang, *Le Phénomène Teilhard: L'aventure du livre Le Milieu Divin* (Paris: Aubin, 1999). Another detailed study from a particular theological perspective is provided by David Grumett's "Action, Passion and Vision in Teilhard de Chardin's *Le milieu divin*" (PhD diss., King's College, Cambridge, 2003).

39. See *The Divine Milieu: Pierre Teilhard de Chardin*. Translated by Siôn Cowell (Brighton and Portland, OR: Sussex Academic Press, 2004). See ibid., vii–xxix, foreword by Thomas M. King.

40. See Louis M. Savary, *Teilhard de Chardin* The Divine

Milieu *Explained: A Spirituality for the 21st Century* (New York and Mahwah, NJ: Paulist, 2007).

41. LT, 154.

42. See Teilhard's French article of 1928, "Les Tendances Intellectuelles de la Chine Moderne," OSc II, 868–71. For a difference of views, see LT, 138f. and LTF, 60 and 64. Whereas his former teacher, and the director of the Musée de l'Homme in Paris, Professor Marcellin Boule, was opposed to a fuller integration into Chinese organizations, Teilhard was emphatic in not wanting to prolong a separatist attitude. He shared this approach with the Swedish explorer Sven Hedin, whom he urged "to trust the Chinese and work with them." The latter was grateful for this advice and gained "the full confidence of even the most anti-foreign Chinese...." See LT, 154.

43. Pierre Teilhard de Chardin, *Letters to Two Friends 1926–1952* (London: Collins, 1972; hereafter abbreviated LTF), 65.

44. LT, 126.

45. Quoted in Cuénot, 77.

46. Quoted in George B. Barbour, *In the Field with Teilhard de Chardin* (New York: Herder & Herder, 1965), 23, where the Chinese characters for Teilhard's name are given.

47. LZ, 80.

48. LZ, 70.

49. LTF, 69.

50. LTF, 67.

51. See LT, 175. Writing to his friend Ida Treat on April 20, 1927, Teilhard said, "I should tell you that I sent a moderately pro-China and humanitarian article to an (intelligent) new Catholic journal in Calcutta, *The Week* (first issue)"; see LTF, 70. It has been difficult to locate this "moderately pro-China" article, which was published anonymously; it has never been published in Teilhard's collected works. An Indian Jesuit, Father George Gispert-Sauch, found it after I had mentioned this article as possibly lost in the first edition of this book. In fact, it consists of two articles that I republished with comments; see "Teilhard's Attitude towards the Modernization of China: Two Documents from 1927," *Teilhard Review* 16/1–2 (1981), 6–15. The complex ques-

tion of Teilhard's attitudes toward contemporary Chinese political developments provides a fascinating topic of research for which these articles are important.

52. LT, 176.

53. Hu Shih, "My Credo and Its Evolution," in *Living Philosophies,* ed. A. Einstein, J. Dewey, Sir J. Jeans, et al. (Simon and Schuster, 1931).

54. LT, 176f.

55. LT, 177.

56. For the entire passage see LTF, 44.

57. LTF, 45.

58. LZ, 79.

59. HE, 19–47.

60. George B. Barbour, *In the Field with Teilhard de Chardin*, 17.

61. Quoted in C. Cuénot, *Teilhard de Chardin*, 81.

62. A fuller discussion of Teilhard's association with this important discovery is found in the chapter on "Peking Man" in my Teilhard biography *Spirit of Fire*, 126–33.

63. See the museum's booklet *The World Culture Heritage in Beijing: Peking Man Site at Zhoukoudian*, purchased on site in May 2008, n.d.

64. See the correspondence edited by P. Leroy, *Dans le sillage des sinanthropes: Lettres inédites de P. Teilhard de Chardin et de J. G. Anderson* (Paris: Fayard, 1971).

65. Stated in "The Scientific Career of Pierre Teilhard de Chardin," written by Teilhard and originally published in *Études,* July–August 1950; see HM, 154.

66. See Jia Lanpo and Huang Weiwen, *The Story of Peking Man: From Archaeology to Mystery* (Beijing: Foreign Languages Press; Hong Kong: Oxford University Press, 1990). See the Appendix, 249–52, for his personal reminiscences on "Father Pierre Teilhard de Chardin and I."

67. Amir D. Aczel, *The Jesuit and the Skull: Teilhard de Chardin, Evolution, and the Search for Peking Man* (New York: Riverhead Books, 2007).

68. Sometimes also translated as Yellow "Crossing," "Cruise," or even "Rally." I have retained the translation used in

Cuénot's Teilhard biography and in the *Teilhard de Chardin Album*.

69. Today this region is called Xinjiang Uyghur Autonomous Region of the People's Republic of China, comparable in size to Iran or Western Europe. Its capital is Urumqi.

70. See G. Le Fèvre, *La Croisière Jaune: Expédition Citroën Centre Asie* (Paris: Plon, 1933, reprinted 1952). Additional information can be found in the special expedition issue of the journal *La Géographie* 58 (Paris, 1932). Both publications were given to me by Teilhard's youngest brother, Monsieur Joseph Teilhard de Chardin, during a visit on October 1, 1973. Le Fèvre's book carries Teilhard's signature, indicating probably that this had been his own copy.

71. Letter by Georges-Marie Haardt, March 1, 1932, quoted in *Teilhard de Chardin Album*, 114.

72. For a description of the Chinese delegation see G. Le Fèvre, 83–85.

73. *La Géographie*, 376.

74. J. Hackin was a well-known specialist on Buddhism in Central Asia. He had translated works from Tibetan and was able to communicate with the Tibetan monks encountered during this expedition. He was a specialist of comparative studies in iconography, and his reason for joining the Yellow Expedition was to trace through Chinese Turkestan one of the ancient routes by which Buddhism had spread eastward from India into China. Since the end of the nineteenth century, this particular route had raised much interest in the scholarly world, particularly through the earlier expeditions of Albert von Le Coq, Paul Pelliot, and Sir Aurel Stein. Later, in 1938, during the International Exhibition of Chinese Art in London, Hackin was invited to deliver one of the official lectures on "Buddhist Art in Central Asia: Indian, Iranian and Chinese Influences (from Bamiyan to Turfan)," chaired by Sir Francis Younghusband. See J. Hackin et al., *Studies in Chinese Art and Some Indian Influences* (London: India Society, 1938).

75. See G. Le Fèvre, 270f. and 254. Jacovleff also painted several members of the expedition (see the reproductions in Le Fèvre's book). The color studies of the various ethnic types were later reproduced in a limited edition. I first saw examples in the

family of Teilhard's younger brother, Joseph. Later I found seven portraits painted by Jacovleff between December 1931 and February 1932 in the Jesuit Campion Hall in Oxford. They consist of color portraits of western and Chinese missionaries. They seem to have been given to Campion Hall on the advice of Sir John Rothenstein (1901–92), director of the Tate Gallery, London, 1938–64. The Campion Hall catalogue of art works includes a note from Jacovleff's executor, L. Brockman, written in 1939: "A few days ago, Mr. John Rothenstein, Director of the Tate Gallery, came to Paris to acquire a few works of the world-known painter, Alexander Jacovleff, who died last year. A. Jacovleff was considered as a leading draftsman and famous for his portrait sketches...as a member of a scientific expedition he visited the interior of China and brought back a number of portraits, among them a few of well-known missionaries. They are wonderful drawings and Mr. Rothenstein urged me not to sell them, but to donate them to Catholic Religious Institutions and preferably to your College. As the executor of the estate, I gladly follow M. Rothenstein's noble suggestion."

76. First published in *La Géographie*, 379–90; reprinted in OSc IV, 1697–1708.

77. See LT, 191. Similarly, the leader of the Yellow Expedition pressed Teilhard to accompany the French group on their return expedition via Indochina. He was unwilling to go, however.

78. See OSc, XI, maps 10 and 11; also Teilhard's report "Observations Géologiques à travers les déserts d'Asie Centrale de Kalgan a Hami," in OSc IV, 1795–1831.

79. See G. Le Fèvre, chap. 16. A detailed travellers' account of the Muslim uprising is found in M. Cable and F. French, *The Gobi Desert* (London: Hodder & Stoughton, 1946), 220–57: "Revolt in the Gobi."

80. G. Le Fèvre, 333–40; *La Géographie*, 256f.

81. Ibid., 337.

82. Teilhard's younger brother Joseph thought that Teilhard's health, especially his heart condition, was permanently affected by the physical and climatic conditions endured during the Yellow Expedition.

83. In 1932, a big exhibition in Paris presented the results

to the public. See *Album de la Croisière Jaune* (Paris, 1932), published on that occasion. A documentary film based on the expedition was released in 1934 and can occasionally still be viewed. See the *New York Times* film review "*La Croisière Jaune*, a Record of a Great Motor Journey," May 6, 1934.

84. LT, 180 and 186. Although the experience of the Gobi desert and Sinkiang is only briefly documented in Teilhard's letters, his descriptions of the physical, social, political, and cultural conditions are corroborated by contemporary accounts of other visitors to this region as, for example, by Sven Hedin and Owen Lattimore.

85. See LT, 184. The final version of these essays are "Sketch of a Personalistic Universe" (1936), HE, 53–92, and "Some Reflexions on the Conversion of the World" (1936), SC, 118–27. Contrary to the original intention, the latter is mainly concerned with Christianity rather than with "various religions."

86. See SC, 126.

87. LZ, 108.

88. TF, 40–59.

89. See Thomas M. King, SJ, and Mary Wood Gilbert, eds., *The Letters of Teilhard de Chardin and Lucile Swan*. Foreword by Pierre Leroy, SJ (Washington, DC: Georgetown University Press, 1993), hereafter cited as LTLS. For a discussion of the letters, see Ursula King, "The Letters of Teilhard de Chardin and Lucile Swan. A Personal Interpretation," American Teilhard Association: *Teilhard Studies* 32 (1995). The French tranlsation of LTLS has been published as *Correspondance Lucile Swan–Pierre Teilhard de Chardin* (Brussels: Éditions Lessius, 2009).

90. LT, 204.

91. New York, 1965.

92. G. Barbour, 40.

93. LI, 305.

94. LT, 219. Teilhard's expedition travel across India and what is now Pakistan (September 20–December 12, 1935) has been described in detail by Gérard-Henry Baudry, "Sur les Pas de Teilhard aux Indes," *Teilhard aujourd'hui* 21 (2007): 9–18. This article also lists Teilhard's correspondence and scientific reports relating to this Indian expedition.

95. LT, 218f.

96. Teilhard remained in contact with him in the following years. Patterson was a Fellow at Trinity College, Cambridge. In 1938, he became director of the Cambridge University Museum of Archaeology and Ethnology.

97. See LT, 207–18 for his impressions of India.

98. H. de Terra, *Memories of Teilhard de Chardin* (London: Collins, 1964), 53.

99. Ibid., 34.

100. See LT, 213.

101. LT, 216.

102. LT, 219.

103. H. de Terra, 64f.

104. Ibid., 66.

105. Ibid.

106. R. Speaight, *Teilhard de Chardin* (London: Collins, 1967), 216.

107. See Beatrice Bruteau, *Evolution toward Divinity: Teilhard de Chardin and the Hindu Traditions* (Wheaton, IL: Theosophical Publishing House, 1974).

108. All quotations are from LT, 222.

109. H. de Terra, 113.

110. See LT, 236–39; H. de Terra, 82–96; details of the itinerary are found in C. Cuénot, 198, n. 1.

111. LT, 236 and 237.

112. H. de Terra, 97.

113. Ibid., 84.

114. Ibid., 102.

115. LT, 173.

116. Interview with Father Leroy, Versailles, February 1974.

117. H. de Terra, 106.

118. Pierre Teilhard de Chardin, *The Phenomenon of Man* (London: Collins, 1959) (abbreviated PM). For the new English translation see *The Human Phenomenon: A New Edition and Translation of Le phénomène humain* by Sarah Appleton-Weber (Brighton and Portland, OR: Sussex Academic Press), 1999. I refer to this translation as HPh.

119. PM, 291–99; HPh, 209–15.

120. PM, 206–12; HPh 142–47.

121. PM, 211. For a somewhat different translation see HPh, 146.

122. PM, 211–12, *passim*; HPh, 146–47 *passim*.

123. See J. Needham's review of *The Phenomenon of Man* in the *New Statesman*, November 7, 1959. He writes there, "To insist that 'during historic time the principal axis of anthropogenesis has passed through the West' is simply to perpetuate a vulgar error."

124. For a much more detailed historical study of this theme, see the authoritative work by W. H. McNeill, *The Rise of the West: A History of the Human Community* (Chicago: University of Chicago Press, 1963).

125. See the chapter "The Collective Issue," PM, 237–53; more appropriately entitled "The Collective Way Out" in HPh, 167–79.

126. His wide range of encounters and experiences are evident from the letters of this period, and from the writings of friends, such as Lucile Swan, Malvina Hoffman, Claude Rivière, Père Leroy, Dominique de Wespin. See also the chapters on China in M. and E. Lukas, *Teilhard* (London: Collins, 1977).

127. New York, 1938. Helen Foster, aged twenty-four, arrived in China in 1931 and married Edgar Snow in 1936. After her death in January 1997 her obituary in the British paper, *The Guardian* (January 17, 1997), stated that "almost every well-known figure connected with China at the time, from Teilhard de Chardin to Pearl Buck, passed through the Snow family house. From there the Snows fostered and introduced to the outside world a score of Chinese writers...."

128. See L. Swan, "With Teilhard de Chardin in Peking," *The Month* 1 (London, 1962): 5–15; the quotation is from 6.

129. Teilhard apparently helped Helen Snow in 1933 to arrange the first exhibition of works by Chinese left-wing artists in Paris. Similarly, Father d'Ouince knew of Chinese students whom Teilhard helped to come to France for their studies—incidents of little importance, but they illustrate Teilhard's concern for individual Chinese he met. Personal information.

130. Teilhard refers to Marxism from the early 1920s

onward, when he met an active member of the French Communist Party, the American Ida Treat, who was married to the French communist activist and politician Paul Vaillant-Couturier who, in 1926, became the editor in chief of the Communist Party's newspaper, *L'Humanité*. Teilhard and Ida Treat became lifelong friends. It seems that extracts of the letters she received from Teilhard between 1926 and 1952 are published in the first section of *Letters to Two Friends*, without an indication of the addressee. Teilhard first met Ida Treat at the Museum in Paris where she worked for a doctorate in paleontology (obtained in 1930). In later years, Ida Treat (1889–1978) returned to the United States and taught at Vassar College, Poughkeepsie, New York. She left her papers, diaries, and letters to the Vassar libraries. The Australian Jesuit John Cowburn has studied this material closely and written a privately circulated monograph about "Paul Vaillant-Couturier, Ida Treat and Pierre Teilhard de Chardin." It contains more details than found anywhere else, but more research needs to be done on these papers. See the Ida Treat Bergeret papers in the Special Collections of Vassar Libraries at http://specialcollections.vassar.edu/findingaids/bergeret_ida.html.

131. Paris, 1968. See especially chap. 9, "Attitude de Teilhard devant la guerre et l'indicible misère de la Chine"; chap. 10, "Un essai d'explication de l'indifférence apparente de Teilhard devant la souffrance"; and chap. 12, "Teilhard et les religions de la Chine."

132. C. Rivière, 128; my translation.

133. Ibid., 221.

134. Ibid., 142.

135. The general state of Buddhism in China, including the Buddhist renaissance movement, is described in detail in K. Ch'en, *Buddhism in China* (Princeton: Princeton University Press, 1964); H. H. Welch, *The Practice of Chinese Buddhism 1900–1950* (Cambridge, MA: Harvard University Press, 1967), and *The Buddhist Revival in China* (Cambridge, MA: Harvard University Press, 1968).

136. L. Swan, 10. Lucile Swan lived in an abandoned temple in the west of Peking. In October 1932 Teilhard wrote to Lucile from Paris, "I like so much to hear from you what you do, and

what you think, in the quiet recess of your small temple" (LTLS, 1). For more information on their relationship, see the chapter on "Lucile Swan" in U. King, *Spirit of Fire* (1996), 144–54.

137. See P. Leroy, "L'Institut de Géobiologie à Pekin, 1940–46. Les dernières années du P. Teilhard de Chardin en Chine," *L'Anthropologie* 69, no. 3–4 (1965): 360–67. For the papers published by Teilhard and P. Leroy from the Peking Institute of Geobiology (including the scientific review *Geobiologia*), see OSc IX.

138. Cuénot lists twenty-seven essays for the Peking period 1939–46; see Teilhard's "Chronological List of Works" in HM, 241–51, where 27 essays are listed as written between 1939 and 1945. Teilhard left China by boat for France on March 27, 1946; some of his shorter notes, published in 1946 in France, may still have been written in China during the preceding years. This makes it difficult to be certain of the definite number of pieces he wrote during the war years.

139. Personal communication. See also P. Leroy, "Teilhard de Chardin tel que je l'ai connu," translated as "The Man" in LT, 15–47, and his personal notes in *Lettres Familières de Pierre Teilhard de Chardin mon ami 1948–1955* (Paris: Centurion, 1976) (LF). I have used the French edition for my quotations; for the American edition see *Letters from My Friend: Correspondence between Teilhard de Chardin and Pierre Leroy 1948–1955* (New York: Paulist, 1979).

140. See LF, 15 and 32; C. Rivière, 61.

141. This is well brought out in M. and E. Lukas, *Teilhard*.

142. It is impossible to gain a complete picture of Teilhard's reading, as only three *carnets de lecture* are known to exist, covering the years 1945 and afterward, and the last 1952, according to C. Cuénot. Whether he took notes on reading in other years is unknown. Valuable supplementary evidence can be found in the diaries from mid-1944 onward. The earlier diaries (1925–44) were lost on his departure from China. The second *carnet* is the only one that has now been transcribed and published by Gérard-Henry Baudry, *Notes de Lectures (1945–1947)* (Paris: Médiasèvres, 2007; abbreviated NL).

143. A list of representative titles is found in C. Cuénot, 236f.

144. Marc Faessler analyzes Teilhard's notes on Karl Barth

in his doctoral dissertation, "Homme réel and Phénomène Humain," University of Geneva, 1967. To my knowledge, no other work has made use of the notes in the *carnets de lecture*.

145. A detailed discussion of Teilhard's notes and comments on the two books is found in appendix IV. For Teilhard's excerpts from Johanns, see the notes reproduced in NL, 15–25.

146. *Carnet de lecture II*, 59 comments on Beverley Nichols, *Verdict on India* (London: J. Cape, 1944) (see NL, 77). According to Teilhard, the author seems to favor Jinnah rather than Gandhi or Nehru.

147. *Carnet de lecture II*, no page number; see NL, 119. Teilhard indirectly referred to Huxley's book in an essay of 1947; see FM, 190, also TF, 200.

148. Paris, 1931. See *carnet de lecture II*, 42 and *cahier XIV*, 5; see NL, 56–57.

149. H. Delacroix, *Études d'histoire et de psychologie de mysticisme* (Paris: Alcan, 1908); J. Baruzi, *St. Jean de la Croix et le Problème de l'expérience mystique* (Paris: Alcan, 1924). Both are listed for further consultation in *carnet de lecture II*, 42 (see NL, 56) and are well-known reference works on the history of mysticism.

150. See LF, 127f.; also C. Cuénot, 246f.

Chapter 4

1. See the interview by Marcel Brion, "Rencontre avec le Père Teilhard de Chardin," in *Les Nouvelles Littéraires* (January 11, 1951).

2. The late diaries consist of nine exercise books, *Cahiers XIII–XXI*, dating from July 1944 to April 1955. They are kept in the Jesuit Archives in France.

3. See especially the valuable correspondence with his friend and former collaborator, Father Pierre Leroy, SJ, *Lettres Familières de Pierre Teilhard de Chardin mon ami 1948–1955* (Paris: Centurion, 1976; abbreviated as LF).

4. In the "Chronological List of Works," drawn up by C. Cuénot on the basis of the thirteen published volumes of Teilhard's *Oeuvres* of religious and philosophical writings (found in HM, 241–51), the following number of titles are listed:

1916–22: 38 titles
1923–31: 19 titles
1932–45: 48 titles
1946–55: 92 titles

5. Among the religious and philosophical thinkers he met were Emmanuel Mounier, Gabriel Marcel, Nicolas Berdyaev, Louis Lavelle, Jean Hippolyte, Vladimir Lossky, and Abbé Pierre. At UNESCO, he met Julian Huxley and Joseph Needham. Ten years after his death, in 1965, UNESCO devoted a symposium to both Teilhard's and Einstein's thought; see P. Maheu, ed., *Science et synthèse* (Paris: Gallimard, 1966); Engl. trans. *Science and Synthesis* (New York: Springer, 1971).

6. LI, 367. The only public statement of Teilhard's ideas at that time is found in the long interview accorded to Marcel Brion in early 1951 (see n. 1 above). It inaugurated a new series of regular encounters with well-known intellectual figures through which the journal *Les Nouvelles Littéraires* presented their life and work to its readers. The interview with Teilhard was the first; it was followed by "Rencontre avec Jean-Paul Sartre," an indication of the equal importance accorded to both thinkers. This is also expressed in the comment of a student chaplain of that time: "If you want to fill an auditorium, all you have to do is advertise that you have Teilhard or Jean Paul Sartre." Quoted in M. and E. Lukas, *Teilhard: A Biography* (London: Collins, 1977), 215.

7. LF, 39, quoted in C. Cuénot, 268.

8. Letter to Father Martindale, February 12, 1943.

9. C. Cuénot, *Teilhard de Chardin: A Biographical Study* (London: Burns & Oates, 1965), 261, mentions it only briefly. A longer account is found in J. Bacot, "Autour du Congrès Universel des Croyants: Quelques Évocations," *Cahiers Pierre Teilhard de Chardin* 2 (Paris: Éditions du Seuil, 1960), 143-50. Teilhard mentions it in a letter of July 6, 1948, to Lucile Swan where he writes, "Last Saturday, in a meeting of the World Congress for the Union of Faiths…I met Aldous Huxley…" (LTLS, 233). For a detailed discussion of Teilhard's links with this movement see U. King, "Teilhard's Association with the World Congress of Faiths," in U. King, *The Spirit of One Earth: Reflections on Teilhard de Chardin and Global Spirituality* (New

York: Paragon House, 1989); see chap. 8, 135–46. See also U. King, "Pierre Teilhard de Chardin, Global Visionary for Our Times," in *Interreligious Insight: A Journal of Dialogue and Engagement* 3/2 (2005): 14–21. This quarterly journal is a joint publication by the World Congress of Faiths, Common Ground, and Interreligious Engagement Project.

10. J. Bacot, 146.

11. See "The Sense of Man" (1929), in TF, 22, n. 4.

12. *Cahier XIII*, 105.

13. *Cahier XIV*, 11.

14. For the development of the French branch see J. Bacot, and cyclostyled papers from the Union des Croyants, Paris: "Le Congrès Universel des Croyants—Historique 1946–1962"; Solange Lemaître, "Le Père Teilhard de Chardin—Sa presence," 1965; J. F. Six, "Louis Massignon, prophète du dialogue entre croyants d'Orient et d'Occident," 1958.

15. FM, 185–92.

16. FM, 192.

17. "Le Congrès Universel des Croyants—Historique 1946–1962," 2.

18. Available in cyclostyled form from Union des Croyants, Paris.

19. "Le Congrès Universel des Croyants" (1950), unpublished. The three talks are published as "A Phenomenon of Counter-Evolution in Human Biology or the Existential Fear" (1949), AE, 181–85; "How May We Conceive and Hope That Human Unanimisation Will Be Realised on Earth?" (1950), FM, 281–88; "The Zest for Living" (1950), AE, 229–43. They are analyzed in U. King, *The Spirit of One Earth*, 135–46. Thus, six contributions can be clearly dated as addressed to the "Union des Croyants" between 1947 and 1950: four published essays, one participation in a discussion, and one outline; the latter two are only available in cyclostyled form. The biography by M. and E. Lukas, 221, incorrectly describes the essay "Ecumenism" (December 1946) as addressed to the Union des Croyants, before this movement had come into existence.

20. This idea is more fully developed in the subsequently written talk "The Zest for Living" (1950); see AE, 229–43.

21. Personal communication from one of the secretaries, Mme d'Hauteville. Also confirmed by Father Leroy who, after Teilhard's death, took the latter's place on the committee of the Union des Croyants.

22. Briefly referred to by Teilhard in TF, 139, n. 2.

23. Personal communication from Swami Ritajananda, Gretz (France).

24. The correspondence, dating from June 1946 to March 1955, is still unpublished. When living in the United States, Teilhard also kept in touch with other members; for example, Louis Massignon saw Teilhard in New York in 1952; Dr. Loriot, the treasurer of the movement, met him during a visit in London in 1954; see C. Cuénot, *Teilhard de Chardin*, 311 and 366.

25. The meetings of the Union des Croyants took place at the Musée Guimet until 1958.

26. Paris, 1955. See also her earlier books *Le Mystère de la Mort dans les religions de l'Asie* (Paris: Presses Universitaires de France), 1943; *Abdul Baha—Une grande figure de l'unité* (Paris: Adrien-Maisonneuve, 1952). Later publications include *Ramakrichna* (Paris: Éditions du Seuil, 1954), and *Hindouisme ou Sanâtana Dharma* (Paris: Fayard, 1957), published in English as *Hinduism* (London: Burns & Oates, 1959).

27. See P. Leroy, "Les 'Textes Mystiques d'Orient et d'Occident,' Hommage à Solange Lemaître," Union des Croyants (Paris, 1961).

28. See Teilhard's letter to S. Lemaître, December 12, 1953: "Ci-joint un projet de 'notice' me concernant, —que je préférerais à celui que vous m'avez envoyé. Je n'ai pas d'objection sérieuse à ce que vous publiez quelques passages de la Messe sur le Monde, —bien que cela puisse faire peut-être se froncer les soucils de qq. supérieur." In 1953, after reading Lemaître's work *Abdul Baha— Une grande figure de l'unité* (which devotes several pages to the work of the World Congress of Faiths), Teilhard described this book as "those beautiful pages on unity" and he expressed the hope that Lemaître's forthcoming anthology of mystical texts would similarly embody the idea of unity as its major theme. See letter to S. Lemaître, January 11, 1953.

29. Letter to Dr. Loriot, December 24, 1952.

30. Letter to S. Lemaître, March 2, 1955.

31. He is reported to have said: "Surtout...faites vivre l'Union des Croyants, c'est le Mouvement de Cîme de demain." See S. Lemaître, *Le Père Teilhard de Chardin—Sa Présence* (Paris: Association des Amis de P. Teilhard de Chardin, 1965), 10.

32. René Grousset (1885–1952) is well known as historian of the Orient and the Crusades. See among others his *Histoire de la Philosophie Orientale* (Paris: Nouvelle Librairie nationale, 1923); *Histoire de l'Extrême-Orient* (Paris: P. Geuthner, 1929); *Les Civilisations de l'Orient* (Paris: G. Crès, 1929–30); *Les Philosophies Indiennes* (Paris: Desclée, 1931); *Le Bilan de l'Histoire* (Paris: Plon, 1946); *L'Inde* (Paris: Éditions d'histoire et d'art, 1949). Teilhard referred to Grousset as early as 1934 (see LI, 274), but a closer study of his works seems to have occurred only after 1946. Unfortunately, his subsequent correspondence with Grousset appears to have been lost.

33. See C. Cuénot, *Teilhard de Chardin*, 297, n. 1. Teilhard's contacts with René Grousset, Solange Lemaître, and the "Union des Croyants" are discussed ibid., 295–98. The readers' register of the Musée Guimet shows no record of Teilhard's borrowing of books. However, one of the former librarians thinks that Teilhard was known well enough to obtain books without going through the formality of signing the register. Personal communication.

34. TF, 134–47.

35. See S. Lemaître, "In Memoriam," in *Réflexions sur le bonheur, Cahiers Pierre Teilhard de Chardin* 2 (Paris: Éditions du Seuil, 1960), 154.

36. Paris 1938, reprinted 1966. Its subtitle is "La Doctrine Morale et Métaphysique de Ramanuja." See *cahier XIV*, 87 and 150, for Teilhard's references to Lacombe's book.

37. Personal communication from Mlle Jeanne Mortier, who kindly allowed me to consult the letters dealing with Indian thought and also Teilhard's preface to this correspondence. The latter consists of two pages, dated August 15, 1947; this was published separately in the French journal *Europe*, March–April 1965, 114–15. The Romain Rolland–Jeanne Mortier correspondence remains unfortunately still unpublished, but it can be found at the Fondation Teilhard de Chardin in Paris.

38. C. Cuénot, 297, n. 1.

39. See *Actes du XXI Congrès International des Orientalistes*, Paris 23.-31.7.1948, published in 1949–50, 5.

40. London, 1943.

41. See *cahier XVI*, 5ff.

42. Written in 1950, the theme of this essay was first announced in English on 4.10.1948 as "the heart of matter," and on October 4, 1948 as "The Golden Glow"; see *cahier XVI*, 4 and 5.

43. *Cahier XVI*, 5. G. Dunbar, vol. I, 163 writes in a section on "Hindu religious movements" that, after the coming of the Moghuls, "the fires of adversity had brought into greater prominence than ever before the doctrine of the essential unity of God, a doctrine which involves a belief that 'every god accepted by Hinduism is elevated and ultimately identified with the central Reality which is one with the deeper Self of Man....'" Here and elsewhere he quotes Radhakrishnan's *The Hindu View of Life* (Oxford: G. Allen & Unwin, 1927).

44. Letter to Solange Lemaître, January 5, 1949. The Neo-Confucian philosopher Chu Xsi of the twelfth century is sometimes described as "both the Herbert Spencer and Thomas Aquinas of China." See J. Needham, *Within the Four Seas: The Dialogue of East and West* (London: Allen & Unwin, 1969), 67, and *Science and Civilisation in China*, vol. 2 (Cambridge: Cambridge University Press, 1956), 455f.

45. The contact with Jacques Masui is definitely established, but it may be that Teilhard first heard about Sri Aurobindo even earlier from his friend Abbé Breuil. Apparently, the latter realized the similarities between the two thinkers and pointed them out to Aurobindo, in a letter written at the end of 1950, which, however, only arrived in Pondicherry after Aurobindo's death. See A. Monestier, *Teilhard et Sri Aurobindo* (Paris: Éditions universitaires 1963), 6. Jacques Masui, who died in November 1975, was the editor of the review *Hermès—Recherches sur l'expérience spirituelle*. Its editorial committee included well-known scholars and writers on eastern religions such as Benz, Conze, Murti, Tucci, and Watts.

46. Personal communication from Jacques Masui. See also his monograph *In Memoriam: P. Teilhard de Chardin* (Brussels,

1955), which is probably the first printed comparison between Teilhard and Aurobindo.

47. Teilhard read several other titles in psychology. In *cahier XVII*, 48, he noted down a plan for a psychoanalytical study of Christianity.

48. Later, after meeting Northrop personally, Teilhard wrote that they held "completely opposite positions." See LF, 129.

49. The Maurice Lectures (King's College, London) for 1951; published London 1952. Teilhard first learned about this book through a review in *Time*. See LF, 175 and 186.

50. Letter to S. Lemaître, January 11, 1953.

51. Letter to S. Lemaître, September 13, 1950.

52. See *cahier XVII*, 6–9.

53. Perhaps his cousin Marguerite? However, the extract, dated September 10, 1948, is not found in any of the published letters to her. This is not unusual, as can be seen from extracts of other letters, found in the *Journal*, but not elsewhere.

54. *Cahier XVII*, 9.

55. See *cahier XIV*, 86; also R. Grousset, 121f.

56. A comparison between Shiva and the cosmic Christ provides a fruitful line of inquiry. A modern tapestry by an Indian Christian shows Christ on the cross, surrounded by Indian symbols, as "Lord of the Sacred Dance," a traditional epithet of Shiva. B. Bruteau explores the wider analogies between the Indian tradition of a "cosmic divinity" and Teilhard's "cosmic Christ" in *Evolution toward Divinity: Teilhard de Chardin and the Hindu Traditions* (Wheaton, IL: Theosophical Publishing House, 1974). A pioneering study of Teilhard's understanding of the cosmic Christ is found in J. A. Lyons, *The Cosmic Christ in Origen and Teilhard de Chardin* (Oxford: Oxford University Press, 1982).

57. C. Cuénot, 299.

58. Ibid.

59. LF, 67f. The book referred to is L. Jugnet, *L'Évolution Rédemptrice du P. Teilhard de Chardin* (Paris: Éditions du Cêdre, 1950).

60. See LF, 93. The interview is found in *Nouvelles Littéraires*, January 11, 1951.

61. See E. Maillart, *Oasis Interdites: De Pékin au Cachemere* (Paris: Grasset, 1937); English translation: *Turkestan Solo: One Woman's Expedition from the Tien Shan to the Kizil Khum* (London: Heinemann, 1938). After reading this work, Teilhard wrote to the author, "If your pilgrimage in Asia has only revealed to you the organic immensity of the world, your effort will have been amply rewarded, a hundred times more than through any so-called scientific results....The goal of all science is only to teach us to become conscious of the unity and movement of everything that surrounds us." Letter of June 21, 1937.

62. *Cahier XVII*, 55. See also Teilhard's discussions on Indian religions reported by Maryse Choisy, *Teilhard et l'Inde* (Paris: Éditions universitaires, 1964).

63. LF, 130.

64. LI, 368.

65. LTLS, 257.

66. LF, 130.

67. LF, 140. This comment was made after hearing a sermon by Cardinal Fulton Sheen in New York.

68. See LF, 163.

69. LI, 463.

70. See LF, 123.

71. See LI, 453 and 462f.; LF, 242. Father Paul Henry, SJ, from Louvain had negotiated with a Swiss publisher to bring out a German translation of some of Teilhard's articles already published in French. The Jesuit General withheld permission for publication in early 1955. Similarly, Teilhard learned shortly before his death that he was not allowed to return once more to France to participate in a scientific symposium.

72. See LF, 36 and 213; M. and E. Lukas, *Teilhard: A Biography* (London: Collins, 1977).

73. LF, 225.

74. Stated in a brief biographical outline, written in the third person by Teilhard himself on his election as a member of the *Académie des Sciences* in Paris. This was published in the Jesuit journal *Études* (July–August 1950); see HM, 152–54; the quotation is on 153 but given here in my translation from the French original; see *Le Coeur de la Matière* (Paris: Éditions du Seuil, 1976), 194.

Chapter 5

1. For a detailed examination of Teilhard's vocabulary see C. Cuénot, *Nouveau Lexique Teilhard de Chardin* (Paris: Éditions du Seuil, 1968); M. C. Deckers, *Le vocabulaire de Teilhard de Chardin* (Louvain: Gembloux, 1968); S. Cowell, *The Teilhard Lexicon* (Brighton: Sussex Academic Press, 2001).

2. See *Journal*, 295: "My Method"; also H. de Lubac, *The Religion of Teilhard de Chardin* (London: Collins, 1967), 161f., "A Reversal of Method"; E. Rideau, *La Pensée du P. Teilhard de Chardin* (Paris: Éditions du Seuil, 1965), 49–59. For the early period, the transference of scientific images to religious thought has been studied by H. C. Cairns, *The Identity and Originality of Teilhard de Chardin* (PhD diss., University of Edinburgh, 1971).

3. D. Gray, *The One and the Many: Teilhard de Chardin's Vision of Unity* (London: Burns & Oates, 1969), 68. See his insightful discussion on "Typology in Teilhard," 68–71.

4. Father Leroy in LT, 34.

5. Claude Cuénot was the first to arrange Teilhard's essays in chronological order; a "Chronological List of Works" is found in his Teilhard biography, and especially in HM, 241–51. A brief summary of the content of all essays and books is given by Fabio Mantovani in his substantial *Dizionario delle Opere di Teilhard de Chardin*, 2006.

6. For a list of the early essays that discuss pantheism, monism, and mysticism, see appendix II.

7. WTW, 13–71.

8. WTW, 115–49.

9. CE, 56–75.

10. WTW, 28. Following the usage of his time, Teilhard expresses himself in exclusive language (*l'homme* translated as "man," referred to as "he"). Whenever possible, I have changed *man* to *human being*, but have left the personal pronoun *he* here, since Teilhard, a man, speaks autobiographically about his own experience in this text.

11. WTW, 101.

12. WTW, 29f. This amazing passage referring to the Earth as *Terra Mater*, as mother, and as divine, resonates with contem-

porary ecological and ecofeminist spirituality, but it was written in 1916.

13. See WTW, 28f. for a discussion of this theme.

14. MM, 58.

15. For the quotations from the diary see *Journal*, 31, 183, 177, and 42; my translation.

16. Ibid., 27.

17. WTW, 14.

18. R. C. Zaehner, *Mysticism Sacred and Profane* (Oxford: Clarendon Press, 1957).

19. *Journal*, 303.

20. Ibid., 175.

21. I cite here the translation of Siôn Cowell (2004), MD, 108, which uses the plural "others" rather than "the other," as in the first translation of MD, 138. Teilhard's development of the sense of the human is expressed in another essay, "The Rise of the Other" (1942), AE, 59–75.

22. See WTW, 120f.

23. Ibid., 124f.

24. Ibid., 129.

25. London: Fontana, 1976. The book is divided into I: The Way of Physics; II: The Way of Eastern Mysticism; III: The Parallels.

26. WTW, 130.

27. Ibid., 135f.

28. Ibid., 122.

29. Ibid., 137.

30. Ibid., 148.

31. See "The Universal Element" (1919), WTW, 289–302.

32. Some of Teilhard's major writings on this theme are found in the collection of essays entitled *Science and Christ*. The christological perspective implied in this convergence has been dealt with at length in the studies of Ch. F. Mooney and D. Gray.

33. See G. M. Hopkins's poems "God's Grandeur" and "As Kingfishers Catch Fire, Dragonflies Draw Flame."

34. See "Creative Union" (1919), WTW, 151–76. An extensive discussion of this theory is found in D. Gray, *The One and the Many*.

35. D. Gray, 16.

36. For "pan-Christism" see SC, 59 and 124; HM, 55. Blondel's use of "pan-Christism" is discussed in TB, 58f. For "'pan-Christic' monism" see CE, 171, and for "'pan-Christic' mysticism," HM, 47.

37. WTW, 177–90.

38. HM, 182–95.

39. See *P. Teilhard de Chardin–M. Blondel Correspondence*, ed. H. de Lubac, abbrev. TB, and the letters to Auguste Valensin in *Lettres Intimes*.

40. See H. de Lubac, *The Religion of Teilhard de Chardin*, 157, and TB, 10.

41. HM, 67–79. This text was first published in *Hymne de l'Univers* (1961), translated into English as *Hymn of the Universe* (1965 and 1969).

42. Ibid., 75f.

43. It is the second essay so appended; it follows an even earlier one, of October 14, 1916, written during the First World War, on the eve of the attack on Douaumont, entitled "Christ in Matter"; see HM, 61–67; a fuller version of this text is found in HU, 39–51. Both appended essays, although written in the third person, encapsulate descriptions of Teilhard's own mystical experience and universal spiritual vision.

44. The first version of "My Universe" (1918) is found in HM, 196–208, the second in SC, 37–85.

45. CE, 56–75.

46. TB, 25.

47. MM, 302.

48. See TB, 52 and 20.

49. See TB, 29 and 39.

50. CE, 68.

51. CE, 65.

52. See CE, 58–60.

53. CE, 65.

54. CE, 72. The translation of *le Tout* as "the Whole" has been replaced by "the All" throughout.

55. CE, 64.

56. CE, 64–70, *passim*.

57. See especially chap. 9, "The Element of Novelty," and chap. 14, "God All in All."

58. H. de Lubac, 155.

59. C. Cuénot, *Nouveau Lexique Teilhard de Chardin* (Paris: Éditions de Seuil, 1968), 145–55.

60. See ibid., 146f.

61. The term *panentheism*, found in the works of Paul Tillich, Jürgen Moltmann, Hans Küng, and Philip Clayton, among others, is not a new invention but was first coined by the nineteenth-century German philosopher and educator Karl Christian Friedrich Krause (1781–1832). The concept remained suspect for a long time, and its general acceptance was much delayed. The German writer Günther Schiwy has argued that it would have greatly helped Teilhard's thinking and clarified his position had he adopted the term *panentheism* rather than *pantheism* in his writings. See chap. 7, "'Pan-en-theismus'—eine Spurensuche" in G. Schiwy's book, *Ein Gott im Wandel: Teilhard de Chardin und sein Bild der Evolution* (Düsseldorf: Patmos, 2001), 123–43.

Chapter 6

1. LZ, 53.

2. TF, 40–59.

3. See the table listing "Later Writings that include Specific Comparisons with Eastern Religions" in appendix 3.

4. LZ, 108. The theme had preoccupied him for some time; see the reference to the "eastern" and "western" solution with regard to the problem of the One and the Many in a letter of February 9, 1931, in LI, 223f.

5. TF, 40.

6. TF, 42.

7. See TF, 42–45, *passim*.

8. TF, 137f.

9. See SC, 105–6, *passim*.

10. TF, 45.

11. TF, 44.

12. SC, 105.

13. As for example "logically" (SC, 106; TF, 48; LI, 251 and 274), "in strict logic," and "in theory" (both TF, 45).

14. TF, 45.

15. TF, 46f.

16. See TF, 47.

17. TF, 54. The original reads, "En somme...le Christianisme, pour demeurer lui-même, doit embrasser, en la sauvant, la mystique occidentale." One could understand this as meaning a marrying of the mystical with the institutional in religion.

18. TF, 55.

19. These notes were taken by C. Cuénot and J. Bousquet at the École Normale Supérieure, Paris, where the lecture was given on January 8, 1933. A brief summary is found in C. Cuénot, *Teilhard de Chardin*, 140f.; a fuller statement is provided in C. Cuénot, *Ce que Teilhard a vraiment dit* (Paris: Stock, 1972), 224–28.

20. C. Cuénot, *Ce que Teilhard a vraiment dit*, 226f.

21. See H. de Lubac, ed., *Lettres Intimes de Teilhard de Chardin*, and H. de Lubac, *Teilhard Posthume*. For H. de Lubac's works on Buddhism, see his *Aspects du Bouddhisme* (Paris: Éditions du Seuil, 1951); *La Rencontre du Bouddhisme et de l'Occident* (Paris: Aubier, 1952); *Amida* (Paris: Éditions du Seuil, 1955).

22. Quoted in C. Cuénot, *Teilhard de Chardin*, 142. However, as de Lubac's letter remains unpublished, this question may have been inferred from Teilhard's answer.

23. LI, 251. Cuénot, *Teilhard de Chardin*, 142, attributes this passage wrongly to Monchanin. Since Teilhard's letters to de Lubac (LI) have been published, it seems that the initial criticism came directly from de Lubac himself rather than from Abbé Monchanin.

24. Monchanin admired in particular Teilhard's essays on "The Phenomenon of Man" (1928) and "The Spirit of the Earth" (1931). Later, after 1946, Teilhard read some of Monchanin's own works (see LI, 252). See the essays on Hinduism and Christianity in J. Monchanin, *Mystique de l'Inde, mystère chrétien*, ed. S. Siauve (Paris: Fayard, 1974). On Monchanin, see S. Rodhe, *Jules Monchanin: Pioneer in Christian-Hindu Dialogue*

(Delhi: Indian Society for Promoting Christian Knowledge, 1993), J. Mattam, *Land of the Trinity* (Bangalore: Theological Publications in India, 1975), and H. de Lubac, *Images de l'Abbé Monchanin* (Paris: Éditions Montaigne, 1967), especially 119–51: "L'Abbé Monchanin et le Père Teilhard de Chardin." Monchanin (1895–1957) was one of the earliest people to compare Teilhard's and Aurobindo's thought in a lecture given in Pondicherry in 1955 or 1956.

25. H. de Lubac, *The Religion of Teilhard de Chardin*, 153.

26. LI, 273f., April 29, 1934; my translation.

27. TF, 134–47.

28. TF, 163–208.

29. TF, 200.

30. See TF, 200–201, *passim.*

31. AE, 215–27.

32. TF, 209–11.

33. TF, 209. The French has *deux voies* instead of *routes.* The English translation renders both *voie* and *route* by "road."

34. LI, 273.

35. See the essays "The Grand Option" (1939) and "The Heart of the Problem" (1949) in FM, 37–60 and 260–69.

36. Teilhard's emphasis on time is a special feature of his typological approach to historical data. Its newness is discussed in F. Bravo, *La Vision de l'Histoire chez Teilhard de Chardin* (Paris: Les Éditions du Cerf, 1970).

37. AE, 383.

38. See M. Weber, *The Sociology of Religion* (London: Methuen, 1966), 166, and also the discussion in R. Bendix, *Max Weber: An Intellectual Portrait* (London: Methuen, 1966), 201ff.

39. C. Cuénot, *Teilhard de Chardin*, 141.

Chapter 7

1. *The Vision of the Past* (London: Collins, 1966), 75.

2. See his essay of 1945, "A Great Event Foreshadowed: The Planetisation of Mankind," FM, 124–39; see also HPh, 171.

3. AE, 242.

4. TF, 47.

5. CE, 199.

6. CE, 121, n. 8.

7. See CE, 61 and AE, 157.

8. See TF, 209. The references to the Sufis date from 1950 and later. Perhaps Teilhard learned more about the Sufis from the great Islam scholar, Louis Massignon, whom he knew well, and through his work with the French branch of the World Congress of Faiths.

9. AE, 219.

10. SC, 104f.

11. SC, 105.

12. See LI, 274.

13. G. Le Brun Kéris, "Teilhard de Chardin et l'Islam," *La Croix*, December 12, 1969.

14. The French translator of Iqbal's work, *The Reconstruction of Religious Thought in Islam*, published an article comparing Iqbal and Teilhard. See Eva Meyerovitch, "Orient et Occident," *New Morality* 1, 1963, 49–68. Other similarities exist between Teilhard and the modern Islamic thinker Fathi Uhman from Egypt.

15. Eva Meyerovitch, 66.

16. SC, 106.

17. See John and Mary Evelyn Grim, "Teilhard de Chardin. A Short Biography" at www.teilharddechardin.org/biography, accessed on March 1, 2010.

18. Mentioned in H. de Lubac, *Images de l'Abbé Monchanin* (Paris: Éditions Montaigne, 1967), 150, n. 1.

19. See LZ, 58.

20. See LI, 274.

21. See CE, 122, n. 9.

22. See CE, 121 and 122.

23. CE, 123.

24. SC, 98–112.

25. CE, 96–132.

26. The French title "L'épreuve des religions" expresses the "trial" situation more clearly than the English translation "Religions put to the test." See the sections in SC, 104–6, CE, 121–26.

27. Entirely concerned with this theme is the essay "A Mental

Threshold across Our Path: From Cosmos to Cosmogenesis," AE, 251–68.

28. See FM, 260–62, *passim*. The translation is partly my own.

29. TF, 21. Written in 1929, Teilhard's affirmation of the human being having "become adult" long antedates similar statements by Dietrich Bonhoeffer and other, more recent theologians.

30. SC, 101f. A fuller discussion of this theme is found in "Modern Unbelief—Its Underlying Causes and Remedy" (1933), SC, 113–17.

31. SC, 103.

32. AE, 240. See the letter of March 16, 1954: "Our age is one of *atheism*.—No, I would say, on the contrary, it is an age of the obscure adoration of a 'God Ahead.'" LF, 232.

33. See, for example, SC, 108; HM, 96; LF, 232.

34. CE, 126.

35. SC, 103; see also LI, 251.

36. TF, 134.

37. SC, 103.

38. TF, 134–47.

39. TF, 135.

40. TF, 136. In Joseph Needham's opinion, it is impossible to overestimate the importance that the Buddhist rejection of the world and the doctrine of *maya* had in Chinese Buddhism. Irreconcilable with Taoism and Confucianism, which, in their different ways, both accept the world, it helped to inhibit the development of Chinese science. He refers to a fifth-century A.D. Chinese observer who considered Buddhism as suitable for Indians, but not for Chinese, and quotes him as saying that "for Confucius and Laotse the regulating of the things in this world is the main objective, but for the Buddhists the objective is the escape from this world." See J. Needham, *Science and Civilisation in China*, vol. 2 (Cambridge: Cambridge University Press, 1956), 403ff.

41. See TF, 139.

42. See TF, 140.

43. See TF, 141. "God and his transcendence" refers to Indian spirituality. Stressing the "religious character of Indian

thought," H. Nakamura has pointed out that Indian languages have an extraordinarily rich vocabulary for the idea of God, in contrast to western classical languages. See his *Ways of Thinking of Eastern Peoples—India—China—Tibet—Japan* (Honolulu: East-West Center Press, 1964), 157 and 159.

44. See TF, 144 and 142.

45. TF, 141 and 143, *passim*.

46. Title of the last subsection of the essay; see TF, 145–47 for the following quotations.

47. See TF, 144, where Teilhard refers to "the humanism of a Tagore." He may have read Tagore in Peking; his diary of 1944 quotes an extract from Tagore's *Gitanjali*. See *cahier XIII*, 59.

48. TF, 146.

49. See J. Needham, "The Role of Europe and China in the Evolution of Oecumenical Sciences," *British Association for the Advancement of Science* (September 1967): 83–98, especially 95. Elsewhere Needham uses the image of different "rivers" flowing into modern science, just as Teilhard talks about the different "rivers" of religion coming together; see TF, 145f.

50. Letter to S. Lemaître, January 11, 1953. Teilhard also expressed his concern that the newly founded Center for World Religions in Harvard might pursue "a lowest common denominator—rather than a new God...except if it may give birth to someone like Newman." See *cahier XVIII*, 137.

51. New York: Newman Press, 1971.

52. R. E. Whitson, 52. See especially the chapters on "Convergence of Religion," 35–53, and "Convergence and Commitment," 166–87.

53. AE, 239.

54. SC, 112.

55. CE, 125.

56. See CE, 208. The axial role of Christianity is discussed in detail in "The Christian Phenomenon" (1950), CE, 199–208. See also the epilogue of the same title in HPh, 209–15 (PM, 291–99).

57. CE, 199.

58. LZ, 79.

59. CE, 130.

60. See CE, 125, pp. 126 and 128, *passim* for quotations from "How I Believe."

61. HE, 91. He also described Christianity in terms of a "personalistic universe," wherein the personal represents the highest form of the spiritual. See "Sketch of a Personalist Universe" (1936), HE, 53–92, and "Some General Views on the Essence of Christianity" (1939), CE, 133–37; also the section on "The Personal Universe" and "The Personalising Universe," HPh, 183–87; PM, 257–64.

62. CE, 128.

63. CE, 130; see the entire section on "The Universal Christ and the Convergence of Religions," CE, 126–30.

64. SC, 112.

65. CE, 130.

66. SC, 112.

67. *The Vision of the Past*, 205.

68. HPh, 168; PM, 239.

69. TF, 145.

70. He distinguished clearly between the coil and a genuinely converging spiral. In cahier XIV, 128, the difference is shown in the following diagram:

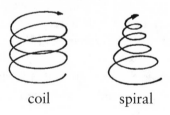

coil   spiral

71. R. E. Whitson, 22. See his chapter on "The Unity of Civilization."

72. LF, 187. Interesting, C. Cuénot's *Nouveau Lexique Teilhard de Chardin* has an entry on "convergence" but not on "confluence."

73. See C. Cuénot, 15 and 48. R. E. Whitson, 21f. indicates as an example: "Our most forceful specification of convergence in process is probably that of biological generation, in which the offspring is clearly a new reality not identifiable singly with the par-

ents. It is not simply an addition of their characteristics, but something quite different; yet in origin of individual existence it is in complete continuity with them: it embodies them in the greater effect of their convergence."

74. See HPh, 69f.; PM, 114f.

75. SC, 110.

76. SC, 197.

77. I have discussed this further under "Exploring Convergence: The Contribution of World Faiths"; see chap. 7 in my book *The Spirit of One Earth: Reflections on Teilhard de Chardin and Global Spirituality* (New York: Paragon House, 1989). Also published as The Third Francis Younghusband Lecture, *World Faiths* 106 (1978): 1–16. An extensive discussion of convergence is found in R. E. Whitson, *The Coming Convergence of World Religions* (New York: Newman Press, 1971).

Chapter 8

1. PM, 219; HPh, 152. See also "The Basis and Foundations of the Idea of Evolution" (1926) in *Vision of the Past*, 116–42, and "The Human Rebound of Evolution and Its Consequences" (1947), FM, 193–213.

2. WTW, 87. The importance of evolution for the comparative study of religions has been recognized in R. C. Zachner, *Evolution in Religion: A Study in Sri Aurobindo and Pierre Teilhard de Chardin* (Oxford: Clarendon Press, 1971), although Zaehner does not explore the theme of evolution in any depth. For the place of evolution in the reinterpretation of Christianity, see Teilhard's collection of essays in *Christianity and Evolution* (CE).

3. HE, 43.

4. SC, 98, 99 and 100, *passim*.

5. AE, 237.

6. *The Vision of the Past*, 140.

7. I have developed these ideas more fully and discussed them in a comparative context in "The One and the Many: The Individual and the Community from a Religious Perspective," in U. King, *The Spirit of One Earth*, chap. 3, previously published in *Teilhard Review* 11/1 (1976): 9–15.

8. TF, 23 and 24, *passim.*

9. See the discussion on secularization in the preface of CE, 9–13. N. M. Wildiers writes there that Teilhard's "religion of the earth" and secularization "cover, in fact, the same ideological and sociological reality"; ibid., 9. R. J. Zwi Werblowsky, *Beyond Tradition and Modernity: Changing Religions in a Changing World* (London: Athlone Press, 1976), 6, argues "that western religion has undergone changes that are, to some extent, paradigmatic for all other religions." This does not imply, however, "that western experience sets the standard by which all other developments have to be measured." Nor does it mean an "inevitable transcultural or intercultural convergence on the western model."

10. TF, 25.

11. See *cahier XVII*, 104; also HM, 53: "All around us, and within our own selves, God is in process of 'changing.'..." These two texts of 1950 may be compared with earlier passages, such as the sections on "The Future of the Spirit" and "The Arising of God," written in 1931; see HE, 38–47. I have discussed Teilhard's reflections on the changing understanding of God in my article "'The Death of God—The Rebirth of God': A Study in the Thought of Teilhard de Chardin," *Modern Churchman* 18 (1974): 18–30. Teilhard's search for an appropriate image of God in the light of evolution is examined in depth by Günther Schiwy, *Ein Gott im Wandel: Teilhard de Chardin und sein Bild der Evolution* (Düsseldorf: Patmos, 2001).

12. See letter to Dr. Loriot, December 24, 1952, and also Teilhard's papers on "The God of Evolution" (1953) and "My Litany" (1953), CE, 237–45. For a discussion of process theology see the contributions in E. H. Cousins, ed., *Process Theology* (New York: Newman, 1971), and John B. Cobb, Jr., and David Griffin, *Process Theology: An Introductory Exposition* (Philadelphia: Westminster, 1976). Process theology emphasizes God's becoming over being and is linked to contemporary discussions on panentheism. Most process theologians have been influenced by Whitehead's process philosophy, but not Teilhard de Chardin.

13. Only found in C. Cuénot, *Teilhard de Chardin*, 216f., from which all quotations are taken. The text can be seen as a preparation for the important essay "How I Believe" (1934) writ-

ten in the following year, where the same ideas were expressed in more detail; see CE, 96–132.

14. Cuénot, 217.

15. Ibid.

16. MM, 58.

17. *The Vision of the Past*, 173; partly my translation.

18. HE, 44; see also SC, 102. "The Spirit of the Earth" is found in HE, 19–52.

19. SC, 100.

20. HE, 100; see the entire essay "The Phenomenon of Spirituality" (1937), HE, 93–112.

21. SC, 104.

22. AE, 229–43.

23. See AE, 232 and 238.

24. AE, 236.

25. PM, 64 and 42; HPh, 30 and 13.

26. FM, 196–213.

27. FM, 204f.

28. This statement is written in capital letters; see AE, 240.

29. AE, 240.

30. CE, 123 and p. 124, *passim*.

31. AE, 241.

32. PM, 11. Sir Julian Huxley's introduction to *The Phenomenon of Man* has not been reproduced in the new English translation, but HPh carries a new foreword by Brian Swimme.

33. Quoted in R. Speaight, 297.

34. See George Gaylord Simpson, *This View of Life* (New York: Harcourt, Brace & World, 1964), 215.

35. LT, 284.

36. AE, 297–309, prefaced by "Written for Huxley."

37. LF, 126 and 138.

38. For references to Huxley see LF, 97, 160 and 166f.

39. Letter to J. Huxley, September 8, 1952; see also LI, 412.

40. HM, 91.

41. The similarities between Teilhard's and Huxley's thought are discussed in M. Gex, "Vers un humanisme cosmologique," *Revue de Théologie et de Philosophie* 3 (1957), 186–205. However, a fuller comparison between Teilhard's and

Huxley's views, taking into account the references in Teilhard's correspondence with Father Leroy (LF), and his unpublished letters to Huxley, is still outstanding.

42. AE, 241 and 242, *passim.*

43. Ibid., 242.

44. "Le goût de vivre." This is the French title of the essay under discussion, translated as "Zest for Living" in AE, 229–43.

45. For the end of the essay see AE, 242; the postscript is in AE, 243.

46. OSc IX, 3936. These words are the conclusion of a scientific article on "Fossil Men," published in Peking in 1943, which summarizes at the end "The Trend and Meaning of Human Evolution."

47. CE, 118 and 119, *passim.*

48. See "On the Possible Bases of a Universal Human Creed" (1941), FM, 76–81, described as "Remarks on a New York Congress of Science and Religion." Teilhard here presents some reflections on convergence as a "personal testimony, the fruit of thirty years spent in close and sincere contact with scientific and religious circles in Europe, America and the Far East."

49. FM, 76f. This theme is more fully developed in "The Heart of the Problem" (1949), FM, 260–69: at the source of the modern religious crisis lies "a conflict of faith between upward and forward."

50. FM, 81.

51. FM, 185–92.

52. See the short note on "Ecumenism" (1946), SC, 197–98.

53. FM, 189.

54. SC, 198.

55. See SC, 197 and 198.

56. *Cahier XVII,* 37; Teilhard used the English word *spearhead* here.

57. Such an integration would require a theological development going beyond Teilhard. In 1945, his *carnet de lecture* included some extracts on Shiva and Kali, taken from Ch. Autran, *Mithra, Zoroastre et la Préhistoire aryenne du Christianisme* (Paris: Payot, 1935). Apart from this, only the diaries of 1949–50 carry some references to Shiva, together with extracts from R.

Grousset, *Bilan de l'Histoire*. There he found South Indian hymns quoted, praising the cosmic forces of Shiva that inspired Teilhard's comparative reflections. See also chap. 4, notes 52 and 54.

58. AE, 48.

59. TF, 105

60. FM, 23.

61. AE, 49.

62. See CE, 120.

63. Personal communication from Father Leroy.

64. B. Bruteau, *Evolution toward Divinity: Teilhard de Chardin and the Hindu Traditions* (Wheaton, IL: Theosophical Publishing House, 1974), 76. At the time of its publication, this was the first comparative study of its kind. The author thinks that Teilhard's basic insights find more or less close parallels in various strands of traditional Hindu thought, as well as in contemporary reinterpretations, such as that of Sri Aurobindo. In particular, she points to a common vision of God in the cosmos, and God as energy, and a similar approach to the problem of action, and the conquest of evil. As Teilhard himself was unaware of such similarities, and to some extent inimical to the Hindu outlook, this study aims to refute his criticisms and to show how the Hindu worldview would have been helpful to the development of Teilhard's own views, had he taken the trouble to study it. The book highlights the similarities rather than the differences between Teilhard and Indian thought. However, it does not examine whether, given certain premises, particular data are comparable.

65. *Carnet de lecture II*, 10; see G. Baudry, *Notes de Lecture (1945–1947)*, 25.

66. See *carnet de lecture II*, 8; see G. Baudry, 23. The difference between emanation and Teilhard's understanding of creation is examined in R. B. Smith, *Towards the Discovery of God* (PhD diss., University of Exeter, 1968).

67. See *carnet de lecture II*, 10 and 9; see G. Baudry, 23 and 24.

68. These differences were first clearly formulated in a lecture given by Abbé Monchanin in Pondicherry in 1956, published in note form in 1974. See "Teilhard et Sri Aurobindo," in J.

Monchanin, *Mystique de l'Inde: mystère chrétien* (Paris: Fayard, 1974), 31f.

69. The difference between Aurobindo's and Teilhard's understanding of involution and evolution is discussed in J. Feys, *The Philosophy of Evolution in Sri Aurobindo and Teilhard de Chardin* (Calcutta: Firma K. L. Mukhopadhyay, 1973), on whose arguments I have drawn here. Feys's book is a detailed philosophical study of the theme of evolution in Teilhard and Aurobindo, the most comprehensive work on the subject in existence. R. C. Zaehner's *Evolution in Religion* and other books notwithstanding, a fully comprehensive and critical comparison of all aspects of the two thinkers has still to be undertaken.

70. PM, 61; HPh, 28.

71. J. Feys, 108. Feys relates Aurobindo's view of involution and evolution to the Indian *sat-karya-vada* theory of causation, which considers the effect in essence as always preexistent in the cause.

72. J. Feys, 231f. Unfortunately, Feys's important study on evolution does not recognize the implications of Teilhard's evolutionary perspective for his understanding of religion, especially not with regard to the further evolution of religion.

73. B. Bruteau completely overlooks this fundamental difference in *Evolution toward Divinity*. For the relationship between the transcendent and immanent in Teilhard's thought, see H. de Lubac's essay "'Ascent' and 'Descent' in the Work of Teilhard de Chardin," TB, 143–68; French edition 1964: 127–53.

74. Ludovico Galleni has discussed three different theories of evolution (genocentric theory; organismocentric theory; biospherocentry theory) in his article "Is Biosphere Doing Theology?" *Zygon* 36/1 (March 2001): 33–48. See also L. Galleni, Darwin, *Teilhard de Chardin e gli altri* (Ghezzano [PI]: Felici Editore, 2010).

75. See the chapter on "Religious Evolution" in R. Bellah, *Beyond Belief: Essays on Religion in a Post-Traditional World* (New York: Harper & Row, 1970), 20–50.

76. See Huxley's preface to G. B. Barbour, *In the Field with Teilhard de Chardin* (New York: Herder & Herder, 1965), 8f.

77. See the passage in CE, 222f., paraphrased here.

78. C. Cuénot, 262.

79. Already announced in PM, 283, HPh, 202.

80. See J. O'Manique, *Energy in Evolution: Teilhard's Physics of the Future* (London: Garnstone, 1969).

81. See LF, 188 and 193.

82. Teilhard wrote these remarks in English. See C. Cuénot, "Un inédit de Pierre Teilhard de Chardin," *Études Teilhardiennes* 1 (1968): 57–60. Teilhard's English use of *Mystic* refers to *Mysticism* and has been changed accordingly.

83. CE, 93.

84. LF, 193.

85. SC, 112.

86. Teilhard had found this expression in J. V. L. Casserley, *The Retreat of Christianity in the Modern World: The Maurice Lectures, King's College, London, for 1951* (London: Longmans, Green, 1952). He was so delighted with it that he quoted it in several letters; see letter to Solange Lemaître, January 11, 1953; LI, 422; LF, 186.

87. LI, 460; also LI, 450.

88. AE, 226 and 227.

89. See Paul Tillich, *Christianity and the Encounter of the World Religions* (New York: Columbia University Press, 1963), 30.

90. FM, 79.

91. See Theodosius Dobzhansky, *The Biology of Ultimate Concern* (London: Collins, 1971). Dobzhansky calls Teilhard "one of the most profound religious philosophers of our time" and points out that his "writings belong really to a class by themselves; an understanding of their singularity is essential for a comprehension of their contents" (ibid., 95 and 114).

92. Dobzhansky, 109 and 110.

Chapter 9

1. CE, 68.

2. See the works of H. de Lubac, M. Barthélemy-Madaule, Ch. Mooney, and F. Nemeck listed in the bibliography. Professor R. C. Zaehner, well known for his contribution to the study of

mysticism, turned from initial enthusiasm to a subsequent rejection of Teilhard, but he still granted at the end that the latter was a mystic. Earlier he had called him "one of the greatest mystics of all time" (*Teilhard Review* 2, 2 [1967]: 42).

3. For a comprehensive contemporary history of Christian mysticism see the highly praised four-volume series by Bernard McGinn, *The Presence of God: A History of Western Christian Mysticism* (New York: Crossroad, 1991–).

4. See, for example the critical discussions in S. T. Katz, ed., *Mysticism and Philosophical Analysis* (New York: Oxford University Press, 1978), and F. Staal, *Exploring Mysticism* (Berkeley: University of California Press, 1975). Other publications taking different approaches are R. C. Zaehner, *Mysticism Sacred and Profane* (Oxford: Clarendon Press, 1957), *Hindu and Muslim Mysticism* (London: University of London Press, 1960); W. T. Stace, *Mysticism and Philosophy* (London: Macmillan, 1960); F. C. Happold, *Mysticism: A Study and Anthology* (Harmondsworth: Penguin, 1970); W. Johnston, *The Still Point* (New York: Fordham University Press, 1971), and *The Inner Eye of Love* (London: Collins, 1978). See also A. Ravier, ed., *La Mystique et les Mystiques* (Paris: Desclée, 1965).

5. Emphasized by H. de Lubac in his commentary on the Teilhard-Blondel Correspondence (TB); see also his study on *The Religion of Teilhard de Chardin*, chap. 9 "The Element of Novelty."

6. Protagonists of the essential unity of all religions can be found in both West and East. Apart from the well-known views of the followers of neo-Vedanta see, among others, the works of A. Huxley, F. Schuon, S. H. Nasr, and other writers representing the *philosophia perennis* school.

7. Teilhard's synthesis between a personal and universal approach is analysed in M. Bartholémy-Madaule, *La Personne et le drame humain chez Teilhard de Chardin* (Paris: Éditions du Seuil, 1967). The importance of a convergent structure is discussed in A. Glässer, *Konvergenz—die Struktur der Weltsumme P. Teilhard de Chardins* (Kevelaer: Butzon & Bercker, 1970).

8. CE, 102.

9. See R. C. Zaehner, *Mysticism Sacred and Profane*.

10. See TF, 209–11, from which all quotations are taken.

11. AE, 215–27.

12. TF, 211.

13. See the title of the essay under discussion, and also the longer text, "A Clarification: Reflections on Two Converse Forms of the Spirit" (July 1950), AE, 215–27.

14. AE, 223.

15. See R.C. Zaehner's article "Teilhard and Eastern Religions," *Teilhard Review* 2, 2 (1967–68): 41–53. The quotation is on 43.

16. The diagram in this form is my own, but it is adapted from a similar diagram found in FM, 269. For a discussion of the *via tertia*, see AE, 56.

17. See the discussion of "Cosmic Life," chap. 5, above.

18. See A. Ravier, "Teilhard de Chardin, et l'expérience mystique d'après ses notes intimes" in *Terre Promise, Cahier VIII*, Fondation et Association Teilhard de Chardin (Paris 1974), 212–32."

19. A rather different assessment of Teilhard as a mystic is found in Ravier's sermon "Homélie pour la Messe du Xe Anniversaire de la mort du Père Teilhard de Chardin" TB, French edition, 155–63.

20. *Cahier XIII*, 113, 96 and 90, *passim*.

21. A point also stressed by M. Barthélemy-Madaule, *Bergson et Teilhard de Chardin* (Paris: Éditions du Seuil, 1963), 475–93: "La Vie Mystique."

22. Cyclostyled discussion of the 1948 conference, Union des Croyants, Paris, 30, 37, and 38.

23. AE, 21–57.

24. AE, 55–57, *passim*; slightly adapted English translation.

25. LTF, 115.

26. HM, 88.

27. TF, 143. Teilhard's inspiring ideas about love as unifying energy have a remarkable, independent parallel in the work of the Russian American sociologist Pitirim A. Sorokin (1889–1968). I have compared their ideas in my article "Love—A Higher Form of Human Energy in the Work of Teilhard de Chardin and Sorokin," *Zygon* 39/1 (March 2004): 77–102. For Sorokin's theory see his book *The Ways and Power of Love:*

Types, Factors, and Techniques of Moral Transformation (Philadelphia: Templeton Foundation Press, 2002).

28. See the discussion on *shakti* in B. Bruteau, *Evolution Toward Divinity*, 122ff.

29. *Journal*, 204.

30. *Carnet de lecture II*, 42. The criticism relates to R. Bastide's book, *Les Problèmes de la Vie Mystique* (Paris: A. Colin, 1931).

31. TF, 117 and 120.

32. TF, 205.

33. It would require a detailed philosophical investigation to decide how far the positing of a self can only be done in con-tradistinction and relation to the other, that is, how far the personal self is a relational concept.

It has been argued that the Upanishadic *tat tvam asi* cannot provide a basis for a personal I-Thou relationship, and that Indian philosophy is undeveloped with respect to the relational concept of love. See P. T. Raju, "The Inward Absolute and the Activism of the Finite Self," in S. Radhakrishnan and J. H. Muirhead, eds., *Contemporary Indian Philosophy* (London: G. Allen & Unwin, 1952), 532f. For a philosophical critique of Teilhard's understanding of the person, see Ch. Winckelmans de Cléty, *The World of Persons* (London: Burns & Oates, 1967), 391–97 and 407–19. The author wrongly assumes, though, that Teilhard thinks in pluralistic terms, whereas he is primarily a monist. It is in fact the attempt to combine a pluralistic and monistic perspective in the process of unification that character-izes Teilhard's synthesis as convergent.

34. A. Huxley, *The Perennial Philosophy* (New York: Harper & Brothers, 1945). Teilhard met Aldous Huxley on sev-eral occasions. He read this book in English and made notes on it, also in English, in his *carnet de lecture*. These are transcribed, translated into French, in G.-H. Baudry, *Notes de lecture* (Paris: Médiasèvres, 2007), 119.

35. HM, 89.

36. CE, 183.

37. CE, 184: "Christian charity is forthwith both dynamized, universalized and (if I may be allowed the word...) 'pantheized.'"

In his diary, he distinguishes two forms of Christian charity: one seeks to "supernaturalize" human beings; the other implies the effort to "superhumanize" them. See *cahier XV*, 89.

38. Quoted by C. Cuénot, "Un inédit de Pierre Teilhard de Chardin," *Études Teilhardiennes* 1 (1968): 57. With reference to the comparison between Christian and Buddhist love, see the remarks found in P. Tillich, 70–72, especially the contention that Buddhist compassion lacks the will to transform individual and social structures.

39. See Teilhard's notes on reading Maréchal in appendix IV on "Teilhard's Reading." The central place given to love by Teilhard is highlighted in an anecdote reported in C. Rivière, *En Chine avec Teilhard*, 204: It seems the Cartesian axiom "I think, therefore I am" was changed by the philosophers Blondel and Valensin (both well known to Teilhard) into "I will, therefore I am," which Teilhard then turned into "I love, therefore I am."

40. F. K. Nemeck, *Teilhard de Chardin et Jean de la Croix: Les "passivités" dans la mystique teilhardienne comparées à certains aspects de la "nuit obscure" de saint Jean de la Croix* (Montreal: Bellarmin, 1975).

41. See ibid., 133.

42. Swami Siddheswarananda, *Pensée Indienne et Mystique Carmélitaine*, Centre Védantique Ramakrichna, Gretz, 1974. These comparisons, first developed in a lecture series given at the Sorbonne in the late 1940s, are perhaps little known outside the Ramakrishna–Mission. The publication contains five studies dealing with Saint John of the Cross, plus a general essay on Indian thought and Carmelite spirituality. But in spite of certain similarities between the mysticism of Saint John and *jnana-yoga*, Swami Siddheswarananda seems to think that there is really no genuine *jnanin* to be found in Europe. The Christian search for union with the Divine is more like the royal path of the *raja-yogin*. He affirms without hesitation that Saint John of the Cross is "like the Patanjali of the West"; see ibid., 156.

43. "The Spiritual Contribution of the Far East" (1947) bears the following editorial footnote: "In 1946, during an interview with Siddheswarananda,...Père Teilhard was at pains to obtain more accurate information about the various forms of

yoga, and to confirm that in India the highest ecstasy corresponded to final loss of consciousness in an impersonal whole." TF, 139, n. 2.

44. TF, 201. Some months before, Teilhard referred to the Swami in a letter as "a very honorable man," but remarked, "one lets him naively take a disproportionate and ridiculous amount of room. I find it humiliating that one lets him give twelve lectures at the Sorbonne (to a private group) to disseminate a nebulous and certainly 'infrawestern' mysticism whilst nothing is said or published where the gentiles might appreciate the 'terrific' (sic) spiritual energy which is accumulating in the Christian 'neo'-mysticism" (LI, 368). This strong reaction must be related to Teilhard's difficult personal situation on his return from China, when he was not allowed to speak publicly on any religious topic.

45. TF, 105.

46. See his article "Teilhard and Eastern Religions," *Teilhard Review* 2, 2 (1967–68): 41–53. Zaehner makes much of Bhagavad-Gita 11.13: "Then did the son of Pandu see the whole [wide] universe in One converged, there in the body of the God of gods, yet divided out in multiplicity." See his commentary *The Bhagavad-Gita* (Oxford: Oxford University Press, 1969). B. Bruteau also points out the similarities with the Bhagavad-Gita.

47. R. C. Zaehner, *Evolution in Religion* (Oxford: Clarendon Press, 1971), 3.

48. See F. von Hügel, *Selected Writings* (London: Collins, 1964), for a modern parallel to Teilhard's understanding of religion and mysticism.

49. See part I on "Taoism, Teilhard de Chardin and Western Thought: A Comparison" in A. Stikker, *The Transformation Factor: Towards an Ecological Consciousness* (Rockport, MA: Element, 1992), 9–7. An earlier study on the affinity between Chinese thought and Teilhard was undertaken by Marie-Ina Bergeron, *La Chine et Teilhard* (Paris: J.-P. Delarge, 1976).

50. HM, 100.

51. R. Robertson, *The Sociological Interpretation of Religion* (Oxford: Blackwell, 1970), 90; emphasis added.

52. See *cahier XIII*, 100, and *cahier XIV*, 11 and 40.

53. See PM, 42, and HPh, 13, where *energy* is defined as "a capacity for action or, more exactly, for interaction."

54. SC, 221, from a letter to the personalist philosopher E. Mounier, in which Teilhard refers to a "theology of modern science."

55. See HM, 95.

56. F. C. Happold, *Mysticism: A Study and an Anthology* (Harmondsworth: Penguin, 1971), 395.

57. See C. E. Raven, *Teilhard de Chardin: Scientist and Seer* (London: Collins, 1962).

58. The three words represent the subtitles of the three parts of Teilhard's essay "My Fundamental Vision" (1948), TF, 163–208.

59. W. Johnston, *The Inner Eye of Love: Mysticism and Religion* (London: Collins, 1978), 179.

Epilogue

1. I have developed these themes at some length in my book *The Search for Spirituality: Our Global Quest for Meaning and Fulfillment* (New York: BlueBridge, 2008; and London: Canterbury Press, 2009). See chaps. 4 and 10.

2. C. G. Jung, *Psychology and Religion: West and East.* Collected Works, vol. 11 (London: Routledge & Kegan Paul, 1969), 537 and 557.

3. See the helpful outline by John F. Haught, *God and the New Atheism: A Critical Response to Dawkins, Harris, and Hitchens* (Louisville, KY: Westminster John Knox, 2008).

4. J. Kelley, "Personal Recollections of Teilhard," *Teilhard Review* 10 (1975): ix.

5. See H. Dumoulin, "Die geistige Vorbereitung des Abendlandes für den Dialog mit Asien," *Stimmen der Zeit* 177 (1966): 13–18.

6. J. Dunne, *The Way of All the Earth: An Encounter with Eastern Religions* (London: Sheldon Press, 1973), 220.

7. I have discussed this in chap. 1 of my book *The Search for Spirituality* (see n. 1 above), especially under "Western Words for the Spiritual" and "The Spiritual in Different Cultures."

8. A. Curle, *Mystics and Militants: A Study of Awareness, Identity and Social Action* (London: Tavistock, 1976).

9. See Gérard-Hendry Baudry, "La Mystique de la Recherche selon Pierre Teilhard de Chardin," *Teilhard aujourd'hui* 23 (September 2007): 57–66, as well as the earlier article by the French philosospher Madeleine Barthélemy-Madaule, "Mystique et recherche scientifique," *Études Teilhardiennes* 1 (1968): 91–106.

10. George Gaylord Simpson, *This View of Life: The World of an Evolutionist* (New York: Harcourt, Brace & World, 1964), 224, where he also says that Teilhard's "two most extensive discussions of evolutionary mysticism" are his book *Man's Place in Nature* (CW 8) and *The Phenomenon of Man* (CW 1). See Simpson's whole chap. 11 on "Evolutionary Theology: The New Mysticism" (213–33), in which he discusses three biologists whom he calls "new mystics": Pierre Lecomte du Noüy, Edmund W. Sinnott, and P. Teilhard de Chardin.

11. William Johnston, *Mystical Theology: The Science of Love* (Maryknoll, NY: Orbis, 1995), 80.

12. See John Grim and Mary Evelyn Tucker, "Introduction" in Arthur Fabel and Donald St. John, eds., *Teilhard in the 21st Century: The Emerging Spirit of Earth* (Maryknoll, NY: Orbis, 2003), 1–12; the quotations are on 66, 67, and 69. The same chapter is reprinted under the title "An Overview of Teilhard's Commitment to 'Seeing' as expressed in his Phenomenology, Metaphysics, and Mysticism" in C. Deane-Drummond, ed., *Pierre Teilhard de Chardin on People and Planet* (London and Oakville, CT: Equinox, 2006), 55–73; the quotations are on 66, 67, 69.

13. See the essays in W. Mark Richardson, Robert John Russell, Philip Clayton, and Kirk Wegter-McNelly, eds., *Science and the Spiritual Quest: New Essays by Leading Scientists* (London and New York: Routledge, 2002).

14. Ursula Goodenough, *The Sacred Depths of Nature* (Oxford: Oxford University Press, 2000).

15. Ibid., 167.

16. Ibid., 174.

Appendix IV

1. See Gérard-Henry Baudry, ed., *Pierre Teilhard de Chardin: Notes de Lectures (1945–1947): Camus, Nietzsche, Sartre, Tolstoï, Toynbee...* (Paris: Médiasèvres, 2007). This is the transcription of the text contained in Teilhard's second notebook, without any comment or analysis. Given Teilhard's compressed form of note taking that includes many abbreviations that are not always easy to decipher, this edition is difficult to use.

2. In 1945, Teilhard read and commented upon three lectures by Karl Barth published under the title *God in Action* (New York, 1936). The notes in the *carnet de lecture* relating to Karl Barth are reproduced and analyzed in M. Faessler, *Homme Réel et Phénomène Humain: Essai sur les fondements christologique et cosmologique de l'anthropologie à partir des oeuvres de K. Barth et de P. Teilhard de Chardin*. PhD diss., University of Geneva, 1967.

3. First published in 1924, a second, enlarged edition appeared in two volumes, Louvain 1937–38. *Studies in the Psychology of the Mystics* (London: Newman Publishing, 1927) is a translation of the 1924 edition. Teilhard's extracts from the second volume of the French edition are found in *carnet de lecture I*, 87–92, which have not been published so far.

4. J. Maréchal, vol. 2, 409–83; Engl. trans., 284–344.

5. See J. Maréchal, 421.

6. Ibid., 423–31; English trans., 294–300.

7. Ibid., 426.

8. J. Maréchal, 431ff.

9. See *cahier XIII*, 139 (July 16, 1945).

10. 2 vols. (Louvain, 1932–33), commented upon in *carnet de lecture II*, 1–10, reproduced in Baudry, 15–25. According to a recent reviewer, Johanns offers a meticulous, systematic examination of major Vedanta thinkers and assesses them sympathetically from a Thomistic perspective.

11. Father Pierre Johanns, SJ (1882–1955), born in Luxembourg and a member of the South Belgian Province of the Society of Jesus, studied philosophy at Louvain and then Sanskrit at Oxford, where he obtained a BLitt. He spent seventeen years in India (1921–38), teaching in Jesuit houses in Calcutta and

Kurseong. After his return to Belgium he taught at Namur. Johanns's work is discussed in J. Mattam's study, *Land of the Trinity: A Study of Modern Christian Approaches to Hinduism* (Bangalore: Theological Publications in India, 1975), chap. 1. Sean Doyle is the first scholar to devote a whole book to Johanns, *Synthesizing the Vedanta: The Theology of Pierre Johanns, SJ* (Bern: Peter Lang, 2006).

12. Published from Calcutta, 1922–46, in association with Father Dandoy, who, after Johanns's return to Belgium in 1939, became its sole editor.

13. Johanns's volume on Vallabha has been described by Norvin Hein as combining a "lucid summary in Western terms with a liberal Christian critique." See N. Hein, "Hinduism," in Ch. J. Adams, ed., *A Reader's Guide to the Great Religions* (New York: The Free Press, 1965), 67.

BIBLIOGRAPHY

This bibliography offers a selection of primary and major secondary sources on Teilhard's life and thought. Further references to articles, theses, and other publications in English, French, Italian, and German are given in the notes to each chapter.

I. Works by Pierre Teilhard de Chardin

The philosophical and religious essays of Pierre Teilhard de Chardin have been published in a series of thirteen volumes entitled *Oeuvres* (Éditions du Seuil, Paris). Their titles are listed here, followed by the English translation, published first by Collins, London, and then in the United States by Harcourt Brace Jovanovich, New York, or Harper & Row, New York. A list of abbreviations for the most frequently used titles is found on the first page of the Notes.

A. Collected Works

1.	*Le Phénomène Humain*	1955	*The Phenomenon of Man*	1959
			The Human Phenomenon	1999
			(new English translation)	
2.	*L'Apparition de l'Homme*	1956	*The Appearance of Man*	1965
3.	*La Vision du Passé*	1957	*The Vision of the Past*	1966
4.	*Le Milieu Divin*	1957	*Le Milieu Divin*	1960
5.	*L'Avenir de l'Homme*	1959	*The Future of Man*	1964
6.	*L'Énergie Humaine*	1962	*Human Energy*	1969
7.	*L'Activation de l'Énergie*	1963	*Activation of Energy*	1970
8.	*La Place de l'Homme dans la Nature*	1963	*Man's Place in Nature*	1966
9.	*Science et Christ*	1965	*Science and Christ*	1968
10.	*Comment Je Crois*	1969	*Christianity and Evolution*	1971
11.	*Les Directions de l'Avenir*	1973	*Toward the Future*	1975

329

12.	*Écrits du Temps de la Guerre*	1976	*Writings in Time of War*	1968[1]
13.	*Le Coeur de la Matière*	1976	*The Heart of the Matter*	1978

[1] This translation is based on an earlier French edition of the war essays, published by Éditions Grasset, Paris, 1965.

B. Other Writings

Hymne de l'Univers. Éditions du Seuil: Paris, 1961. Translated by Simon Bartholomew as *Hymn of the Universe*. London: Collins, 1965; New York: Harper & Row, 1969.

Journal, vol. 1 *(Cahiers 1–5: 26 août 1915–4 janvier 1919)*. Texte integral. Eds. N. & K. Schmitz-Moormann. Fayard: Paris, 1975.

L'Oeuvre Scientifique, 11 vols., eds. N. & K. Schmitz-Moormann. Walter: Olten and Freiburg im Breisgau, 1971.

Let Me Explain. Texts by P. Teilhard de Chardin selected and arranged by J.-P. Demoulin. London: Collins, 1970; New York: Harper & Row, 1972; new ed. in French *Je m'explique*. Paris: Éditions du Seuil, 2005.

Notes de Lectures (1945–1947): Camus, Nietzsche, Sartre, Tolstoï, Toynbee..., ed. G.-H. Baudry. Paris: Médiasèvres, 2007.

Notes de Retraites 1919–1954, ed. G.-H. Baudry. Paris: Éditions du Seuil, 2003.

Pierre Teilhard de Chardin: Writings. Selected with an introduction by U. King. Modern Spiritual Masters Series. Maryknoll, NY: Orbis, 1999.

C. Letters

Dans le sillage des sinanthropes: Lettres inédites de P. Teilhard de Chardin et de J. G. Anderson (1926–1934), ed. P. Leroy. Paris: Fayard, 1971.

Génèse d'une Pensée, eds. A. Teillard-Chambon and M. H. Bégouën. Paris: B. Grasset, 1961. Translated as *The Making of a Mind: Letters from a Soldier-Priest (1914–1919)*. London: Collins, 1965.

Lettres à Édouard Le Roy (1921–1946): Maturation d'une pen-

sée, ed. F. Euvé, SJ. Paris: Éditions Facultés Jésuites de Paris, 2008.

Lettres à Jeanne Mortier (1939–1955). Paris: Éditions du Seuil, 1984.

Lettres à l'Abbé Gaudefroy et à l'Abbé Breuil, ed. G.-H. Baudry. Monaco: Éditions du Rocher, 1988.

The Letters of Teilhard de Chardin and Lucile Swan, eds. T. M. King, SJ, and M. Wood Gilbert. Foreword by P. Leroy, SJ. Washington, DC: Georgetown University Press, 1993.

Lettres d'Égypte (1905–1908), ed. H. de Lubac. Paris: Aubier, 1963.

Lettres d'Hastings et de Paris (1908–1914), eds. A. Demoment and H. de Lubac. Paris: Éditions Montaigne, 1965.

Lettres Familières de Pierre Teilhard de Chardin Mon Ami: Les dernières années (1948–1955), ed. P. Leroy. Paris: Centurion, 1976. Translated as *Letters from My Friend Teilhard de Chardin*. New York/Mahwah, NJ: Paulist, 1976.

Lettres Intimes à Auguste Valensin, Bruno de Solages, Henri de Lubac, André Ravier (1919–1955), ed. H. de Lubac, 2nd ed. Paris: Aubier-Montaigne, 1974.

Letters from a Traveller (1923–1955), ed. C. Aragonnès. London: Collins, 1962 and 1966.

Letters to Two Friends (1926–1952), ed. R. d'Ouince. London: Collins, 1972.

Letters to Léontine Zanta (1923–1939), eds. R. Garric and H. de Lubac. London: Collins, 1969.

Pierre Teilhard de Chardin–Maurice Blondel Correspondence (1919), ed. H. de Lubac. New York: Herder & Herder, 1967. French edition, Paris: Beauchesne, 1965.

Répertoire de la correspondance de Pierre Teilhard de Chardin. 2600 lettres recensées (de 1893–1955). Présentation par François Euvé, SJ. Paris: Facultés Jésuites: Médiasèvres, 2010.

D. Unpublished Material

Cahiers XIII–XXI (diaries 1944–55). Jesuit Archives, Paris.
Carnets de lecture I, II, and *III*. Jesuit Archives, Paris. *Carnet II*

has been published by G.-H. Baudry in 2007; see *Notes de Lectures* under "Other Writings" above.

Correspondence with Madame Solange Lemaître; private collection.

Unpublished letters to J. Huxley, Dr. Loriot, Ella Maillart, Father Martindale, Mlle Mortier, Dr. Needham, Father d'Ouince. Fondation Teilhard de Chardin, Paris.

II. Works on Pierre Teilhard de Chardin

A. Biographies

Album based on publications and letters of P. Teilhard de Chardin and on papers preserved at the Fondation Teilhard de Chardin, Paris. Designed by J. Mortier and M. L. Aboux. London: Collins, 1966.

Boudignon, P. *Pierre Teilhard de Chardin: Sa vie, son œuvre, sa réflexion.* Paris: Éditions du Cerf, 2008.

Cuénot, C. *Teilhard de Chardin: A Biographical Study.* London: Burns & Oates, 1965.

Hemleben, J. *Teilhard de Chardin in Selbstzeugnissen und Bilddokumenten.* Hamburg: Rowohlt Taschenbuch, 1966.

Héronnière, É. de la. *Teilhard de Chardin: Une mystique de la traverseé.* Paris: Pygmalion/Gérard Watelet, 1999.

King, U. *Spirit of Fire: The Life and Vision of Teilhard de Chardin.* Maryknoll, NY: Orbis, 1996.

Lukas, M. and E. *Teilhard: A Biography.* London: Collins, 1977.

Raven, C. E. *Teilhard de Chardin: Scientist and Seer.* London: Collins, 1962.

Speaight, R. *Teilhard de Chardin: A Biography.* London: Collins, 1967.

B. Books on Teilhard's Thought

Aczel, A. D. *The Jesuit and the Skull: Teilhard de Chardin, Evolution, and the Search for Peking Man.* New York: Riverhead Books, 2007.

Barbour, G. *In the Field with Teilhard de Chardin*. New York: Herder & Herder, 1965.

Barthélemy-Madaule, M. *Bergson et Teilhard de Chardin*. Paris: Éditions du Seuil, 1963.

Baudry, G.-H. *Dictionnaire des correspondants de Teilhard de Chardin*. Lille: G.-H. Baudry, 1974.

———. *Teilhard de Chardin et l'appel de l'Orient: La convergence des religions*. Saint-Étienne: Aubin, 2005.

Bergeron, M.-I. *La Chine et Teilhard*. Paris: J.-P. Delarge, 1976.

Bruteau, B. *Evolution toward Divinity: Teilhard de Chardin and the Hindu Traditions*. Wheaton, IL: Theosophical Publishing House, 1974.

Choisy, M. *Teilhard et L'Inde*. Paris: Éditions universitaires, 1964.

Corbishley, T. *The Spirituality of Teilhard de Chardin*. London: Collins, 1971; Paramus, NJ: Paulist, 1971.

Cowell, S. *The Teilhard Lexicon*. Brighton and Portland, OR: Sussex Academic Press, 2001.

Cuénot, C. *Ce que Teilhard a vraiment dit*. Paris: Stock, 1972.

———. *Nouveau Lexique Teilhard de Chardin*. Paris: Éditions de Seuil, 1968.

Deane-Drummond, C., ed. *Pierre Teilhard de Chardin on People and Planet*. London and Oakville, CT: Equinox, 2006.

Delfgaauw, B. *Evolution: The Theory of Teilhard de Chardin*. London: Collins, 1961.

Demoment, A., SJ, ed. *Françoise Teilhard de Chardin (1879–1911): Lettres et Témoignages*. Paris: Beauchesne, 1975.

Duffy, K., SSJ, ed. *Rediscovering Teilhard's Fire*. Philadelphia: St. Joseph's University Press, 2010.

Fabel, A., and D. St. John, eds. *Teilhard in the 21st Century: The Emerging Spirit of Earth*. Maryknoll, NY: Orbis, 2003.

Faricy, R. L., SJ. *Teilhard de Chardin's Theology of the Christian in the World*. New York: Sheed & Ward, 1967.

Feys, J. *The Philosophy of Evolution in Sri Aurobindo and Teilhard de Chardin*. Calcutta: Firma K. L. Mukhopadhyay, 1973.

Galleni, L. *Darwin, Teilhard de Chardin e gli alteri...Le tre teorie dell'evoluzione*. Ghezzano, PI: Felici Editore, 2010.

Gray, D. *The One and the Many: Teilhard de Chardin's Vision of Unity*. London: Burns & Oates, 1969.

Grumett, D. *Teilhard de Chardin: Theology, Humanity and Cosmos*. Leuven (Louvain) and Dudley, MA: Peeters, 2005.

King, T. M. *Teilhard's Mass: Approaches to "Mass on the World."* New York, Mahwah, NJ: Paulist, 2005.

———. *Teilhard de Chardin*. The Way of the Christian Mystics, vol. 6. Wilmington, DE: Michael Glazier, 1988.

———. *Teilhard's Mysticism of Knowing*. New York: Seabury, 1981.

King, U. *Christ in All Things: Exploring Spirituality with Teilhard de Chardin*. Maryknoll, NY: Orbis, 1997; London: SCM, 1997.

———. *The Spirit of One Earth: Reflections on Teilhard de Chardin and Global Spirituality*. New York: Paragon House, 1989.

———. *Towards a New Mysticism: Teilhard de Chardin and Eastern Religions*. London: Collins, 1980; New York: Seabury, 1980.

Lubac, H. de. *Teilhard Posthume: Réflexions et souvenirs*. Paris: Fayard, 1977.

———. *The Religion of Teilhard de Chardin*. London: Collins, 1967.

———. *The Faith of Teilhard de Chardin*. London: Burns & Oates, 1965.

Maheu, R., ed. *Science and Synthesis: An International Colloquium Organized by UNESCO on the Tenth Anniversary of the Death of A. Einstein and P. Teilhard de Chardin*. New York: Springer, 1971.

Mantovani, F. *Dizinario delle Opere di Teilhard de Chardin*. Verona: Gabrielli editori, 2006

Meynard, Th., ed. *Teilhard and the Future of Humanity*. New York: Fordham University Press, 2006.

Monestier, A. *Teilhard et Sri Aurobindo*. Paris: Éditions universitaires, 1963.

Mooney, C. F. *Teilhard de Chardin and the Mystery of Christ.* London: Collins, 1966.

O'Manique, J. *Energy in Evolution: Teilhard's Physics of the Future.* London: Garnstone, 1969.

Ouince, R. d'. *Un prophète en procès*, vol. 1: *Teilhard de Chardin dans l'Église de son temps;* vol. II: *Teilhard de Chardin et l'avenir de la pensée chrétienne.* Paris: Aubier-Montaigne, 1970.

Rideau, E. *Teilhard de Chardin: A Guide to His Thought.* London: Collins, 1967.

Rivière, C. *En Chine avec Teilhard, récit suivi des lettres inédites de P. Teilhard de Chardin.* Paris: Éditions du Seuil, 1968.

———. *Teilhard, Claudel et Mauriac.* Paris: Éditions universitaires, 1963.

Savary, L. M. *Teilhard de Chardin*, The Milieu Divin *Explained: A Spirituality for the 21st Century.* New York/Mahwah, NJ: Paulist, 2007.

Schiwy, G. *Ein Gott im Wandel: Teilhard de Chardin und sein Bild der Evolution.* Düsseldorf: Patmos, 2001.

Stikker, A. *The Transformation Factor: Towards an Ecological Consciousness.* Rockport, MA: Element, 1992.

Terra, H. de. *Memories of Teilhard de Chardin.* London: Collins, 1964.

———, ed. *Perspektiven Teilhard de Chardins.* Munich: C. H. Beck, 1966.

Wang, Hai-Yan. *Le Phénomène Teilhard: L'aventure du livre Le Milieu Divin.* Saint-Étienne: Aubin, 1999.

Wildiers, N. M. *An Introduction to Teilhard de Chardin.* London: Collins, 1968.

Zaehner, R. C. *Evolution in Religion: A Study in Sri Aurobindo and Pierre Teilhard de Chardin.* Oxford: Clarendon Press, 1971.

D. Book Chapters and Articles

Aldwinckle, R. F. "Science and Mysticism in Teilhard de Chardin." *Canadian Journal of Theology* 12 (1966): 184–93.

Barthélemy-Madaule, M. "Milieu Mystique et Milieu Divin." In *Le Message Spirituel de Teilhard de Chardin*, ed. C. Cuénot, 36–45. Colloque de Milan. Paris: Éditions du Seuil, 1969.

———. "Mystique et recherche scientifique." *Études Teilhardiennes* I (1968): 91–106.

Baudry, G.-H. "Ninety Years Ago: Teilhard at Verdun." *Teilhard Newsletter* 26 (March 2009): 7–12. Published online by the British Teilhard Association at www.teilhard.org.uk.

———. "Sur les Pas de Teilhard aux Indes." *Teilhard aujourd'hui* 21 (2007): 9–18.

———. "La Mystique de la Recherche selon Pierre Teilhard de Chardin." *Teilhard aujourd'hui* 23 (2007): 57–66.

Brion, M. "Rencontre avec le Père Teilhard de Chardin,' *Les Nouvelles Littéraires* (January 11, 1951).

Déletie, H. "Teilhard de Chardin et la philosophie traditionelle de l'Extrême-Orient." *Rencontre Orient-Occident* 4 (1962): 13–18.

Dumoulin, H. "Die geistige Vorbereitung des Abendlandes für den Dialog mit Asien." *Stimmen der Zeit* 177 (1966): 275–88.

Grim, J. A. and M. E. Tucker. "An Overview of Teilhard's Commitment to 'Seeing' as expressed in his Phenomenology, Metaphysics, and Mysticism." In *Pierre Teilhard de Chardin on People and Planet*, ed. C. Deane-Drummond, 55–73. London and Oakville, CT: Equinox, 2006.

Grootaers, W. A. "When and Where Was the 'Mass on the World' Written?" *Teilhard Review* 12/3 (1977): 91–94.

Grumett, D. "Teilhard de Chardin's Evolutionary Natural Theology." *Zygon* 42/2 (2007): 519–34.

Huxley, J. Foreword to *In the Field with Teilhard de Chardin* by G. Barbour, 7–9. New York: Herder & Herder, 1965.

———. Introduction to *The Phenomenon of Man*, by P. Teilhard de Chardin, 11–28. London: Collins, 1959.

Kelley, J. "Personal Recollections of Teilhard." *Teilhard Review* 10/2 (1975): *Centre to Centre '75* insert, ix–xi.

King, U. "Spirit of Fire: Teilhard's Cosmic Spirituality." In *Rediscovering Teilhard's Fire*, ed. K. Duffy, SSJ, 9–31. Philadelphia: St. Joseph's University Press, 2010.

336

———. "Feeding the Zest for Life: Spiritual Energy Resources for the Future of Humanity." In *Teilhard and the Future of Humanity*, ed. T. Meynard, SJ, 3–19. New York: Fordham University Press, 2006.

———. "Pierre Teilhard de Chardin, Global Visionary for Our Times." *Interreligious Insight* 3/2 (2005): 14–21.

———. "Love—A Higher Form of Human Energy in the Work of Teilhard de Chardin and Sorokin." *Zygon: Journal of Religion and Science* 39/1 (March 2004): 77–102.

———. "The Letters of Teilhard de Chardin and Lucile Swan." In *Teilhard in the 21st Century: The Emerging Spirit of Earth*, ed. Arthur Fabel and Donald St. John, 44–66. Maryknoll, NY: Orbis, 2003.

———. "'Consumed by Fire from Within': Teilhard de Chardin's Pan-Christic Mysticism in Relation to the Catholic Tradition." *Heythrop Journal* 40/4 (1999): 456–77.

———. "Teilhard's Reflections on Eastern Religions Revisited." *Zygon: Journal of Religion and Science* 30/1 (March 1995): 45–70.

———. "Teilhard's Attitude towards the Modernization of China: Two documents from 1927." *Teilhard Review* 16/1–2 (1981): 6–15.

———. "Teilhard's Fundamental Vision." *Ampleforth Journal* 83 (1978): 11–21.

———. "'The Death of God—the Rebirth of God': A Study in the Thought of Teilhard de Chardin." *Modern Churchman* 18 (1974): 18–30.

———. "The Phenomenology of Teilhard de Chardin." *Teilhard Review* 6/1 (1971): 33–45.

Knights, P. "'The Whole Earth My Altar': A Sacramental Trajectory for Ecological Mission." *Mission Studies* 25 (2008), 56–72.

Le Brun Kéris, G. "Teilhard de Chardin et l'Islam." *La Croix*, December 17, 1969.

Lemaître, S. "In Memoriam." *Cahiers Pierre Teilhard de Chardin* 2 (1960): 151–58.

———. "Le Père Teilhard de Chardin. Sa Présence." Monograph, Association des Amis de Pierre Teilhard de Chardin, Paris, 1965.

337

Leroy, P. "Teilhard tel que je l'ai connu." Trans. as "The Man," in *Letters from a Traveller* by P. Teilhard de Chardin, 15–47. London: Collins, 1966.

———. "L'Institut de Géobiologie a Pékin 1940–1946. Les dernières années du P. Teilhard de Chardin en Chine." *L'Anthropologie* 69 (1965): 360–67.

———. "Les 'Textes Mystiques d'Orient et d'Occident.'" *Hommage à Solange Lemaître.*" Cyclostyled, Union des Croyants, Paris, 1961.

Masui, J. *In Memoriam: P. Teilhard de Chardin.* Monograph, Brussels, 1955.

Meyerovitch, E. "Orient et Occident." *New Morality* 1 (1963): 49–68.

Needham, J. "The Phenomenon of Man." *New Statesman*, November 7, 1959.

Ouince, R. d'. Prologue. In *Letters to Two Friends*, by P. Teilhard de Chardin, 1–19. London: Collins, 1970.

Process Studies 35/1 (2006). Special number on Teilhard de Chardin and Process Thought.

Simpson, G. Gaylord. "Evolutionary Theology: The New Mysticism." In *This View of Life: The World of an Evolutionist*, by G. Gaylord Simpson, 213–33. New York: Harcourt, Brace & World, 1964.

Stiernotte, A. P. "An Interpretation of Teilhard as Reflected in Recent Literature." *Zygon: Journal of Religion and Science* 4 (1968): 377–425.

Swan, L. "With Teilhard de Chardin in Peking." *The Month* 1 (1962): 5–15.

Zaehner, R. C. "Teilhard and Eastern Religions." *Teilhard Review* 2/2 (1967–1968): 41–53.

III. Works on Related Subjects

A. Books

Actes du XXI Congrès International des Orientalistes. Paris: Imprimerie Nationale, 1949.

Bellah, R. N. *Beyond Belief: Essays on Religion in a Post-Traditional World*. New York: Harper & Row, 1976.

Black, D., P. Teilhard de Chardin, C. C. Young, and W. C. Pei. *Fossil Man in China: Geological Memoirs*, Series A, Number 11. Beijing: Geological Survey of China 1933. Reprinted in P. Teilhard de Chardin, OSc V, 1903–2080.

Cable, M., and F. French. *The Gobi Desert*. London: Hodder & Stoughton, 1946.

Capra, F. *The Tao of Physics*. London: Fontana, 1976.

Casserley, J. *The Retreat of Christianity from the Modern World: The Maurice Lectures, King's College, London, for 1951*. London: Longmans, Green, 1952.

Ch'en, K. *Buddhism in China*. Princeton: Princeton University Press, 1964.

Chaudhuri, H., and F. Spiegelberg. *The Integral Philosophy of Aurobindo*. London: Allen & Unwin, 1960.

Cobb, J. B. Jr., and D. Griffin. *Process Theology: An Introductory Exposition*. Philadelphia: Westminster, 1976.

Cousins, E. H., ed. *Process Theology*. New York: Newman Press, 1971.

Curle, A. *Mystics and Militants: A Study of Awareness, Identity and Social Action*. London: Tavistock, 1976.

Dobzhansky, T. *The Biology of Ultimate Concern*. London: Collins, 1971.

Dunne, J. *The Way of All the Earth: An Encounter with Eastern Religions*. London: Sheldon, 1973.

Geertz, C. *Islam Observed: Religious Developments in Morocco and Indonesia*. New Haven: Yale University Press, 1968.

Ghose, Aurobindo. *The Life Divine*, 3rd ed. New York: India Library Society, 1965.

Goodenough, U. *The Sacred Depths of Nature*. Oxford and New York: Oxford University Press, 2000.

Grumett, D. *De Lubac: A Guide for the Perplexed*. London: T & T Clark, 2007.

Hackin, J., et al. *Studies in Chinese Art and Some Indian Influences*. London: India Society, 1938.

Happold, F. C. *Mysticism: A Study and an Anthology*. Harmondsworth, UK: Penguin, 1971.

Haught, J. F. *Making Sense of Evolution: Darwin, God, and the Drama of Life*. Louisville, KY: Westminster John Knox, 2010.

Hillman, A. *Awakening the Energies of Love: Discovering Fire for the Second Time*. Putney, VT: Bramble Books, 2008.

Huby, J. *Christus: Manuel d'Histoire des Religions*. Paris: Beauchesne, 1913.

Hu Shih. "My Credo and Its Evolution." In *Living Philosophies*, edited by A. Einstein, J. Dewey, Sir J. Jeans et al. New York: Simon and Schuster, 1931.

Huxley, A. *Perennial Philosophy*. London: Harper, 1945.

Iqbal, M. *The Reconstruction of Religious Thought in Islam*. London: Oxford University Press, 1934.

Jacovleff, A. *Dessins et Peintures d'Asie exécutées au cours de l'expédition Citroën Centre-Asie*. Paris: Meynial, 1934.

James, W. *Pragmatism: A New Name for Some Old Ways of Thinking*. London: Longmans, Green, 1907.

———. *The Varieties of Religious Experience*. New York: Collier, 1961; 1st ed. London: Longmans, Green, 1902. Trans. into French as *L'expérience religieuse*. Paris: F. Alcan, 1906.

Johanns, P. *Vers le Christ par le Vedanta*, 2 vols. Louvain: Museum Lessianum, 1932–33.

Johnston, W. *Mystical Theology: The Science of Love*. Maryknoll, NY: Orbis, 1995.

———. *The Inner Eye of Love: Mysticism and Religion*. London: Collins, 1978.

Katz, S. T., ed. *Mysticism and Philosophical Analysis*. London: Sheldon, 1978.

King, U. *The Search for Spirituality: Our Global Quest for a Spiritual Life*. New York: BlueBridge, 2008, and Norwich: Canterbury Press, 2009.

Lacombe, O. *L'Absolu selon le Vedanta*. Paris: Geuthner, 1937, repr. 1966.

Lammens, H. *Islam: Beliefs and Institutions*. London: Methuen, 1929, repr. 1968.

Lanpo, J., and H. Weiwen. *The Story of Peking Man*. Beijing:

Foreign Languages Press; Hong Kong: Oxford University Press, 1990.

Le Fèvre, G. *La Croisière Jaune*. Paris: Plon, 1933.

Lemaître, S. *Textes mystiques d'Orient et d'Occident*, 3 vols. Paris: Éditions d'histoire et d'art-Plon, 1955.

Lubac, H. de. *Images de l'Abbé Monchanin*. Paris: Éditions Montaigne, 1967.

———. *Aspects du Bouddhisme II—Amida*. Paris: Éditions du Seuil, 1955.

———. *La rencontre du Bouddhisme et de l'Occident*. Paris: Aubier, 1952.

———. *Aspects du Bouddhisme I*. Paris: Éditions du Seuil, 1951.

Maillart, E. *Oasis Interdites: De Pékin au Cachemire*. Paris: Grasset, 1937. Trans. into English as *Turkestan Solo: One Woman's Expedition from the Tien Shan to the Kizil Khum*. London: Putnam, 1934.

Maréchal, J. *Études sur la Psychologie des Mystiques*. Paris: Alcan, 1924. Trans. into English as *Studies in the Psychology of the Mystics*. London: Burns, Oates & Washburne, 1927. Enl. 2nd ed., 2 vols. Paris: Desclée de Brouwer, 1937–38.

Mattam, J. *Land of the Trinity: A Study of Modern Christian Approaches to Hinduism*. Bangalore: Theological Publications in India, 1975.

McNeill, W. H. *The Rise of the West: A History of the Human Community*. Chicago: University of Chicago Press, 1963.

Monchanin, J. *Mystique de l'Inde, mystère chrétien: Ecrits et inédits*. Paris: Fayard, 1974.

Needham, J. *Science and Civilisation in China*, vol. 2. Cambridge, UK: Cambridge University Press, 1956.

———. *Within the Four Seas: The Dialogue of East and West*. London: Allen & Unwin, 1969.

Rasmussen, O. D. *Tientsin: An Illustrated Outline History*. Tientsin: Tientsin Press, 1925.

Richardson, W. M., R. J. Russell, P. Clayton, and K. Wegter-McNelly, eds. *Science and the Spiritual Quest: New Essays by Leading Scientists*. London and New York: Routledge, 2002.

Ruskin, John. *Modern Painters*. Edited and abridged by David Barrie. London: Pilkington Press, 1987 [original edition, 3 volumes, 1856].

Samson, P. R., and D. Pitt, eds. *The Biosphere and Noosphere Reader: Global Environment, Society and Change*. London and New York: Routledge, 1999.

Schuré, E. *Les Grands Initiés: Esquisse de l'Histoire Secrète des Religions*. Paris: Perrin, 1889.

Siddheswarananda, Swami. *Pensée Indienne et Mystique Carmélitaine*. Gretz/France: Centre védantique Rama-krichna, 1974.

Snow, E. *Red Star over China*. New York: Random House, 1938.

Snow, H. *Inside Red China*. New York: Doubleday, Doran, 1939.

Tillich, P. *Christianity and the Encounter of the World Religions*. New York: Columbia University Press, 1963.

Welch, H. H. *The Buddhist Revival in China*. Cambridge, MA: Harvard University Press, 1968.

―――. *The Practice of Chinese Buddhism 1900–1950*. Cambridge, MA: Harvard University Press, 1967.

Whitson, R. E. *The Coming Convergence of World Religions*. New York: Newman Press, 1971. Revised edition, Lima, OH: Wyndham Hall Press, 1992.

Zaehner, R. C. *Hindu and Muslim Mysticism*. London: Athlone, 1960.

―――. *Mysticism Sacred and Profane*. Oxford: Clarendon Press, 1957.

B. Book Chapters and Articles

Auclair, M. "Solange Lemaître." In *À la grâce de Dieu* by M. Auclair, 95–103. Paris: Éditions du Seuil, 1973.

Bacot, J. "Autour de Congrès Universel des Croyants: Quelques Evocations." *Cahiers Pierre Teilhard de Chardin* 2 (Paris, 1960): 143–50.

Bulletin Citroën. *Numéro Spécial consacré a l'Exposition des Expéditions Citroën Centre-Asie et Centre-Afrique*. Paris, 1932.

Cuttat, J. A. "L'expérience chrétienne est-elle capable d'assumer la spiritualité orientale." In A. Ravier, ed., *La Mystique et les Mystiques*. Paris: Desclée de Brouwer, 1965.

Eliade, M. "Cultural Fashions and the History of Religions." In *The History of Religions*, ed. J. M. Kitagawa, 21–38. Chicago: University of Chicago Press, 1967.

Géographie, La. Special number devoted to the Yellow Expedition, vol. 8. Paris, 1932.

Hu Shih. "My Credo and Its Evolution." In *Living Philosophies*, ed. A. Einstein, J. Dewey, Sir J. Jeans et al. New York: Simon and Schuster, 1931.

Klostermaier, K. K. "Hindu-Christian Dialogue: Its Religious and Cultural Implication." *Sciences Religieuses/Studies in Religion* 1 (1971): 83–97.

Needham, J. "The Roles of Europe and China in the Evolution of Oecumenical Sciences." *British Association for the Advancement of Science* (1967): 83–98.

Six, J. F. "Louis Massignon, prophète du dialogue entre croyants d'Orient et d'Occident." Cyclostyled, Union des Croyants, Paris, 1958.

Smart, N. "Sri Aurobindo and History." In *Sri Aurobindo 1872–1972: A Centenary Symposium*. Sri Aurobindo Society of Great Britain, London, 1972, 15–22.

———. "Interpretation and Mystical Experience." *Religious Studies* 1 (1965): 75–87.

Union des Croyants. "Le Congrès Universal des Croyants, Historique 1946–1962." Cyclostyled, Paris, 1962.

———. *Hommage à Solange Lemaître*. Monograph, Paris, 1969.

Viney, D. W. "Teilhard: *Le Philosophe Malgré L'Église*." In *Rediscovering Teilhard's Fire*, ed. Kathleen Duffy, SSJ. Philadelphia: St. Joseph's University Press, 2010: 69–88.

———. "Teilhard and Process Philosophy Redux." *Process Studies* 35/1 (Spring–Summer 2006): 12–42.

The World Culture Heritage in Beijing. *Peking Man Site at Zhoukoudian*. Museum Brochure, n.d.

IV. Interviews with Teilhard de Chardin's Acquaintances, Friends, and Relatives

Dr. Claude Cuénot	Paris, March 1973
Mme Béatrice d'Hauteville	Paris, February 1974
Dr. Joanna Kelley	London, March 1974 and June 1975
Fr. Pierre Leroy, SJ	Versailles, March 1973 and February 1974
	Chantilly, September 1975
Fr. Henri de Lubac, SJ	Lyons, September 1973
Mr. Gabriel Marcel	Paris, March 1973
Fr. Gustave Martelet, SJ	Lyons, September 1973
	Chantilly, September 1975
Mr. Jacques Masui	Paris, February 1974
	Geneva, May 1975
Mlle Jeanne Mortier	Paris, Mary 1973 and February 1974
	Orléans, September 1973
	Chantilly, September 1975
Dr. Joseph Needham	Cambridge, May 1973 and May 1975
Fr. René d'Ouince, SJ	Paris, March 1973
M & Mme Joseph Teilhard de Chardin	Paris, March 1973 and February 1974
	Les Moulins (Auvergne), September 1973
Mlle Alice Teillard-Chambon	Paris, March 1973

INDEX

ANNOTATED STUDY GUIDE

This guide offers reading suggestions for examining selected themes of my book *Teilhard de Chardin and Eastern Religions* (Mahwah, NJ: Paulist, 2011) in more depth. It gives readers the opportunity to extend their knowledge of Teilhard's works and vision and to discover more of the richness of his experience and thought. I also wish to convey something of the intensely mystical quality of his faith and to relate his ideas to some important contemporary debates.

Reference to Teilhard's *Collected Works* (his religious and philosophical writings) are made to the number of each volume, followed by page numbers. The sequence of volumes follows.

Pierre Teilhard de Chardin's Collected Works in English Translation (hereafter CW), by Volume Number

1. *The Phenomenon of Man*	1959	(newly translated as *The Human Phenomenon*, 1999)	
2. *The Appearance of Man*	1965		
3. *The Vision of the Past*	1966		
4. *The Divine Milieu*	1960		
5. *The Future of Man*	1964		
6. *Human Energy*	1969		
7. *Activation of Energy*	1970		
8. *Man's Place in Nature*	1966		
9. *Science and Christ*	1968		
10. *Christianity and Evolution*	1971		
11. *Toward the Future*	1975		
12. *Writings in Time of War*	1968		
13. *The Heart of the Matter*	1978		

Organization of This Guide

The annotated bibliographical references of this guide do not closely follow my book outline but relate to its major themes and contexts. Any of the topics may be chosen for further study and discussion, either in the order presented or independently from each other. Most publications are in English, although a few references to French, German, and Italian works are included that complement what is available in English. The discussion has been arranged under the following headings:

1. **Teilhard's Life and Thought:** Biographies—Reference Works—Teilhard's Writings and Correspondence
2. **His China Years, Paleontology, and Peking Man:** Life in Tientsin and Peking—Paleontological Excavations, Geology, and Peking Man
3. **Science, Evolution, Biosphere, Noosphere, and Ecosphere:** Teilhard the Evolutionary Scientist—God and Evolution—Christ and Evolution—Biosphere and Noosphere—The Ecosphere
4. **Religious Pluralism and Interreligious Dialogue:** Teilhard and Chinese Thought—Teilhard, Hinduism, and Comparative Theology—Theology of Religions)
5. **Spirituality and Mysticism:** Teilhard's Writings on Spirituality (including "The Mass on the World" and *The Divine Milieu*)—Jesuit Authors on Teilhard's Spirituality—Reference Works on Spirituality and Mysticism
6. **Teilhard's Legacy:** Teilhard Associations—Library Resources and Recent Studies—Teilhard and the World Wide Web

1. Teilhard's Life and Thought

Several biographical studies are especially helpful in getting to know Teilhard's life and thought in greater depth, and to become acquainted with his religious, philosophical, and scientific writings. There are also his extensive correspondence, some still unpublished, and his diaries and retreat notes, only partly published and not yet translated into English. I have provided an extensive list of publications by Teilhard, as well as on him, in the bibliography of my book *Teilhard de Chardin and Eastern Religions* (2011). I therefore draw attention only to a few particularly helpful titles here.

References to Websites and to Teilhard associations in France and England can be found at the end of this guide, in section 6 on "Teilhard's Legacy." But I mention at the start that in the United States information about Teilhard can easily be obtained from the American Teilhard Association (ATA). It publishes a bulletin (*Teilhard Perspective*) twice a year for members, and also two monographs on particular themes (*Teilhard Studies*). About sixty of these have appeared during the past thirty-five years, and I refer to several of them later. A rich selection of these *Teilhard Studies* has been published in book form by Arthur Fabel and Donald St. John, eds., *Teilhard in the 21st Century: The Emerging Spirit of Earth* (Maryknoll, NY: Orbis, 2003). This can serve as an excellent introduction since it covers different aspects of Teilhard's life and thought, and such themes as ecology for the twenty-first century, cosmogenesis, and theological and social dimensions.

Further material can be found on the ATA Website, www.teilharddechardin.org, which includes an excellent short biography by John Grim and Mary Evelyn Tucker (also included as chapter 1 in *Teilhard in the 21st Century* mentioned previously), a list of writings, pictures, quotations, and other information about Teilhard. For the purchase of *Teilhard Studies* or past numbers of *Teilhard Perspective*, contact the American Teilhard Association, c/o John Grim, 29 Spoke Drive, Woodbridge, CT 06525.

An engaging entry may be made by first reading **Teilhard's own words** as he began to develop and live out his vision. Several of the books listed following are no longer in print, but most titles can be found in a good university or college library and sometimes in secondhand bookshops. Moreover, books by and about Teilhard that are out of print or rare may be available for purchase online at Amazon.com.

An easy and enjoyable way into Teilhard's life are his *Letters from a Traveller* (London: Collins, 1962), covering the years 1923–55. They were edited by his cousin Marguerite Teillard-Chambon (note the slightly different spelling of the family name

"Teilhard"), who published under the name Claude Aragonès. She was very close to Teilhard, especially during the years of the First World War. From that period we have a substantial correspondence between her and Teilhard entitled *The Making of a Mind: Letters from a Soldier-Priest 1914–1918* (London: Collins, 1965). These reveal the emergence of Teilhard's thinking (in French these letters are aptly called *Genèse d'une Pensée*) and the beginning of his writing within the disturbing context and upheavals of the First World War. The letters are a companion volume to Teilhard's first set of essays, *Writings in Time of War* (London: Collins, 1968), written between 1916 and 1919, which are foundational for all his later writings. The two volumes—*The Making of a Mind* and *Writings in Time of War*—shed much light on each other. This is complemented by Teilhard's diary of that period, but it is not available in English. See Pierre Teilhard de Chardin, *Journal Tome 1 (26 août 1915–4 janvier 1919)* edited by Nicole and Karl Schmitz-Moormann (Paris: Fayard, 1975).

Another way of approaching Teilhard is through reading some selected texts, such as *Let Me Explain: Texts by P. Teilhard de Chardin Selected and Arranged by J.-P. Demoulin* (London: Collins, 1970; New York: Harper & Row, 1972); new edition in French *Je m'explique* (Paris: Éditions du Seuil, 2005), or *Pierre Teilhard de Chardin: Writings: Selected with an Introduction by U. King*. Modern Spiritual Masters Series (Maryknoll, NY: Orbis, 1999).

Biographies

As to currently available full book-length **biographies**, there is the widely read study by the American writers Mary and Ellen Lukas, *Teilhard: A Biography* (New York: Doubleday & Company, 1977) and more recently, my own biography *Spirit of Fire: The Life and Vision of Teilhard de Chardin* (Maryknoll, NY: Orbis, 1996; 13th repr., 2010). Of the earlier Teilhard biographies, now out of print, it is still worthwhile to consult the fine study by the Anglican theologian Charles E. Raven, *Teilhard de Chardin: Scientist and Seer* (London: Collins, 1962). This is less a biography than a reflection on a series of important themes relating, among others, to Teilhard and human origins, Teilhard and emergent evolution, Teilhard and the problem of evil, Teilhard and his critics. There is also the acclaimed biography by the well-known British writer Robert Speaight, *Teilhard de Chardin* (London: Collins, 1967), and the superbly illustrated *Teilhard de Chardin Album*, edited by Jeanne Mortier and Marie-Louise Aboux (London: Collins, 1966).

A standard reference work on Teilhard's life is the early, wide-ranging study by Claude Cuénot, *Teilhard de Chardin: A Biographical Study* (London: Burns & Oates, 1965), which provides more factual details than any other. A well-received **biography in French** is Édith de la Héronnière, *Teilhard de Chardin: Une mystique de la traversée* (Paris: Pygmalion, 1999). The most recent biographical study to appear in France is by Patrice Boudignon, *Pierre Teilhard de Chardin: Sa vie, son oeuvre, sa réflexion* (Paris: Les Éditions du Cerf, 2008). It contains extensive quotations from Teilhard's writings, and its main focus is the future development of humanity in Teilhard's thought and several of his women correspondents.

Much factual and visual documentation is included in **two German biographies:**

Johannes Hemleben, Kurt Kusenberg, Wolfgang Müller, Uwe Naumann, eds., *Pierre Teilhard de Chardin: Mit Selbstzeugnissen und Bilddokumenten* (Hamburg: Rowohlt Taschenbuch, 1998 [a revised text of the first edition in 1963]).

Günther Schiwy, *Teilhard de Chardin: Sein Leben und seine Zeit*, 2 vols. (Munich: Kösel, 1981); vol. 1 covers 1881–1923, vol. 2 1923–55.

Reference Works

An excellent **survey of Teilhard's ideas** is provided by Émile Rideau's large volume *Teilhard de Chardin: A Guide to His Thought* (London: Collins, 1967; the original French edition was published in 1965 by Éditions du Seuil, Paris). The particular value of this work consists in its thematic chapters, which include essays on Teilhard's cosmology, anthropology, theology, spirituality, and his vocabulary and language.

An indispensable **reference work** of more recent date is Siôn Cowell, *The Teilhard Lexicon* (Brighton, Sussex & Portland, OR: Sussex Academic Press, 2001). It bears the subtitle *Understanding the Language, Terminology and Vision of the Writings of Teilhard de Chardin* and is the first English-language dictionary of his vocabulary. It is based on an earlier work by Cuénot that deals with Teilhard's sometimes very difficult and unusual words and ideas.

For those who read Italian, there exists a helpful **chronological dictionary of all Teilhard's religious and philosophical writings,** providing a short synopsis of the themes of each of Teilhard's essays, and of his books *The Phenomenon of Man* (in a new translation now entitled *The Human Phenomenon*) and *The Divine Milieu.* See Fabio Mantovani, *Dizionario delle Opere di Teilhard de Chardin* (Negarine de S. Pietro in Cariano, VR: Il Segno dei Gabrielli editori, 2006).

Detailed information about Teilhard's correspondence, with a chronological list of all letters published until 1974 and descriptions of their recipients, is found in Gérard-Henry Baudry, *Dictionnaire des correspondants de Teilhard de Chardin*, published by the author in Lille, 1974. But quite a few additional collections of letters have been published since then that are not covered by this early reference work.

Teilhard's Writings and Correspondence

For the rich collection of Teilhard's philosophical, theological, and religious writings, see the **Bibliography of Collected Works (13 volumes) in English and French** in my book *Teilhard de Chardin and Eastern Religions*. These works are distinct from his scientific articles, memoirs, and books published as *L'Oeuvre Scientifique* (11 volumes).

Teilhard was a great friend to many; he maintained an **extensive correspondence** throughout his life with his friends and family as well as with professional contacts all over the world. Several thousand letters have been preserved. I draw special attention to

Teilhard's letters to his women friends and to his Jesuit friends and colleagues.

Besides the already mentioned correspondence with his cousin Marguerite Teillard-Chambon, a lively exchange of ideas is found in the *Letters to Léontine Zanta* (Paris: Desclée de Brouwer, 1965), a fascinating woman philosopher whose Paris *salon* Teilhard regularly attended in the years after the First World War and from whom he learnt much about classical Greek philosophy. She was also a remarkable early feminist of influence in France, not least with Simone de Beauvoir. It was especially Léontine Zanta who prompted Teilhard to reflect on the changing role of women in society and in the church.

Then there are the *Letters to Two Friends 1926–1952* (New York: New American Library, 1968). This book does not mention the friends by name, but it is known that the first set of letters was addressed to Ida Treat, whom Teilhard had met as a graduate student at the Musée de l'Homme in Paris, where she was working for her doctorate in paleontology. The second set was written to Rhoda de Terra, the wife of the German paleontologist Helmut de Terra, with whom Teilhard had worked in the Far East. Teilhard saw much of Rhoda de Terra during the last years of his life, when both lived in New York.

Another very important and substantial correspondence, covering the years 1932–55, is that with the American sculptor Lucile Swan, whom Teilhard first met at a dinner party in Beijing some time in 1929. This correspondence became known much later than other letters; it first entered the public domain when Father Thomas M. King and Mary Wood Gilbert, the daughter of Lucile's cousin, edited *The Letters of Teilhard de Chardin and Lucile Swan* (Washington, DC: Georgetown University Press, 1993). The *Letters* were only published in French translation in 2009 and are still awaiting much closer analysis. For a brief discussion of their content see "The Letters of Teilhard de Chardin and Lucile Swan: A Personal Interpretation" by Ursula King, *Teilhard Studies* 32 (1995); reprinted in *Teilhard in the 21st Century: The Emerging Spirit of Earth*, ed. Arthur Fabel and Donald St. John, 44–66. Maryknoll, NY: Orbis, 2003.

The important letters to his Jesuit friends and superiors are only available in French. Of exceptional interest is the large collection entitled *Lettres Intimes de Teilhard de Chardin à Auguste Valensin, Bruno de Solages, Henri de Lubac, André Ravier* (Paris: Aubier Montaigne, 1972; revised edition 1974). Ranging from 1919 to 1955, these letters cover Teilhard's entire life span after the First World War. They touch on many decisions and reflections affecting his religious and scientific activities. As such, they are indispensable for understanding Teilhard's inner development and thinking. For the last years of his life this is supplemented by the letters to his friend and scientific collaborator, the Jesuit Pierre Leroy, who published *Lettres familières de Pierre Teilhard de Chardin mon ami, 1948–1955* (Paris: Centurion, 1976), translated as *Letters from My Friend Teilhard de Chardin* (Mahwah, NJ: Paulist, 1976). These give an insight into the difficulties and loneliness of Teilhard's last years in Paris and New York, but they also convey the strength of his continuing commitment to pioneering scientific research and to a deeply sustaining vision of faith. Of special interest are also the untranslated *Lettres à Jeanne Mortier* (Paris: Éditions du Seuil, 1984), addressed to the legatee of Teilhard's writings who played a unique role in getting them published. Without her, they might never have appeared in print. For in-depth research on Teilhard's entire correspondence, consult the chronological list of his published and unpublished letters and their recipients and location in *Répertoire de la correspondance de Pierre Teilhard de Chardin. 2600 lettres recensées (de 1893–1955)*. Présentation par François Euvé, SJ. Paris: Facultés Jésuites: Médiasèvres, 2010.

2. His China Years, Paleontology, and Peking Man

Life in Tientsin and Peking

Teilhard first went to China in 1923 for a scientific expedition supported by the Natural History Museum in Paris, of which Marcellin Boule was the director. Then, and during his subsequent stays in China, Teilhard lived in the city of **Tientsin**, a port city with an international flavor because of its foreign concessions. The city's atmosphere in the 1920s is vividly described in a lively memoir by the Englishman Brian Power. He grew up there, and as a boy he even met Teilhard when serving at Mass in the chapel of the Jesuit college in Racecourse Road at the edge of the British concession; see Brian Power, *The Ford of Heaven: A Childhood in Tianjin, China* (Oxford: Signal Books, 2005). The earlier name of *Tientsin* has been replaced in the revised edition of this book by today's *Tianjin*, now a large international city with global trade links, where the former concession buildings have been transformed into museums.

In 1929, Teilhard was made official adviser to the Chinese Geological Survey. Soon afterward he moved permanently to Peking, where he collaborated with the Chinese and several international scientists based in that city. He was happier there, since Peking reminded him of Paris, whereas, according to Cuénot's biography (78), he was less charmed by Tientsin, "that city of bankers and warehousemen, a sort of endless shopping center in which any intellectual or spiritual contact was inconceivable." His scientific work took him to many regions in China to study the geology of the whole continent. He undertook several expeditions with the American geologist George B. Barbour, who later became the dean of the College of Arts and Sciences, University of Cincinnati (1938–58), where copies of his correspondence with Teilhard are deposited.

Barbour's book *In the Field with Teilhard de Chardin* (New York: Herder & Herder, 1965) provides detailed descriptions of their geological expeditions and of Teilhard as a colleague and friend, who was always so happy to undertake practical field work. It also contains fascinating vignettes of life in Tientsin and Peking, of later visits to Europe and South Africa, and an appreciative foreword by Sir Julian Huxley. Moreover, it shows us the Chinese characters and transcription of the name given by the Chinese to Teilhard: it translates as "Father Daybreak Virtue" (ibid., 23).

Paleontological Excavations, Geology, and Peking Man

Teilhard's scientific work was closely associated with the excavations at Chou-Kou-Tien (now called **Zhoukoudian**), not far from Peking, where the first skull of **Peking Man** (or **Sinanthropus**) was found in 1929, with many more fossil finds in later years. The original fossils of Peking Man were lost during the Second World War. This has led to many worldwide speculations about their possible fate and has produced a spate of writings. The most exciting read about this, a real detective story of many personalities and parts that continues to fascinate, is

> Amir D. Aczel, *The Jesuit and the Skull: Teilhard de Chardin, Evolution, and the Search for Peking Man* (New York: Riverhead Books, 2007). A reviewer has described this book as "probably the best recounting of the disappearance of the Peking Man bone collection during the Japanese occupation and subsequent intense efforts to solve the mystery and attain their recovery" (*Teilhard Perspective* 40/2 [2007]: 2).

> More technical and less colorful but very informative are **Teilhard's own writings on Peking Man.** They provide clear evidence and proof of his meticulous expert work on fossils. See for example the *Geological Memoir* (Series A, Number 11) published early in Peking on *Fossil Man in China: The Choukoutien Cave Deposits with a Synopsis of Our Present Knowledge of the Late Cenozoic in China* by Davidson Black, Teilhard de Chardin, C. C. Young, and W. C. Pei, edited by Davidson Black (Peiping: The Geological Survey of China and the Section of Geology of the National Academy of Peiping, May 1933); the text is reproduced in OSc 5, 1903–2080). It contains detailed descriptions as well as many drawings and maps relating to the site and its finds. Teilhard's excellent scientific work, here and elsewhere, provides the concrete context for his "seeing" of the tangible material world, of matter and life, in which all his philosophical and religious thinking is deeply rooted.

> Teilhard's two essays "Sinanthropus Pekinensis: An Important Discovery in Human Palaeontology" (1930) and "The Discovery of Sinanthropus" (1937) are included in **The Appearance of Man** (CW 2—see 58–67 and 84–92). The same volume contains a final, substantial

essay on "The Singularities of the Human Species" (with an appendix on "Complementary Remarks on the Nature of Point Omega") on 208–73. Written in 1954, one year before Teilhard's death, this is an excellent summary of his views on human evolution and its significance, providing one of the best introductions to his understanding of the human phenomenon.

Teilhard's involvement with and early assessment of the significance of Peking Man is also evident from the regular letters he wrote to his mentor, Marcellin Boule, at the Natural History Museum in Paris during the 1930s. These letters were published in French in 2004; nine of the most significant ones had already been thoroughly analyzed earlier by Ludovico Galleni and Marie Claire Groessens-Van Dyck, "Lettres d'un paléontologue: Neuf lettres inédites de Pierre Teilhard de Chardin à Marcellin Boule," *Revue des Questions Scientifiques* (Tome 172, 5–104, Brussels, 2001).

The **history of the excavations of Peking Man** is amply documented by **two leading Chinese scientists,** Jia Lanpo and Huang Weiwen, *The Story of Peking Man from Archaeology to Mystery* (Beijing and Hong Kong: Foreign Languages Press; Oxford and New York: Oxford University Press, 1990). It contains many photographs and references to the scientific contributions of the Canadian Davidson Black and Teilhard de Chardin. Jia Lanpo, who worked as a young man with Teilhard and others at Chou-Kou-Tien, has also added a personal tribute to Teilhard in commemoration of the hundredth anniversary of Teilhard's birthday in 1981 (249–51). He speaks of "this scientist of towering stature" who quickly put the young Chinese scientist "at ease with his amicable manner and his patience and tirelessness in educating the young learner" (249). Teilhard's contribution as well as that of other western scientists to the study of the important discovery of Peking Man is also acknowledged in the contemporary Zhoukoudian Museum near the caves, which is now a World Heritage site (see the museum's publication *The World Culture Heritage in Beijing: Peking Man Site at Zhoukoudian*, 2004). Recently, new dating methods have shown that Peking Man is older than previously thought. On reexamination, the site was found to be 680,000–780,000 years old; earlier estimates had put the age at 230,000–500,000 years.

Further information on "His China Years, Paleontology, and Peking Man" can be gleaned from my Teilhard biography *Spirit of Fire* (1996); see especially the chapters "Discovery of China" (90) and "Peking Man" (126).

The modern debate between philosophy and science in China is examined in Thierry Meynard's article "The Role of Science in Contemporary China and according to Teilhard" (in Thierry Meynard, SJ, ed., *Teilhard and the Future of Humanity* (New York: Fordham University Press, 2006, 135–55). This includes a discussion of the eminent Chinese geologist Ding Wenjiang (1887–1936), who was the founder of the Chinese Geological Survey, which he directed from 1916 to 1921, and of the Museum of Natural History in Peking. Teilhard knew him well and refers to him as V. K. Ting in his writings. Father Meynard has provided a helpful description of Teilhard's research situation in China: "At the beginning of the twentieth century, many research institutions were created on the model of those in the West, and in which Western institutions played an important role. When Teilhard de Chardin came to China, he first worked with the museum of natural history, founded by the Jesuit Émile Licent in Tianjin. Later on he worked as advisor to the Geological Survey of China founded in 1916. While the Chinese directed the Survey, many research programs were in fact directed by Western scientists, such as Amadeus W. Grabau, an American, and J. G. Anderson, a Swede. With the discovery of the Zhoukoudian site and its famous 'Peking Man,' the Survey collaborated with the Anatomy Department of the American Hospital School in Beijing, also called Peking Union Medical College. Davidson Black, an American, directed this unit, which benefited from the financial support of the Rockefeller Foundation. Teilhard worked within this research unit in the 1920s and 1930s" (op. cit., 136).

Many studies exist on the history of the Jesuit missions in China of which Teilhard was well aware. Fascinating is the detailed study of their early beginnings, recently presented under new perspectives gleaned from previously unknown Portuguese and Latin sources by Liam Matthew Brockey, *Journey to the East: The Jesuit Mission to China, 1579–1724* (Cambridge, MA, and London: Harvard University Press, 2007). This study reveals a vast canvas of cross-cultural traffic in ideas, beliefs, objects, religious and cultural practices between early modern Europe and East Asia. It provides a fitting historical background to Teilhard's encounter with China during the twentieth century.

3. Science, Evolution, Biosphere, Noosphere, and Ecosphere

Teilhard the Evolutionary Scientist

The dynamic process of evolution and all it entails for understanding the whole of life, including that of the human being, was always central to Teilhard's thinking. Sir Julian Huxley met Teilhard in 1946 and later wrote appreciatively about what they shared in their view of evolution:

> I began to realize that for many years we both had been thinking along parallel lines, trying to consider man *sub specie evolutionis*, at one and the same time a product of past evolution and an active agent in its further course.
>
> We both realized that, in the million-year passage from subhuman to human, man had stepped across a critical threshold, and left the slow-moving biological phase of evolution for the new, faster-moving, and increasingly mind-directed psychosocial phase, in which evolution is manifested by changes in ideas and societies and cultures rather than in organisms and their genetic constitution.

In this, we were both backed by long years of professional concern with evolution—myself as a general evolutionary biologist of neo-Darwinian brand, but with excursions into religion and other psychosocial fields, Teilhard as geologist, paleontologist, and anthropologist, as well as a Christian priest and member of a religious order.

It was because he knew the facts of his science at first hand in the field, all over the world from Europe to China and Africa, that he was able—or rather, compelled—to attempt the task of applying them to his religious beliefs.

This linking of evolutionary biology with Christian theology, it seems to me, is his unique contribution to thought, enabling thousands of Christians to accept the greatest scientific discovery since Newton—Darwin's discovery of the evolutionary process as a fact and as a scientifically explicable phenomenon—and so pave the way for the eventual reconciliation of science and religion, which will come when the religiously minded understand that theology needs a scientific foundation, and grasp the fact that religion itself evolves, and when the scientifically minded accept the equally basic fact that religion is part of the evolutionary process, and an important element in its psychological phase, of human history. (Huxley's foreword in G. Barbour, op. cit., 8f.)

This is a fine testimony from one great scientist to another. It sums up the immense significance of evolution in a few sentences and expresses a strong recognition of Teilhard's reputation as an internationally recognized scientist and Christian priest by Sir Julian Huxley. The theories of evolution prevalent in the first half of the twentieth century shaped Teilhard's scientific work throughout his life. His initial research training in paleontology took place under the eminent French scientist Marcellin Boule at the Musée National d'Histoire Naturelle in Paris, opened in 1898 in preparation for the Paris World Fair in 1900. Paleontology is the science that studies the history and evolution of life on Earth during more than 3 billion years. It is based on the study of fossils—a term that refers to any traces of animal or plant life preserved in sedimentary rocks. The impressive galleries of comparative anatomy and paleontology at the Paris Museum, with their vast collections of fossils from all over the world, would have been well known by Teilhard, and their greatly enlarged displays can still be visited today. The Gallery of Paleontology was created by Albert Gaudry, after whom the most prestigious prize of the Geological Society of France is named. Teilhard was awarded the Prix Gaudry for his scientific research in 1952. The eulogy for the award, given by the distinguished French vertebrate paleontologist Jean Piveteau, lists Teilhard's major achievements, his expeditions and research in China and also his early promotion of the notion of the biosphere, his study of the history of life and of human origins, and the emergence of the noosphere, of the same size and importance as the biosphere (see next section on **Biosphere** and **Noosphere**). Piveteau finished by saying, "One can see what imposing perspectives the work of Père Teilhard de Chardin opens up for us....There can be no doubt that it marks a turning point in our science of paleontology and in our view of the world" (my translation; for the whole text in French see OSc X, 4595–98).

Piveteau also wrote the preface to the eleven volumes of Teilhard's *Oeuvres Scientifique* (see OSc I, XXI–XXIII), where he highlights Teilhard's synthesis of two immense evolutionary processes, that of the Earth (and its continents) and that of life (leading to the emergence of the human phenomenon). As Piveteau rightly points out, during his life Teilhard was hardly known except as a paleontologist, but after his death, the publication of his essays, until then only familiar to a small number of friends, revealed a profound thinker whose sudden fame among a large public then caused the neglect of the immense reputation of the scientist. Yet Teilhard's thinking is profoundly embedded in and deeply nourished by his scientific research and evolutionary understanding. The two important strands of his thought—his scientific work and his philosophical and religious reflections—must be studied together to perceive their integral connections.

His passion for collecting fossils began at an early age and was sustained throughout his years of philosophical and theological studies as a young Jesuit, leading eventually to his scientific research training in Paris and culminating in a brilliant doctoral dissertation in 1922, for which he was awarded two prizes, the Prix Visquenel and the Prix Gustave Roux (see OSc I, 420 and 423). Teilhard had already collected fossils during his stay in Egypt (1905–8) and continued collecting during his years of theological studies in Hastings (1908–12), where he discovered the full meaning of evolution (see following). He even collected fossils during the First World War, which he later studied for his doctorate.

His early collections are well documented:

> During his years in Hastings, Teilhard developed an enthusiasm for paleobotany, collecting ferns and other fossilized plants (still housed today in the Hastings Museum collection). This interest was later carried over into China, where his fossilized plant specimens gathered in the country can still be seen in Beijing Natural History Museum. While at Hastings, Teilhard had continued to collect minerals on the Channel island of Jersey, where he had lived earlier during his philosophical studies (1901–5). At that time he had carried out joint researches on the geology and mineralogy of Jersey with the somewhat older Jesuit Felix Pélletier. Later Teilhard spent two years in Hastings editing the printed catalogue of the Jersey minerals for the *Annales de la Société Jersiaise*. Descriptions of these activities are given in Pierre Teilhard de Chardin, *Letters from Hastings 1908–1912* (New York: Herder & Herder, 1968, 89f. and 137; the same correspondence also mentions some of the specimens collected during his 1905–8 stay in Egypt). See also the essay "Teilhard and the Geology of Jersey" by Arthur E. Mourant in David P. Taylor-Pescod, ed., *Links with Britain*, which accompanies the catalogue of *The Teilhard de Chardin Centenary Exhibition*, London: Westminster Abbey, June 16–July 30, 1983 (mounted by La Délégation à l'Action Artistique de la Ville de Paris et Le Musée National d'Histoire Naturelle de France). After this London exhibition, two further essays with more geological details about Jersey were published. See the following:

A. E. Mourant, "The Geological Collection from Maison Saint Louis, Jersey," *Annual Bulletin Société Jersiaise* 23/4 (1984): 517–19. The French Jesuits had set up the Maison St Louis in 1880. It became an important center of teaching and research, especially in geology and later in archaeology. The Jesuits undertook pioneering work on minerals and assembled what was then by far the best collection of the minerals of Jersey, which was later sadly disbanded. This article tells the story of the mineral collection and lists three articles by Teilhard published in the same *Annual Bulletin* of the Jersey Society in 1911, 1920, and 1921 (two are reprinted in OSc I; 53–67, and one in OSc I: 199–204).

A. E. Mourant, "Teilhard de Chardin and the Geology of Jersey," *Annual Bulletin Société Jersiaise* 24/2 (1986): 199–214. This is the most informative study about Teilhard's scientific work on the geology of Jersey. Dr. Mourant knew Teilhard personally. He has collected 132 references to Jersey from Teilhard's letters to his family (1908–13), two letters to Father Pelletier, and a personal letter to Dr. Mourant written in English from "The Geological Society of China," Peking, on October 20, 1933. Teilhard refers in it to his "honeymoon" with geology during his years in Jersey. He writes: "I send to you...two papers on the geology of North China (Jehol) in which you will recognize a striking parallelism with Jersey. The likeness is so strong that, for my personal convenience, I used to characterize my Chinese rocks by Jerseyan names" (op. cit., 210). Mourant's comments provide a chronology of Teilhard's work on Jersey and assess the contribution of his 1920 paper "La structure de l'île de Jersey" (reprinted in Teilhard's OSc X, pp. 199–204) to the understanding of the island's geology. He mentions meeting Teilhard in New York in 1953, when "we discussed Jersey geology for the whole of a long lunch hour" (op. cit., 214).

Most of Teilhard's essays and notes on evolution from 1920 to 1955 are grouped together in his book *Christianity and Evolution*

(CW 10, 1971). This collection also contains the "Note on Some Possible Historical Representations of Original Sin" (1922, 45–55), which got him into trouble with the Roman authorities of the Catholic Church. For the discussion of evolution see especially the essays "Christology and Evolution" (1933, 76–95); "Christianity and Evolution: Suggestions for a New Theology" (1945, 173–86), and "The God of Evolution" (1953, 237–43). The same volume also contains one of the key statements of Teilhard's faith, "How I Believe" (1934, CW 10, 96–132). It speaks of "the evolution of faith" and the elements of Teilhard's faith, about the confluence of religions, the universal Christ, and the shadows of faith. This essay deserves close study. It is preceded by the often-quoted epigraph:

> I believe that the universe is an evolution.
> I believe that evolution proceeds towards spirit.
> I believe that spirit is fully realized in a form of personality.
> I believe that the supremely personal is the universal Christ.

In addition you may like to read the essay "The Basis and Foundations of the Idea of Evolution" (1926) in Pierre Teilhard de Chardin, *The Vision of the Past* (CW 3, 116–42), and also in the same volume the brief, late note on "Evolution of the Idea of Evolution" (1950, CW 3, 245–47).

Teilhard's own interest in evolution first developed during his theological studies in Hastings when he read Henri Bergson's *Creative Evolution* (published in 1907), which made Bergson famous during his own lifetime (1859–1941). With the great contemporary interest in evolutionary theories, there has been a revival of interest in this philosopher, and a new edition of his famous work has been published. See Henri Bergson, *Creative Evolution*, edited by Keith Ansell Pearson, Michael Kolkman, and Michael Vaughan (New York & Basingstoke: Palgrave Macmillan, 2007).

> For an excellent discussion of the impact of evolutionary theory on theological reflection, see John F. Haught, *Making Sense of Evolution: Darwin, God, and the Drama*

of Life (Louisville: Westminster John Knox, 2010). This includes extensive references to Teilhard's thought.

For a briefer discussion of evolution in relation to theology, see the article by Ludovico Galleni, "Is Biosphere Doing Theology?" *Zygon* 36/1 (March 2001): 33–48; and his book *Darwin, Teilhard de Chardin e gli alteri...Le tre teorie dell'evoluzione* (Ghezzano, PI: Felici Editore, 2010). See also Ludovico Galleni and Marie Claire Groessens-Van Dyck, "A Model of Interaction Between Science and Theology Based on the Scientific Papers of Pierre Teilhard de Chardin," in William Sweet and Richard Feist, eds., *Religion and the Challenges of Science* (Aldershot: Ashgate, 2007: 55–71).

See also David Grumett, "Teilhard de Chardin's Evolutionary Natural Theology," *Zygon* 42/2, 2007: 519–34; and Noel Keith Roberts, *From Piltdown Man to Point Omega* (New York: Peter Lang, 2000).

Teilhard's grand vision of synthesis based on his evolutionary research and personal reflection is found in his magnum opus, *The Phenomenon of Man* (CW 1, 1959), written during 1938–40 in Peking and preceded by several essays of the same title. Sir Julian Huxley wrote an appreciative introduction to Teilhard's *Phenomenon of Man*. This book demonstrates in great detail how Teilhard understood evolution, but it is best read in the much improved, new translation by Sarah Appelton-Weber:

Pierre Teilhard de Chardin, *The Human Phenomenon* (Brighton, Surrey & Portland, OR: Sussex Academic Press, 1999). Important here is the editor-translator's introduction on "Teilhard's Transforming Thought" (xvii–xxi), and the new foreword by the well-known mathematical cosmologist Brian Swimme (xiii–xvi), which replaces Julian Huxley's introduction to the first translation. According to John Grim's and Mary Evelyn Tucker's "Short Biography"(in A. Fabel and D. St. John, eds., *Teilhard in the 21st Century*, 2003 [for details see Section 1 previous]), "An important contribution of this work is

381

the creative manner in which it situates the emergence of the human as the unifying theme of the evolutionary process. *The Human Phenomenon* in its presentation of the fourfold sequence of the evolutionary process [galactic evolution, Earth evolution, life evolution, and consciousness evolution] establishes what might almost be considered a new literary genre" (24).

Teilhard's comprehensive approach to all aspects of evolution, evident from his linking the evolution of the Earth and its continents with the evolution of life, led him and his scientist friend, Father Pierre Leroy, SJ, to found the Institute of Geobiology in Peking from where they published the review *Geobiologia* (1943–45). Its publications are included in Teilhard's *Oeuvre Scientifique* (see OSc IX). Of particular interest is the overview provided by the monograph *Fossil Men: Recent Discoveries and Present Problems* (Peking, 1943). It discusses *Sinanthropus*, Neanderthal Man, and *Homo Sapiens* and concludes with a "General Outline of Human Evolution" and "The Significance of our Evolution" (see OSc IX, 3905–36).

Several essays in the *Teilhard Studies* series of the American Teilhard Association provide further helpful reflections on different scientific aspects of Teilhard's scientific work:

James Salmon, "Teilhard and Prigogine," *Teilhard Studies* 16 (1986). This deals with complexity theory.

Edward O. Dodson, "The Teilhardian Synthesis, Lamarckism, and Orthogenesis," *Teilhard Studies* 29 (1993). See also Dodson's earlier book, *The Phenomenon of Man Revisited: A Biological Viewpoint on Teilhard de Chardin* (New York: Columbia University Press, 1984).

John Haught, "Chaos, Complexity, and Theology," *Teilhard Studies* 30 (1994). This connects Teilhard's thought with scientific theories about chaos and complexity.

Kathleen Duffy, SSJ, "The Texture of the Evolutionary Cosmos: Matter and Spirit in Teilhard de Chardin," *Teilhard Studies* 43 (2001).

For an extensive discussion of contemporary approaches to evolution see the **Special Issue** on the **Epic of Evolution,** *Teilhard Perspective* 31/1 (Spring 1998).

God and Evolution

In response to contemporary debates about Darwin, evolution, and religion, a vast literature has come into existence, but this often ignores Teilhard's writings or misinterprets them. One of the great exceptions is the theologian **John F. Haught** from Georgetown University, who knows Teilhard's work in depth. His constructive theology develops some of Teilhard's ideas much further. See

> John F. Haught, *God after Darwin: A Theology of Evolution* (Boulder, CO: Westview, 2000); see especially "A God for Evolution," 81–104. This widely acclaimed book engages deeply with Darwinian thinking and argues convincingly that Darwin's disturbing picture of life, instead of being hostile to religion, actually provides fertile ground for innovative reflections on the idea of God. A most stimulating source for reading about theology and evolution.

> John F. Haught, *Deeper Than Darwin: The Prospect for Religion in an Age of Evolution* (Boulder, CO: Westview, 2003). This takes the argument of Haught's previous book even further by looking at religious belief in the light of evolutionary biology, showing that while Darwin's understanding of life is essentially correct, the religions of the world provide us with a still deeper and fuller vision of the phenomenon of life and of the universe.

> Of similar interest are the writings by Ian G. Barbour, the son of Teilhard's friend, George Barbour. See especially Ian G. Barbour, *Nature, Human Nature, and God* (Minneapolis: Fortress, 2002), which surveys major issues in contemporary discussions on science and religion. Several sections deal with "God and Evolution," "Evolution and Human Nature," "God and Nature" as well as "Theology, Ethics, and the Environment" within

the larger context of process thought. See also the *festschrift* for Ian Barbour produced by Robert Russell, ed., *Fifty Years in Science and Religion: Ian Barbour and His Legacy* (Burlington, VT: Ashgate, 2003), which contains a chapter by John Haught on "'Seeing the Universe': Ian Barbour and Teilhard de Chardin."

The impact of evolutionary thinking on the understanding of God is much discussed by process theologians influenced by the philosopher Alfred North Whitehead (1861–1947). The leading exponent of process theism is Charles Hartshorne (1897–2000), whereas Teilhard's thought has not been given sufficient attention by process theologians. The journal *Process Studies* 35/1 (Spring/Summer 2006) devoted a special issue to Teilhard and process thought, with contributions by J. F. Haught, J. McDaniel, and D. W. Viney. The last argues that Teilhard should be considered one of the founders of modern process metaphysics, alongside Whitehead and Hartshorne.

Several essays in the *Teilhard Studies* series offer discussions on **evolution and the Christian understanding of God**. See especially

John A. Grim and Mary Evelyn Tucker, "Teilhard's Vision of Evolution," *Teilhard Studies* 50 (2005).

John F. Haught, "In Search of a God for Evolution: Paul Tillich and Pierre Teilhard de Chardin," *Teilhard Studies* 45 (2002).

Gloria L. Schaab, SSJ, PhD, "The Divine Welling Up and Showing Through: Teilhard's Evolutionary Theology in a Trinitarian Panentheistic-Procreative Paradigm," *Teilhard Studies* 55 (2007).

Michael Heller, "Teilhard's Vision of the World and Modern Cosmology," *Teilhard Studies* 58 (2009).

For those able to read **German**, I refer to some helpful **studies on evolution in German:**

Karl Schmitz-Moormann, *Pierre Teilhard de Chardin: Evolution—die Schöpfung Gottes* (Mainz: Mathias Grünewald, 1996). This small monograph by an internationally known Teilhard specialist, who with his wife Nicole edited Teilhard's scientific works, looks at evolution theologically, by linking it to creation and redemption. There is also a chapter on Teilhard's image of God.

Of considerable interest is a set of essays by Günther Schiwy, *Ein Gott im Wandel: Teilhard de Chardin und sein Bild der Evolution* (Dusseldorf: Patmos, 2001). Particularly helpful are chap. 3, "Der Gott der Evolution" (50–65); chap. 4, "Der kosmische Christus" (66–80); and chap. 7, "'Pan-en-theismus'—eine Spurensuche" (123–43). The last essay discusses the meaning of *panentheism* (literally "God-in-all," meaning that God is in everything, and everything is held in God). Unfortunately Teilhard did not use the word *panentheism*, which is much more suitable for describing what he calls "Christian pantheism" in his essays. Pantheism means that God is all, and all is God; there is identity between God and the universe rather than intimate interdependence, as understood in panentheism.

For contemporary discussions on panentheism, see John W. Cooper, *Panentheism: The Other God of the Philosophers. From Plato to the Present* (Grand Rapids, MI: Baker Academic, 2006), which contains a chapter on Teilhard entitled "Christocentric Panentheism."

Perhaps Teilhard was unaware of the existence of the term *panentheism*, which had been coined by the early nineteenth-century German philosopher Karl Krause and was then adopted by Hegel, followed by later philosophers and theologians, for example, Tillich and Moltmann. It is possible that the word remained unknown in France so that Teilhard never came across it. This is the view of Thomas M. King, SJ, who briefly comments on panentheism and Teilhard's use of *pantheism* in his book *Teilhard's Mass: Approaches to "The Mass on the World"* (Mahwah, NJ: Paulist, 2005, 61 and 63).

Schiwy's book includes the additional feature that it quotes relevant passages on Teilhard written by Cardinal Joseph Ratzinger before he became pope, especially from his *Einführung in das Christentum*, Munich: Kösel, 1968 (*Introduction to Christianity*, London: Burns & Oates, 1969; current ed. San Francisco, CA: Ignatius Press, 2004).

These positive comments find a parallel in Pope Benedict's remarks made during a vespers service in the cathedral of Aosta, northern Italy, on July 24, 2009, when he praised Teilhard's cosmic vision. See John L. Allen's article "Pope Cites Teilhardian Vision of the Cosmos as a 'Living Host'" in the *National Catholic Reporter*, July 28, 2009; Allen highlights the pope's ambivalence about Teilhard, whose cosmic vision he seems to like while worrying about some of his interpretations as being at odds with orthodox faith.

Christ and Evolution

Much has been written on Teilhard's Christology in general, a theme I have not dealt with in my book *Teilhard and Eastern Religions*. One of the most challenging theological issues today concerns the question of how to think about Christ in an evolutionary world. Fewer authors have dealt with this burning issue than with those on more traditional christological themes. For Teilhard the body of Christ is the center for humanity and the whole world. The world is seen as a divine body, as "divine milieu" (for which references are provided later), and its final evolution culminates in "Christ-Omega." These ideas are already clearly stated in the early essay "My Universe" (1924), another of Teilhard's key texts that discusses the universal Christ, Christ-Omega, and the evolution of the world. See his collection of essays entitled *Science and Christ* (CW 9, 37–85).

Teilhard's mystical love for Christ is movingly expressed in one of the last essays of his life, "**The Christic**," which speaks of the consummation of the universe by Christ and the consummation of Christ by the universe. This is found in the last volume of his Collected Works, **The Heart of Matter** (CW 13, 80–102). See also the text of "**My Litany**," found at Teilhard's death, written on both sides of a picture of a radiant heart of Christ (CW 10, 244–45).

Among earlier publications on Teilhard's understanding of Christ, two books stand out:

> Christopher F. Mooney, SJ, *Teilhard de Chardin and the Mystery of Christ* (London: Collins, 1966). A seminal study on Teilhard's Christology, very clearly structured and easy to read. It deals among others with such central themes as the body of Christ for Teilhard and Saint Paul; physical and moral evil in the context of evolution; creation as a Christogenesis toward the final plenitude in Christ.

> J. A. Lyons, *The Cosmic Christ in Origen and Teilhard de Chardin: A Comparative Study* (Oxford: Oxford University Press, 1982). This is a pioneering study regarding the cosmic nature of Christ and of Christ as Omega. It contains many ideas and references to textual passages on Teilhard's "cosmic Christ" that invite further constructive theological development.

Other studies on Christ and evolution to which I draw attention:

> Ilia Delio, *Christ in Evolution* (Maryknoll, NY: Orbis, 2008). In his Foreword John F. Haught recommends "the fresh evolutionary theology" of this book and points out, "The cosmological and evolutionary framework of this study allows for a renewal of Christology." It also shows "that a cosmic and evolutionary sensitivity need not stand in contradiction to the Christian emphasis on the personhood of God." Besides Teilhard, Delio also discusses Raimon Panikkar, Thomas Merton, Bede Griffiths, and other approaches to Christ.

> Celia Deane-Drummond, *Christ and Evolution: Wonder and Wisdom* (London: SCM Press and Minneapolis: Fortress, 2009). A substantial but difficult study that presents itself as "an exercise in the development of a Christology that takes due account of evolutionary theory without succumbing to an identification with or alienation from it"

(xviii). Teilhard de Chardin's, Rahner's, and Moltmann's engagement with Christ and evolution are each considered in turn, albeit briefly, and so are John Haught's, Arthur Peacocke's, and Ian Barbour's thought, but all are found wanting. The author draws instead on Hans Urs von Balthasar's "theodrama" and on the Sophiology of the Orthodox theologian, Sergii Bulgakov, to develop an evolutionary Christology.

I also recommend an earlier study in French by Soeur Ina Bergeron and Anne-Marie Ernst, *Le Christ Universel et l'Évolution selon Teilhard de Chardin* (Paris: Les Éditions du Cerf, 1986). With a preface by Pierre Leroy, SJ, this book offers a well-chosen selection of Teilhard's texts on evolution with a helpful commentary on evolution and the universe, the human being, revelation, Christian life, and Christ as animator of evolution.

Agustin Udias, SJ, "Christogenesis: The Development of Teilhard's Cosmic Christology," *Teilhard Studies* 59 (2009). This essay by Father Udias, for many years a professor of geophysics at the Universidad Complutense de Madrid, provides a brilliant summary of what he calls Teilhard's "evolutive cosmovision." The emergence of the "universal Christ" is traced very clearly and systematically: first in Teilhard's early writings (1908–20); then "from cosmogenesis to Christogenesis 1920–1935"; followed by "a new Christology 1930–1950," and the last writings from 1950 to 1955, leading to "The Christic." I know of no other author who has provided such a clear, succinct analysis of the major elements of Teilhard's cosmic Christology.

Biosphere and Noosphere

Descriptions of the **biosphere** and **noosphere** abound in Teilhard's writings. The word *biosphere* was first suggested by the Austrian scientist Eduard Suess in 1875, in his book *The Origin of the Alps*. He then developed this new concept in his multivolume work *Das Antlitz der Erde* (1883–1901), translated as *The Face of the Earth* (1909–24). Teilhard was an early supporter of the idea of the biosphere. He liked the title "The Face of the Earth" so much that he used it in 1921 for one of his own articles. However, before that, in January 1918, when still in the trenches, he wrote an essay about "The Great Monad" (CW 13, 182–95)—describing the rise of a unified, thinking Earth; this vision was originally inspired by his sight of the full moon in the night sky above the Earth. He first gave it the subtitle "A Serious Fantasy...in the Moonlight," but then crossed it out. He saw

over the torn and blackened earth, there rose the great Monad....

...This evening, as I saw the single block into which we are all on the point of solidifying, for the first time I had the feeling of *emerging* from our race and of seeing it as a self-contained whole—and I felt as though we were all linked together and floating in the void.... When the thinking Earth has completed its closing in upon itself, then only shall we know the true nature of a Monad!...

...This evening, in the agony of the bloody schism which at this moment is dividing the World....I saw *the frontiers* of Mankind—I became conscious of the blackness and emptiness around the Earth....

...Even in this century, people are still living as chance circumstances decide for them, with no aim but their daily bread or a quiet old age. You can count the few who fall under the spell of a task that far exceeds the dimensions of their individual lives...unless adult Humanity is to drift aimlessly and so to perish, it is essential that it rise to the concept of a specifically and integrally *human effort*. After having for so long done no more than allow itself to live, Humanity will one day understand that the time has come to undertake its own development and to mark out its own road....

One and the same influence animates and holds together everything that thinks....One single circle embraces all spirit, and *imprisons nothing*....

We can hardly perceive this higher and uncircum-
scribed unity of the Universe....

(For the texts cited above see CW 13, *The Heart of Matter*, 185,
186, 188, 191. This essay of 1918, "The Great Monad," is
included in the original French collection *Écrits du Temps de la
Guerre*, but not in its English translation *Writings in Time of War*.)

These passages from "The Great Monad" express the perception of an intrinsic human oneness that is slowly emerging but
in the main still has to be created. It was, strangely, through the
war that Teilhard realized that humankind forms a single organic
Earth-wide reality that transcends individuals and groups. It can
be studied like a living organism covering the entire globe, a network that stretches over the face of the whole world. He also
described this vision as an **immense Thing**, like the rising of the
pale moon over the sleeping earth.

But Teilhard was still looking for the right word to describe
this. The "**great Monad**" was soon replaced by the idea of an
"**anthroposphere**"—a sphere of the human—and in February
1920 Teilhard asked, "Who will be the Suess of the anthroposphere?" (quoted in CW 13, 182).

Eventually, through clarifying discussions with the philosopher Édouard Le Roy during the mid-1920s, Teilhard formulated
the new word *noosphere*, a word derived from the Greek word
nous for mind in the sense of an integrating vision. This became one
of his major ideas, central to his vision of the world. Just as the zone
of life, the biosphere, is a living layer above the nonliving geo-
sphere, there exists another, thinking layer, a sphere of mind and
spirit surrounding the globe. The emergence of the noosphere is an
important step forward in becoming human, in the process of
transformation that Teilhard called "hominization." All human
beings are part of this thinking envelope of the Earth. Through their
thinking, feeling, connecting, and interacting with each other, and
above all through their powers of love, all humans contribute to the
growth and expansion of the noosphere.

While Teilhard was the person who coined the word *noosphere*, it was first made known through Le Roy's philosophical
writings, and then through the Russian geochemist Vladimir I.

Vernadsky. The latter lived in Paris during the mid-1920s, and Teilhard met Vernadsky along with Le Roy at that time, so that the creation of the word *noosphere* is sometimes attributed to all three together. In fact, Teilhard clearly stated this himself in an article he wrote at the end of his life. Referring to the revolutionary transformation that took place at the end of Tertiary time, he says, "Our planet developed the psychically reflexive human surface, for which, together with Professor Edouard Le Roy and Professor Vernadsky, we suggested in the 1920s the name 'noosphere'" (see OSc X, 4580). Teilhard himself used the term *noosphere* first in 1925, in a long essay on "Hominization" that bears the subtitle "Introduction to a Scientific Study of the Phenomenon of Man" (in *The Vision of the Past*, CW 3, 51–79). This formulation already anticipates his future major book on this subject, not begun until the late 1930s. The human being is the key to the understanding of evolution by making the effort of moving it forward, but the noosphere also points beyond itself to "a higher pole or center that directs, sustains and assembles the whole sheaf of our efforts" (ibid., 78).

Teilhard's vision in the trenches of the oneness of the Earth as if seen from the moon conjures up the much later iconic photograph of our bluish-green planet suspended in space, surrounded by blackness, an unforgettable image so aptly named "Earth Rise." Ideas about the biosphere and noosphere are closely interconnected with debates about the environment, ecology, the future of humanity, and that of our planet. John Grim and Mary Evelyn Tucker describe the biosphere as "Earth-layer of living things" and the noosphere as "the Earth layer of thinking beings" (in A. Fabel and D. St. John, *Teilhard in the 21st Century*, 2003, 22 [for publication details see under section 1 previous]). The literature about these topics is enormous and continues to grow at a surprising rate. The seminal idea of the noosphere and its diffusion among scientists of different nationalities is well documented in the excellent, innovative publication by

Paul R. Samson and David Pitt, eds., *The Biosphere and Noosphere Reader: Global Environment, Society and Change* (London and New York: Routledge, 1999). With a foreword by Mikhail S. Gorbachev, this reader provides the first comprehensive history of the ideas of the biosphere and noosphere. Drawing on classical influences, modern parallels, and insights into the future, it traces the emergence of these two concepts within the context of environmental change. It includes passages from seminal works by Bergson, Le Roy, Teilhard de Chardin, Vernadsky, Lovelock, Margulis, Russell, Needham, Huxley, Toynbee, and others. The editors describe the noosphere as lying "at an intersection where science and philosophy meet" (xi) and see this concept as "intrinsically linked to the notion of a continuously evolving planet Earth" (2). They provide a thorough analysis of common themes and competing ideas associated with the noosphere. They also examine the potential application of noospheric ideas to current debates about culture, education, and technology in such realms as the Internet, space colonization, and the emergence of super-consciousness (see especially section 5, "The Future of the Noosphere," and section 6, "The Noosphere and Contemporary Global Issues," where the editors discuss "noospheric institutions," such as the UN and increasingly the nongovernmental organization [NGO] movement). They speak of an exploding interest in noospheric ideas and point to the thousands of references to this new concept on the Internet. This is remarkable for two reasons: "First, it highlights an enormous interest in the noosphere among those who are active on the Internet, many of whom claim it as a useful concept to describe the ultimate evolution of the World Wide Web into an unprecedented form of super-consciousness. Second, it shows that much of the use of the term 'noosphere' is in secondary literature or at least not in the main titles and keywords of more traditional databases" (xi). Besides mentioning Teilhard, Le Roy, and Vernadsky as joint inventors of the word *noosphere*, Samson and Pitt also quote Teilhard as confiding in his biographer that "I believe, so far as one can ever tell, that the word 'noosphere' was my invention; but it was he [Le Roy] who launched it" (4).

Teilhard considered the noosphere to be "the object of the science of tomorrow," of "a superior and distinct science," as he wrote in 1927 from Tientsin to his philosopher friend Édouard Le Roy. See their correspondence in French: Pierre Teilhard de Chardin, *Lettres à Édouard Le Roy (1921–1946)* (Éditions Facultés Jésuites de Paris, 2008; I have quoted briefly from 77; my translation).

The Ecosphere

Teilhard's holistic, life-enhancing vision is presently a source of inspiration for twenty-first-century environmental concerns. Here are some good examples:

Mary Evelyn Tucker, "The Ecological Spirituality of Teilhard" (*Teilhard Studies* 51 [2005]). This revised version of an earlier *Teilhard Studies* (no. 13) articulates the rich resources, and limitations, of Teilhard's ecological thinking. His comprehensive vision of the Earth and its interconnected life processes "is a well spring of hope for the critical work ahead to create a sustainable future" (1).

William E. Rees, "Sustainable Development and the Ecosphere: Concepts and Principles," *Teilhard Studies* 54 (2007). A perceptive discussion of the distinction between environment and ecosphere, the special case of ecosystems, the limits to the human-carrying capacity of the Earth, and of sustainability in the real world.

Celia Deane-Drummond, ed., *Pierre Teilhard de Chardin on People and Planet* (London and Oakville, CT: Equinox, 2006). This rich collection of essays deals with Teilhard's thinking in relation to cosmos, environmental responsibilities and ethics, science and theology, ecotheology, mysticism, and some aspects of Eastern Christianity.

The growing environmental crisis and the need to re-envision our role as citizens of the planet and members of the Earth community present a tremendous challenge to the world's religions. This topic is explored in much detail in a full-length book by Mary Evelyn Tucker, *Worldly Wonder: Religions Enter Their Ecological Phase* [with a commentary by Judith A. Berling] (Chicago and La Salle, IL: Open

Court, 2003). It develops further some of the ideas mentioned in Tucker's *Teilhard Study* listed previously. Particularly informative are the appendices, with the texts of the Global Forum, Moscow, 1990; the Summit on Environment, New York, 1991; the Union of Concerned Scientists' Warning to Humanity, 1992; the Earth Charter, 2000; and the Catholic-Orthodox Joint Declaration, Venice, 2002. These provide excellent materials for further study and discussion.

Steven C. Rockefeller, "Teilhard's Vision and the Earth Charter," *Teilhard Studies* 52 (2006). This essay was first prepared for a panel on "The Spirit of the Earth: Global Ethics and a Sustainable Future" at the Teilhard conference held at the United Nations on April 8, 2005. The Earth Charter, promulgated in 2000, is the outcome of a decade-long, worldwide consultation process involving numerous groups and faiths around the world. It is a declaration of fundamental principles for building a just, sustainable, and peaceful global community. Rockefeller skillfully draws out the connections with Teilhard's vision, especial his understanding of love as "the internal propensity to unite" and other comments that suggest that ethical values have a critical role to play in the evolutionary advance of civilization.

John Grim and Mary Evelyn Tucker, "Thomas Berry: Reflections on His Life and Thought," *Teilhard Studies* 61 (2010). This insightful introduction to the great ecological thinker also discusses Teilhard's influence on Thomas Berry.

Other helpful titles on religion and ecology include:

David L. Gosling, *Religion and Ecology in India and Southeast Asia* (London and New York: Routledge, 2001), unusual for its discussion of ecological resources in Hinduism and Buddhism and of contemporary environmental struggles in India and Thailand. This book also includes a unique list of "Medicinal Plants Identified in Thailand" (176–80) and a record of the Indian nongovernmental organizations that participated in the Earth Summit in Rio de Janeiro in 1992.

An earlier set of essays complementing Gosling's study is *Buddhism and Ecology*, eds. Martine Batchelor and Kerry Brown (London: Cassell and Worldwide Fund for Nature, 1992). The same publishers have produced other titles dealing with Christianity, Hinduism, Islam, Judaism, and ecology.

Mark Hathaway and Leonardo Boff, *The Tao of Liberation: Exploring the Ecology of Transformation* (Maryknoll, NY: Orbis, 2009) brings together rich perspectives drawn from liberation theology, creation theology, cosmology and ethics, science and spirituality steeped in a deep ecumenism nourished by the wisdom of the *Tao Te Ching*. The book offers first a perceptive analysis of the pathologies threatening our globe and then traces alternative paths of liberation and wholeness, much influenced by Thomas Berry, among others. The Earth Charter is presented as a common framework, and "The Tao of Liberation" includes "Spirituality for an Ecozoic Era" and "The Ecology of Transformation."

The most comprehensive information on religion and ecology is found on the *Forum on Religion and Ecology Website* at Yale University. The forum has been described as the largest international multireligious project of its kind. It lists ecological resources from the world's religions, statements on Climate Change Science and Ethics, a science bibliography, and the latest news and events. See www.yale.edu/religionandecology. Additional information is provided by the *Alliance of Religions and Conservation* (ARC) based in Britain; see www.arcworld.org.

4. Religious Pluralism and Interreligious Dialogue

The study of **eastern religions** along with **worldwide ecumenical studies** has progressed enormously since Teilhard's death in 1955. Many specialized in-depth studies are available in each of these areas. It is impossible to provide a study guide to these large subjects here; ample bibliographical references can be found in many contemporary handbooks to the study of religion, and informative overviews on all religions are given in the fifteen volumes of the excellent *Encyclopedia of Religion*, 2nd ed., easily found in all major libraries (ed. Lindsay Jones, Macmillan Reference USA. An imprint of Thomson Gale, Farmington Hills, MI, 2005).

Teilhard's experience and knowledge of eastern religions are analyzed in detail in my book *Teilhard de Chardin and Eastern Religions* (2011). This aspect of Teilhard's thought has been little studied, although there exists now a brief treatment in French by Gérard-Henry Baudry, *Teilhard de Chardin et l'appel de l'Orient: La convergence des religions* (Paris: Aubin, 2005). It provides a good overview but contains little new information.

Although Teilhard never acquired an in-depth historical and textual knowledge of religions outside Christianity, he reflected on the diversity and complementarity of the different faiths and spoke of their possible future convergence. Already in the 1920s, he was seeking religious insights in the East to complement those of Christianity, and he stressed the central importance of mysticism for contemporary spirituality. One may even consider him as an early pioneer of interfaith dialogue, since he became an active participant and supporter of the French group Union des Croyants, founded after the Second World War in Paris as a branch of the World Congress of Faiths. I have discussed this at length in my book *The Spirit of One Earth: Reflections on Teilhard de Chardin and Global Spirituality* (New York: Paragon House, 1989); see chap. 7, "Exploring Convergence: The Contribution of the World Faiths," and chap. 8, "Teilhard's Association with the World Congress of Faiths, 1947–1950." A more recent discussion of this material is found in my article "Pierre Teilhard de Chardin: Global Visionary for Our Times," *Interreligious Insight: A Journal of Dialogue and Engagement* 3/2 (Autumn 2005): 14–21.

Teilhard and Chinese Thought

Teilhard de Chardin acquired much practical knowledge of Asian religious cultures indirectly through his travels and expeditions, and he read widely. It is rather disconcerting, though, that there is no written evidence to suggest that he enquired much about **Chinese religions**, especially Taoism or Confucianism, when he lived in China for so many years. Yet unbeknown to him, there exist some remarkable parallels between Taoism and Teilhard's thought, as several authors have shown:

> The French Franciscan Missionary of Mary, Sister Marie-Ina Bergeron, who lived in China from 1939 to 1951, undertook a pioneering study on the parallels between Teilhard's thought and Chinese thought. After being imprisoned by the Chinese communists for twenty-eight months, where she first learned about Chinese philosophy from a Chinese fellow prisoner, she returned to the West, trained as a sinologist, gained a doctorate in Paris in 1971, and published widely until her death in 1999. See Marie-Ina Bergeron, *La Chine et Teilhard* (Paris: Jean-Pierre Delarge, 1976).
>
> For a comparison between Teilhard's thought and Taoism, see Allerd Stikker, "Teilhard, Taoism, and Western Thought," *Teilhard Studies* 15 (1986). This is only a brief introduction. The same author has undertaken a much more fully documented comparison of Taoism, Teilhard de Chardin, and western thought applied to present trends in the world. See Allerd Stikker, *The Transformation Factor: Towards an Ecological Consciousness* (Rockport, MA, Shaftesbury, Dorset and Brisbane, Queensland: Element, 1992).
>
> Detailed information about religion in contemporary China is found in Xinzhong Yao and Paul Badham, *Religious Experience in Contemporary China* (Lampeter: University of Wales Press, 2008). Based on the first comprehensive survey of religion and religious experience in China carried out in 2004–7 by western and Chinese scholars, this book assesses the relation between religion and other aspects of Chinese life and thought after fifty years of atheist communism. It includes chapters on Confucianism, folk religion, Buddhism, and Christianity in

China; it also compares the differences between religion in urban and rural China.

Teilhard, Hinduism, and Comparative Theology

Teilhard was always most interested in Hinduism and its conception of ultimate unity, but he held no specialist knowledge of the Hindu religious tradition and traveled only once to India. Teilhard's expedition across India and what is now Pakistan (September 20–December 12, 1935) has been described in detail by Gérard-Henry Baudry, "Sur les Pas de Teilhard aux Indes," *Teilhard aujourd'hui* 21 (2007): 9–18, which also lists Teilhard's correspondence (where observations on land and people can be found; see especially *Letters from a Traveller*, 1962) as well as scientific reports relating to this Indian expedition.

With regard to Teilhard and **Hinduism**, there exists a remarkable study comparing his views to those of Ramanuja, a famous theologian of medieval Hinduism. See Anne Hunt Overzee, *The Body Divine: The Symbol of the Body in the Works of Teilhard de Chardin and Ramanuja* (Cambridge: Cambridge University Press, 1992). This is a fine example of comparative theology, wherein Teilhard's vision of the cosmic Christ is compared with the eleventh-century Hindu theologian Ramanuja's view of the body of Brahman. Both thinkers regard the world as inherently divine and use the symbol of the body to express this.

A more fully developed comparative theology, not directly related to Teilhard but meeting many of his expectations about a "convergence" of religions, is the innovative study by Francis X. Clooney, SJ, *Hindu God, Christian God: How Reason Helps Break Down the Boundaries between Religions* (Oxford and New York: Oxford University Press, 2001). It greatly broadens the theological conversation in today's pluralistic context by looking at Christian and Hindu debates about God's existence and identity, divine embodiment, revelation, and the process of theologizing. A nuanced study the reasoning of which is deeply grounded in specific texts from two different religions whose encounter reveals exciting new theological possibilities.

Late in his life Teilhard read and made extensive notes on the detailed study by Pierre Johanns, SJ, *Vers le Christ par le Vedanta* (2 vols., Louvain, 1932–33). These notes are discussed in appendix IV on "Teilhard's Reading" in my book *Teilhard de Chardin and Eastern Religions* (2011). For an up-to-date analysis of Johanns's understanding of Hinduism, see the study by

Sean Doyle, *Synthesizing the Vedanta: The Theology of Pierre Johanns, SJ* (Oxford, Bern, etc.: Peter Lang, 2006). This recent study has been well received for showing clearly Johanns's contribution to the history of Indian Christian theology, his serious dialogue with the Indian tradition, and his presentation of Vedantic spirituality, filtered through a Christian consciousness. Johanns is a much-forgotten pioneer of inculturation whose work prepared the way for the emergence of an indigenous Indian theology, and as such it deserves more general recognition and study.

Theology of Religions

A Christian perspective on religious pluralism has been worked out by several authors who have developed what is called a "theology of religions." This field of lively debate first took off after the Second Vatican Council. A large literature exists in this area, and good overviews can be obtained from two recent studies published in the same year:

Jacques Dupuis, SJ, *Christianity and the Religions: From Confrontation to Dialogue* (Maryknoll, NY: Orbis, and London: Darton, Longman & Todd, 2002). Dupuis refers to Teilhard in this book, and even more so in his earlier magisterial work, *Toward a Christian Theology of Religious Pluralism* (Maryknoll, NY: Orbis, 1997) that got him into trouble with the Roman authorities. The next title by Knitter does not discuss Teilhard, but it presents by far the best and most accessible introduction to the many complex discussions surrounding religious pluralism.

Paul F. Knitter, *Introducing Theologies of Religions* (Maryknoll, NY: Orbis, 2002). Knitter groups the numerous positions in the theological interpretation of religious diversity into four different models: (1) replacement model; (2) fulfillment model; (3) mutuality model; (4) acceptance model. His conclusion states the need for inter-Christian dialogue and for interreligious cooperation. Each section of his argument is well supported by references to further readings.

Another widely acclaimed writer on religious pluralism and interreligious dialogue is the Catalan-born Hindu-Christian Raimon Panikkar. His large corpus of writing contains a number of perspectives that bear strong resemblance to Teilhard's thought. For an in-depth study of his theology of religions and understanding of **interreligious dialogue** see the fine study by the Finnish theologian Jyri Komulainen, *An Emerging Cosmotheandric Religion? Raimon Panikkar's Pluralistic Theology of Religions* (Leiden and Boston: Brill, 2005). Komulainen speaks of "the striking similarity of the basic orientation of these two thinkers" and states that Panikkar's vision "seems to fulfill Teilhard's desire for a new mysticism that takes account of the complementary insights of other religions and finds unity through tension, instead of reducing the multiple to a common ground" (123 and 122).

Also recommended is the thought-provoking essay by Ewert H. Cousins, "Teilhard's Concept of Religion and the Religious Phenomenon of Our Time," *Teilhard Studies* 49 (2004). This essay was originally written in 1981 for a UNESCO conference in Paris marking the centennial of Teilhard's birth and deals with the evolution of religious consciousness. It also refers to Panikkar but sees him as going beyond Teilhard, since Panikkar advocates a "dialogic dialogue" that goes beyond a "dialectic dialogue" that is mainly concerned with defending oneself and refuting the claims of other religions (8). See also Ewert Cousins's article, "The Convergence of Cultures and Religions in the Light of the Evolution of Consciousness," *Teilhard Perspective* 32/2 (Fall 1999), first published in *Zygon* 34/2 (June 1999): 209–19.

For wider background reading relating to contemporary discussions, see David Ray Griffin, ed., *Deep Religious Pluralism* (Louisville: Westminster John Knox, 2005). This provides stimulating essays on religious pluralism and dialogue from the perspective of Whiteheadian process thought. Examples deal with Buddhist, Chinese, Christian, Hindu, Islamic, and Jewish versions of "deep religious pluralism," which is presented as an alternative to the kind of pluralism that has dominated recent discussions, especially among Christian thinkers.

5. Spirituality and Mysticism

Teilhard's powerful spiritual vision is centered on the cosmic Christ. His spirituality, described as a new "mysticism of action," is presented as a kataphatic rather than an apophatic mysticism, where knowledge of God is obtained through affirmation (**kataphatic**) rather than negation (**apophatic**). This mystical spirituality has deep roots in the New Testament, especially in Saint Paul, in the Ignatian *Spiritual Exercises*, and in the Christian mystical tradition, all reinterpreted within an evolutionary perspective.

Teilhard's Writings on Spirituality

Elements of Teilhard's thought on spirituality, intimately connected to his own mystical experience and spiritual practice, are found throughout his writings. Teilhard referred more often to "mysticism" than "spirituality," but he used both terms. Essays on both can be found especially in his early *Writings in Time of War* (CW 12; see particularly the essays "The Mystical Milieu" [1917] and "The Priest" [1918], which anticipates "The Mass on the World" [1923]), and in the volumes on *Human Energy* (CW 6), and *The Activation of Energy* (CW 7 VII). *Human Energy* contains the essay "The Phenomenon of Spirituality" (1937; CW 6: 93–112) as well as "The Mysticism of Science" (1939; CW 6: 163–81). Several essays in *The Activation of Energy* deal with the understanding of spirit, energy, and evolution. See this volume also for the inspiring reflections on "The Zest for Living" (1950; CW 7: 229–43) and "The Spiritual Energy of Suffering" (1950: CW 7: 245–49), preceded by "The Significance and Positive Value of Suffering" (1933; CW 6: 48–52). A succinct selection of texts together with an introduction to his spirituality is found in *Pierre Teilhard de Chardin: Writings Selected with an Introduction by Ursula King* (Maryknoll, NY: Orbis, Modern Spiritual Masters Series, 1999, 10th repr. 2009).

The early essay "The Priest" and "The Mass on the World" are commented upon as a particular form of sacramental panentheism that can orientate Christian approaches to the present ecological crisis in Philip Knights's essay, "'The Whole Earth My Altar': A Sacramental Trajectory for Ecological Mission," *Mission Studies* 25/1 (2008): 56–72.

Of the greatest importance are Teilhard's deeply mystical works "The Mass on the World" (1923; CW 13: 119–34), the book *The Divine Milieu* 1927; CW 4), and the late essays "The Heart of Matter" (1950; CW 13, 15–79) and "The Christic" (1955; CW 13, 80–102). These four form a spiritual quartet of extraordinary richness and splendor. They deserve dedicated, attentive study, each in its own right, and all four together. So far, commentaries exist on two of them:

Thomas M. King, SJ, *Teilhard's Mass: Approaches to "The Mass on the World"* (Mahwah, NJ: Paulist, 2005). Besides commenting on passages of "The Mass on the World," this work discusses Teilhard's priesthood, his scientific work, and his spirituality. It contains the text of "The Mass on the World," accompanied by a prayer service to celebrate this Mass.

A superb, detailed commentary on all the passages of *The Divine Milieu* is provided by Louis M. Savary, *Teilhard de Chardin—The Divine Milieu Explained: A Spirituality for the 21st Century* (Mahwah, NJ: Paulist, 2007). It is a

remarkable example of explaining Teilhard's book systematically, by relating his thought to evolution, modern
science, and the contemporary world, as well as to practical spiritual exercises that readers can try out for themselves in order to learn the new kind of spirituality needed
for the twenty-first century. Working through these exercises alone or together in a group makes one realize what
it truly means to live in the "divine milieu"—a milieu that
Teilhard also sometimes called a "mystical milieu"—to
breathe in divine presence and strive toward union and
communion with God within all experiences of life.

The author reflects in detail on (1) "The Attributes of the
Divine Milieu" (173–200); (2) "The Nature of the Divine Milieu,
the Universal Christ, and the Great Communion" (200–15); and
(3) "The Growth of the Divine Milieu" (216–37). The second section speaks of the evolving cosmic Christ and describes Teilhard's
ideas about Christ's "third," cosmic nature as "a new theological
position" (215), a view also taken by J. A. Lyons's book (1982;
see previous under **Christ and Evolution**).

I would have liked to have seen two more aspects further
developed in Savary's book: the first concerns the question of how
the divine milieu is related to Teilhard's understanding of the
growth of the **noosphere** (see previous section on **evolution**); the
second relates to the central place given to the all-transforming
energy and power of love in the development of humanity, and in
the growth and universal communion of the divine milieu (mentioned only briefly on 203). *The Divine Milieu* is dedicated to
those who love the world, and it has been said that it articulates
Teilhard's "vision of the human as 'matter at its most incendiary
stage'" (Grim and Tucker in Fabel & St. John, 2003, 23; for
details see under section 1 previous).

Jesuit Authors on Teilhard's Spirituality

Several **eminent Jesuit authors** have commented at length on
Teilhard's spirituality. Foremost among them is his longtime
friend and correspondent, Henri de Lubac, one of the most emi-

nent Catholic theologians of the twentieth century. **Henri de Lubac, SJ,** *The Religion of Teilhard de Chardin* (London: Collins, 1967—a translation of *La Pensée religieuse du Père Teilhard de Chardin* [Paris: Aubier, 1962]). This is a pioneering, profusely annotated study that discusses, among others, Teilhard's basis in the Christian tradition, his stature as "scientist, prophet, and mystic," his method, his element of novelty, evolution and freedom, and his works such as *The Divine Milieu*, his understanding of the human phenomenon, and of being a Christian. It also contains some important letters. This book remains foundational.

Since de Lubac knew Teilhard intimately, he is one of the best-qualified interpreters to weigh up the strengths and weaknesses of his work. He has written several other works on Teilhard, of which I only list the following:

Henri de Lubac, SJ, *The Faith of Teilhard de Chardin* (London: Burns & Oates, 1965—a translation of *La Prière du Père Teilhard de Chardin* [Paris: Fayard, 1964]). The American edition of the same text is identical except for a different title (and two subheadings): *Teilhard de Chardin: The Man and His Meaning* (New York: New American Library, Mentor Omega Books, 1967). This book complements de Lubac's earlier title listed previously. The first part deals with Teilhard's spiritual development (with extensive discussion of divine presence, and of the cosmic Christ, Teilhard's annual retreats, the Ignatian tradition, and limitations of Teilhard's work). The second part discusses Teilhard's defense of Christianity, his apologetics, the axis of Rome, and comments by other writers on his work.

Henri de Lubac's final reflections are gathered in his book *Teilhard Posthume: Réflexions et souvenirs* (Paris: Fayard, 1977). This book contains a whole chapter on Teilhard's "Omega Point," comparisons with several other French thinkers, and reflections on Teilhard's relationship to Vatican II.

Other Jesuits have written brief introductions to Teilhard's spirituality that are easier to read but less comprehensive than de Lubac's work. See the succinct reflections by the

English Jesuit **Thomas Corbishley**, *The Spirituality of Teilhard de Chardin* (London: Collins, Fontana Library, 1971), and the fuller account by the American **Robert Faricy, SJ**, *All Things in Christ: Teilhard de Chardin's Spirituality* (London: Collins, Fount Paperbacks, 1981). This is one of the few books that briefly discusses Teilhard's devotion to the Sacred Heart, on which further work needs to be done.

Another well-known Jesuit writer is **Thomas M. King**, who produced a nuanced study of great depth, *Teilhard's Mysticism of Knowing* (New York: Seabury, 1981), which invites close study and critical engagement since it presents a very personal interpretation of Teilhard's mysticism. One may wonder whether the latter is not even more a "mysticism of loving" than a "mysticism of knowing."

The same author has subsequently written a more general, simpler introduction to Teilhard, also centered on his mysticism. See Thomas M. King, SJ, *Teilhard de Chardin* (Wilmington, DE: Michael Glazier, 1988), published in the series "The Way of the Christian Mystics."

A very brief, attractive introduction that connects Teilhard's scientific work with his mysticism has been produced by the Boston College scientist **James W. Skehan, SJ**, "Geology and Grace: Teilhard's Life and Achievements," *Teilhard Studies* 53 (2006). The same author has also published prayerful meditations that show without a doubt what a deep Christian mystic Teilhard was. See James W. Skehan, SJ, *Praying with Teilhard de Chardin* (Winona, MN: St. Mary's Press, 2001).

Reference Works on Spirituality and Mysticism

General studies on spirituality and mysticism often overlook the twentieth-century Christian mystic, Pierre Teilhard de Chardin. An exception is the book by

Harvey D. Egan, SJ, *Christian Mysticism: The Future of a Tradition* (Collegeville, MN: Liturgical Press, 1990), which devotes a whole chapter to Teilhard (see chap. 7, 260–302). This includes a discussion of Teilhard's scientific and mystical view of evolution, and of his radical Christocentrism as well as his basic distinction between the road of "eastern mysticism" and that of "Christian mysticism."

A major reference work on mysticism is the four volumes by Bernard McGinn, *The Presence of God: A History of Western Christian Mysticism* (New York: Crossroad; London: SCM, 1991–). See McGinn's chapter "Theoretical Foundations: The Modern Study of Mysticism" in the first volume of this series, *Foundations of Mysticism*, 1991: 265–343.

For a wide overview relating to different figures, movements, and studies of Christian spirituality and mysticism consult:

Richard J. Woods, *Christian Spirituality: God's Presence through the Ages* (Maryknoll, NY: Orbis, 2006), which contains one page on Teilhard and Merton together (252).

A wide choice of academic articles on the history and theology of spirituality, ending with two contributions on "Spirituality and Feminism," is found in Kenneth J. Collins, ed., *Exploring Christian Spirituality: An Ecumenical Reader* (Grand Rapids, MI: Baker Books, 2000).

For a more inclusive global approach to spirituality, partly inspired by Teilhard's planetary and evolutionary perspectives, see my book, *The Search for Spirituality: Our Global Quest for a Spiritual Life* (New York: BlueBridge, 2008; Norwich, UK: Canterbury Press, 2009). It discusses spirituality in relation to interfaith dialogue, the human life cycle, health and education, gender issues, science and the arts, our understanding of nature and ecology, and of the struggle for life. Its overall vision is one of hope and flourishing for people and planet, animated by the zest for life and the power of love. Particularly helpful is the extensive annotated bibliography for each chapter.

A valuable **reference work** is provided by the Canadian theologian David B. Perrin, *Studying Christian Spirituality* (New York and London: Routledge, 2007), described as "the ideal introduction for students wishing to discover how spirituality can be understood beyond the conventional boundaries that religions have established" (frontispiece). It covers a great variety of perspectives and methods and includes rich bibliographical resources for further study (but none on Teilhard's spirituality or on ecological or evolutionary spirituality). It ends on a lively note by asking "Questions of Critical Edges" that explore science, politics, gender, cyberspace, and other promising perspectives. David Perrin has also provided a brief overview on "Mysticism" in the *Blackwell Companion to Christian Spirituality*, ed. Arthur Holder (Oxford: Blackwell, 2005: 442–58).

The well-known German feminist theologian Dorothee Soelle takes a different, more activist approach to mysticism in *The Silent Cry: Mysticism and Resistance* (Minneapolis: Fortress, 2001). A similarly embodied and actively engaged approach to mysticism is advocated by Beverly J. Lanzetta, *Radical Wisdom: A Feminist Mystical Theology* (Minneapolis: Fortress, 2005). She redefines the mystical journey from a feminine perspective as a "radical mysticism" for both women and men.

Wayne Teasdale, *The Mystic Heart: Discovering a Universal Spirituality in the World's Religions* (Novato, CA: New World Library, 1999). The further evolution of mysticism and spirituality can only occur if more dialogical thinking is developed among different faith communities and the secular world. Wayne Teasdale argues for a "universal communal spirituality," even a new "interspirituality" that emerges when people from different faith traditions discover the mystic heart of the world's faiths and of the world itself.

Beverly Lanzetta, *Emerging Heart: Global Spirituality and the Sacred* (Minneapolis: Fortress, 2007). Rooted in the author's own spiritual experiences, this is another probing reflection on the mystical heart of the world faiths, the significance of interreligious dialogue, and the newly emerging global spirituality that the world needs.

An extensive list of **key internet resources** on Christian spirituality (major individuals or schools of thought; textual sources; general themes) is given in Alister E. McGrath, *Christian Spirituality* (Oxford and Malden, MA: Blackwell, 1999).

For printed sources, see the large series Classics of Western Spirituality (Mahwah, NJ: Paulist, 1978–), which numbers more than 120 volumes with original texts from the Catholic, Protestant, Eastern Orthodox, Jewish, Islamic, and American Indian traditions.

A wide selection of spiritual writings from twentieth-century authors of different faiths is available in the Modern Spiritual Masters series (ed. Robert Ellsberg), published by Orbis Books, Maryknoll, New York, since 1998. They include texts from Teilhard de Chardin, Simone Weil, Bede Griffiths, Thomas Merton, Thich Nhat Hanh, Evelyn Underhill, Mohandas Gandhi, Howard Thurman, Etty Hillesum, and many others.

Additional aspects of Teilhard's spirituality are discussed in my book *The Spirit of One Earth: Reflections on Teilhard de Chardin and Global Spirituality* (New York: Paragon House, 1989). It contains, among others, reflections on "Science and Mysticism," on Teilhard's essay "The Phenomenon of Spirituality," and on "Aurobindo's and Teilhard's Vision of the Future of Humankind." I have discussed Teilhard's fire and heart mysticism in "'Consumed by Fire from Within': Teilhard de Chardin's Pan-Christic Mysticism in Relation to the Catholic Tradition," *Heythrop Journal* 40/4 (October 1999): 456–77.

For the central place assigned to the powers of love in Teilhard's and Sorokin's work see my article "Love—A Higher Form of Human Energy in the Work of Teilhard de Chardin and Sorokin," *Zygon: Journal of Religion and Science* 39/1 (March 2004), 77–102. Often quoted is Teilhard's famous saying: "The day will come when, after mastering space, the winds, the waves, the tides, and gravity, we shall harness for God the energies of love. And on that day, for the second time in the history of the world, humanity will have discovered fire" (1934; see CW 11, 87). An innovative and inspiring study, which has developed this ideal with much imagination and benefit, is by:

> Anne Hillman, *Awakening the Energies of Love: Discovering Fire for a Second Time* (Putney, VT: Bramble Books, 2008). This book engages readers with the path and work of positive transformation. It takes in so much of human experience (and of the evolutionary history of our species) and shows through many practical examples how we can develop a qualitatively different kind of love to build a common future for humanity on Earth.

6. Teilhard's Legacy

Teilhard's writings are studied widely in their original French editions and in their translations into many other languages. His ideas have influenced debates in science and religion, philosophy, theology, mysticism, spirituality, the comparative study of religions, as well as developments in the arts and in applied areas such as palliative care (where Cicely Saunders, the founder of the modern hospice movement, has acknowledged the influence of Teilhard's ideas about the value of suffering) or architecture, for example, in the construction of Arcosanti in Arizona (see reference under **Teilhard and the World Wide Web** following).

Many consultations and conferences continue to be held to commemorate and advance Teilhard's ideas. UNESCO organized one in Paris in 1965, ten years after Teilhard's death, and again in 1981, for his birth centennial (for the 1965 conference see R. Maheu, ed., *Science et Synthèse*, Paris 1966; trans. as *Science and Synthesis: An International Colloquium Organized by UNESCO on the Tenth Anniversary of the Death of A. Einstein and Teilhard de Chardin* [New York: Springer, 1971]). In 2005, for the fiftieth anniversary of Teilhard's death, a conference focusing on ecological issues was held in memory of Teilhard at the United Nations headquarters in New York, and during the same year, several other conferences took place in the United States, France,

Britain, and China. In 2006, an international conference on Teilhard's significance for planetary ethics and creation spiritualities was organized in Manila in the Philippines (see the report in *Teilhard Perspective* 39/1 [Spring 2006]).

Teilhard will also be remembered by the various professional and scientific organizations to which he belonged. Besides his association with several scientific organizations in China, he was among others a member of the Académie des Sciences and a director of research at the Centre National de La Recherche Scientifique in France, an honorary member of the New York Academy of Sciences, and since 1937 also an honorary fellow of the Royal Anthropological Institute in London. The eminent British prehistorian, Professor Dorothy A. E. Garrod, who had known Teilhard since 1921 (she had studied at some stage with Teilhard's friend, the famous Abbé Breuil) wrote movingly in the obituary notice of the Royal Anthropological Institute's journal *MAN* that Teilhard's sudden death on April 10, 1955, had "deprived the scientific world of a very distinguished geologist and paleontologist....In him, the scientist was doubled by a Christian thinker of great originality and vision—two sides of his character which were facets of a singularly well knit and integrated spirit, whose philosophy of the Universe developed continuously right up to the time of his death." She already spoke of "the many people in various walks in life who have been influenced by his ideas" and concluded that Teilhard's "keenly intelligent face with vivid eyes lit by an inner flame of enthusiasm will not soon be forgotten by those who had the privilege of knowing him" (*MAN*, May 1955).

Since Teilhard's death, many different associations have been founded in different countries around the globe to preserve, hand down, and study Teilhard's seminal ideas and large corpus of writings. It would be difficult to compile a comprehensive list of all the Teilhard associations that exist today around the world, but I mention briefly what is available in France, England, and the United States.

Teilhard Associations

A large collection of primary and secondary sources on Teilhard, his life, thought, and works can be consulted at the French **Fondation Teilhard de Chardin**, 38, rue Geoffroy-Saint-Hilaire, 75005 Paris, France. See their Website, www.teilhard.org. Through an annual subscription, access can be gained to a research Website where Teilhard's writings are available in digitalized format if the necessary ID and password have been obtained: see www.teilhard-recherche.com.

The French Jesuits hold Teilhard's diaries and other original texts at their Jesuit house in Vanves near Paris; their study house in central Paris, the **Centre Sèvres—Facultés Jésuites de Paris** has a Chair in Teilhard Studies; see www.centresevres.com/s/chaires/49 (for more information contact francois.euve@centresevres.com).

The French **Association des Amis de Pierre Teilhard de Chardin** (B.P. 90 001, 75221 Paris Cedex 05, France) publishes a regular journal entitled *Teilhard aujourd'hui*. See also their international Website giving information about activities in Europe, www.teilhard-world.com.

Details about the **British Teilhard Association** and their *Teilhard Newsletter* can be found at www.teilhard.org.uk.

As mentioned at the beginning of this guide, the Website of the **American Teilhard Association** (ATA) is www.teilharddechardin.org; it should be consulted for all further information.

I next draw special attention to some library resources and recent studies.

Library Resources and Recent Studies

PIERRE TEILHARD DE CHARDIN COLLECTION AT THE GEORGETOWN UNIVERSITY LIBRARY

At this premier Jesuit college in Washington, D.C., is housed the most extensive repository of materials by and about Teilhard in North America. Due to the good offices of its late professor of theology and Teilhard scholar, Thomas King, SJ (1929–2009), and others, a gathering of more than seven hundred items can be viewed through its online catalogue at www.library.georgetown. edu/.

From this home page, type "Teilhard" in the upper-right search box. This will bring you to an item-by-item chronological presentation, clearly done with many images. Other search approaches are available there, and with some negotiation an extraordinary research facility is achieved. In addition, when the American Teilhard Association closed its small office on 72nd Street in New York City, circa 1980, its library of many works found a new home at this Georgetown Library. Moreover, in the Special Collections of Georgetown University Library, the Pierre Leroy Papers (1947–84), the Robert T. Francoeur Papers (1938–75), the Lucile Swan Papers (1907–85), and many other papers of people connected with Teilhard de Chardin can be found.

Another helpful bibliographical research tool is the Internet site "WorldCat," a composite collection of information from some 71,000 libraries. Their Teilhard page is http://worldcat.org/ identities/lccn-n79-32934. This can be sorted by date, author, and title.

Among recent studies published on Teilhard, I draw attention to some new publications and also to several volumes mentioned earlier that provide extensive further bibliographical references:

> Arthur Fabel and Donald St. John, eds., *Teilhard in the 21st Century: The Emerging Spirit of Earth* (Maryknoll, NY: Orbis, 2003; see remarks under **Teilhard's Life and Thought**, section 1 previous.
>
> Celia Deane-Drummond, ed., *Pierre Teilhard de Chardin on People and Planet* (London and Oakville, CT: Equinox, 2006); see remarks under **Science, Evolution, Biosphere and Noosphere**, section 3 previous.
>
> Kathleen Duffy, SSJ, ed., *Rediscovering Teilhard's Fire* (Philadelphia: St. Joseph's University Press, 2010). This book of essays by prominent Teilhard scholars (among others Kathleen Duffy, John F. Haught, Ludovico Galleni, John Grim, Thomas King, James Skehan, Mary Evelyn Tucker, and Donald Wayne Viney) examines Teilhard's

contributions to theology, philosophy, science, spirituality, and aesthetics and suggests ways in which his synthesis and vision continue to be relevant today.

Thierry Meynard, SJ, ed., *Teilhard and the Future of Humanity* (New York: Fordham University Press, 2006); see remarks under **His China Years, Paleontology, and Peking Man**, section 2 previous.

James Salmon, SJ, and John Farina have edited *The Legacy of Teilhard de Chardin* (Mahwah, NJ: Paulist, 2011) with contributions by theologians Ewert Cousins, John Haught, Thomas King, SJ, and Philip Hefner, and by scientists Harold Morowitz, James Skehan, SJ, Ludovico Galleni, and Mark McMenamin. The preface is by John Farina, and James Salmon, SJ, has written the introduction.

Teilhard and the World Wide Web

Abundant references to Teilhard's thought can be found on the World Wide Web. In fact, Google listed 526,000 references to Teilhard in 2010 (as compared to just over 1,000 in 1997), but not all are equally trustworthy. As always, discernment in using information from the Web is essential. There are many sites pointing to helpful discussions and articles, such as those dealing with Teilhard's major works *The Human Phenomenon* or *The Divine Milieu*, or with his ideas about complexity-consciousness, the noosphere, the Omega point, God and evolution, and other philosophical, theological, and spiritual views expressed by him.

Some philosophers and members of the worldwide media community consider Teilhard's ideas about the noosphere—a sphere or globe surrounded by a thinking layer—as an anticipation of cyberspace and the Internet. In fact, the suggestion has been made that Teilhard may be considered as "patron saint" of the Internet.

The Websites of the different Teilhard associations mentioned earlier provide links to further sites where more information on Teilhard's works, thought, and influence around the world can be found. To mention a few other sites:

www.teilhardforbeginners.com: A most helpful brief introduction. It centers explicitly on presenting Teilhard's spirituality based on *The Divine Milieu* and *The Human Phenomenon* and was created by Louis Savary, the author of *Teilhard de Chardin*: The Divine Milieu *Explained* (see details under **Spirituality and Mysticism**, section 5 previous).

Information about the Global Consciousness Project, an international, multidisciplinary collaboration of scientists, engineers, artists, and others housed at Princeton University can be accessed at http://noosphere.princeton.edu.

Among the myriad Web references to the **Noosphere**, it is especially encouraging to see that the president of the United Nations General Assembly, Miguel d'Escoto Brockmann, in an address to the UN Conference on the World Financial and Economic Crisis on June 26, 2009, made a reference to Teilhard, saying that his vision of an emergent worldwide noosphere could provide much guidance. The address is posted online at a number of sites; Google "**Noosphere announced at the United Nations.**"

A filmed interview on "**The Noosphere, Internet and Global Community**" with the late Dr. Ewert H. Cousins was posted on YouTube on September 1, 2009, by somedayfire.

Of great importance are the resources on religion and ecology provided at www.yale.edu/religionandecology (see details under **The Ecosphere**, section 3 previous).

Also worth investigating is the site of the Cosanti Foundation (www.arcosanti.org), a foundation relating to architecture and ecology created in connection with the construction of Arcosanti in Arizona. This is an innovative complex and a community designed by the Italian-born American architect Paolo Soleri, a visionary planner of the twentieth century for whom Teilhard's thought was a prime inspiration. His Arcosanti was conceived in the 1970s to include "The Pierre Teilhard de Chardin Complex" as an ecumenical "neomonastic" cloister and retreat facility. At present, this is still in course of further development, in line with the current expansion of the foundation's program.

Concluding Reflection

The rich resources of this bibliographical essay give you a taste of the wealth of perspectives, ideas, and connections to be discovered in Pierre Teilhard de Chardin. His ardent love of the world and love of God fused together in a passionate commitment to "seeing" and conveying a new vision of the world, the human, and the Divine. He wanted to inspire people to see more and thereby become more—to see things as they really are and develop a new synthesis of our vastly extended experience of Earth, of life, of what it means to be human and discover the fire of the Spirit.

The inspirational, prophetic power of "seeing" was beautifully expressed by John Ruskin, the visionary English writer and social reformer, in words that seem to apply admirably to Teilhard:

The greatest thing a human soul ever does in this world is to see something, and tell what it saw in a plain way. Hundreds of people can talk for one who can think, but thousands can think for one who can see.

To see clearly is poetry, prophecy, and religion,—all in one.

John Ruskin, *Modern Painters*,
1987 (1856), 403